Immigrants outside Megalopolis

Immigrants outside Megalopolis

Ethnic Transformation in the Heartland

EDITED BY
RICHARD C. JONES

LEXINGTON BOOKS

A division of
ROWMAN & LITTLEFIELD PUBLISHERS, INC.
Lanham • Boulder • New York • Toronto • Plymouth, UK

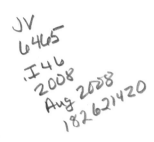

LEXINGTON BOOKS

A division of Rowman & Littlefield Publishers, Inc.
A wholly owned subsidiary of The Rowman & Littlefield Publishing Group, Inc.
4501 Forbes Boulevard, Suite 200
Lanham, MD 20706

Estover Road
Plymouth PL6 7PY
United Kingdom

British Library Cataloguing in Publication Information Available

Library of Congress Cataloging-in-Publication Data

Immigrants outside megalopolis : ethnic transformation in the heartland / edited by Richard C. Jones.
p. cm.
Includes bibliographical references and index.
ISBN-13: 978-0-7391-1919-8 (cloth : alk. paper)
ISBN-10: 0-7391-1919-2 (cloth : alk. paper)
1. United States—Emigration and immigration. 2. Small cities—United States. 3. United States—Population. I. Jones, Richard C., 1942–
JV6465.I46 2008
305.9'069120973—dc22 2007047336

Printed in the United States of America

The paper used in this publication meets the minimum requirements of American National Standard for Information Sciences—Permanence of Paper for Printed Library Materials, ANSI/NISO Z39.48–1992.

Contents

PART THREE: EASTERN UNITED STATES

PART FOUR: EPILOGUE

Preface

The idea for this book originated during research stays in Spain (1999) and Ireland (2002) where I had gone to investigate parallels between the EU periphery and Mexico in regards to emigration and return migration, but where I found these countries far more concerned about *immigration*. They were having considerable difficulties adjusting to new "Third World" immigrants whose entry had transformed them from countries of emigration to countries of immigration almost overnight. I became aware of something unique about the relatively successful U.S. experience with these same immigrants—something that might be instructive in a world where immigrant maladjustment is more the exception than the rule. I felt compelled to enlarge my traditional focus on Mexican migrant patterns and impacts to take account of the experiences of other groups. In the ensuing years, I have done so by writing on immigrant segregation and assimilation in U.S. cities, particularly in San Antonio, and by expanding my global interest to include cities such as Madrid, Dublin, and Buenos Aires. The current volume is a continuation of this new research direction.

This volume addresses the dynamic interaction between two processes: the formation of cultural landscapes and the negotiation of socio-economic adjustment, for particular immigrant nationalities in specific U.S. cities outside the major urban conurbations referred to jointly as megalopolis (Boston-to-Washington, Chicago-to-Pittsburgh, San Diego-to-San Francisco, and peninsular Florida). Each of the chapters takes one non-megalopolitan city and one national or ancestry group as its focus. Different authors emphasize one or the other of the two processes noted above, but both processes appear in each contribution. Each contributor also investigates the historical origins and the spatial patterns of his or her group.

When I began to search for potential contributors in 2003, there were relatively few geographers concentrating on these "heartland" cities. My deep appreciation goes to colleagues Stan Brunn, Dennis Conway, Kavita Pandit, and Curt Roseman for making me aware of the contributors whose work appears within. Otherwise, I relied on presentations at the Association of American Geographers meetings as well as recent journal articles and book chapters to inform me about who was currently researching these topics. Among the twelve authors and co-authors in this book are eight geographers, in addition to two sociologists, a demographer, and an anthropologist. The latter four authors, including two from the countries whose groups they discuss, add significantly to the depth of discussion on socio-economic adjustment of immigrants in the United States.

The number of researchers formally addressing this topic has multiplied exponentially since 2002, with at least eight new edited books (five of them by geographers) treating the new geography of immigration in the U.S., and with other contributions in press. These volumes have documented a cultural transformation in cities and towns of the heartland, and a glimpse of the future of "mainstream" America. The current volume remains unique, however, in the diversity of immigrant nationalities and regions it considers, and in addressing the dual themes of cultural landscape and social adjustment.

I could not have carried this book to fruition without my "internal editorial board"—migration and development scholars in three disciplines whom I chose to review the chapter manuscripts. So let me personally thank Jim Allen, Dan Arreola, Tom Boswell, Mansour El-Kikhia, Ines Miyares, Kavita Pandit, and Thankam Sunil for their splendid efforts. Their calls for broader contexts, deeper discussion, tighter conceptual frameworks, and clearer methodologies immeasurably improved the chapters without too much grief for the authors.

Acquisitions Editor Patrick Dillon with Lexington Books has been most helpful and efficient in bringing this book to production. The longer-term process had various several twists and turns owing to the dissolution of AltaMira Press, who originally expressed interest in the book, and the re-structuring of Rowman and Littlefield Publishers, of which Lexington Books is a scholarly division. Let me also thank Jessica Dribble and MacDuff Stewart for their efforts on the book's behalf.

I have incurred family debts as well. My daughter Katrina, who has a Boston University B.A. and a San Francisco State M.A. in Museum Studies has been a real inspiration and provider of insights on the contributions of immigrants in New England and northern California. My wife Maria, an M.A. in Bilingual Studies from UTSA and an immigrant herself (from Mexico) has been my constant sounding board and companion in the research that constitutes my contributions to this volume. Finally, my sons Rick and Chris, and my daughter Alexis, have patiently endured the interminable weekend and week-night hours spent in labor with my PC.

I am aware that the sacrifices of immigrants are the precondition for any scholarship on the subject, including my own. In that light I can only hope that this book humanizes their struggles, shows their contributions, and promotes their understanding and accommodation. I have tremendous respect for these new Americans. But even if I fail—if distrust and anger towards immigrants continue unabated—the immigrants themselves will continue to adjust and adapt and contribute. Moreover, they will continue to feel affection for this country, coming here at the risk of their lives and fortunes and self-esteem, to serve the country in capacities too numerous to detail. They have the conviction that they can outmaneuver the obstacles—be they geography, language, prejudice, or abuse—and still be useful in American society. Their strategy is well-stated by the poem, "Outwitted," by Edwin Markham:

He drew a circle that shut me out—
Heretic, rebel, a thing to flout.
But love and I had the wit to win:
We drew a circle that took him in!

PART ONE

INTRODUCTION

Chapter 1

Immigrants Transform and Are Transformed by the U.S. Heartland

Richard C. Jones

The fact that we have such a wonderfully diverse population here, a very, very good thing for this community, and for the young people in this community to be in school with people from all over the world. That's amazing. And so you're sitting next to someone from somewhere else in the world; what a great geography lesson. What a great sociology lesson; what a great history lesson. So, so I think that our children are having the opportunity to be more accepting, to have a bigger world view. I see this as extremely positive for our community, on every level that I can possibly think of. (Foundation leader, Utica, New York; from Ellen Kraly, Chapter 12, this volume).

[Dora:] You come to work, for a better life. You don't come to commit crimes, like robbery and other things. [Maria:] I tell you that at the beginning, I didn't go out, because I said "it isn't my place, it isn't my people, I am here without permission. It felt like it said here on my forehead, 'illegal.'" (Mexican migrants, Leadville, Colorado; from Nancy Hiemstra, Chapter 6, this volume).

The Changing Cultural and Social Geography of Immigration

Over the past few decades, immigrants to the United States have chosen to live in large cities whose cosmopolitan, ethnically-mixed populations have absorbed them with relative ease. *Megalopolis*—the metropolitan conurbations of Boston-Washington [Bosnywash], Chicago to Pittsburgh [Chipitts], San Diego to San Francisco [Sansan], Peninsular Florida [Penflor], and occasionally others—has attracted a disproportionate number of these foreign-born (three-fourths in 1990). However, the 1990s saw a distinct shift away from megalopolis towards *non-megalopolitan areas* distributed throughout the country. Smaller places such as Utica and Leadville, the source of the above quotes, have participated in this trend, but two-thirds of the non non-megalopolitan immigrant growth was in cities of one million population and above—Dallas, Atlanta, Charlotte, Nashville, Denver, Phoenix, Seattle, and others. The causes for this are conjectural and are discussed below. The result, however, has been a cultural transformation of the U.S. Heartland, that broad pool of states beyond the peripheral metropolitan swaths. The implantation of new features on the cultural landscape (businesses, homes, churches, schools, possessions, and the people themselves) is giving many Americans a geography lesson on the "Third World"—at a time when increased world understanding is something the country cannot do without. In some cases these new groups have revitalized declining communities.

But this geographic dispersion of immigrants has created more than new cultural landscapes. It has also created landscapes of conflict and suffering as the immigrants and their hosts adjust to each other. The differences between immigrants and residents tend to stand out starkly on the social landscape of smaller, more demographically homogenous or bi-cultural places. Some traits, for example religious rituals, marriage practices, economic pursuits, house styles, and language, may come into conflict with local norms and laws and generate animosity towards the immigrant group. This animosity may hinter the immigrants' primary goal (arguably, the host society's goal for them as well): socio-economic integration.

The purpose of this book is to investigate the dynamic interaction between these two processes—the creation of new cultural landscapes and the negotiation of social adjustment—in cities outside of the large urban agglomerations at the eastern and western flanks of the country. The contributors to this volume deal principally with first generation immigrants who struggle and face and the need for cultural anchors to see them through the hard times. In some of the places detailed in this book, conflict—fed by a daily infusion of new immigrants—is still fresh and unresolved. In others, the initial sparring between newcomers and hosts has given way to accommodation of various kinds. There are indications that the second generation will have an easier time of it than the first.

Geographers, whose contributions are highlighted in this volume, are uniquely trained to appreciate the evolution of cultural landscapes and the adjustment difficulties faced by immigrants in their daily activity spaces—in neighborhoods, schools, workplaces, shops, and public agencies. Migration geographers have recently combined the quantitative techniques of migration analysis with the ethnographic case study approach, to yield new insights. The advantages of this mixed-methods approach are evident in this book. The volume also includes contributions by other social scientists, representing the fields of anthropology, sociology, and demography. Their approaches to issues of social adjustment greatly enrich the volume. In two cases the contributors write about groups that represent their own ancestry—offering personal insights on the adaptational hurdles presented by U.S. society.

Trends in Megalopolitan and non-Megalopolitan Growth of the Foreign Born

In 2000, an astonishing 95 percent of the U.S. foreign-born population lived in metropolitan areas—compared to only 80 percent of the native population. The fact that only 5 percent live in non-metropolitan areas implies that the job opportunities and social climate in these areas present a special challenge for immigrants. Besides being overwhelmingly metropolitan, the foreign-born were concentrated in the largest U.S. cities: 55 percent in the nine largest metropolitan areas alone, where only 27 percent of the native population lived (Schmidley 2001, 16). These nine largest metros (all above five million population) are, however, quite different from those included in the definition of "megalopolis" given above and used in this book. These largest metros omit adjacent metro areas that are arguably part of a continuous demographic and economic core region (megalopolis), and they omit peninsular Florida as well. The larger, more comprehensive entity of megalopolis serves us better than an arbitrary urban size cut-off point.

The term "megalopolis" was originally coined by Gottmann (1961) to refer to the northeastern seaboard—Bosnywash. The concept was expanded by Hartshorn (1992, 36-37) and De Blij and Muller (1994) to include three other regions of "megalopolitan growth": Chipitts, Sansan, and peninsular Florida (referred to here as Penflor). The definition has been further expanded in recent years. However, to meet our purposes (identification of a traditional immigrant core region), the early-1990s definition encompassing only the four major concentrations will be used.

Table 1.1 examines growth rates in the foreign-born population over the 1990s, using the data sets extracted from the 1990 and 2000 U.S. Censuses and calibrated by researchers with the Lewis Mumford Center at the University of Albany (Mumford Center 2005). In 1990, 77 percent of the foreign-born lived in Megalopolis. By 2000, this figure had dropped to 71 percent, suggesting immigrant dispersion outside megalopolis between the two censuses. The U.S. foreign-born population grew 56 percent over the decade, over four times as fast as the population overall, 13 percent. The table reveals that growth in the foreign born population was quite uneven among the size classes of cities. In Megalopolis, the foreign-born grew at below average (national) rates for all the conurbations with the exception of Penflor. At the other end of the distribution, the non-metropolitan foreign-born also grew at below average rates. The spike in the foreign percentage growth column occurs for the non-megalopolitan areas of one million and more population, where the foreign-born population more than doubled, with a phenomenal growth rate of 138 percent—from approximately two million in 1990 to five million in 2000.

Table 1.1 Distribution and Growth of Total and Foreign-Born Populations, by U.S. Metropolitan Category, 2000

Metropolitan Category	Total Population, 2000 (thousands)	Foreign-born Population, 2000 (thousands)	% of Total Population	% of Total Foreign-born	% Growth in Population, 1990-2000	% Growth in Foreign-born, 1990-2000
Megalopolis:	**134,234**	**21,855**	**47.8**	**70.9**	**10.5**	**43.9**
Bosnywash	49,965	7,874	17.8	25.6	8.2	44.1
Chipitts	37,860	2,696	13.5	8.7	6.7	52.7
Sansan	32,587	8,731	11.6	28.3	13.8	37.2
Penflor	13,822	2,554	4.9	8.3	23.7	59.8
Outside Megalopolis:	**147,188**	**8,960**	**52.3**	**29.0**	**15.2**	**95.3**
Large metro[a]	47,144	4,945	16.8	16.0	24.9	138.3
Small metro[b]	44,604	2,568	15.8	8.3	13.9	68.4
Non-metro	55,440	1,447	19.7	4.7	8.9	46.6
Total population	**281,422**	**30,814**	**100.0**	**99.9**	**12.9**	**55.8**

[a] one million population and above in 2000.
[b] less than one million population in 2000.
Source: U.S. Census, 2000.

Where are the cities that constitute this spike in foreign-born growth? As shown in Figure 1.1, they are twenty-four in number and located all across the United States. There is no immediately apparent common denominator that identifies them. Upon closer inspection, however, their regional locations suggest certain principles at work. One set of cities is in the Upper South/Lower Midwest, where economic restructuring in resource-oriented sectors (the corporate and spatial concentration of meat packing, poultry, commercial forestry, tobacco, etc.) has drawn Latino migrants in large numbers. These migrants, especially Mexicans, gravitate to larger cities seasonally and permanently when their primary sector jobs are finished or after they have become adjusted to U.S. life (Guthey 2001; Driever 2004; Rich and Miranda 2005; Gouveia et al. 2005). Other groups besides Mexicans also select these cities, for their low unemployment rates and variety of job opportunities (Dakan 2006; Johnson-Webb 2003). An equally prevalent set of cities is located in the Southwest, where rapid growth in tertiary and quaternary sectors (including tourism and retirement) has created a demand for "high-touch" jobs to serve the "high-tech" professionals and businesses who demand them. Among these are high-growth Texas cities (Dallas, Houston, Austin) and amenity cities of the mountain West (Denver, Phoenix, Las Vegas, and Salt Lake City). Finally, a small group of high-growth cities are located in the north (Minneapolis, Seattle, Portland). These cities have been culturally receptive to immigrants, mediated by voluntary refugee resettlement agencies including Lutheran, Episcopal, and Catholic organizations that cooperated with the U.S. government to locate early waves of Indochinese (Airriess and Clawson 2000) and refugees from the former Soviet Union (Hardwick and Meacham 2005). All of these cities—whether upper southern, midwestern, mountain western, or Pacific Northwest—provide economic opportunity and cultural mass, stemming from their large size. Concentrations of co-ethnics provide the cultural and social capital that immigrants need for identity and adjustment in an alien environment (Kibria 2002; Dhingra 2003; Hardwick 2002).

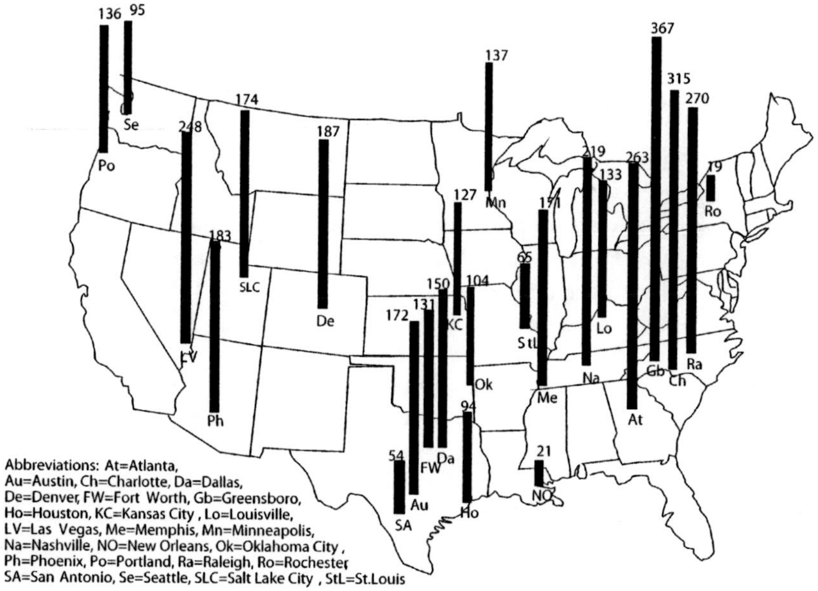

Figure 1.1 Percentage Growth Rates in Foreign-born Population, 1990-2000: Non-Megalopolitan Cities of 1 Million+ Population in 2000

These large high-growth cities outside megalopolis are key to the theme of this book. Over the 1990s, these twenty-four metro areas accounted for two-thirds of the total increment in the foreign born outside megalopolis. Six of them (Charlotte, Dallas, New Orleans, Phoenix, Portland, and San Antonio) are the focus of studies in this volume.

Three other contributors to this volume consider smaller metropolitan areas (Iowa City, Sheboygan, and Utica), and two consider non-metropolitan areas (Garden City, Kansas, and Leadville, Colorado). These smaller places have drawn immigrants for many of the same reasons (concentration of agricultural industries, high-tech and amenity growth, and a welcoming social milieu) that drew immigrants to larger places. The above analysis of non-megalopolitan places illustrates that immigrants respond sensitively to growth points and opportunities in the U.S. economy and society.

Immigrant Dispersion to Smaller Places: Evidence from the Literature

The deconcentration trend documented above has attracted relatively little attention until recently. For example, it is scarcely mentioned in several comprehensive statistical profiles of immigration (del Pinal and Singer 1997; Lee 1998; Schmidley 2001; Martin and Midgeley 2003). In their portrayal of immigrant America, Portes and Rumbaut (1996) indicate the importance of space and place in migration, in their chapter "Moving: Patterns of Immigrant Settlement and Spatial Mobility." They examine cross-sectional data (around 1990) showing a high degree of immigrant concentration in the U.S., and furthermore, they champion such clustering as quite desirable—providing (for an immigrant group) "preservation of a valued life-style, regulation of the pace of acculturation, greater social control over the young, and access to community networks for both moral and economic support" (54).

The trend towards spatial dispersion has not gone unnoticed, however. Gober (1999), one of the first to recognize this trend, found a decrease in concentration of the foreign-born across the states in the 1980s, particularly for Latinos—a finding tending to refute the "demographic Balkanization" thesis previously advanced by Frey and Liaw (1999). In their pathbreaking book, Alba and Nee (2003) devote part of a chapter to spatial patterns, cautiously suggesting that racial and ethnic diversity are increasing in most parts of the United States, and that ". . . one future possibility is the emergence of a much larger number of immigrant cultural centers, especially of Spanish speakers" (249), a trend they see as desirable and in keeping with their spatial assimilation hypothesis. In support of this statement, Durand, Massey, and Capoferro (2005) find that Mexican migration is much more spatially diversified today than in 1990, with cities like Houston, Dallas, Las Vegas, Phoenix, and Minneapolis leading the trend, and with many more "gateway states" than before.

In related analyses, Singer (2004, 2006) has recently called attention to the fact that in the 1990s, rates of growth of the foreign-born were fastest in metropolitan areas that she identifies as "emerging gateway cities." Her typology is basically congruent with the megalopolis/non-megalopolis distinction drawn in this book. Specifically, cities that she identifies as "former, continuous, or post-World War II gateways" are almost exclusively in Megalopolis, while her "emerging, re-emerging, and pre-emerging gateways" are largely large non-megalopolitan cities such as those researched in this volume.

Perhaps the clearest sign of immigrant decentralization is that scholars are beginning to undertake ethnographic field research in emerging gateway cities. In Table 1.2, I document this trend for immigrant groups addressed in this volume. This table includes only a representative sample of studies; it does not attempt to be comprehensive. Studies that deal with several different immigrant groups, or that treat a specific group's experiences nationwide, are not included in this compendium. The table shows that the literature before 2000, and especially before 1995, cast its spotlight on such megalopolitan cities such as New York, Los Angeles, Miami, Chicago, Philadelphia, and Washington D.C. The exceptions are Indo-Chinese groups (Vietnamese, Laotian or Hmong) in smaller places such as New Orleans, Denver, Atlanta, and Fresno—whose more dispersed locations were partly a result of U.S. refugee resettlement policies. After 2000, the sample includes such non-megalopolitan cities as Kansas City (Mexicans); Phoenix (Cubans); Dallas (Asian Indians); Rochester [MN] (Hmong); Minneapolis, Portland, and Sacramento (Russians); and Utica (Bosnians). In the case of Mexicans, even smaller places have been studied: Grand Island [NB], Marshallton [IA], and Dalton [GA]. These smaller places are becoming crucibles for new forms of accommodation that are tracing the future of Mexican adjustment to the heartland. In such places, "reactive accommodation," marked by conflict, may be superseded over a period of time by "participatory accommodation," in which newcomers and established residents make an active effort to understand each other (Bach et al. 1993). The chapters in this book that deal with Leadville [CO] and Garden City [KS] are good examples of reactive and participatory accommodation, respectively.

The Integration and Acculturation of U.S. Immigrant Groups

The geographic profile of immigrant growth and dispersion, its causes and consequences, is incomplete without a consideration of impacts on the immigrants themselves. How are they are adjusting to life in the United States? This adjustment encompasses two separate processes (Berry 1990; Marger 1994, 118-20).

Table 1.2 Case Studies of "New Immigrants" in the Research Literature, by Group Nationality and Year of Publication (cities outside Megalopolis **in bold**)

	Year of Publication of Immigrant Case Studies		
Nationality	Before 1995	1995-2000	After 2000
Mexican	So.California (Mines & Anzaldua 1982) Los Angeles (Dagadog 1984)	New York City (Smith 1996) Los Angeles (Ortiz 1996) **San Antonio** (Jones 1996) Los Angeles (Vigil 1997)	New York City (Smith 2001) **Dalton, Ga** (Engstrom; Zuniga & Hernandez Leon, 2001) **Kansas City** (Driever 2004) **Grand Island, Neb** (Gouveia et al. 2005) **Marshallton, Iowa** (Grey & Woodrick 2005
Cuban	Miami (Portes 1984; Stepick & Grenier 1993)	Los Angeles (Potocky 1996) Miami (Garcia 1996; Potocky 1996)	**Phoenix** (Skop & Menjivar 2001)
Asian Indian		New York City (Lessinger 1995) Chicago (Rangaswamy 2000)	**Dallas** (Dhingra 2003)
Vietnamese	Los Angeles (Desbarats & Holland 1983) **New Orleans** (Airriess & Clawson 1991; Zhou & Bankston 1994) Philadelphia (Kibria 1993)	**Denver** (Do 1999)	**New Orleans** (Airriess 2002)
Laotian		**Atlanta** (Duchon 1997) **Fresno** (Miyares 1997)	**Rochester, Minn.** (Faruque 2002)
Russian	Washington, DC (Birman & Tyler 1994)		**Sacramento** (Hardwick 2002) **Minneapolis/St.Paul** (Fennelly & Palasz 2003) **Portland** (Hardwick & Mecham 2005)
Bosnian			**Utica, NY** (Kraly & van Valkenburg 2003) **Bowling Green, Ken.** (Snyder et al. 2005)
Iranian	Los Angeles (Bozorgmehr & Sabagh 1987)	**Iowa City** (Chaichian 1997)	

Source: author.

Integration involves immigrants' social and economic consolidation with the host society. Socially, immigrants establish contacts with the dominant ethnic group(s) as neighbors, friends, club or society members (*social integration*), while economically, they make strides towards parity in occupational status and income (*economic integration*). *Acculturation* involves adoption by the immigrants of host-society culture—language, religion, food, music, and attitudes towards their countries of origin and destination.

Viewed from the perspective of different immigrant groups, integration and acculturation may act independently of each another. In Figure 1.2, the upper-case labels in each quadrant of the graph delineate a four-category typology. An integrated group may be acculturated, as with immigrants from northern Europe; or not, as in the case of high-SES (socio-economic status) Asian and Latino immigrants. Conversely, a non-integrated group may be acculturated, as with Anglophone Caribbeans and sub-Saharan Africans (who acculturate to black subculture in the U.S.); or not, as with low-SES Asians and Latinos (who adhere strongly to their own cultures). In this typology, the clearest distinction appears to be between high socio-economic status groups at the top of the graph (certain Asian and Latino groups, and Europeans), and lower-SES groups at the bottom. The lower and higher status groups are separated by *barriers to integration*—indicated by the horizontal dashed line in the figure. According to the literature, these barriers may include (1) low levels of immigrant community and family resources; (2) discrimination by the host society; (3) undocumented status; (4) lack of incentives to interact with the host society (such as temporariness and intentions to return home); (5) recent vintage; and (6) the pressure to conform to dissonant norms (Berry 1990; Marger 1994, 125-29; Portes and Rumbaut 1996, 247-53).

To illustrate this typology, I make use of 2000 U.S. Census ancestry data (U.S. Bureau of the Census 2000). Only a few illustrative groups are used in this exercise. I define *economic integration* as *the percentage of a foreign-born group living above the poverty level in 2000*; and *acculturation* as *the percentage of the group that spoke only English at home in 2000*. These groups are located as points on the graph of Figure 1.2. In its upper left quadrant—high integration accompanied by low acculturation—we find Filipinos (fil), Asian Indians (asi), Chinese (chi), Iranians (ira), and Cubans (cub). These groups—all high-SES Asian or Latino groups that exhibit strong cultural cohesiveness in the face of pressures to acculturate—have been extensively researched (e.g., Rieff 1993; Chaichian 1997; Lozada 1999; Rangaswamy 2000; Kibria 2002; Dhingra 2003). They serve as examples of what Portes and Rumbaut (1996, 241-51) refer to as *selective acculturation*—the adoption or exercising of cultural traits that benefit their integration (such as language, education, and hard work) coupled with the refusal to give up those that provide cultural refuge or reinforce cultural pride even though they may lack direct integrative value (religion, food preferences, meeting family obligations, honoring one's history, etc). In the upper right quadrant—high integration accompanied by high acculturation—are northern European groups such as Germans (ger) and English (eng), who have been in the United States for generations and form the white Anglo-Saxon mainstream. In the lower right quadrant we find the unusual situation of low integration accompanied by high acculturation—represented by sub-Saharan Africans (ssa) and British West Indians (bwi). Limited economic and cultural resources often compel immigrants to live in inner city areas where powerful and persuasive contingents of their own ethnic group may force them to acculturate into a group that rejects host society treatment and norms. Such *dissonant acculturation* (Portes and Rumbaut 1996, 243-47; Hintzen 2001; Stoller 2001) may have negative repercussions for their eventual integration into the host society. Portes and Rumbaut write:

> Immigrants today (enter) a pluralistic society in which a variety of racial and ethnic subcultures coexist. Hence, the central question is not whether children of immigrants acculturate, but to what sector of American society they acculturate to (Portes and Rumbaut 1996, 247).

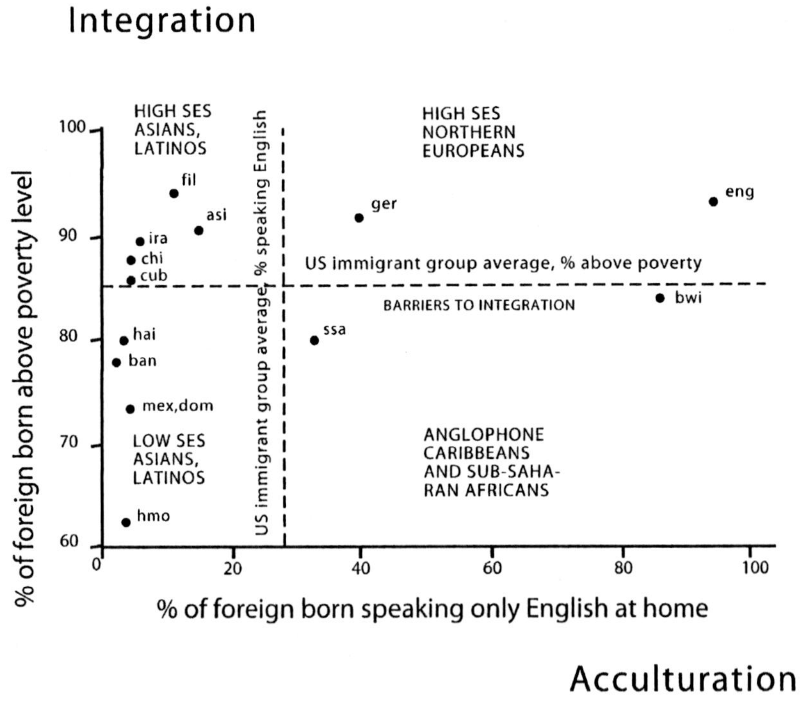

Figure 1.2 Integration/Acculturation Typology, U.S. Immigrant Groups

In the lower left quadrant of Figure 1.2 we have a situation of low integration and low acculturation—the condition today of most Mexicans (mex), Dominicans (dom), Haitians (hai), Bangladeshis (ban), and Hmong (hmo). These groups, whose marginal situations have been the focus of some research (Stepick 1992; Haddad and Smith 1994; Ortiz 1996; Vigil 1997; Pessar and Graham 2001; Smith 2001; Faruque 2002), are separated by low socio-economic status and discrimination from the traditional mainstream as well as from "model minorities" of more recent vintage (such as Cubans and Asian Indians).

Summary of the Chapters

The chapters—all original contributions written for this volume—are organized by broad geographic regions (West and East), which represent two different immigration histories. The West traditionally has been identified with Mexican immigration, and three of the six chapters in this section deal with that group. The West is also the area traditionally preferred by Asian groups—Chinese, Japanese, and Filipinos. The rapid growth of high-tech Western gateway cities has attracted new higher-status immigrants such as Asian Indians, Russians, and Cubans. The East has entertained a great diversity of immigrants for a long period of time. Its traditional industrial cities were forged by the labor of European immigrants, and its modern-day industrial cities have often owed their revitalization to immigrants from Eastern Europe, Central and South America, and the Caribbean. It has developed institutions (governmental and non-governmental) to accommodate new flows, including refugees from Eastern Europe, the Middle East, Vietnam, and Laos. New urban and agribusiness economies have readily employed Mexicans and some Central Americans, but the recency, volume, and undocumented status of these workers has hindered their accommodation into host cultures. The five chapters in this section illustrate this diversity of immigrant experiences.

The section on the *Western United States* begins with Chapter Two, "Slavic Dreams: Post Soviet Refugee Identity and Adaptation in Portland, Oregon," by Susan Hardwick. Hardwick points out that post-Soviet Slavs from the former USSR now comprise the largest refugee group in the Pacific Northwest. Her specific study group is Russian and Ukranian Protestants whose white skin color and religion, in addition to well-developed economic support systems provided to refugees by local social service agencies, would be expected to help them to blend rapidly into the mainstream society. However, the "bonds and bounds" of religious networks tie them together into a cohesive ethno-religious group that excludes outsiders. They exemplify a pattern of selective or segmented adjustment to U.S. life that is typified by so many new immigrant groups, and illustrate the dynamic tension between preservation of culture and social adjustment that is the hallmark of this book. First generation refugees hold onto their Slavic identities with surprising vigor, and their residential patterns provide additional evidence in support of this premise since the majority of post-Soviet era arrivals reside in dispersed nodes of Slavic ethnicity that cluster near Russian and Ukranian

Protestant churches. Their strong religious affiliation emerges as both a help and a hindrance in the larger assimilation experience. They live in what Hardwick calls a "culture of betweenness." An interesting conclusion of the study is that this group identifies more with "groups of color" than with mainstream U.S. society with whom they share many ethno-cultural attributes.

Chapter Three, "Emigrés Outside Miami: The Cuban Experience in Metropolitan Phoenix," by Emily Skop, points out that a number of cities outside of Miami have become home to significant numbers of Cuban émigrés. Unlike the case of Russians and Ukranians in Portland, Cubans in Phoenix have a numerically much smaller presence. Furthermore, a large Latino community (25 percent) helps the Cubans to blend in with relative ease. Skop discovers that her study group is highly selected and dramatically different from the Miami enclave of Cubans. Compared to their Miami compatriots, the Phoenix Cubans are largely second generation and thus less tied to the old Cuba before Castro, and more likely to be single males of moderate or low socio-economic status. In the absence of a Cuban enclave in Phoenix, they depend primarily upon themselves and upon the larger Phoenix community for support. The lack of a Cuban cultural landscape and political presence in Phoenix (and the concomitant lack of Cuban identity there) does not appear to affect their adjustment to the city.

Chapter Four highlights a third group of relatively high-status immigrants—Asian Indians—in still another emerging gateway city of the U.S. West. In "Trying to Be Authentic, But Not *Too* Authentic: Second Generation Hindu Americans in Dallas, Texas," Pawan Dhingra presents evidence for segmented adjustment in which the second generation embraces their culture as a way of dealing with their racial minority status, while at the same time shying away from strong spiritual ties to temple religion, because they do not see its relation to their lives in the U.S. Instead, they seek out secular organizations such as the Indian American Network Association (IANA), that fosters social and economic integration. Nevertheless, both first and second generations consider religion central to their ethnic identities, in that it serves as a lens for cultural adaptation and a mechanism for relating to both others in the Indian community, and to other groups. Asian Indians are not refugees; unlike Russians, Ukranians, Cubans, Hmong, or Vietnamese, they have a relationship with their homeland not truncated by political events. Their cultural ties are strong at the same time their educational backgrounds prepare them for well-paying jobs in the U.S. This presents them with the dilemma of preserving their cultural landscape or integrating into U.S. life, a dilemma that is a core theme of this book.

Chapter Five, "Spatial Disjunctures and Division in the New West: Latino Immigration to Leadville, Colorado," is written by Nancy Hiemstra. In relation to the three previous chapters, she takes us from large metro to non-metro (a tourist area high in the Rockies), and from a high to a low SES immigrant group (Mexicans). We see in Leadville a situation of reactive accommodation in which Anglo residents still hold stereotypical and largely negative views of the new

Latino/a population, which tripled from 1990 to 2000 and which is largely undocumented. In a sense, Leadville's Latinos are facing some of the same problems as those in the Midwest and South, where their recency, salience, and legal status have hindered their successful adjustment. Mexicans in Leadville are meeting the increased demand for low wage service labor in the booming mountain resort industry in such nearby towns as Vail and Breckenridge, 45-90 minutes away. They live in Leadville for its lower cost of living; in so doing, however, they are removed from the support they presumably receive in their places of employment, and face instead suspicion and aloofness on the part of the local population. This is heightened by their residence at the edge of town in low-rent apartments and trailer parks, where they have few opportunities to interact with townspeople. There is little shared space between newcomers and residents in Leadville, and scant evidence of a Mexican cultural landscape. This chapter provides poignant insights on the obstacles that newly-arrived undocumented immigrants face in small towns.

Similarly, Chapter Six, "Meatpacking and Mexicans on the High Plains: From Minority to Majority in Garden City, Kansas," by Donald Stull and Michael Broadway, also deals with how Mexicans adjust to a small town. Compared to Leadville, however, Garden City immigrants are better-integrated into the community. The lure is large meat packing firms locating nearby. Initially, Southeast Asian "boat people" provided a labor source, but as their and their children's mobility drew them to better opportunities elsewhere, the 1990s saw them supplanted by Mexican workers. These workers have transformed the cultural landscape of Garden City—its labor force, schools, businesses, and political landscape. In 2005, Garden City—now almost 50 percent Hispanic—elected its first Hispanic mayor—a Latina. In concluding, Stull and Broadway address the arguments of Samuel Huntington, who fears racial division between Hispanics and Anglos and sees Hispanic immigration as a disturbing challenge to our national identity. They find Huntington's fears and assertions completely groundless. Instead, they believe that Garden's city's future is in good hands—those of its emerging Hispanic majority.

Chapter Seven, "Cultural Retrenchment and Economic Marginality: Mexican Immigrants in San Antonio," by Richard Jones, examines the adjustment of new immigrant Mexicans into an established Hispanic community with its own cultural institutions—Tejano (Texas Mexican American) lifeways and language, Hispanic-run businesses, social services serving the Latino population, and strong political representation. I begin with the observation that in San Antonio, Mexican immigrants would appear to not have to face the same problems as outside the Southwest—because a mediating culture already exists there, that of Mexican Americans. Indeed, in San Antonio, Mexican cultural landscapes (homescapes, gardens, fences) appear embedded within established Hispanic neighborhoods. However, the emotional prism through which Mexico and the U.S. see each other makes social adjustment difficult, and in fact two different adjustments must be negotiated—first to Tejano culture and then to Anglo culture. Interviews with Mexican immigrant families reveal perceptions of discrimination against Mexican migrants by both Mexican Americans and Anglos that worsen their situation of economic marginality and contribute to their strong adherence to Mexican (as opposed to Tejano or Texan) culture.

The section on the *Eastern United States* begins with Chapter Eight, "Spaces and Places of Adaptation in an Ethnic Vietnamese Cluster in New Orleans, Louisiana," by Christopher Airriess. Airriess has been studying the Versailles community, at the eastern extremity of New Orleans, for almost two decades. The community is thirty years old and began with the settlement of higher-status first wave refugees; today less affluent families who came in later waves largely comprise its population. As with the Hmong, their generations-long journey from north to south in Vietnam and then halfway around the world to the United States, coupled with the trauma that accompanied those moves, has left a profound sense of loss and longing for familiar landscapes of home. Airriess documents how they have attempted to re-create these landscapes in New Orleans. Two community spaces and places are especially evocative of their origins: (1) agricultural spaces, rooted in their farming and fishing backgrounds, especially those of the early waves; and (2) religious spaces, stemming from their (persecuted) experiences as Roman Catholics. Finally, (3) commercial spaces, although Buddhist/Chinese and urban in origin, are nevertheless important places of Vietnamese interaction and exercising of cultural preferences. The author ends with a description of the evacuation and partial return of the community after Hurricane Katrina.

Chapter Nine, "The Quest for Home: Sheboygan's Hmong Population," by Karl Byrand, presents a similar theme to Airriess' New Orleans' Vietnamese. The Hmong and later-wave Vietnamese share some similarities in terms of motives, remembered political trauma, poor economic resources, rural backgrounds, and refugee status. However, as Byrand shows, the Hmong come from a tribal, shamanistic, decidedly non-Western tradition, making their integration to the U.S. more difficult than in the case of the Vietnamese. Also, the Hmong are a historically persecuted people, the latest example of which is that since they aided the U.S. efforts in Indochina, after 1975 they were forced to flee as refugees from new Communist regimes. Many were resettled in the United States with the help of church groups and voluntary organizations concentrated in the West as well as in north-central states such as Minnesota and Wisconsin. Byrand expounds in detail upon the halting assimilation process undergone by Hmong in Sheboygan, including mistrust of Western health care practices; language difficulties; low educational attainment; and limited occupational prospects. On a more positive note, the author notes that as Sheboygan's Hmong population has expanded, so has its visual imprint on the cultural landscape, including Hmong-owned and -operated grocery stores and video stores; a mutual assistance association; churches; and radio and TV programs on local public access stations that help maintain Hmong culture.

Chapter Ten, "Getting Settled in the Heartland: Community Formation among First- and Second-Generation Iranians in Iowa City, Iowa," by Mohammad Chaichian, examines the experiences of a very different group of Asian migrants from the Indochinese migrants just discussed. A relatively small contingent of about 700 Iranians, including 300 in Iowa City, have made Iowa their home since the 1979 Iranian Revolution that triggered emigration on a massive scale. In Iowa City they are highly educated and economically successful, with 85 percent of the first generation having completed a college degree. The Iranian community is a cohesive one, promoted by an active Iowa Cultural Association, despite its heterolocal nature. This cohesiveness is partly a function of the feelings of loneliness and isolation that the Iranians attribute to prejudice in a small-city environment—a situation that has been amply documented among other Asian groups (Asian Indians, Koreans, Chinese) in small cities. Chaichian makes the interesting observation, based on his interviews, that the second generation's good schooling, high socio-economic status, strong cultural identity (inculcated by their parents), and extensive friendship networks help insulate them from this prejudice and help them feel more at home in Iowa City. Ironically, their professional aspirations and willingness to take their parents away with them leads the author to conclude that "this small Iranian-American community has a limited chance, if any, of a long-term and sustained inter-generational survival."

In Chapter Eleven, "The Untraditional Geography of Hispanic Settlement in a New South City: Charlotte, North Carolina," by Heather Smith, we return to Mexican immigration—in this case into a city and state that since 1990 have exhibited among the highest growth rates of Mexican foreign-born in the country. Unlike the movement of Mexicans to Garden City or Leadville, the principal draw has been urban jobs in construction and landscaping (secondarily, extractive/manufacturing job opportunities in Charlotte's larger urban region have been important), and unlike those of Western cities, Charlotte's Mexicans are moving into a black/white racial binary in which they do not readily fit. The magnitude of the Mexican influx has led to concerns among community leaders about growing poverty levels, low English language proficiency, and pressure on schools. Nevertheless, tension between resident blacks and Hispanics has been much less than expected, which Smith attributes to the cushion of rapid growth in Charlotte (generating many jobs) and to the availability of suburban housing. The Hispanic community has located not in the inner city but in the near-suburbs, where a landscape of Mexican restaurants and stores has sprung up almost overnight. Although adjustment to U.S. urban life is proving difficult for some (especially women), the prospect for eventual integration appears good.

It is especially appropriate to end the case studies with Ellen Kraly's "'An Anchor of Hope': Refugees in Utica, New York." Other contributors to this volume (Airriess, Broadway and Stull, and Smith) have briefly touched upon the role of immigration in the revitalization of cities and communities, but in Kraly's case, this is the principal focus of her chapter. Utica/Rome was the third-fastest declining

MSA in the nation over the 1990s (losing 5.3 percent of its population). Yet the city doubled its number of foreign-born over the period. This influx, anchored by Bosnians (one-third of the total) but including significant numbers of Vietnamese, Belorussians, Ukranians, Italians, and others, has led to a "rebirth" of the city in terms of home buying and renovation, the emergence of new businesses (e.g., restaurants) in deteriorating parts of the city, more close-knit neighborhoods, new school programs (e.g., ESL) that benefit the larger community, and a young and ambitious new population to replace an aging one. Moreover, the immigrants have been very well received by the community and this has greatly facilitated their adjustment.

In the final chapter book, I address the extensive literature on the benefits and costs of immigration, coming to a positive assessment of the overall impacts both inside megalopolis and outside.

This first chapter thus ends as it began, with a positive view of the role immigrants can play in smaller places outside of megalopolis, as initial reactions give way to participatory accommodation and appreciation. Kraly's chapter suggests that both preservation of immigrant lifeways *and* successful social adjustment are possible.

References

Airriess, Christopher. 2002. "Creating Vietnamese Landscapes and Place in New Orleans." Pp. 228-254 in *Geographical Identities of Ethnic America: Race, Space, and Place,* ed. by Kate Berry and Martha Henderson. Reno: Univ. of Nevada Press.

Airriess, Christopher, and David Clawson. 1991. "Versailles: a Vietnamese Enclave in New Orleans, Louisiana." *Journal of Cultural Geography* 12:1-15.

———. 2000. "Mainland Southeast Asian Refugees: Migration, Settlement, and Adaptation." Pp. 311-346 in *Ethnicity in Contemporary America: a Geographical Appraisal,* edited by Jesse O. McKee. Lanham, Maryland: Rowman and Littlefield.

Alba, Richard, and Victor Nee. 2003. *Remaking the American Mainstream.* Cambridge, MA: Harvard University Press.

Bach, Robert, Rodolfo de la Garza, Karen Ito, Louise Lamphere, and Niara Sudarkasa. 1993. *Changing Relations: Newcomers and Established Residents in U.S. Communities.* New York: The Ford Foundation.

Berry, John W. 1990. "Acculturation and Adaptation: a General Framework." Pp. 90-102 in *Mental Health of Immigrants and Refugees*, edited by Wayne H. Holtzman and Thomas H. Bornemann. Austin, TX: Hogg Foundation for Mental Health.

Birman, Dina, and Forrest B. Tyler. 1994. "Acculturation and Alienation of Soviet Jewish Refugees in the United States." *Genetic, Social, and General Psychological Monographs* 120(1):103-49.

Bozorgmehr, Mehdi, and George Sabah. 1987. "Are the Characteristics of Exiles Different from Immigrants? The Case of Iranians in Los Angeles." *Sociology and Social Research* 71:77-84.

Chaichian, Mohammad. 1997. "First Generation Iranian Immigrants and the Question of Cultural Identity." *International Migration Review* 31(3):612-27.

Dagodag, W. Tim. 1984. "Illegal Mexican Workers in Los Angeles: Locational Characteristics." Pp. 199-217 in *Patterns of Undocumented Migration: Mexico and the United States*, edited by Richard C. Jones. Totowa, NJ: Rowman and Allanheld.

Dakan, William. 2006. "Changes in the Heartland: Emerging Ethnic Patterns in Louisville, Kentucky." Pp. 367-77 in *Race, Ethnicity, and Place in a Changing America*, edited by John Frazier and Eugene Terry-Fio. Binghamton, NY: Global Academic Publishing, Binghamton University.

de Blij, Harm J., and Peter O. Muller. 1994. *Geography: Realms, Regions, and Concepts*. New York: John Wiley.

del Pinal, Jorge, and Audrey Singer. 1997. *Generations of Diversity: Latinos in the United States. Population Bulletin* 52(3), October.

Desbarats, Jaqueline, and Linda Holland. 1983. "Indochinese Settlement Patterns in Orange County." *Amerasia Journal* 10(1):23-46.

Dhingra, Pawan. 2003. "The Second Generation in 'Big D': Korean American and Indian American Organizations in Dallas, Texas." *Sociological Spectrum* 24:247-278.

Do, Phuong. 1999. "A Girl Called Hoai." Pp. 101-109 in *Struggle for Ethnic Identity: Narratives by Asian American Professionals*, edited by Pyong Gap Min and Rose Kim. Walnut Creek, CA: Altamira Press.

Driever, Steven. 2004. "Latinos in Poly-Nucleated Kansas City." Pp. 207-223 in *Hispanic Spaces, Latino Places: Community and Cultural Diversity in Contemporary America*, edited by Daniel Arreola. Austin: Univ. of Texas Press.

Duchon, D. A. 1997. "Home is Where you Make It: Hmong Refugees in Georgia." *Urban Anthropology and Studies of Cultural Systems and World Economic Development* 26(1):71-93.

Durand, Jorge, Douglas Massey and Chiara Capoferro. 2005. "The New Geography of Mexican Immigration." Pp. 1-20 in *New Destinations: Mexican Immigration in the United States*, edited by Victor Zúñiga and Rubén Hernández León. New York: Russell Sage Foundation.

Engstrom, James. 2001. "Industry and Immigration in Dalton, Georgia." Pp. 44-56 in *Latino Workers in the Contemporary South*, edited by Arthur Murphy, Colleen Blanchard, and Jennifer Hill. Athens: University of Georgia Press.

Faruque, Cathleen Jo. 2002. *Migration of the Hmong to the Midwestern United States*. Lanham, MD: University Press of America.

Fennelly, Katherine, and Nocole Palasz. 2003. "English Language Proficiency of Immigrants and Refugees in the Twin Cities Metropolitan Area." *International Migration* 41(5):93-125.

Frey, William, and Kao-Lee Liaw. 1999. "Internal Migration of Foreign-Born Latinos and Asians: Are They Assimilating Geographically?" Pp. 212-30 in *Migration and*

Restructuring in the United States: A Geographic Perspective, edited by Kavita Pandit and Suzanne Davies Withers. Lanham, Md.: Rowman and Littlefield.

Garcia, Maria Cristine. 1996. *Havana U.S.A.* Berkeley: University of California Press.

Gober, Patricia. 1999. "Settlement Dynamics and Internal Migration of the U.S. Foreign-Born Population." Pp. 231-49 in *Migration and Restructuring in the United States: a Geographic Perspective*, edited by Kavita Pandit and Suzanne Davies Withers. Lanham, Md.: Rowman and Littlefield.

Gottmann, Jean. 1961. *Megalopolis*. New York: The Twentieth Century Fund.

Gouveia, Lourdes, Miguel Carranza, and Jasney Cogua. 2005. "The Great Plains Migration: Mexicanos and Latinos in Nebraska." Pp. 23-49 in *New Destinations: Mexican Immigration in the United States*, edited by Victor Zúñiga and Rubén Hernández León. New York: Russell Sage Foundation.

Grey, Mark, and Anne Woodrick. 2005. "Latinos have Revitalized our Community: Mexican Migration and Anglo Responses in Marshalltown, Iowa." Pp. 133-154 in *New Destinations: Mexican Immigration in the United States*, edited by Victor Zúñiga and Rubén Hernández León. New York: Russell Sage Foundation,.

Guthey, Greig. 2001. "Mexican Places in Southern Spaces: Globalization, Work, and Daily Life in and around the North Georgia Poultry Industry." Pp. 57-67 in *Latino Workers in the Contemporary South*, edited by Arthur Murphy, Colleen Blanchard, and Jennifer Hill. Athens: University of Georgia Press.

Haddad, Yvonne, and Jane Smith, ed. 1994. *Muslim Communities in North America*. Albany: State University of New York Press.

Hardwick, Susan. 2002. "Russian Acculturation in Sacramento." Pp. 255-78 in *Geographical Identities of Ethnic America: Race, Space, and Place*, edited by Kate Berry and Martha Henderson. Reno: University of Nevada Press.

Hardwick, Susan, and James Meacham. 2005. "Heterolocalism, Networks of Ethnicity, and Refugee Communities in the Pacific Northwest: the Portland Story." *The Professional Geographer* 57(4):539-57.

Hartshorn, Truman. 1992. *Interpreting the City: An Urban Geography*. New York: John Wiley and Sons, Inc.

Hintzen, Percy. 2001. *West Indian in the West: Self-Representations in an Immigrant Community*. New York: New York University Press.

Johnson-Webb, Karen. 2003. *Recruiting Hispanic Labor: Immigrants in Non-Traditional Areas*. New York: LBF Scholarly Publishing.

Jones, Richard C. 1996. "Spatial Origins of San Antonio's Mexican-born Population." *Rio Bravo* 5(1):1-26.

Kibria, Nazli. 1993. *Family Tightrope: the Changing Lives of Vietnamese Americans*. Princeton, NJ: Princeton University Press.

Kibria, Nazli. 2002. *Becoming Asian American: Second Generation Chinese and Korean American Identities*. Baltimore: Johns Hopkins University Press.

Kraly, Ellen, and Kristin van Valkenberg. 2003. "Refugee Resettlement in Utica, New York: Opportunities and Issues for Community Development." In *Multicultural*

Geographies: the Changing Racial and Ethnic Patterns of the United States, edited by John Frazier and Florence Margai. Binghamton, NY: Binghamton Univ. Press.

Lee, Sharon. 1998. "Asian Americans: Diverse and Growing." *Population Bulletin* 53(2), June.

Lessinger, Johanna. 1995. *From the Ganges to the Hudson: Indian Immigrants in New York City*. Boston: Allyn and Bacon.

Lozada, Eriberto P. 1999. "What Being Filipino American Means to Someone Called Fuji." Pp. 143-55 in *Struggle for Ethnic Identity: Narratives by Asian American Professionals*, edited by Pyong Gap Min and Rose Kim. Walnut Creek, CA: Altamira Press.

Marger, Martin. 1994. *Race and Ethnic Relations: American and Global Perspectives*. Belmont, CA: Wadsworth.

Martin, Philip, and Elizabeth Midgeley. 2003. "Immigration: Shaping and Reshaping America." *Population Bulletin* 58(2), June.

Mines, Richard, and Ricardo Anzaldúa. 1982. *New Migrants vs. Old Migrants: Alternative Labor Market Structures in the California Citrus Industry*. San Diego: Monographs in U.S.-Mexican Studies 9, Program in U.S. Mexican Studies, Univ. of California, San Diego.

Miyares, Ines. 1997. "Changing Perceptions of Space and Place as Measures of Hmong Acculturation." *The Professional Geographer* 49(2):214-24.

Mumford Center. 2005. The Lewis Mumford Center for Comparative Urban and Regional Research, American Cities Project. Albany, NY: The University of Albany. Available at www.albany.edu/mumford.

Ortiz, Vilma. 1996. "The Mexican-Origin Population: Permanent Working Class or Emerging Middle Class?" Pp. 247-77 in *Ethnic Los Angeles*, edited by Roger Waldinger and Mehdi Bozorgmehr. New York: Russell Sage Foundation.

Pessar, Patricia, and Pamela Graham. 2001. "Dominicans: Transnational Identities and Local Politics." Pp. 251-73 in *New Immigrants in New York*, edited by Nancy Foner. New York: Columbia University Press.

Portes, Alejandro. 1984. "The Rise of Ethnicity: Determinants of Ethnic Perceptions among Cuban Exiles in Miami." *American Sociological Review* 49: 383-97.

Portes, Alejandro, and Ruben Rumbaut. 1996. *Immigrant America: A Portrait*. Berkeley: University of California Press.

Potocky, Miriam. 1996. "Refugee Children: How Are They Faring Economically as Adults?" *Social Work* 41(4): 364-73.

Rangaswamy, Padma. 2000. *Namasté America: Indian Immigrants in an American Metropolis*. University Park: The Pennsylvania State University Press

Rich, Brian, and Marta Miranda. 2005. "The Sociopolitical Dynamics of Mexican Immigration in Lexington, Kentucky, 1997-2002: an Ambivalent Community Responds." Pp. 187-219 in *New Destinations: Mexican Immigration in the United States*, edited by Victor Zúñiga and Rubén Hernández León. New York: Russell Sage Foundation.

Rieff, David. 1993. *The Exile: Cuba in the Heart of Miami.* New York: Simon and Schuster.

Schmidley, Dianne. 2001. *Profile of the Foreign-Born Population in the United States: 2000, Current Population Reports*: Series P23-206. Washington, DC: U.S. Government Printing Office, December.

Singer, Audrey. 2004. "The Rise of New Immigrant Gateways." *The Brookings Institution, Living Cities Census Series.* February, p. 35.

———. 2006. "The New Metropolitan Geography of Immigration: Washington, DC, in Context." Pp. 45-55 in *Race, Ethnicity, and Place in a Changing America,* edited by John Frazier and Eugene Terry-Fio. Binghamton, NY: Global Academic Publishing, Binghamton University.

Skop, Emily, and Cecilia Menjívar. 2001. "Phoenix: the Newest Latino Immigrant Gateway?" *Yearbook of the Association of Pacific Coast Geographers* 63:63-76.

Smith, Robert. 1996. "Mexicans in New York City: Membership and Incorporation of a New York Immigrant Group." In *Latinos in New York,* eited by S. Baver and G. Haslip Viera. South Bend, IN: University of Notre Dame Press.

———. 2001. "Mexicans: Social, Educational, Economic, and Political Problems and Prospects in New York." Pp. 275-300 in *New Immigrants in New York,* edited by Nancy Foner. New York: Columbia University Press.

Snyder, Cindy, J. Dean May, Nihada Zulcic, and W. Jay Gabbard. 2005. "Social Work with Bosnian Refugee Children and Families: a Review of the Literature." Child Welfare League of America.

Steppick, Alex. 1992. "The Refugees Nobody Wants: Haitians in Miami." In *Miami Now! Immigration, Ethnicity, and Social Change*, edited by Guillermo Grenier and Alex Stepick. Gainesville: University of Florida Press, chap. 4.

Stepick, Alex, and Guillermo Grenier. 1993. "Cubans in Miami." Pp. 79-110 in *In the Barrios: Latinos and the Underclass Debate,* edited by Joan Moore and Raquel Pinderhughes. New York: Russell Sage Foundation.

Stoller, Paul. 2001. "West Africans: Trading Places in New York." Pp. 229-249 in *New Immigrants in New York*, edited by Nancy Foner. New York: Columbia Univ. Press.

U.S. Bureau of the Census. 2000. Summary File 4 (SF4). Washington, DC: U.S. Census Bureau, Public Information Office.

Vigil, James Diego. 1997. *Personas Mexicanas: Chicano High Schoolers in a Changing Los Angeles.* Fort Worth: Harcourt Brace.

Zhou, Min, and Carl Bankston. 1994. "Social Capital and the Adaptation of the Second Generation: the Case of Vietnamese Youth in New Orleans." *International Migration Review* 28(4):821-845.

Zúñiga, Victor, and Rubén Hernández-León. 2001. "A New Destination for an Old Migration: Origins, Trajectories, and Labor Market Incorporation of Latinos in Dalton, Georgia." Pp. 126-36 in *Latino Workers in the Contemporary South*, edited by Arthur Murphy, Colleen Blanchard, and Jennifer Hill. Athens: University of Georgia Press.

PART TWO

WESTERN UNITED STATES

Chapter 2

Slavic Dreams: Post-Soviet Refugee Identity and Adaptation in Portland, Oregon[1]

Susan Hardwick

> Sometimes I feel like I belong here and sometimes I don't. I mean, the Soviet Union does not exist anymore so I don't really come from anywhere now. I feel confused and pretty empty sometimes even though being an American has always been my biggest dream (Elizabeta, Portland, 2005).

The first decade of the twenty-first century is both the best of times and the worst of times for scholars interested in issues related to the migration, settlement, identity, and adjustment experiences of foreign-born migrants in the United States. As anti-immigrant rhetoric continues to be widely promulgated by the media, and discussed and debated in school classrooms and public and political discourse, understanding more about the experiences of immigrants, refugees, and asylees has become an increasingly important field of study. However, despite this increased attention to issues related to international migration, new and more challenging questions continue to emerge—with increasingly complex answers. Perhaps none are as challenging (or as fascinating, relevant, or timely) as questions about the ever-shifting terrain of the relationship between the spatial patterns of immigrants and refugees and their identities, adjustment, and adaptation to American life. This chapter delves into these topics in a search for new ways to answer a set of unexpected questions about two new groups of migrants who now reside in the Portland, Oregon metropolitan area, Russians and Ukrainians.

Along with other social scientists, human geographers have a long history of interest in the socio-spatial dynamics of immigrant adjustment in North American cities. Of particular importance most recently have been ongoing efforts to provide new ways of thinking about the relationship between the settlement patterns of new migrants and their assimilation experiences (see, for example, Portes and Rumbaut 1996; Li 1998). Critiques of classic Chicago School "acculturation-assimilation" models (that focused on inner cities being places where poor, unassimilated ghettoized minorities reside, and suburbs being places where new immigrants live who are more assimilated into mainstream American or Canadian life), continue to be debated in the scholarly literature (see, for example, Skop and Li 2003). Today however, many foreign-born migrants settle in multicultural suburbs located far from downtown neighborhoods (Portes and Jensen 1987, Thompson 1989, Portes and Zhou 1993, Wright and Ellis 2000, Wright, Ellis, and Parks 2004).

Zelinsky and Lee added another new twist to this debate with yet another new model called *heterolocalism* (1998). Following their original publication on the relationship between the spatial patterns of new immigrants, Zelinsky expanded upon and refined this new model in a seminal book on ethnicity, race, and space (2001). During the past five years or so, heterolocalism has encouraged geographers to re-examine their traditional thinking about spatial patterns of immigrants. This theory (and the follow up research and critiques it engendered) provided the motivation for this chapter and my other related publications on Russians and Ukrainians in the Pacific Northwest (see, for example, Hardwick and Meacham 2005; Hume and Hardwick 2005).

Along with heterolocalism, of particular relevance to this chapter and to the ongoing debate on the relationship between immigrant assimilation and residential location patterns is the notion of ethnic *communities of choice*. Work published by White and Glick on what they called the "self-segregation" of certain immigrant groups (1999), and a follow-up study on San Antonio conducted by Jones (2003), found that certain relatively invisible European groups such as Russian Jews may *choose* to remain relatively segregated despite their high socioeconomic status (SES). Jones' findings on twenty-eight ancestry groups in San Antonio, (based on the use of dissimilarity indexes that analyzed 1990 *Census of Population* data), for example, revealed that the socioeconomic status of a particular group exerts a non-linear influence on segregation, reducing it for below-average SES groups (as in older traditional assimilation models) and increasing it for above-average SES groups (a new pluralism model based on the decision-making of professional class and higher earnings groups). The analysis presented in this chapter integrates the findings on the processes of immigrant *segregation by choice* and on the heterolocalism model.

Because it is located far from traditional immigrant gateway cities such as New York and Los Angeles, one of the most surprising stories to emerge in the past decade and a half has been the migration of post-Cold War refugees from the former Soviet Union to this Pacific Northwest region (see Gunderson 1999; Suo and Chuang 2001; Hardwick 2002). Even more surprising are the religious identities and affiliations of these groups since most belong to evangelical Protestant faiths. Since 1990, post-Soviet migrants have settled in the Pacific Northwest in particularly large numbers, making Washington and Oregon the top two states for Russian and Ukrainian refugee arrivals in the year 2000 (*U.S. Census of Population* 2000). Most surprising of all has been the very large numbers of these two related groups who have settled in the Portland metropolitan area.

During the past two decades, the state of Oregon has become a rapidly changing place in terms of its overall population growth and the diversification of its population. Oregon now ranks eleventh in the nation in the total number of new refugees. Russians and Ukrainians accounted by far for the largest number of new refugee arrivals each year for the past decade and a half. Other much larger numbers of new *immigrants* from Mexico and other parts of Latin America, and South and Southeast Asia add diversity to these *refugee* arrivals each month.

Most of the incoming Russians and Ukrainians (along with most other migrants from the former USSR), are still classified as *refugees* by the American government despite the end of the Cold War more than a decade ago. This classification allows them to enter the country in larger numbers than other non-refugee groups, and also requires them to have a sponsor in place before being allowed to enter the country. Refugee status is defined in the U.S. based on the Geneva Convention and the U.S. Refugee Act passed in 1980. It granted "a permanent and systematic procedure for the admission . . . of refugees of special humanitarian concern in the U.S." (Kritz 1983, xviii). After 1980, refugees included all groups defined as persons who lived outside their homeland who were unable or unwilling to return because of persecution or a well-founded fear of persecution. Because of their religious belief systems—and the government opposition to them during the Socialist years of rule in the former USSR—most Russians and Ukrainians are able to enter the U.S. with refugee status. This guarantees housing for each family or individual, as well as monthly stipends that are paid in return for regular attendance at language and employment training during their first months of residency here.

This chapter reports on the results of a long-term ethnographic and spatial analysis of the shifting identities; residential, economic, and religious patterns; and adjustment experiences of Russians and Ukrainians in northern California and the Pacific Northwest (see Hardwick 1993, 2002; Hardwick and Meacham 2005). The emphasis on ethnic identity in this chapter emerged when I made the seemingly obvious assumption that the white skin color and Protestant religious belief systems (in addition to the well-developed economic support systems provided to refugees by local social service agencies), would assist groups such as Russians and Ukrainians to blend rapidly into the mainstream society of their new place of residence. The results of this analysis illustrate, however, that a complex interplay of social, political, economic, and cultural processes are at work that encourage many of these new migrants to cling steadfastly to their distinctly non-American identities. Chief among these interrelated factors are: (1) the role of religion as a potent force that dramatically slows the acculturation process of new Slavic migrants in the study area; and (2) a set of survival skills fostered in their homeland that allow these particular groups to work within (and outside) the political system in Oregon to assert their identity and meet pressing economic needs.

Thus, even though their white, mainstream Protestant identities would seem to provide Russian and Ukrainian migrants with an ideal setting for rapid integration into mainstream society, the tight bonds of religion tie them together into a distinctive group that excludes outsiders. The majority of the residents of the study area who were born in the former USSR continue to hold onto their Slavic identities with surprising vigor in the first decade after resettlement in the U.S. Their residential pattern (Figure 2.1) provides additional evidence in support of this premise since the majority of post-Soviet era arrivals reside in *nodal clusters* instead of in the more dispersed patterns that often typify groups who are assimilating rapidly into American society and space (Figure 2.1).

This map shows a broad pattern of such clusters, with two principal zones of concentration—Vancouver, Washington, just north of the Columbia River; and Portland, Oregon, east of the Willamette River. Both of these parts of the metro area have affordable housing and a plethora of social service agencies to provide support for newly arriving refugees. Therefore, these are the two zones where the densest populations of Russians and Ukrainians currently reside. A third, less concentrated pattern is found in a more suburban zone in Portland, west of the Willamette River. Besides housing and services, another key to understanding and interpreting these patterns is acknowledging the important role of religion in the lives of most of these Slavic residents of the study area. The location of Russian-speaking churches, shown in Figure 2.1, shows a strong correspondence with the population map. The majority of these Slavic fundamentalist churches are clustered in the first two zones. There are fewer churches in the third zone, Portland's Westside suburbs, serving smaller populations of Russian and Ukrainian Christians who moved away from the larger eastside and Vancouver Slavic population clusters into more expensive West Hills suburbs during the past decade as their incomes increased through time (in keeping with more traditional assimilation models).

Since the vast majority of the Russians and Ukrainians in western Oregon arrived in the area with refugee status because they belonged to groups that were persecuted for their religious beliefs in the former Soviet Union, these Baptist, Pentecostal, and Seventh Day Adventist believers often arrived with their entire congregations from home. Most were sponsored by church congregations already in place in the Portland-Vancouver urban area. Thus, they prefer to reside in a neighborhood or suburb located close to the church that sponsored them or near to other believers from their homeland.

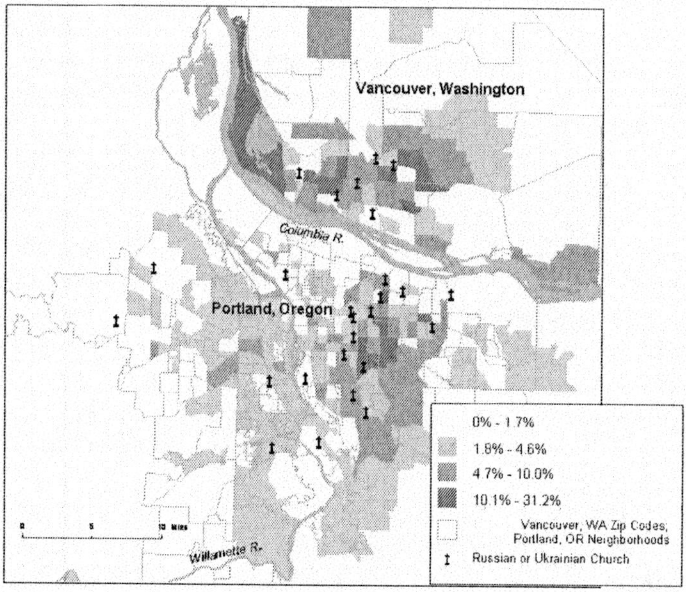

Figure 2.1 Percent of Population Russian or Ukranian, and Russian/Ukranian Churches (Sources: Census TIGER/Line 2000; Slavic Directory, 2002).

The central role of religious institutions in the creation of nodal heterolocalism in the city analyzed in this chapter contributes to several of the larger themes of *Immigrants Outside Megalopolis*. My primary focus here is to document and analyze the shifting identities and adjustment experiences of recently arriving refugees as they continue their struggle to create new lives and landscapes in a strange and unknown place.

Research Methods Used in this Study

The data analyzed in this chapter came from a variety of quantitative and qualitative sources. Census reports for 1990 and 2000, along with information from refugee and immigrant resettlement agency files, church records, and business directories, provided the information needed for the spatial analysis of Slavic residential, religious, and economic patterns in the Portland CMSA. This locational data was built upon by a series of "on the ground" ethnographic methods including structured and unstructured interviews and participant observation, and field observation. I build here on the prior work of Herbert (2000) and other geographers who have called for studies based on the lives of real people for more than a decade (see, for example, Herbert 2000; Lawson 2000; McHugh 2000). I also administered a survey questionnaire to newcomers from the Russian Federation and Ukraine in 2003 to gather additional information about their perceptions and feelings related to identity and adjustment.

This mixed methods approach was necessary for this study because quantitative data alone cannot accurately tell the story of migrant experiences and processes. *Census of Population* figures gathered in 1990 and 2000 provide information only on Russians and Ukrainians who understand enough English to be able to fill out census forms. Those who possess the language skills needed to complete census forms may also resist doing so, however. Based on experiences in their homeland, many find it difficult if not impossible to trust government requests and so refuse to mail back census information for fear of later repercussions by the government. As with many other groups of foreign-born migrants, this makes it difficult to obtain reliable statistics on their residential patterns or social and economic status.

Records kept by area churches and refugee relief agencies proved to be much better indicators of how many migrants from the former USSR have come into the area and where they live than do census statistics. I also used Immigration and Naturalization Service databases from 1982-1997 to track refugee destinations by zip code as well as to establish that most of these newcomers in the Pacific Northwest came in as a part of a large extended family, were unskilled operators, fabricators, or laborers, married, and entered the country through San Francisco, Portland or Seattle processing centers.

Data analyzed from the IPUMS (Integrated Public Use Microdata Series 2000) files of the *U.S. Census of Population*, 2000, also proved helpful in the analysis presented in this chapter. The IPUMS contains only a 5 percent sample of all Russians and Ukrainians in the Portland metropolitan area, but made possible a greater understanding of their places of origin and other relevant data between 1995 and 2000. Information gathered from this selected sample of Russians who resided in the Portland area in 2000 reveals that ¾ of them lived in the Portland area in 1995. That is, Portland Russians are surprisingly tied to their area of initial settlement. By way of contrast, most Cubans in Portland in 1995 had already moved to Miami by 2000. This finding provides additional evidence that Portland is perceived as a positive settlement locale for people from the former USSR, despite the region's serious economic problems (since Oregon currently has the highest unemployment rate in the nation). As we will see later in this chapter, their positive *perception of place* in Oregon, and the long-term residency patterns that are emerging for Russians and Ukrainians in the region, also speak to the importance of religious ties and the role of emerging political savvy and empowerment in maintaining ethnic identity and cultural and religious systems and values.

Ultimately, as in most ethnographic studies, it was data gathered and analyzed from structured and unstructured interviews that yielded the most useful information for this chapter. During the past four years as I worked with Slavic migrants in the Willamette Valley, I very slowly built up the trust needed to learn more about their feelings and perceptions related to identity and adaptation experiences. Since, as Piirainen (1997) has pointed out, xenophobia was a central element in the official Soviet propaganda during their formative years prior to coming to the United States and even brief and random conversation with a foreigner might, in the worst case, have implied the loss of a job and social status in the Soviet Union only ten years ago. Thus, I was forced to make contact very slowly and with great caution to gain enough trust to be able to conduct interviews, especially with newly arriving individuals. The assistance of a former refugee gatekeeper at IRCO (the Immigrant and Refugee Community Organization) in northwest Portland proved invaluable in making the contacts needed to conduct interviews. My Russian language skills and more than two decades of prior work in the field with Russians and Ukrainians in the western United States and Canada, (as well as many months spent conducting interviews in their homeland in the Russian Federation and Ukraine), also helped me gain the trust of this often untrusting group of migrants.

On the other hand, as Piirainen and others have reminded us, Russian culture is extremely verbal. So once the initial moment of gaining trust with interviewees had been established, I found it relatively easy to become involved in long discussions about their migration and adaptation experiences, as well as their perceptions and feelings about their desire to cling to their Russian-ness and Ukrainian-ness in the process.

Situating Portland Refugees within an International Context

In 2000, the United Nations Population Division estimated that there were 175 million international migrants in the world with one in every thirty-five people living in a country other than where they were born. This estimate has more than doubled since 1960, when it was estimated that 79 million international migrants existed worldwide (United Nations 2000). Many of the world's displaced people relocate to the United States, with the 2000 census reporting an estimated 31.3 million foreign-born residents here (a 57 percent increase from the number reported in the 1990 Census).

Refugees make up a large proportion of these numbers, both internationally and in the United States. Since 1975, more than 2.3 million refugees have settled in the United States (see Massey et al. 1998, Hirschman et al 1999). Because the

United States government has long monitored human rights conditions and political change in Russia/Soviet Union, certain residents of this large state (who could prove they were being persecuted for their religious beliefs) were able to secure refugee status beginning in the late 1980s (Hardwick 1993). This policy continues today for evangelical Christians and Jews who wish to resettle in places like Israel, Germany, Australia, and the United States and Canada.

The 1980 Refugee Act in the United States was passed to try to remedy the patchwork of refugee programs in the United States that had emerged during the Cold War years. For three decades following World War II, refugee admissions had been limited to people fleeing Communism. After 1980, refugees were defined as persons living outside their homeland who were unable or unwilling to return because of persecution or a well-founded fear of persecution. In effect, the new law created a worldwide eligibility for admission of political refugees provided they are determined to be of "special humanitarian concern" to the United States (Kritz 1983, xix).

Most of the Russians and Ukrainians who relocated to the U.S. in the past decade arrived as a response to the easing of emigration laws in the former USSR during the late Cold War years, and the subsequent passage of the Lautenberg Amendment to the 1980 Refugee Act by the U.S. Congress in 1989. Chief among the groups who were able to prove they fit the definition of *refugees* were Jews and evangelical Christians such as Pentecostals, Baptists, and Seventh Day Adventists who were persecuted for their religious beliefs under the Soviet system. Following the breakup of the USSR in 1991, out-migration began in earnest. American immigration policies do not classify Russian Orthodox, Ukrainian Orthodox or Catholic believers, or atheists from Russia or Ukraine as "refugees" (since they are perceived to have been less persecuted in their homeland during the Cold War years). However, fundamentalist Protestant groups from the former Soviet Union are classified as refugees by the U.S. government because of their many years of persecution under Soviet regimes. This explains the large numbers of evangelical Christians who now live in the Portland-Vancouver urban area (as opposed to these other groups).

The majority of better educated Jewish migrants from the former USSR have relocated to Israel, western European cities, or larger cities in North America such as New York, Toronto, Boston, Chicago, and Los Angeles due to the availability of higher wage, professional employment in these larger urban centers. There are currently only about eighty Russian or Ukrainian Jewish families in the Portland area and their experiences have been very different from the evangelical refugees (because of the educational and socioeconomic differences that separate these groups). Therefore, due to the much larger numbers and internal cohesiveness of the Russian and Ukrainian Christian migrants in urban Oregon, these groups serve as the focus of the analysis presented in this chapter.

Others who migrate to the United States come on diversity visas. These newcomers, like refugees, are allowed into the United States for humanitarian reasons but have no benefits except green cards and must survive on their own or with the help of family and friends. Tabulations of all post-1980 United States Immigration and Naturalization Service records (up until the time of the dissolution of the IRS when it was subsumed under recent Homeland Security legislation), revealed that no Russian or Ukrainian migrants arrived between 1980 and 1997 on diversity visas. All who were officially listed in these records settled in the Portland area with refugee status.

When new refugees arrive in Oregon, as elsewhere in the United States, they are required to enroll in the federal government's Refugee Case Services Project legislated in the early 1980s by an amendment to the Refugee Act. This revision to the law emerged as a reaction to the concern that too many refugees were staying on welfare. Motivation for new arrivals to register is enhanced by information shared by their personal network of friends, family, and acquaintances met on the journey to North America. This personal network provides information for new arrivals about how to secure cash assistance, medical care, help finding a place to live, and employment ideas from the United States government after they register. This means that many of the choices made during this first stage of a new migrant's life are shaped by outsiders working through government agencies or social service networks.

In 2001, more than $7 million was budgeted by the United States government to help resettle refugees in Oregon alone (Kanal 2001). Most under the age of sixty-five are urged to enroll in beginning English language classes and workshops and classes on much-needed employment skills in their first weeks in the United States to begin preparing for employment. Records kept by social service agencies indicate that 70-90 percent are employed within four to eight months (Immigrant and Refuge Community Organization data files, 2001-2005). Many find jobs in low wage occupations in construction, restaurants, small shops, or industrial and business firms (Figure 2.2). Others drive taxis or work at the Portland Airport or the port of Portland. In 2003, there were more than 400 businesses in the area that catered to Russian-speaking consumers providing services for their compatriots from home (*Slavic Yellow Pages* 2003).

These ethnic businesses, along with the multitude of churches discussed earlier in this chapter, are the only visible evidence in the cultural landscape that Russians and Ukrainians reside in such large numbers in the Portland Metropolitan Area.

Russian and Ukrainian Push-Pull Factors

The vast majority of post-Soviet migrants from the former USSR first left their homeland because of changes in emigration laws before and after the break-up of the Soviet Union in the late 1980s and early 1990s. As mentioned above, chief among the groups who were given permission to emigrate by these new laws were Jews and evangelical Christians. After the USSR was completely dissolved in 1991, emigration began in earnest.

Figure 2.2 Russian Video and Bookstore in Portland, 2003

The Pacific Northwest in particular, a region more often perceived as a place dominated by extreme environmental consciousness, high unemployment rates, and support of alternative lifestyles, would seem to be an unlikely destination for migrants with evangelical Slavic backgrounds. However, tightly structured religious networks linking Russia with towns and cities located on the northwest coast of the United States make this region an especially popular choice for settlement by religious refugees who are intensely connected by their shared religious beliefs (Suo and Chuang 2001). Many if not most decided to leave home after listening to a Russian-language radio broadcast or reading a church newsletter featuring stories about fellow Slavic believers who lived in the American West. The following comment from a young woman born in the Siberian city of Irkutsk who now resides in Salem, a small town located in close proximity to Portland, confirms this finding:

> I heard a sermon one Sunday morning on my old radio in Siberia. The pastor talked about the tulip fields and the freedom that waited for us here. He encouraged us all to come so we could worship in freedom here in Oregon (Galina, Salem, OR, 2004).

The migration of groups of other Russian and Ukrainian immigrants who now reside in California's Central Valley was the result of these same political decisions in the former Soviet Union and the United States in the late 1980s (see Hardwick 1993, 2002).

A series of well-organized local-to-transnational networks are maintained and encouraged by members of local church congregations, ministers, and missionary organizations. As a result, many of the refugees who live in Russian and Ukrainian settlement nodes were members of the same church congregations in their hometowns in the former Soviet Union. According to a Russian refugee now living in northeast Portland, in fact, "In a short time, you've almost moved an entire village to Portland."

Once newcomers arrive, social, cultural, and economic connections and relationships continue to sustain them, especially in their first few years in the United States. As with the migrants discussed in Faist's seminal study of transnationalism and international migration, communication networks are maintained by e-mail messages, phone conversations, and letters connecting migrants in Oregon with family and friends residing in various parts of the region as well as with those who stayed at home (Faist 2000).

Identity Politics and Adaptation

These religious networks, and the spiritual, social and economic support systems they provide for newcomers in Oregon, are complemented by support provided by governmental and private agencies operating actively in the receiving area. For example, sponsors for refugees are identified and selected by voluntary agencies such as the Lutheran Social Services and SOAR (Sponsors Organized to Assist Refugees). A state office of refugee resettlement provides support to other resettlement agencies in the region such as IRCO. This agency is one of the largest social service operations in the country with more than 150 employees (who speak literally every language needed to work with incoming migrants). IRCO's programs provide a layered network of activist political and private agencies provide language and employment training, up to eight months of financial support, housing, medical care, and psychiatric support for new arrivals from Russia, Ukraine and elsewhere to help cushion the shock of arrival in a new place with a new culture.

Impacts of Religious Affiliations

Despite the critically important role of the support systems mentioned above, for the vast majority of post-Soviet refugees from the USSR, the role of religious institutions remains the centerpoint for maintenance of their ethno-religious identity and their ongoing cultural survival. This fervent response from a forty-two year old Ukrainian man to my interview questions about the role of religion in his personal life dramatically illustrates this feeling:

> But you see, having the same God in our lives holds us all together. When we sing our songs in church and listen to the teaching of our same Russian Bible, nothing else can tear us apart. We are Russian Christians. That's just all there is to know, you see? (Victor, Portland, 2003).

Victor and literally all of the other Russians and Ukrainians interviewed for this project spoke from the heart when I questioned them about the role of religion in their lives. But many also identified some of the more practical reasons why belonging to the same church as their friends and family from home was helpful in terms of adjusting to life in Oregon. According to a fifty year-old Baptist from Kiev:

> My church helps me stay connected to my culture and my beliefs for sure. But it is also where I make my connections for jobs. You know, I can't open my own business because it costs too much here—and I need work to be a plumber like I did at home. So sometimes I hear about jobs people need done when we talk at church (Sasha, Beaverton, OR, 2005).

From findings gathered through personal interviews like this one with Sasha and survey questionnaires, it was clear that identifying with membership in particular congregations is the glue that helps hold Slavic refugees together, at least in the early years of settlement. The sense of belonging provided by religious and spiritual bonds holds Russians and Ukrainians together tightly as they fend off the "sins" of the outside world. Their shared behavioral norms, dress codes, and values bind believers to each other and to their places of origin and common culture. However, the safety and security of being a part of a larger group can both empower members to feel confident to venture out into the outside world (thereby speeding the adaptation process) or slow down their willingness to move beyond the comfort of their insider church group. Religious affiliations thus emerged as both a help and a hindrance to the larger assimilation experience for these and other groups of refugees and immigrants.

Impacts of Political Empowerment: The Slavic Coalition

The cohesive power of Russian and Ukrainian religious and economic networks in western Oregon's towns and cities is played out in other, more political ways as well. A second contributing network that helps explain some of the reasons for an emerging sense of "we-ness" among Russians and Ukrainians in Portland has been the formation of the Slavic Coalition. With the support of a civic empowerment grant that funded an initiative called the Interwoven Tapestry Project, Russians and Ukrainians recently formed this increasingly active organization at a retreat in 2004. Since that time, goals of the Coalition have been refined and plans laid out for accomplishing two primary objectives: (1) finding ways to work within the larger community's social and economic infrastructure; and (2) insuring that the ethnic and religious identities of its members are maintained to provide insider support for helping with adaptation and adjustment to life in Portland.

As with other refugee groups, the economic needs of this community are very real. Helping their members find safe and affordable housing, meaningful employment, and health and education care remain critical concerns of the Coalition. But because they are white, foreign-born migrants, Russians and Ukrainians were not initially considered to be a part of the larger community's Coalition of Color (a political group charged by the county government to make funding decisions related to support for various immigrant and refugee groups). Therefore, they had to come up with ways to convince the leadership of this diverse group at city, county, and regional levels that the Slavic Coalition should be included as a community of color. This insider membership status would allow the Coalition to gain access to funding and programs such as the Coalition of Educational Excellence and other social and educational service support initiatives in Portland. This goal was accomplished by late 2003 by active participation and debate at public meetings, networking with the leaders of other minority groups over coffee, and numerous e-mail and cell phone conversations that spread across the region.

Secretary Vladmir Golovan's report of the outcomes of this first organizational meeting of the Coalition laid the groundwork for redefining their white ethnic identity as follows:

> It is not easy for a Slavic community to be recognized by officials as a minority group (we do not look like a minority group based on our skin color) . . . but we already made steps to succeed in this field. Coalition of Color finally recognized us as a minority group (it's an organization that unites coalitions of different minority groups like Latino Network, Asian-Pacific Islanders, African Americans, African Immigrants, Native Americans).

Key to declaring this group's status as a community of color is understanding the new county and city funding system in Portland. Beginning in late 2001, Multnomah County and other government jurisdictions in the metropolitan region reorganized the process of grant distribution for services to minority groups. The county declared that it would no longer fund individual groups or agencies for programs, but rather wanted to limit funding to partnerships of minority coalitions and service providers. As a result of their successful coalition building effort, IRCO and the Slavic Coalition received a $340,000 grant from Multnomah County in 2004 to provide "culturally-specific school-based and school-linked programming for the Slavic community" (McDonald interview 2004). Gaining this funding would have been impossible without membership in the city's Community of Color Coalition. Not coincidentally, these funds address the overarching goal of the Slavic Coalition: "to advocate for the Slavic community" (Slavic Coalition Retreat Agenda 2004).

Clearly the Slavic Coalition's status as a member of the Portland Community of Color Coalition carries important messages about the changing meanings and definitions of race in local and national politics. As constructed whiteness is expressed and exposed in differing ways among and between refugee and immigrant communities in the United States and native-born people of color, the implications for the impact of these evolving definitions for funding minority programs in Portland and elsewhere in the Willamette Valley are immense.

The Co-Chairs of the Slavic Coalition presented their position to the Director of the U.S. Office of Refugee Resettlement at a community-based conference held at IRCO in May, 2005. Clarifying the goals of the Coalition, one of these two speakers stated emphatically that:

> We are a community of color just like the rest of you sitting here in this room today. Even though some of you are black Africans or Cubans or Asians or are from some other place, we are all truly people of color and we all need support.

Both the Portland-based Slavic Coalition (and its efforts to empower Russian and Ukrainian refugees to identify themselves as apart from other whites in the region) and the exclusiveness of tightly bound evangelical Slavic religious congregations (who bind its members together to protect them from the "evil" outside influences of the majority culture) are working to maintain a distinctive ethnic and religious identity for refugees in the Portland urban area. At the same time, these groups also lend economic and social support that helps newcomers cope with the challenges of life in a new and often confusing place. Interestingly, then, these insider networks and institutions are engaged both in helping maintain ethnic identity and assisting with adjustment to the receiving society in a role located in-between the two extremes of identity maintenance and involvement in the Americanization process.

Conclusions: Identity, Adaptation, and Ethnic Transformation in Oregon's Heartland

Although there are a large number of well organized refugee support systems in place in Portland, this chapter has shown that two primary networks are key to sustaining and maintaining the ethnic and religious identities of Russians and Ukrainians in the region—religious institutions and political empowerment coalitions. Although these types of support systems may also be helpful for other groups of refugees and immigrants in North America, migrants from the former Soviet Union are particularly poised to hang onto and use these two networks of support because of the conditions in their homeland prior to departure for Oregon.

In the Soviet Union, the importance and power of local and regional support systems was integral to surviving day to day life where scaled-up authoritarian rule dominated individual lives. It was the power of internal groups that held people and culture together within a Socialist society. These ground-level solidarities became ever more intense within a society that made gathering together, especially for religious purposes, illegal. Thus, "the solidarities that developed in this particularized society were, in the first place, personal solidarities towards the members of a primary group or a social network, and not abstract solidarities towards the social order in general (Piirainen 1997, 46). This helps explain why active participation in religious networks and membership in church congregations helps hold Russians and Ukrainians together in Oregon and elsewhere, even after migrating to a place far from home.

Sociologist Max Weber's classic arguments about the cohesiveness of insider support in traditional cultures add substance to this argument with his discussion of the importance of maintaining social solidarity with a restricted number of people based on kinship and other close ties. This sharp division between insiders and outsiders—us and them—he reminds us, is a characteristic of a traditional society. Weber writes:

> In the inside, there was the attachment to tradition, a relation of mutual respect among the fellow members of the same tribe, family or house, and a corresponding restraint in the quest for the unscrupulous acquisition inside this circle of fellow men, united by this relation of mutual respect; the inside morals. And second, in the relations with the outside, an absolute lack of restraint and consideration was predominant, whereby every stranger initially was an enemy, towards whom there were no ethical constraints: the outside morals (Weber 1972, 303).

The power of Russian and Ukrainian religious and political networks in Portland, then, lies in the importance of clinging to insiders who are part of a shared value system and common history. Both are critical to maintaining and defining and re-defining the shifting tides of ethnic identity. Renaming their insider group as a "community of color" to gain the advantages from a system geared to help *diverse* groups (rather than historically *white* groups) makes sense based on this long tradition of finding ways to survive in a closed system—not only for economic reasons, but also for other, deeper reasons that emanate from long, hard years depending on insider networks in their Slavic homeland.

As white Protestant, foreign-born residents of a predominately white Protestant region of the country, the experience of post-Soviet Russians and Ukrainians illustrates a distinctive type of ethnic community, a *community of choice*. Despite ongoing linguistic and employment challenges in a new place of residence that is very difference from the former Soviet Union, these two related groups are adjusting selectively to life in America. Anchored firmly within their identities and congregations of choice, at least in the first decade and a half of settlement in the Pacific Northwest, Slavic migrants are seeking a new path—a path of *cultural betweenness*. Here, choices can be made about what to cling to from home (e.g. religious beliefs), what to reject in their new society, and what pieces of American society to accept. This path is littered with confusing moments, but is also lined with possibilities of forging an as yet uncharted new way to move towards acculturation, assimilation, and adjustment to American life in the years to come.

Notes

1. Thanks are extended to the National Science Foundation for support from grant # BCS-0214467 who generously funded the field research, travel costs, and cartography for this article. I also am deeply indebted to the expert cartographic assistance of James E. Meacham and Anika Juhn, and to Victoria Libov and Susan E. Hume for their invaluable research support, as well as the gently rigorous content editing of Richard C. Jones.

References

Faist, Thomas. 2000. *The Volume and Dynamics of International Migration and Transnational Social Spaces*. Oxford: Oxford University Press.

Gunderson, Kevin. 1999. Russians New Wave. *The Oregonian.* May 16: 1, 5.

Hardwick, Susan W. 2002. "Russian Acculturation in Sacramento." Pp. 255-78 in *Geographical identities of ethnic America: Race, space, and place*, edited by Kate A. Berry and Martha Henderson. Reno: University of Nevada Press.

———. 1993. *Russian Refuge: Religion, Migration, and Settlement on the North American Pacific Rim*. Chicago: University of Chicago Press.

Hardwick, Susan W., and James E. Meacham. 2005. "Heterolocalism, networks of ethnicity, and refugee communities in the Pacific Northwest: The Portland story." *The Professional Geographer* 57(4):539-557.

Herbert, Steven. 2000. "For ethnography." *Progress in Human Geography* 24:550-568.

Hirschman, Charles, Philip Kasanitz, and Josh DeWind. 1999. *The Handbook of International Migration: The American Experience.* New York: The Russell Sage Foundation.

Hume, Susan E., and Susan W. Hardwick. 2005. "Migration, culture, and place: The impacts of refugee resettlement on the Portland Urban Area." *The Geographical Review* 95:189-209.

Immigrant and Community Organization Refugee Files. 2001-2005. Portland, OR.

Immigration and Naturalization Service Annual Databases, 1982-1997. Washington, DC.

Integrated Public Use Microdata Series (IPUMS). 2000. *U.S. Census of Population.* Washington, DC.

Jones, Richard C. 2003. "The segregation of ancestry groups in San Antonio." *The Social Science Journal* 40:213-232.

Kanal, Nehru. 2001 and 2004. Personal interview. Office of Refugee Resettlement, Salem, OR.

Kritz, Mary. 1983. *U.S Immigration and Refugee Policy.* Lexington, MA: Lexington Books.

Lawson, Victoria. 2000. "Arguments within the Geographies of Movement: the Theoretical Potential of Migrants' Stories." *Progress in Human Geography* 24:173-189.

Li, Wei. 1998. "Los Angeles' Chinese Ethnoburb. From Ethnic Service Center to Global Economy Outpost." *Urban Geography* 19(6):502-517.

Massey, Douglas S., J. Arango, G. Hugo, A. Kouaouci, A. Pellegrino, and J. E. Taylor. 1998. *Worlds in Motion: Understanding International Migration at the End of the Millennium.* Oxford: Clarendon Press.

McDonald, Jeffrey. 2004. Personal interview. Immigrant and Refugee Community Organization, Portland, OR.

McHugh, Kevin E. 2000. "Inside, Outside, Upside Down, Backward, Forward, Round and Round: A Case for Ethnographic Studies in Migration." *Progress in Human Geography* 24:71-89.

Piirainen, Timo. 1997. *Towards a New Social Order in Russia: Transforming Structures and Everyday Life.* Aldershot, England: Dartmouth Publishing Company, Ltd.

Portes, Alejandro, and Leif Jensen. 1987. "What's an ethnic enclave? The case for conceptual clarity." *American Sociological Review* 52(5): 768-771.

Portes, Alejandro, and Ruben Rumbaut. 1996. *Immigrant America: A portrait.* Berkeley: University of California Press.

Portes, Alejandro and Min Zhou. 1993. "The New Second Generation: Segmented Assimilation and its Variants." *Annals of the Academy of Political and Social Science* 530:74-96.

Skop, Emily, and Wei Lee. 2003. "From the Ghetto to the Invisiburb: Shifting Patterns of Immigrant Settlement in Contemporary America." Pp. 113-24 in *Multicultural Geographies*, edited by John W. Frazier and Florence Margai. New York: Academic Publishing.

Slavic Coalition Minutes. 2004. Founding Meeting. Portland, OR.

Slavic Coalition Retreat Agenda. 2004. Portland, OR.

Slavic Yellow Pages. 2003. Portland, OR.

Suo, Steve, and Angie Chuang. 2001. "Russians, Ukrainians call Northwest Home." *The Oregonian*, August 6:1,4.

United Nations High Commission for Refugees. 2000. *The State of the World's Refugees.* Oxford: Oxford University Press.

United States Census of Population. 2000. Washington, DC.

Weber, Max. 1972. *Wirtschaft und Gesellschaft.* Tubingen, Germany.

White, Michael, and Jennifer Glick. 1999. "The Impact of Immigration on Residential Segregation." Pp. 345-72 in *Immigrant and Opportunity: Race, Ethnicity, and Employment in the United States*, edited by Frank D. Bean and Stephanie Bell-Rose. New York: Russell Sage Foundation.

Wright, Richard, and Mark Ellis. 2000. "Race, Region and the Territorial Politics of Immigration in the U.S." *International Journal of Population Geography* 6:197-211.

Wright, Richard, Mark Ellis, and Virginia Parks. 2004. "Work Together, Live Apart? Geographies of Racial and Ethnic Segregation at Home and at Work." *Annals of the Association of American Geographers* 94(3):620-637.

Zelinsky, Wilbur. 2001. *The Enigma of Ethnicity. Another American Dilemma.* Iowa City: University of Iowa Press.

Zelinsky, Wilbur, and Barrett A. Lee. 1998. "Heterolocalism: An Alternative Model of the Sociospatial Behaviour of Immigrant Ethnic Communities." *International Journal of Population Geography* 4:1-18.

Chapter 3

Émigrés Outside Miami: The Cuban Experience in Metropolitan Phoenix

Emily Skop

Miami is well-known as the Cuban capital in the United States, home to well-over half of all U.S. Cubans (Boswell 1994; Garcia 1996; Skop 2001). Yet there are a number of cities besides Miami which have become home to Cuban émigrés, largely as a result of the Cuban Refugee Resettlement Program. Because resettlement was seen as the "most immediate, effective, and economical means" of accelerating the adjustment process for the refugees (Thomas 1963, 8), over the past forty-odd years the U.S. government program, with the help of volunteer agencies like Catholic Social Services, International Rescue Committee (IRC), United Hebrew Immigrant Aid Society, and Church World Service, has dispersed refugees throughout the United States. Cuban émigrés have been resettled in more than fifty cities. New York, Jersey City, Los Angeles, and Tampa received large numbers of refugees (more than 30,000 each), while cities like Dallas, San Diego, Detroit, Denver, and Hartford received fewer numbers of refugees (fewer than 3,000 each). It is true that many of the refugees initially resettled by the Cuban Refugee Resettlement Program eventually returned to Miami (McHugh, Miyares, and Skop 1997), yet a significant minority of the émigrés continue to live in both larger secondary communities, as well as in smaller and more isolated communities.

Surprisingly little research has documented Cuban refugee settlement outside of the Miami megalopolis. In effect, "the Miami Model" has become so popularized that the Cuban population living in other areas has been virtually ignored and potential consequences of these émigrés living in their new communities have largely been disregarded. Yet what happens in those areas where smaller numbers of the Cuban population reside? Do the refugees exhibit the same characteristics as those émigrés living in Miami? Is *cubanidad* reinforced at a smaller scale? Or do forces that are hidden at the larger scale become pervasive in the smaller community? This chapter explores these questions by examining how Phoenix, with a Cuban population of just fewer than four thousand, has been transformed with the arrival of Cuban émigrés. The study relies on the 2000 U.S. Census PUMS 5 percent files, supplemented with intensive interviews of refugee resettlement workers and community organizers, along with field observations conducted from 1997-2002. The results indicate that members of the Phoenix Cuban community are highly selected and dramatically different from those émigrés living in the Miami enclave. Indeed the forces and divisions that are more hidden in Miami (including the role of year of arrival and generation) become pervasive in the smaller community. At the same time, population size, refugee resettlement policy, and the context of reception reinforce a lack of collectivity. As a result, many émigrés lose their sense of *cubanidad*, and identify with and adapt instead to the broader Latino subculture that predominates in Phoenix.

Cuban Migration to the United States

The onset of the Cuban revolution spurred a migration to the United States that has continued to the present day. More than a million Cubans have emigrated since January 1959, when Fidel Castro overthrew the government of Fulgencio Batista. Labeled *Los Batistianos* by the Castro government, many emigrants from 1959 onward were former supporters of the Batista regime, relatives of these exiles, or other elites who may have caused problems for the revolution if they remained on the island (Olson and Olson 1995, 55). As one author stated it, "Many of the migrants actually constitute the most pro-American segment of the Cuban population; that is, those that were more susceptible to the cultural penetration of the United States in the island, or to put it differently, who were more Americanized" (Wong 1974, 88). Fear of imprisonment, harassment and persecution by the revolutionaries (which included both the disruption of daily life and the failure to integrate into the revolution), the loss of jobs, possessions and sources of income as a result of new government policies, and disagreement with the socialist philosophy of the revolution were all motivations for leaving.

Despite a common desire to flee Cuba, the émigré communities before and after 1980 were actually quite different.[1] Pre-1980 Cuban refugees came with a variety of resources, including cash, education, and occupational skills. Many of these exiles had close ties with American enterprises; many of whom provided jobs and contacts immediately upon arrival. During this period of emigration, there were a large proportion of exiles with professional occupations—doctors, lawyers, teachers, businessmen, etc. More than two-thirds of the refugees completed at least high school (Fagen, Brody, and O'Leary 1968, 19). Many fled Cuba before Castro had the ability to take their financial resources, giving the refugees some support when they entered the United States. The exiles generally brought a "'middle class' ethic and style of life similar to that shared by the established sectors of American society" (Portes 1969, 507).

Post-1979 émigrés were different people and Cuba was a different place. Socioeconomic factors set apart the more recent arrivals. The makeup of exiles during the 1980 Mariel boatlift, especially, was significantly different from earlier periods (Council for Inter-American Security 1981; McCoy 1985; Cros Sandoval 1986; Bach 1987; Ackerman and Clark 1995; Skop 2001). Most Cubans from this period came from working-class backgrounds, with skills concentrated in craft, laborer, machine operative, and transport operative occupations; few post-1979 migrants had professional experience (Bach, Bach, and Triplett 1981; Ackerman and Clark 1995; Masud-Piloto 1996). The educational background of most post-1979 arrivals indicates that these émigrés had fewer educational skills as well; most averaged less than eight years of schooling (McCoy 1985; and Ackerman and Clark 1995).

Race was also a characteristic that became significant with those arriving post-1979. Until 1980, the white Cuban population was vastly over-represented in the United States; more than 95 percent of Cuban exiles defined themselves as white. Yet a significant proportion of blacks and mulattos entered the United States during the Mariel Boatlift and after (McCoy 1985, 23; and Skop 1997).[2] Since 1980, the racial composition of entrants has more closely represented the racial composition of the Cuban island population. In fact, according to the 2000 U.S. Census, nearly thirty percent of Cubans identified themselves as either "Black" or "Two or more races."

As a result of such dramatic differences, a conflict of values emerged between pre-1980 refugees and post-1979 arrivals, specifically in reference to self-discipline, attitudes toward privacy, work and money, and life expectations. Golden Exiles and Freedom Flight refugees grasped onto their memories and turned to Miami, "where the Cuba they loved still exists" (Rieff 1993, 134). Yet Mariels and other post-1980 émigrés were unwilling to accept this highly romanticized version of *cubanidad*. It served as a reminder of a bourgeois past that many had originally rebelled against, fought for, and/or been propagandized against, during the last thirty-five years (or, for the youngest émigrés, at least that their parents had rebelled against). Despite the fact that many felt betrayed by the Castro government (demonstrated by their migration to the U.S.), post-1979 Cuban émigrés remembered a time when they faced high levels of unemployment, low income levels, and insufficient social services before 1959. They remembered being tired of the oppressive control of the upper-classes and the corrupt Batista regime during the 1950's (Olson and Olson 1995, 35). While pre-1980 and post-1980 Cuban émigrés generally shared an anti-Castro sentiment, their visions of Cuba were extremely different. The pre-1980 Cuban American community inwardly blamed the Marielitos for shattering the romantic ideal and nostalgic view they had so arduously preserved of Cuba and Cubans (Cros Sandoval 1986, 11), while post-1980 Cuban arrivals attempted to reconfigure *cubanidad* in their own images, rather than accept that version created by pre-1980 Cuban migrants.

The Cuban Refugee Resettlement Program

In the midst of the Cold War with the USSR in the 1960's and 1970's, the United States government perceived that the image (and actuality) of Cuban exiles fleeing Communism was ideologically advantageous. Thus, before 1980, Cuban exiles were welcomed with open arms. Indeed, the U.S. government and society in general welcomed the exiles and implemented many programs to facilitate adjustment, including the aforementioned Cuban Refugee Resettlement Program. When Fidel Castro gained power in Cuba, the United States quickly seized a political opportunity. The unusually positive reception of Cubans was a direct consequence of the perceived congruity between the values for which refugees "left everything behind" and the predominant anti-Communist orientation of American culture (Portes 1969). As an official Cuban Refugee Resettlement Program document states: "From the beginning, Cuban refugees were considered not as intruders but as friends. Efforts on their behalf were regarded not as burdens but as opportunities for service to fellow Americans, to be given with understanding and generosity" (U.S. Department of Health, Education, and Welfare 1967, 12). Thus, émigré claims of political persecution in Cuba were promptly accepted by the U.S. government and the exiles were admitted with refugee status. This refugee status was significant because it gave exiles access to numerous public resources and encouraged a positive reception by the host community. Not only was the largest refugee program in U.S. history set up during these initial years, but the general reception of the exiles was "magnificent" (Thomas 1963, 50).

During the initial wave of the exodus many of the exiles settled in Miami largely because of the city's proximity to Cuba. However, it soon became evident to local government officials in South Florida that the area could not support such a heavy increase in population. As a result, President Kennedy set up the nine-point Cuban Refugee Resettlement Program to assist Miami and provide services for refugees. The plan was comprehensive and acknowledged the role of the Federal Government in the process of satisfactorily situating refugees into a new life in the United States.

A main goal of the Cuban Refugee Resettlement Program was (and continues to be) the resettlement of refugees away from Miami. Volunteer agencies coordinated and carried out the program of resettlement for Cuban exiles and the Federal Government agreed to reimburse the agencies for the costs of transportation to the new resettlement location and for "reasonable expenses incidental to such travel" (Taft et al. 1979, 84). As a result, more than 2,400 Cuban refugee communities now exist in all 50 states. Today, there are concentrations of Cubans in Florida (outside of Miami—where of course, the largest population exists), New York, New Jersey, California, Illinois, and Texas; smaller numbers of refugees are scattered throughout the U.S. Still, more than half of Cuban refugees live in the Miami Metropolitan Area. This suggests that while the Cuban Refugee Program did initially disperse the exiles, it did not prevent some émigrés from making a secondary migration to Miami, which continuously acts as a magnet for Cuban exiles (McHugh, Miyares, and Skop, 1997).

In 1980, a series of complicated events resulted in a dramatic shift in U.S. refugee policy, especially in regards to the way in which Cuban refugee admissions would be handled. The Refugee Act of 1980 represented the first major reform of the refugee provisions of American immigration law in nearly three decades. Most importantly, the Refugee Act of 1980 repealed previous discriminatory treatment of refugees by providing a new definition of a refugee. "The new definition no longer applies only to refugees 'from communism' or certain areas of the Middle East; it now applies to all who meet the test of the United Nations Convention and Protocol on the Status of Refugees" (Kennedy 1981, 143). The 1980 Refugee Act and the 1995 Amendments to the 1990 Immigration and Naturalization Act contain considerable changes from previous admission policy towards Cuban refugees. Post-1979, automatic political asylum and preferential treatment of Cubans based strictly on political considerations no longer characterized refugee admissions policy (Masud-Piloto 1996, 129). And because of the shift in policy, the numbers of Cuban refugees arriving on American shores has dramatically declined since 1980.

Even so, refugee resettlement agencies have continued to play an important role in resettling émigrés outside of the Miami enclave. At times it has proven to be a challenging process, especially because many of the post-1979 émigrés are single males with no relations in the U.S. and because most voluntary agencies prefer to sponsor women, children, or entire families (Garcia 1996, 71). Two organizations, Catholic Social Services and the International Rescue Committee (IRC), have been largely responsible for the majority of Cuban refugee resettlements since 1979. Because the two agencies maintain key offices in a few states, refugee resettlements since 1979 have been highly concentrated, with the vast majority in Florida, New Jersey, New York and California. Interestingly, as the voluntary agencies set up additional offices in new areas, small Cuban settlements have begun to emerge outside traditional areas of settlement. This is the case in Metropolitan Phoenix, which has seen its Cuban population grow dramatically—from fewer than 500 individuals in 1980 to nearly 4,000 residents in 2000.

Comparative Analysis: Cuban Communities in Phoenix and Miami

The highly institutionalized manner in which Cuban émigrés become settled in Phoenix means that the Cuban community in Phoenix, while at first concentrated because of refugee resettlement agency policy, eventually becomes largely invisible on the urban landscape. At the same time, as a result of decision making by the U.S. federal government and the policies of the Cuban Refugee Resettlement Program, members of this particular community are highly selected and dramatically different from those émigrés living in the Miami enclave. These geographic, social, and demographic differences converge to create a unique experience for the Cuban émigrés living outside the Miami megalopolis. For one, it makes it extremely difficult to reinforce a particular, Cuban identity (*cubanidad*) at the smaller scale. For another, it means that the forces and divisions that are more hidden in the larger enclaves become pervasive in the smaller community. As a result, many émigrés come to identify with and adapt to the broader Latino subculture that predominates in Phoenix.

Settlement Patterns

Cubans in Miami are heavily concentrated in two areas of Metropolitan Miami. The largest number live along a corridor that extends directly west from Little Havana in the city's center through Sweetwater and Westchester, and diminishes towards the outer limits of the metropolitan area (Boswell 1993, 20). The other main concentration is northwest of downtown, in Hialeah (Boswell and Skop 1995, 41). Little Havana was the original Cuban area of settlement in the 1960's. This concentration continued through the 1990's. Waves of migrants were attracted to a four-square mile area defined by Southwest 8th Street (Calle Ocho) and Flagler Street. The Cuban neighborhood had shops and *bodegas* (grocery stores) that catered to the new émigrés' needs; low-rent houses and apartments were available; and there was plenty of public transportation (Garcia 1996, 86). As émigrés became more upwardly-mobile, middle- and upper-class Cubans moved west along the Flagler/Calle Ocho corridor into the growing suburbs of Miami, primarily to Coral Gables, West Miami, Sweetwater, and Westchester. Hialeah is an area of blue-collar Cubans. The high proportion of manufacturing plants in that neighborhood acted as a significant magnet for settlement. Hialeah also drew many post-1979 Cubans because of the jobs available at Miami International Airport and the Hialeah race tracks (Garcia 1996, 86).

We might expect that Cubans in Phoenix would follow the same model of concentrated settlement that Cuban exiles in Miami exhibit. But, while they tend to settle initially in refugee resettlement program-sponsored apartment complexes, Cuban émigrés do not remain densely clustered for long. After six months or so, most of the émigrés find new homes and these are highly scattered throughout the Phoenix Metropolitan Area. Few concentrations exist; the population is spread out in many of the residential areas of Phoenix, as well as in Tempe, Gilbert, Mesa, and North Scottsdale. Even in their most densely populated areas, Cubans do not represent more than 100 residents in more than one census tract. In fact, in the Phoenix Metropolitan Area, because Cubans live in census tracts with fewer than 100 Cubans (which represents less than one percent of the entire census tract population), the U.S. Census Bureau will not release the data because of required population thresholds and confidentiality/privacy issues! Lillie, a Cuban refugee who has lived in Phoenix since 1982, compares Phoenix with Miami, where she initially arrived in 1979 and lived for three years:

> Oh no, they aren't the same. Miami is the second largest Cuban city in the world after Havana and you can literally live there and not speak English if you like . . .There is no such thing as a Cuban community in Phoenix. We are all spread out.[3]

Cuban organizations in Miami don't know about Cubans in Phoenix either. Guarione Diaz, the president of the Cuban American National Council, gauged the connections between Phoenix and Miami. He exclaimed: "Cubans in Phoenix? Oh, I don't think there are any!"

Of course, this is not true. While it is a small community, emigrants from Cuba have made Phoenix a destination and have diversified the city's Latino population (Skop and Menjivar 2001). Also important is the fact that Cuban settlement in the city is just over two decades old; few Cubans lived in Phoenix in 1980. By 1990, there were approximately 1,000 Cubans living in the Phoenix Metropolitan Area. Since then, the IRC has sponsored as few as 72 and as many as 400 Cuban refugees each year (Shipman 2004). As a result, in 2000, the Cuban population in Phoenix exceeded 3,500 with the influx of IRC refugees and other Cubans (including second-generation Cuban Americans) since 1990. Pedro, Reception and Placement Coordinator for The International Rescue Committee, describes the process by which refugees are resettled in Phoenix:

> IRC initially places refugees in apartment complexes located nearby the agency's central main office so there is easy access to the agency. But refugees rarely stay in their initial settlements for long (no more than six months generally). We placed five or six families in one nearly apartment complex, but they have already moved. Once they find jobs and become familiarized with the city, most of the refugees relocate to new apartments and for many, eventually new houses. But they do not concentrate in any area of the city.

Because of the highly institutionalized and systematic manner in which Cuban refugees become resettled in Phoenix, then, very small clusters of Cuban newcomers do emerge and become visible in particular apartment complexes and neighborhoods for brief periods of time. Supported with government funds that provide substantial help and orientation, recently arrived Cuban émigrés begin their experience in various Catholic Social Services and IRC-sponsored apartment complexes scattered in and around the northern section of the metro area (Figure 3.1).

But none of the émigrés remain in the same agency-sponsored apartment complexes through time; primarily because they become more familiar with their surrounding environment and move into housing that fits their particular needs more specifically (like being near jobs, locating near better schools, etc.). One result is that the refugees eventually become highly dispersed, oftentimes living in larger apartment complexes with thirty or more apartments. As Skop and Menjivar (2001) discovered in their intensive interviews with new Latino immigrants in the Phoenix Metropolitan Area, the émigrés typically reside in small apartments with less than 800 square feet of living space, though their housing arrangements and luxuries vary tremendously. Their housing experiences range from five people living in a dilapidated two-bedroom apartment, to a four-person family living in a spacious four-bedroom, two-story home with a pool.

Cultural and Social Landscape

Compared with Miami, the cultural imprints of the Cuban community in Phoenix are few and far between. Creating a Cuban community and a sense of *cubanidad* is difficult to do in such a dispersed environment. Lidia, a key leader in the Cuban community, claims:

> There is no Cuban organization in Phoenix. At times, some of the refugees have come to see me to ask me to head up a foundation. But I just don't have time. And no one else is volunteering.

This statement could be compared with that of René Jose Silva, who is the Miami area director of the Cuban American National Foundation:

> This is almost a religious commitment in a sense. Sometimes I look around and I say, you know, I could be doing a lot more, money-wise... for my family. But the compensation I get back in personal rewards from being able to play a role historically... is way beyond anything you could pay (me)" (René Jose Silva, cited in Geldof, 1991).

Perhaps the only Cuban signatures in metropolitan Phoenix are the two restaurants owned by B.J. and Gilbert Hernandez (Figure 3.2). The Havana Café (opened in 1989) and the Havana Café Patio (opened more recently in 1991) serve "Cuban cuisine and culture to the Valley of the Sun" (Hernandez, 2005). With a large sign outlining the island of Cuba, and signs like "90 miles to Cuba" hanging inside the restaurant, the Havana Café serves as a small reminder of the past, as Gilbert Hernandez remembers it before he left the island and came to Phoenix in the 1980s. "We believed that the area was ready for a new international food experience, and our instincts must have been right, because the response was almost overwhelming right from the start." Cubans appear to only represent a small minority of his customers. But he didn't open the restaurant for them—he wanted to expose the entire community to foods unique to Latino culture.

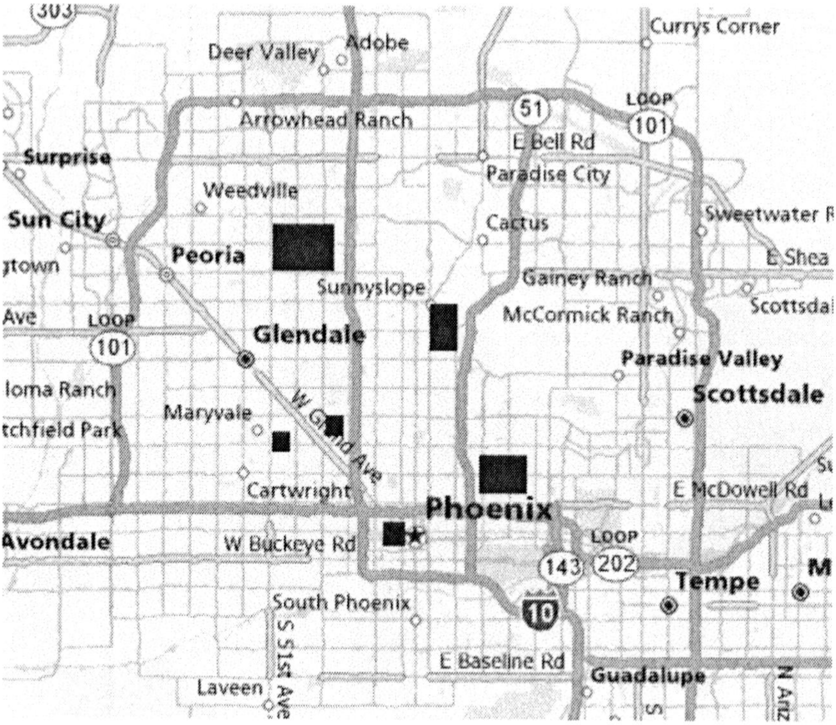

Figure 3.1 Neighborhoods In Metropolitan Phoenix Where Cuban Émigrés Live In Agency-Sponsored Apartment Complexes, 2002

This idea of catering to and identifying with a broader, more pan-ethnic Latino identity reaches beyond this business owner in Phoenix. The lack of Cuban businesses and community organizations in the city indicates that émigrés are looking to other sources for a sense of identity and collectivity. For many émigrés, this means becoming incorporated into the broader Latino community that forms a significant minority in the metropolitan area (in 2000, Phoenix had a Latino population of nearly 35 percent). Institutions targeted to the Latino population provide an important arena where some Cuban émigrés also gather to worship, celebrate festivals and become involved in community interactions.

In contrast, in Miami, the Cuban presence permeates the city:

> Small Cuban-owned businesses line the major thoroughfares. Spanish-language services are scheduled at churches and synagogues . . . Statues of saints and la Virgen de la Caridad are visible on front lawns . . .Street venders sell guarapo (a sugarcane drink) and granizados (snow cones). The "foreign" smells of puros

> (cigars), pasteles (pastries), and café cubano fill the air. Cuban and Latin American brands line the shelves of groceries and supermarkets . . .Outside city limits, small farmers harvest vegetables important to the émigré diet: malanga, boniato, carambola, yuca, and calabaza (Garcia 1996, 88-89).

The Cuban population in Miami has had a tremendous visible cultural impact on that city since émigrés began arriving in 1959. The influx of thousands of refugees settling in Miami enabled Cubans to maintain the culture that they associated with being Cuban. With each new wave of exiles, the identity of Cubans living in Miami was bolstered with memories of pre-Castro Cuba. As the prospect of returning to Cuba became more dim, the exiles used *cubanidad* (a mixture of memories and present-day realities) to preserve their customs, values and traditions. Cuban exiles began shaping the myths of their exile (Rieff 1993, 131). These myths define the Cuban community in Miami. The early refugees created "Little Havana" in an attempt to recreate the Cuban capital city as they remembered it.

Even though nearly thirty percent of the émigrés in Miami arrived post-1979, *La Cuba de Ayer* (the Cuba of yesterday) dominates the cultural landscape, as do memories of pre-1959 Cuba (Garcia 1996, 90). As a result, a particular version of Cuban culture in the city is ubiquitous. Streets named after Cuban patriots, like Jose Marti Avenue (NW 27th Avenue), architecture, stores (*Las Fruterias* and *Las Botánicas*), and the widespread use of Spanish, reflect the cultural influence of pre-1979 Cubans in Miami. The large influx of post-1979 émigrés view Cuban Miami as "sanitized and folkloric," but there is no disagreement that Cubans have left an indelible mark on the landscape of the city.

Demographic Profile of the Phoenix and Miami Cuban Refugee Populations in 2000

Generation is a factor that differentiates Cubans in Phoenix from those living in Miami.[4] Forty-five percent of Cubans living in Phoenix were born in the United States. These American-born Cubans represent a significant minority of Cubans in Phoenix. However, only twenty percent of Miami's Cuban population is American-born. More than 55 percent of Cubans living in Phoenix in 2000 and 80 percent of Miami Cubans came to the U.S. over the past forty years.

As discussed earlier, Cuban migrants tended to come in waves to the U.S. While the Miami sample generally represents the overall pattern of Cuban migration, Phoenix Cubans over-represent those who arrived well before the revolution, as well as those arriving after 1980; they significantly under-represent those who arrived from 1960-1979 (Table 3.1).

There are also dramatic dissimilarities between foreign-born Cubans in Phoenix and Miami in terms of their demographic characteristics (Table 3.2). The variations in racial composition of Miami Cubans and Phoenix Cubans are also notable when the race alone and in combination question in the census is used to identify those Cubans who identified themselves as "White" versus those

Cubans who identified themselves as "Nonwhite" by indicating their race as either "Black" and/or "Two or more races" (Table 3.2, Panel 1). While just eight percent

Figure 3.2 Cuban Restaurants in Phoenix

of the Cuban-born population in Miami is nonwhite, 49 percent of foreign-born Cubans living in Phoenix are nonwhite. The Miami sample is more representative of Cuban migration to the U.S., which was characterized during the 1960's and 1970's as a largely "white" migration. But since the Mariel Boatlift, nonwhites made up a significant portion of those leaving Cuba. Because a significant number of foreign-born Cubans in Phoenix arrived during the 1980's and 1990's, nonwhites are over-represented in the 2000 Phoenix sample.

Table 3.1 Year of U.S. Entry: Cuban Émigrés in Phoenix and Miami, 2000

Year of Entry	Foreign-born Cubans in Phoenix (%) n=1,981	Foreign-born Cubans in Miami (%) n=513,974
Before 1959	15.4	7.0
1960 to 1979	40.1	63.6
1980 to 1989	22.5	24.4
1990 to 1999	22.0	5.0
Total	100.0	100.0

Source: U.S. Bureau of the Census, *2000 Public Use Microdata Sample.*

At the same time, compared to a sex structure where females represent 53 percent of the Cuban-born Miami population, females only represent 21 percent of Cubans in Phoenix (Table 3.2, Panel 2). This disparity in the sex structure of the two groups is again partly due to the nature of migration from Cuba to the U.S. Forty-five percent of Cubans in Phoenix arrived in the 1980's and 1990's, when a significantly higher number of Cuban males also arrived in the U.S. Women were over-represented among pre-1980 exiles. They predominated during the Golden Exile and Freedom Flight periods of migration because regulations in Cuba required males to stay in the country from the age of fifteen to twenty-seven to serve their military duty (Prieto 1984, 7).

Table 3.2 Demographic Composition of the Cuban-born Population in Phoenix and Miami, 2000

Demographic Characteristic	Foreign-born Cubans in Phoenix (%) n=1,981	Foreign-born Cubans in Miami (%) n=513,974
Race: White	50.7	92.3
Nonwhite	49.3	7.7
Sex: Male	79.4	47.3
Female	20.6	52.7
Age: 0-9 Years	7.6	.8
10-19 Years	18.4	5.3
20-29 Years	4.3	12.3
30-39 Years	15.2	16.4
40-49 Years	40.9	15.6
50-59 Years	4.3	18.0
60-69 Years	9.2	15.9
70 Years +	0.0	15.7
Mean Age (in Years)	36.2 Years	48.7 Years
Median Age (in Years)	43.0 Years	49.0 Years
Household Size: 1 person	9.2	9.0
2 persons	13.6	24.6
3-4 persons	66.9	42.7
> 4 persons	10.3	23.7
Median Household Size	4	3
Structure: Married Couple	53.9	70.0
Male-headed	15.7	4.7
Female-headed	21.1	13.0
Other	9.3	12.3

Source: U.S. Bureau of the Census, *2000 Public Use Microdata Sample*. (Washington, DC: Data User Services Division, 2000).

Interestingly, 15 percent of Phoenix Cubans arrived in the U.S. before 1960, compared with just seven percent of Miami arrivals. While 64 percent of Cubans in Miami arrived between 1960 and 1979 (the Golden Exile, Freedom Flight, and 1973-1979 waves), only 40 percent of Cuban-born persons in Phoenix entered the U.S. during this time. The highest percentage of Cubans in Phoenix arrived after 1979. Nearly 45 percent of Cubans in Phoenix arrived during the 1980's and 1990's, compared to only 29 percent of Miami Cubans. Not only is the Cuban population in Phoenix largely second-generation; foreign-born Cubans generally represent a more recent, post-1979, group of arrivals.

Additionally, more than 25 percent of the Cuban émigré population in Phoenix is under the age of nineteen, compared with just six percent of foreign-born Cubans in Miami (Table 3.2, Panel 3). The Phoenix population is considerably younger (with a mean age of thirty-six years) than the Miami Cuban-born population (with a mean age of forty-nine years). But there are disparities within the Phoenix group as well. While Miami foreign-born Cubans demonstrate a relatively even age distribution (tending towards an older age), the Phoenix Cuban age structure peaks twice; 26 percent of the population is 0-19 years of age, while another 41 percent are 40-49 years old. The majority of these older Cubans arrived in the U.S. when they were very young and are part of the "1.5 generation," those born in Cuba but socialized in the United States (Portes 1994, 633). Thus, while Cuban exiles in Miami have at least some memory of Cuba before the revolution, Phoenix Cubans most likely remember two other versions of "home." Cuba, for the "1.5 generation," is little more than a word, a place they have heard about, but barely remember. Younger Cubans in Phoenix recall Cuba as it was during the Castro revolution. Few similarities thread through the three conceptions.

Cuban émigrés in Phoenix also live in relatively larger households than those of foreign-born Cubans in Miami (Table 3.2, Panel 4). The median household size for Cubans in Phoenix is four; one person larger than the median household size for the Miami Cuban-born population. This may be related to the age structure of the two populations. Cuban émigrés in Miami are considerably older than Cubans in Phoenix. Cubans in Miami also have relatively low fertility rates (Boswell and Skop 1995, 22). The presence of children within the Miami foreign-born Cuban household is thus less likely, which makes households smaller. Of interest, however, is the large number of Cuban exiles in Miami that live in households with five or more members. Upon closer inspection, it is revealed that more Cuban exiles in Miami live in extended households, with both an immediate family *and* either other relatives (like grandparents, brothers/sisters, etc.) or unmarried partners, boarders, and/or roommates.

The household structures of Cubans in both Miami and Phoenix are quite different (Table 3.2, Panel 5). Households are classified by type as either a "married-couple" household (where both the householder and his or her spouse are enumerated as members of the same household), a "male- or female-headed" household (a family with a male or female householder and no spouse present), or an "other" household (a male/female living alone, or a male/female not living alone). While seventy percent of the Cuban-born population in Miami lives in married couple households, fewer than fifty-five percent of Phoenix Cubans live in the same household type. Indeed, thirty-seven percent of foreign-born Cubans in Phoenix live in male/female-headed households. This is compared to Miami, where only eighteen percent of Cuban émigrés live in male/female-headed households.

Table 3.3 Profiles of Five Households in Phoenix with at Least One Foreign-born Cuban, 2000

Relation	Sex	Age	Race	Ancestry	Year of Immigration
Head	M	45	NW	Cuban	1980-1981
Spouse	F	39	W	Mexican	Born U.S.
Child	M	2	W	Mexican	Born U.S.
Non-rel.	M	21	W	Mexican	1987-1990
Non-rel.	M	21	W	Mexican	1987-1990
Head	M	37	W	Cuban	1960-1964
Spouse	F	36	W	Dominican	1970-1974
Child	F	3	W	Cuba/Dom	Born U.S.
Child	M	0	W	Cuba/Dom	Born U.S.
Head	F	42	NW	Cuban	1980-1981
Child	F	15	NW	Cuban	1980-1981
Child	F	15	NW	Cuban	1980-1981
Child	M	19	NW	Cuban	1980-1981
Head	M	62	W	German	Born U.S.
Spouse	F	68	W	Cuban	< 1950
Head	M	56	NW	Cuban	1980-81

Source: U.S. Bureau of the Census, *2000 Public Use Microdata Sample*. (Washington, DC: Data User Services Division, 2000).

Information from PUMS also allows for a detailed portrait of the familial and household situations of Cuban émigrés (Table 3.3). Cuban émigrés in Phoenix reside in a variety of situations with respect to their household size, ethnic composition, and year of arrival. Analysis of five Cuban household types provides some interesting (though indirect) evidence of the émigré experience in Phoenix. The first example shows one child living with his Cuban father and Mexican-American mother. Two non-relatives also live in the household; they arrived from Mexico between 1987 and 1990. The father arrived in 1980 when the Cuban Mariel boatlift was in full effect. The second household consists of a Cuban-born father who arrived in the U.S. during the Golden Exile phase. Between 7 and 12 years of age when he arrived in the U.S., this Golden Exile represents the "1.5 generation" (though he was born in Cuba, most of his life experiences were in the U.S.). He is married to a Dominican-born woman who came to the U.S. between 1970 and 1974. They have two American-born children.

In the third household, a Cuban-born Mariel female lives with her three children who also arrived in the Mariel boatlift. The fourth household represents another mixed marriage, the husband is American-born and the wife is Cuban, though she came before 1950. Finally, the fifth household contains one Cuban male who arrived during the Mariel boatlift. Each of these households illustrates just how disparate are the living arrangements of Cubans in Phoenix. Cuban exiles in Phoenix are more likely to live in mixed households (those containing non-Cubans) than in households containing only Cubans. Indeed, nearly sixty percent of all households containing foreign-born Cubans also had members that were non-Cuban, including American-born persons, as well as Mexican-, German-, and Dominican-born persons. This is compared to the less than twenty percent of foreign-born households in Miami that contained non-Cubans. The existence of *cubanidad* as it relates to living arrangements, intimate relationships, and marriage appears to be less important in Phoenix. Cubans in Phoenix are more likely to seek out and interact more with other groups than they are in Miami. As a result, this inhibits the growth of a cohesive Cuban community; rather émigrés are identifying with, and acculturating to broader conceptions of Latino identity.

Discussion and Conclusions

A collective Cuban community has not formed in Metropolitan Phoenix. Little clustering exists, community organizations have not been formed, and cultural imprints are hard to find. At the same time, Cuban émigrés are acculturating into the Latino subculture. There are several possible factors that may contribute to this outcome. First, Cubans have not formed a community in Phoenix because their *numbers are small.* With a population of fewer than four thousand members in a metropolitan area with over two million residents, the émigrés are hard-pressed to create a community infrastructure of Cuban-specific organizations, businesses, and institutions. Indeed, because there are so few Cubans residing in the metropolitan area, the émigrés have become reliant on the larger Latino community for social, cultural, and economic activities. In an effort to cater to the rapidly increasing (and diversifying) Latino community in Phoenix, most Latino small businesses stock specialty items for regional markets (Oberle 2004). Thus, *cubanidad* has become more like *latinidad* in Metropolitan Phoenix.

This compares to Miami, where more than 650,000 Cubans make up nearly thirty percent of the 2 million residents there. In Miami, Cubans have built a viable cultural and economic enclave which allows them not only maintain, but to strengthen their sense of *cubanidad.* The absolute size and diversity of the émigrés has worked advantageously for Cubans living in Miami, and the interaction between the earlier elite and subsequent cohorts goes a long way toward explaining the Miami Cuban exile's economic and social adaptation (Portes and Rumbaut 1990, 24). Newly-arrived exiles had, upon arrival, a significant pool of resources and support to draw from (Portes, Clark, and Bach 1977). Newcomers can find jobs in the shops and small businesses that earlier exiles established around Little Havana. This is repeated year after year with each new group of émigrés directly from Cuba, along with those return migrants resettled by the Cuban Refugee Resettlement Program who have made their way back to the Miami enclave from other parts of the United States. The hiring of refugees is good business for those Cuban-operated enterprises in Miami. Not only do recent arrivals accept low wages in exchange for preferential access to employment within the enclave, they also provide a growing demand for culturally defined goods and Spanish language services (Portes and Stepick 1993; Logan, Alba, and Stolz 2003).

A second reason for the lack of a Cuban community in Phoenix compared to Miami is the *generation gap* between these two populations. As discussed earlier, sixty-five percent of Cubans in Phoenix in 2000 were second-generation Cubans. Yet the vast majority of Cuban-origin persons currently residing in Miami were actually born on the island. In other words, most Miami Cubans are persons who have lived the experience of exile (Garcia 1996). As a community significantly made up of second and third-generation Cubans, Cubans living in Phoenix are less likely to identify with the Cuban exile experience. Those of the "1.5" generation also lack allegiance to the Cuban exile mentality so predominant in Miami, since the majority of their memories have been formed since coming onto American shores. As a result, living within and expressing a Miami-like *cubanidad* (by creating visible cultural and economic landscapes) is less of a reality for Cubans in Phoenix. Rochelle, a second-generation Cuban-American, though she does not live in Phoenix, expresses her feelings about being Cuban, and why she decided to leave the Miami enclave, where her parents live. As she explains (in perfectly non-accented English):

> Everyone is too Cuban in Miami. I couldn't even go to one restaurant where I didn't hear Spanish. It was amazing. I needed to escape; I didn't want to hear about 'the crisis' anymore. My parents were resistant to me leaving, but I had to go.

A third (and closely-related) reason for the non-salience of Cuban culture in Phoenix is its *relatively recent vintage.* Forty-five percent of foreign-born Cubans in Phoenix arrived in the U.S. since 1980, compared to only thirty percent of foreign-born Cubans in Miami. For Cubans, (1) pre-conditions of exit (whether their experiences and memories are based on a pre-1959 or post-revolution environment), (2) socioeconomic composition (whether they come from the upper and middle classes or the lower class in Cuba), and (3) racial characteristics (particularly comparing the racial composition of pre-1980 with post-1980 Cuban migrants) depend a great deal upon when they arrived in the United States. Because Cubans in Phoenix over-represent the post-Mariel Boatlift years and under-represent the pre-Mariel Boatlift years, their acculturation processes may be different from Cuban émigrés living in Miami. Miami's Cuban community is disproportionately composed of those who arrived from Cuba in the 1960's and 1970's. The two groups have come to the U.S. with different experiences, different resources, and different receptions. While earlier Cuban arrivals (coming from the upper and upper-middle levels of the socioeconomic structure of Cuban society) tend to predominate in the political and social hierarchy of the Miami community, the presence of pre-revolution arrivals, those of the "1.5 generation" (with fewer attachments to a Cuban identity), and later arrivals (with fewer resources) tends to disable community formation in Phoenix.

Finally, *the context of settlement* leads to a situation in which Cubans in Phoenix are likely to be unattached refugees. Most Cuban refugees, including those who later move to Phoenix and other cities, arrive first in Miami-- where the large Cuban community is able to absorb those with close family ties to that community. The situation is different for unattached Cubans, however. Because they have no other relatives in the U.S., they are forced to resettle wherever the refugee resettlement agency decides to locate them. Thus, many Cuban émigrés come to Phoenix without a familial or kin social support network in place. Linda McAllister, the IRC's "acculturation center" coordinator in Phoenix—though qualifying her statements as simple observations—maintained that at least ninety percent of the new Cuban refugees coming to the center since 1990 have been younger nonwhite males. As a result, these émigrés seek out alternative sources of collectivity, oftentimes turning to the larger Latino subculture in Phoenix for friendship networks, community support, and intimate relationships.

In Phoenix, without the support of the enclave, Cubans are forced to depend primarily on themselves, focusing their energies on the Latino community already in place, and on the broader Phoenix community for support. More limited in their awareness of social, economic, and cultural opportunities within the Cuban community, these exiles face a dramatically different situation than those exiles that live in the Miami megalopolis, where social connections and intimate ties are highlighted *within* the Cuban enclave. Given the significant number of Cubans living in mixed households in Phoenix, it appears that the émigrés have enmeshed themselves *outside* of a singularly Cuban support system, and now rely on a positive reception from the expansive Phoenix host community for social and cultural identification. The reactions, values, and prejudices of this host community are elements of the circumstances that confront new arrivals (Portes and Borocz 1989, 618), and can channel immigrants into widely divergent courses of adaptation.

In conclusion, the Phoenix population continues to support a group of émigrés considerably different from the "average" Cuban profile, with a higher percentage of younger, nonwhite males, living in a spatially dispersed community with no real focus. As a result, it becomes extremely difficult to reinforce a particular Cuban identity (*cubanidad*) at this scale. At the same time, it means that the forces and divisions that are more hidden in the larger enclaves (including year of arrival, race, and generation) become pervasive in the smaller community.

Throughout the United States, this pattern is being replicated in the smaller Cuban communities created by the Cuban Refugee Resettlement Programs. At the same time, pre-1980 Cuban exiles "worry that these new immigrants will never fit into their community. They are too different: in age, class, race and experiences. Between them lay twenty years of social and ideological differences" (Garcia 1990, 194). It appears that these differences have clearly had an effect on Cubans in Phoenix, where memories, class, race, and support networks have divided the small community and resulted in a largely invisible group.

Notes

1. The 1980 Mariel boatlift represents a profound moment in the history of Cuban migration to the United States. Thus, this chapter refers to pre-1980 and post-1979 arrivals as distinctive groups. For an extensive description of the Mariel boatlift, and its impacts, see Skop 2001.

2. A set of complex historical circumstances explains why nonwhite Cuban exiles were under-represented until 1980 (Casal and Prieto 1981, 314). First, during its first months in power, the revolutionary government attacked the Cuban upper classes; whites over-represented the elite in Cuba. With the most to lose from the revolution, upper- and middle-class persons left; hence whites predominated amongst those escaping Cuba. Second, as the first émigrés settled to life in exile, they set up a chain migration through extended family networks. When the Freedom Flights began, the over-representation of whites continued. "Whether intended or not, this policy (family reunification) automatically excluded categories of persons in the Cuban population that had migrated least during the first years of the exodus; the Negro was thus systematically excluded" (Aguirre 1976, 112). Third, the significant improvement for nonwhites in terms of equality of opportunity since the Cuban revolution naturally dampened their desire for escape. Finally, the perceived expectation that racial discrimination would be encountered in the United States contributed to the low levels of black emigration from Cuba (Stepick and Grenier 1993). Eventually, however, economic and political conditions in Cuba by the late 1970s created a scenario that increased the likelihood of nonwhite emigration.

3. Interviewee names, except those belonging to community leaders and organizers, have been changed to ensure anonymity.

4. Records were extracted from the 2000 U.S. Census Public Use Microdata Sample (PUMS), 5 percent files for every individual who classified themselves as Cuban on the Hispanic origin question. Further filtering using the MSA/PMSA question identified those individuals living in the Miami Metropolitan Area and the Phoenix Metropolitan Area. The analysis that follows relates to the weighted sample of 3,537 Cubans identified in PUMS as Cubans in Phoenix and the 650,601 Cubans identified as Cubans in Miami.

References

Ackerman, Holly, and Juan M. Clark. 1995. *The Cuban Balseros: Voyage of Uncertainty*. Miami: Cuban American Policy Center, Cuban American National Council.

Aguirre, Benigno E. 1976. "Differential Migration of Cuban Social Races: A Review and Interpretation of the Problem. *Latin American Research Review* 11(1):103-24.

Bach, Robert L. 1987. "The Cuban Exodus: Political and Economic Motivations." Pp. 87-137 in *The Caribbean Exodus*, edited by Barry B. Levine. New York: Praeger Publishers.

Bach, Robert, Jennifer B. Bach, and Timothy Triplett. 1981. "The Flotilla 'Entrants': Latest and Most Controversial." *Cuban Studies* 11/12: 29-48.

Boswell, Thomas. 1993. *The Cubanization and Hispanicization of Miami*. Miami: Cuban American Policy Center, Cuban American National Council.

———. 1994. *A Demographic Profile of Cuban Americans*. Miami: Cuban American Policy Center, Cuban American National Council.

Boswell, Thomas, and James R. Curtis. 1983. *The Cuban-American Experience: Culture, Images and Perspectives*. Totowa, NJ: Rowman & Allanheld.

Boswell, Thomas, and Emily Skop. 1995. *Hispanic National Groups in Metropolitan Miami*. Miami: Cuban American Policy Center, Cuban American National Council.

Casal, Lourdes, and Yolanda Prieto. 1981. "Black Cubans in the United States: Basic Demographic Information." Pp. 314-55 in *Female Immigrants to the United States: Caribbean, Latin American, and African Experiences*, edited by Delores M. Mortimer and Roy S. Bryce-LaPorte. Washington, DC: Research Institute on Immigration and Ethnic Studies, Smithsonian Institution.

Council for Inter-American Security. 1981. *The 1980 Mariel Exodus: An Assessment and Prospect*. Washington, DC: Council for Inter-American Security.

Cros Sandoval, Mercedes. 1986. *Mariel and Cuban National Identity*. Miami: Editorial SIBI.

Diaz, Guarione M. Diaz. President/Director, Cuban American National Council. Interviewed October 10, 1997.

Fagen, Richard, Richard A. Brody, and Thomas J. O'Leary. 1968. *Cubans in Exile*. Stanford, CA: Stanford University Press.

Garcia, Maria Cristina. 1990. *Cuban exiles and Cuban Americans: A history of an immigrant community in South Florida, 1959-1989*. Ph.D. dissertation, University of Texas at Austin.

———. 1996. *Havana USA*. Berkeley: University of California Press.

Geldof, Lynn. 1991. *Cubans*. London: Bloomsbury Publishing Limited.

Hernandez, Gilbert. 2005. *The Havana Café*. http://www.rapidaxcess.com/havanacafe/start.html.

Logan, John R., Richard D. Alba, and Brian J. Stults. 2003. "Enclaves and Entrepreneurs: Assessing the Payoff for Immigrants and Minorities." *International Migration Review* 37(2):344-388.

Kennedy, Edward M. 1981. "The Refugee Act of 1980." *International Migration Review* 15(1):141-56.

Masud-Piloto, Felix. 1996. *From Welcomed Exiles to Illegal Immigrants: Cuban Migration to the U.S., 1959-1995*. Lanham, MD: Rowman & Littlefield.

McCoy, Clyde. 1985. *Cuban Immigration and Immigrants in Florida and the United States: Implications for Immigration Policy.* Gainesville: Bureau of Economic and Business Research, University of Florida.

McHugh, Kevin, Ines Miyares, and Emily Skop. 1998. "The Magnetism of Miami: Segmented Paths in Cuban Migration." *Geographical Review* 87(4):504-519.

Oberle, Alex. 2004. "*Se Venden Aquí*: Latino Commercial Landscapes in Phoenix, Arizona." Pp. 239-76 in *Hispanic Spaces, Latino Places: Community and Cultural Diversity in Contemporary America*, edited by Daniel D. Arreola. Austin, Texas: University of Texas Press.

Olson, James S., and Judith E. Olson. 1995. *Cuban Americans: From Trauma to Triumph.* New York: Twayne Publishers.

Portes, Alejandro. 1969. "Dilemmas of a Golden Exile: Integration of Cuban Refugee Families in Milwaukee." *American Sociological Review* 34(4):505-18.

———. 1994. "Introduction: Immigration and Its Aftermath." *International Migration Review* 28(4):632-39.

Portes, Alejandro and Jozsef Borocz. 1989. "Contemporary Immigration: Theoretical Perspectives on its Determinants and Modes of Incorporation. *International Migration Review* 23(3):606-30.

Portes, Alejandro, Juan M. Clark, and Robert L. Bach. 1977. "The New Wave: A Statistical Profile of Recent Cuban Exiles to the United States." *Cuban Studies* 7(1):1-32.

Portes, Alejandro, and Ruben Rumbaut. 1996. *Immigrant America: A Portrait.* Berkeley: University of California Press.

Portes, Alejandro and Alex Stepick. 1993. *City on the Edge: The Transformation of Miami.* Berkeley: University of California Press.

Prieto, Yolanda. 1984. *Cuban Migration of the '60s in Perspective.* New York: New York University, Faculty of Arts and Science, Center for Latin American and Caribbean Studies.

Rieff, David. 1993. *The Exile: Cuba in the Heart of Miami.* New York: Simon & Schuster.

Shipman, Charles. 2004. "Cuban and Haitian Communities Present Different Challenges." *Arizona Refugee Resettlement Journal* 6(1):5.

Skop, Emily. 1997. *Segmented Paths: The Geographic and Social Mobility of Mariel Exiles.* Thesis, Arizona State University.

———. 2001. "Race and Place in the Adaptation of Mariel Exiles." *International Migration Review* 35(2):449-471.

Skop, Emily, and Cecilia Menjivar. 2001. "Phoenix: The Newest Latino Immigrant Gateway?" *Yearbook of the Association of Pacific Coast Geographers* 63:63-76.

Stepick, Alex, and Guillermo Grenier. 1993. "Cubans in Miami." Pp. 79-100 in *In the Barrios: Latinos and the Underclass Debate,* edited by Joan Moore and Raquel Pinderhughes. New York: Russell Sage Foundation.

Taft, Julia, et al. 1979. *Refugee Resettlement in the U.S.: Time for a New Focus.* Washington, DC: New TransCentury Foundation.

Thomas, John F. 1963. "Cuban Refugee Program." *Welfare in Review* 1(3):1-20.

U.S. Bureau of the Census. 2000. Public use microdata sample. *2000 Census of Population.* Washington, DC: Data User Services Division.

U.S. Department of Health, Education, and Welfare, Social and Rehabilitation Services, Children's Bureau. 1967. *Cuba's children in exile.* Washington, DC: GPO.

Wong, Francisco. 1974. *The Political Behavior of Cuban Migrants.* Thesis, University of Michigan.

Chapter 4

Trying to Be Authentic, But Not *Too* Authentic: Second Generation Hindu Americans in Dallas, Texas

Pawan Dhingra

The religious landscape of the U.S. today differs widely from a quarter century ago, due to the arrival of immigrants from throughout the world following the Immigration Act of 1965 (Eck 2000). As they settled into occupations and local residences, immigrants started cultural and religious organizations. Driving through urban and rural areas along the coasts and even into the country's "Heartland" and the South, one sees Buddhist, Hindu and Jain temples, mosques, Sikh *gurduwaras*, and more. The transplantation of religions and of affiliated institutions strengthens ethnic communities and furthers the growing pluralism in the country. For Indian American Hindus, religion is one of the foundations of their ethnic culture (Yang and Ebauh 2001). Cultural centers are frequently attached to temples, symbolizing religion's role in defining the ethnicity.

Part of why immigrants create religious organizations is to inculcate their offspring into their faith and ethnic culture overall, in the face of external pressures that children encounter through popular media, in school, in discriminatory treatment, and elsewhere. The success of the first generation's efforts to pass on an appreciation of religion remains unclear. Some scholars fear that second generation Asian Americans (those born and/or raised in the U.S. to immigrant parents) have a weak interest in religion as a result of acculturation (Williams 1998; Chai 1998), despite a commitment to ethnic lifestyles marked by values, symbols, customs, norms, etc. (Maira 2002; Min and Kim 1999). Rather than concentrating on whether second generation Indian American Hindus care about religion or are assimilated, this paper primarily addresses how they approach religion over time, in particular what religion means to them, how they practice it, and with what impact on future adaptation.[1] The broader theoretical interests involve how a group boundary, in this case religion, changes in meaning over the life course and in response to local factors. As for other types of group identities, people's investment in a religious community can fluctuate due to factors external and internal to a group, discussed in more detail below (Cornell and Hartmann 1997). How do people enact a newer, preferred definition of a group identity and ignore a previous one? Assessing people's trajectory in how they make sense of an identity, as opposed to taking a snapshot approach, can explain more clearly their expressions of it.

Religion deserves particular attention because of its unique set of dimensions. It refers to a philosophy of life, rituals, symbols and practices, and so is more complicated than other cultural markers. Furthermore, the first generation often builds religious sites as a primary way of establishing an ethnic community, and so how the second generation approaches religion per se takes on special significance. Religion links individuals to both local and transnational communities. For Hindus, it also reinforces their minority status, especially within religiously-conservative settings. The second generation of the post-1965 immigration wave is now coming into adulthood, working full time and starting their own families, and so is a key population in understanding religious pluralism in the diaspora.

The study is situated in Dallas, Texas. Immigrant communities consistently remain overlooked outside of the major destination hubs, namely New York City (and surrounding area), Miami, San Francisco, and Los Angeles. The South in particular is a region whose Asian immigrants are receiving attention only recently (Bankston 2003). This chapter first reviews the history of Indian Americans in order to explain the context in which immigrants established temples in Dallas. It then explains how second generation adults approached Hinduism within Dallas, with attention to the theoretical factors that shape people's relationship to group boundaries.

"Hindoos" in America

The first sizeable wave of Indian Americans, mostly men, arrived in the U.S. in the early 1900s and were predominantly Sikhs from Punjab (Leonard 1992). They worked on railroads and in agriculture, with most located on the West Coast. Many moved to California to escape hostility in other states but still encountered derogatory images as an inferior race as they competed for jobs with Whites (Takaki 1989). These Sikh Americans constructed temples and maintained strong personal networks with one another as they struggled to earn a living and build a home on the West Coast. Even though most were Sikh, they became known as "Hindoos" based on the popular image of Indians, with a supposedly debased religion that contributed to their moral suspicion. Many of these Sikh Americans married and had children with Mexican American women, while still remaining attached to their religion and homeland (Leonard 1992).

Indian laborers lost the ability to enter the U.S. with the passage of the Immigration Act of 1917 (Takaki 1989). Those still in the U.S. could not own land unless they were citizens. Citizenship itself was denied to all Indians by the 1923 U.S. Supreme Court case of the United States v. Bhagat Singh Thind. Thind had argued that Indians were racially Caucasian, and thus qualified for citizenship under U.S. law, but the court decided that while Indians may officially be Caucasian, they were not plainly "White" and thus were ineligible for citizenship. Before 1920, over 2000 returned home, most being deported (Maira 2002). Ultimately, Indians were included in the Asian Exclusion Act of 1924, which established a limited quota system for Asian countries and practically ended Asian immigration for forty years.

Migration to the U.S. from India would not begin again in large numbers until the Immigration Act of 1965. This act has reshaped the American landscape, largely by accident. Following WWII and the U.S. Civil Rights Act of 1964, pressure was on the U.S. government both within and outside its borders to shed its clearly discriminatory policies, such as the exclusion of Asian migrants. The 1965 immigration law retracted the limited national origins quotas and so allowed for greater migration from Asia. Lawmakers, however, expected little increase because of the preference system built into the law that mainly privileged immigrants with relatives already in the U.S., i.e., Europeans (Chan 1991). Instead, large numbers of Asians entered through the law's preference for skilled professionals in the medical, teaching, and engineering fields. Most South Asians arriving between 1965 and 1980 came under this selection criteria, which created a large professional class of Indian (and other Asian) migrants. Unlike other Asian immigrants of this time, these Indian Americans did not consolidate in urban centers such as Chinatowns or Koreatowns. Instead, with proficiency or fluency in English and professional jobs, they spread throughout the U.S. Still, the greatest numbers are in the metropolitan areas of New York City/New Jersey, Los Angeles, Chicago and Houston (Leonard 1997).

The image of the Indian doctor or engineer is slowly being accompanied by that of the computer programmer, motel owner, cab driver, and convenience store clerk (Kibria 2006). These post-1980 migrants came over as relatives sponsored by the 1965 wave. With the telecommunications boom of the 1980s and 1990s, Indian computer specialists, often from South India, have migrated to the U.S., with significant representation in the Silicon Valley. At the other end of the occupational ladder, many arrivals since the 1980s have entered one of the nation's most dangerous jobs—cab drivers in metro areas. In addition, many motel owners are of South Asian, in particular Indian, origin.[2] The relationship between these newer arrivals and post-1965 professionals is still unfolding, but few signs of inter-class unity appear on the horizon (Prashad 2000).

While South Asian migration has changed since a century ago, some things have altered little. South Asians remain racially stereotyped as a hard-working model minority, who become the vilified dirty foreigners bent on taking American jobs when they are viewed as working *too* hard (Okihiro 1994). A notorious example is the "dotbuster" episode, when a group of New Jersey youth in and around Jersey City targeted Indian immigrants in 1987, killing one and severely injuring another (Lessinger 1995). The attackers called themselves "dotbusters" in reference to the bindi, or "dot," women often wear on their foreheads. Southern Baptists characterized Hinduism and Islam as debased religions in a prayer booklet published in October 1999, and even entered temples *in the U.S.* to proselytize. Since September 11, 2001, attacks on South Asians, who already suffered the highest rate of hate crimes among Asian Americans,[3] have intensified. Following September 11th, a Sikh and a Pakistani American, in Arizona and Texas, respectively, were killed by individuals who were angry about the attacks. Mosques have been desecrated. Many South Asians, regardless of religion, worry about mistaken classification as terrorists by both lay individuals and government agencies.[4]

Indian Americans in Dallas

The Indian Americans of this study live in metropolitan Dallas, Texas. Dallas has changed significantly from its days of cattle ranches and big oil, made famous in the 1970s television drama named after the city. It has recovered from the recession of the 1980s, which a drop in oil prices and collapse of the savings-and-loan industry exacerbated for the city (Hazel 1997). Today Dallas is part of the "New South," with a diverse economy and society, and dynamic growth. For instance, one in ten workers in Dallas is involved in the high tech economy.[5] This joins with the city's business-friendly history and culture, and its major medical facilities, to attract Asian American professionals.[6] Indian Americans arrived here predominantly after 1965 because of their good fit with the Dallas labor market, particularly in medicine, engineering (including computer-based fields), and small business (Brady 2004; Ghosh-Pandey 1998). With strong educational credentials, migrants relied less on social networks and more on job opportunities in choosing locations. The climate also appealed to those Indian Americans who preferred warmer weather.

The city, along with other Southern metropolitan areas, has experienced a significant rise in population generally. More than one fourth of the nation's immigrants live below the Mason Dixon line, and the proportion is increasing (Bankston 2003). Dallas, along with Texas generally, is an emerging gateway city for Asian immigration, and Asians make up over 4 percent of Dallas

County's population. This percentage is just above the national average. In 1990, there were 17,331 Indian Americans in Dallas/Ft. Worth.[7] These numbers have grown considerably with the influx of first and second generation immigrants for employment, and with the growth of the second generation in general. According to the Census, 63,386 Indian Americans lived in the Dallas/Ft. Worth metropolitan area in 2000, and 25,830 in Dallas county alone.[8] (see Table 4.1). This latter figure is over twice that for Dallas County in 1990 (10,114). Foreign-born South Asian Americans, the majority of whom are of Indian origin, comprise the greatest number of Asian Americans in Texas.

Table 4.1 Total Persons and Persons Self-Designated as Asian Indian, 1990 and 2000 (U.S. Census)[9]

	United States	South Region	Texas	Dallas Co.,Texas
Total, 1990	248,709,873	85,445,930	16,986,510	1,852,810
Total, 2000	281,421,906	100,236,820	20,851,820	2,218,899
Asian Indian, 1990	815,447	195,525	55,795	10,114
Asian Indian, 2000	1,899,599	498,197	142,689	25,830

As in other parts of the nation, Indian Americans in Dallas have an economic position above the city average. They have a median household income of $56,759, while the city average in Dallas is $43,324.[10] Politically, Asian Americans do not exhibit a significant presence at the city level. As of 2006, city council members were White, African American, and Latino, with no Asians represented. The Indian American population is dispersed throughout the city as a result of their proficiency or fluency in English, economic standing, and employment that draws them to various locations. Still, greater concentrations exist around the rim of the city and its suburbs, most notably the northern section with its preponderance of high-tech occupations there (see Figure 4.1). The northern suburbs of Richardson and Plano are referred to as the "telecom corridor." About 25 percent of Texas employees in high tech industries are from India.[11] While there is no "Little India" comparable to that found in New York City or Chicago, there is a collection of grocery stores, clothing shops, and restaurants in Richardson. There is even a for-profit center targeted to first generation South Asian Americans, which houses a restaurant and reception area, plus a movie theater, open in the northern and western suburbs of Dallas, where many Indian Americans live. In addition, there are Indian radio shows, theaters that show predominantly Hindi films, and numerous voluntary cultural, social, religious, and small business organizations. The major South Asian religious traditions—Hindu, Jain, Sikh, Muslim, Hare Krishna, Christian, and Parsis—are found here.

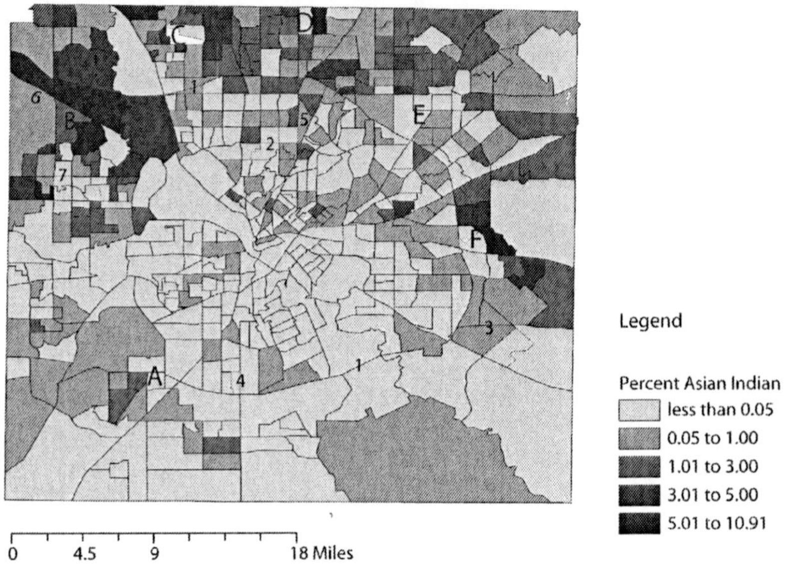

Source: U.S. Census 2000, SF3

Figure 4.1 Percentage of Foreign-Born Indian Americans by Census Tract, Dallas, 2000 (Key to map: A = Duncanville; B = Irving; C = Carrolton; D = Richardson; E = Garland; F = Mesquite; 1 = Interstate 645/LBJ Freeway; 2 = Loop 12; 3 = Interstate 20; 4 = Interstate 35E; 5 = North Central Expressway/Highway 75; 6 = Highway 114; 7 = Airport Freeway/Highway 183)

There are three Hindu temples in the Dallas area. The largest and most well known, the Metroplex temple, unites various forms of Hinduism. Lining its walls in the main room, which seats about 300 people, are statues of Hindu gods from different parts of India. It is an ecumenical temple of the sort found throughout the country, that bridges various regions of India with its particular forms of worship (Eck 2000). (There are multiple varieties of Hinduism that are regionally specific within India.) It is located in a western suburb of Dallas, in the direction of Ft. Worth, but attracts attendees from throughout Dallas. A BAPS Swaminarayan Hindu temple, located in Dallas, places more specific group boundaries; the religion stems from a region within Gujurat, a state in western India (Williams 1998). Figure 4.2 presents the Shri Swaminarayan Temple.

There are also organizations for other institutionalized religions, including a Jain temple, a center for the International Society for Krishna Consciousness, mosques, Sikh *gurduwaras*, and at least one Indian Christian church. These organizations are located in Dallas itself or one of its immediate suburbs. No particular religious or sub-ethnic groups formed communities particularly close to one another. This dispersal limits the sense of geographic focus and salience for the Indian community. In turn, it makes the temples and other organizations all the more important as community sites and as spaces to develop ethnic and religious identities. The population's general economic success and employment status means that many can afford cars and know how to drive (many immigrants who arrived as elderly are a prime exception), and can reach the temples without relying on public transportation or close proximity to one's residence. So, geographic concentration is not necessary to have a tightly-bound cultural and social community (Zelinsky and Lee 1998). While people often visit in one another's homes, "community" spaces must be created. Otherwise, the population would not mingle outside of friendship networks.

Figure 4.2 Dallas BAPS Shri Swaminarayan Temple

Dallas' sophisticated, dynamic economy and growing population contrast with its conservative, traditional religiosity. The city is known as the "buckle of the Bible Belt." There are over 5,000 religious organizations in the Dallas/Ft. Worth area.[12] Driving through neighborhoods both in and outside of Dallas, one sees churches of all sizes, including mega-churches along suburban highways and small congregations in urban strip malls. There is The Biblical Arts Center in the city which features historical and modern religious art from around the world. The city newspaper is one of the few in the nation with a weekly religion section, for which it has won awards; it features articles on religious groups and patterns, as well as notices on religious holidays and events sponsored by organizations. It is not odd to see people praying before meals in public restaurants.[13] Dallas' large Mexican American population also strongly adheres to religious observances, both Catholic and Protestant. Texas as a whole is known for its religiosity. As an example, Southern Baptists have more congregations in Texas than does any other denomination.[14] The state constitution requires, although this is not necessarily enforced, that one must acknowledge the existence of a "supreme being" in order to be elected to public office.[15]

Research Design

The data on how Indian Americans approach religion are based on interviews conducted over the whole of 1999 and during the summers of 2000 and 2002.[16] Initial contact with these individuals occurred mainly outside of any religious context. Using snowball sampling methods, I initially contacted members of social and economic organizations targeting Indian Americans and Asian Americans generally, and then branched outwards. I made significant efforts to reach those with very few ties to an Indian American community. Ultimately, I interviewed thirty-five second generation Indian Americans, aged 22-33. The in-depth interviews ranged from one-and-one-half to three hours.[17] Given their prominence demographically in Dallas as throughout the nation, Hindus made up the vast majority of interviewees (compared to Jains, Sikhs, Muslims, Christians, etc.)—about two-thirds of which attended a temple on major holidays.[18] Few attended regularly, as discussed below. The second generation had completed college and was comprised of doctors, engineers, financial consultants, teachers, and other white collar professionals. About half of the second generation interviewees had moved to Dallas for their work, and the other half had grown up there. Those with family in Dallas more likely attended temples if their parents did also. Those raised in Texas reported stronger incidents of religious discrimination, but those from outside of Texas encountered it as well, as discussed below. I also interviewed a youth group of male high school and college students in the Swaminarayan temple, one of the three major temples in Dallas.[19]

In addition, I conducted participant observation in religious and secular organizations in Dallas. I attended ten Sunday services: five at the Metroplex temple, three at the Swaminarayan temple, and one each at the Jain and Hare Krishna temples. As relevant for this study, I interviewed temple representatives: Mr. Maraj and Dr. Mehta of the Metroplex temple, Mr. Kuba of the Swaminarayan temple, and Mr. Jain of the Jain temple.[20] I also attended youth group meetings, lunches and dinners at the temples; a Health Fair; cultural events sponsored by the temples; children's cultural classes; and guest lectures at the temples.

In addition to temples, Indian Americans participate in secular professional, social, and cultural organizations. Most relevant for this paper is the Indian American Network Association (IANA), a social and professional organization designed to link second generation Indian American adults to one another.[21] It has on average between 100 and 180 paid members in Dallas and an email list of 750, who attend events and can be active but have not paid any dues. It is the only organization in Dallas dedicated to Indian American young adults of primarily the second generation. As explained below, this secular organization, ironically, has become a central site for the second generation to experience its religion along with, and for some in place of, the temple.

I first discuss why immigrants started the temples, then how the second generation made sense of religion, and finally, how the IANA functions as a religious institution.

Establishing Religious Organizations

Immigrants generally use religious and cultural organizations to maintain an ethnic identity (Warner and Wittner 1998). People often become more religious after migrating than they had been in their homeland because of a greater urgency to stay connected to their ethnic heritage (Williams 1988). Religious organizations not only serve spiritual and cultural needs but also provide opportunities to mingle and assume positions of authority (for men and women) that may be denied to them outside of their ethnic community (and for women, inside of it) (Gans 1962; George 1998). Individuals also learn of job opportunities and build social capital through religious institutions (Zhou et al. 2002), as well as becoming acclimated to their cultural environment (Bankston 2000). In addition and most importantly for immigrants, religious organizations allow for the socialization of the second generation into the parents' vision of their ethnic group (Williams 1998). Because the U.S. is one of the most religious societies among industrialized nations, as measured by degree of participation and by Gallup polls on stated religious beliefs (Chaves 2002), immigrants use religious organizations as a socially-acceptable way to assert their culture. Religion and culture fuse for those whose religion is dominant in their homeland but marginal in the U.S. (Ebauh and Chafetz 2000). By teaching religion, parents hope to socialize children into broader ethnic values, namely to respect elders, to be sexually and socially conservative, and to prioritize the family over the individual. Immigrants in general hope to maintain their religious and cultural traditions while selectively assimilating, that is adopting those behaviors that are necessary for success in the host country, such as learning English, attending college, and so forth (Gibson 1988; Portes and Rumbaut 2001). Parents hope that the youth will not invest in "unwelcome" elements of the immediate host culture, such as divorce, teen pregnancy, and prioritizing individual wants at the expense of family-based consensus. Religion appears to them as insurance against these behaviors.

The first generation in Dallas started temples for these reasons. Kuba, one of my informants, notes that immigrant parents go out of their way to pass on their way of life to their children, with religion as a central ingredient: "You keep your cultural values and keep passing them through the generations. Through temples, through all these cultural activities . . . I see the grassroot is obviously the religion. The religion drives it" (1999).

Zhou and Bankston (1998) find similar trends for Southeast Asians in New Orleans, who started ethnic organizations to socialize their children into pursuing education and to keep them away from the peer culture of native minorities living near them.

Second Generation Religiosity

The question becomes, then, in what ways did the second generation pick up or transform these teachings and make use of the temples to strengthen their ethnic identity. This paper concentrates less on whether the second generation practices religion (or not), and more on how its interests in religion changed over time. According to assimilation theory, as groups acculturate they may at most keep a symbolic appreciation of their heritage but remain relatively removed from it (Alba and Nee 2003; Gans 1979). Those who emphasize a constructionist approach, however, contend that group boundaries fluctuate in meaning and salience over time, and so there is not a linear progression from more to less commitment (Cornell and Hartmann 1997). I first analyze how second generation Hindu Americans made sense of their religion while young and then later in their life course. I then concentrate on how they actually try to practice their religion.

Second generation Americans often claim ethnic boundaries comprised of such values as respecting elders, working hard, and being socially conservative, as well as of such cultural traits as language, food, customs, and popular culture (Chong 1998; Kibria 2002; Min and Kim 1999; Portes and Rumbaut 2001). Such values and symbols are promoted by the first generation as a way of preserving cultural identity. However, they also receive tolerance and respect from outsiders, including the host culture, when they coincide with traditional host culture values. These ethnic attributes claimed by Indian Americans suit the current multicultural era. Within multiculturalism all groups celebrate those ethnic characteristics that add to the nation's diversity without causing serious tensions between lifestyles (Wolfe 2000).

Religious practices among new immigrant descendants have remained overlooked until recently, which is especially surprising given the centrality of religion to ethnicity according to immigrants. Research on second generation Hindus' religiosity tends to concentrate on children. Prema Kurien (2000) finds that Hindu temples have become more successful in giving youth pride in their ethnicity and a solid grounding in the principles of their faith (see also Ebaugh and Chafetz 2000). Religious and social organizations educate them in their ancestry which, as anticipated by the first generation, entice them to learn more about their heritage generally. Yet, how second generation adults feel about religion remains uncertain, especially because such supportive institutional contexts for youth are relatively new. Current adults are starting families of their own and so are influential in the next generation's understandings of religion.

Many informants may have grown up practicing elements of their religion but are not comfortable with their degree of comprehension. As Mahiya states:

> It's hard to get into culture and religion and all that stuff, because we don't understand it. And our parents were so busy when we were growing up to really sit down and say, 'here.' Like we'd sit and do pooja, but we don't know really what's going on. My mom would explain it to us sometimes, but you're still sitting through something you don't really register (2002).[22]

My interviewees do not interpret religion as a distinct spiritual or moral philosophy, but instead as supportive of their generic ethnic culture, namely family ties, community bonding, and values. Mahiya, for example, had moved into her own place and voluntarily maintained religious icons, but it would be a mistake to equate that with a commitment to a faith. She continued the pattern she learned as a child, to engage in a ritual that connected more to a family than to a clear religious meaning. As she said, "I keep this astrological thing because my father was a big follower. So, you know, so he always wants to see something in the house" (2002). Among my informants, religion often signifies a social community rather than spiritual or Hindu one per se. As Rajeev explains, "I tell my American friends that going to a garba is like going to a party. Going to a pooja is the thing to do. It's not because we are all religious freaks, it's part of the culture" (1999).

Given the association of Hinduism with community and family, it is not surprising that few informants could articulate a clear notion of distinct religious principles. The following quote by Lukshmi typifies respondents' impressions. She worked at a designer department store:

> An attitude I encounter a lot is snobbishness. It's nice to dress well, but that's not who you are. And, my parents would laugh at me if I said they had to wear something designer. That's just not them, and it's not me. [That] comes from Hindu values (1999).

This quote illustrates that for many informants, religion means commonplace values, such as not to be vane and materialistic.

For a minority of informants, religion does not represent simply culture or family, but a philosophy with understood rituals. Rahul speaks of his and his wife's religious practices:

> We have a small temple at home and on certain religious days we pray there. I pray every morning. We do a ceremony at home, maybe once every two months. I go to the [Metroplex] temple once every 4 to 6 weeks. I used to go to a religious camp (2002).

In contrast to Rahul, most informants attended temples on occasion while growing up but none had attended a Hindu camp and few had temples at home where they consistently prayed. A few informants did not have established temples in their geographic vicinity when young, and many who did lacked organized activities in them. Temple visits were buttressed by practices inside the home, which could be frequent or intermittent depending on one's parents.

Changing Conceptions of Religiosity

Despite the conclusion that adherence to Hindu values is more cultural and family-based than strictly religious per se, over time my informants tend to seek out more strongly the religious underpinnings to their beliefs. That is, they gradually seek a more "authentic" appreciation of their religious roots. I now explore how this change is brought about by factors external as well as internal to the group, namely treatment from others, shared culture, shared interests, and shared institutions (see Cornell and Hartmann 1997; Espiritu 1992; Jenkins 1994). These factors altered the meaning that religion had for informants as they grew older.

External reasons include labeling and discrimination by others based on physical and/or cultural factors. Racist images and treatment as "non-Americans," "smelly," "towel-heads," and "terrorists" indicate to Indian Americans that they are distinct from the majority, regardless of their degree of acculturation. Recurrent questions and critiques of their religion in a socially conservative state made participants keenly aware of this difference. They feel defined as non-Christians and so want to better understand what their religion truly means so as to understand themselves. One's spirituality becomes all the more important in forming group boundaries given the location of Texas. A few participants experienced religious prejudice from Christians. For instance, Usha, who attended a religiously conservative university in the state, says:

> When I was in college, it was mainly Baptists. I would have people come up to me and say you need to be Baptist, and people come up to me and say do you believe that Jesus Christ is blah blah blah. And I would say no. They would try to make me go to one of their sessions. And, being open minded, I'd go. At the beginning they would go, do you think you could convert to Christianity? But I would say no because I don't believe in that religion. And they were like . . . you are going to go to hell. And I'm like . . . I'm going to your hell. That's fine because I don't believe that there is a hell (1999).

A couple of other interviewees similarly reported Christians in Texas trying to convert them. This intolerance contrasts with a long-term trend in the country of appreciation for cultural differences. To some degree religious tolerance remains contested and at times limited to those cultural beliefs that fit in with the main tenants of the society.[23] Distinct faiths that lack references to Jesus Christ or to the Old or New Testament may arouse hostilities, especially at a time when the country feels at war with non-Christian religious fundamentalists (Prashad 2000).

Some informants encountered few direct challenges to their religion, but frequent questions about their cultural practices. As Rajish notes:

> Actually, some of the people I come across really don't understand [our culture]. They ask about religion, and they ask about the red dot on the head, . . . why the ladies wear what they wear and that kind of stuff. My only problem is, I'm not as knowledgeable about it as I should be (1999).

As a result, outsiders kept my informants interested in an authentic notion of religion and gradually motivated them to articulate it in terms of a presentable creed with clear principles, like Western religions (McDermott 2000). This is despite the fact that Hinduism has no fixed form of worship nor text that one must be able to recite. The religious nature of the area led, then, to both a concern over expressing one's Hindu faith and a simultaneous commitment to doing so.

Respondents also cared about defining their religious boundaries because of factors internal to their group. Religion formed such a central element of ethnic culture for Hindu Americans that informants did not feel comfortable treating it as merely a subset of ethnicity broadly. For instance, Joshi hoped to have a deeper knowledge of religion rather than simply carry out ritualistic motions.

> I have had a growing respect for Hinduism and its approach to religion. I can see that as becoming a true asset in going forward. I think in Indian culture it is so closely tied to religion, more than any other culture. I think (that if) you maintain the religion, the relevant cultural aspects will follow (1999).

Another reason for the increasing interest in religion among the second generation is active endorsement by the first generation of religion as the anchor of their cultural identity. Jain, a first generation leader of the Jain temple, while not Hindu, makes this point strongly:

> We believe that India is a rich culture. And our children, though not born in India, still carry those genes. Genes alone are not of any value if we can't steer them in the right direction. I really believe that the parents have a responsibility to pass on our best to our children. The traditions, family values, the religion itself. If we follow the religion, the values come with it (2000).

Finally, and related to the previous point, second generation Indian Americans imagine themselves as parents and express a desire to instill the same morality to their children, as their own parents gave to them. This meant a renewed interest in religion. They believe that future children would have to deal with the same challenges to their cultural and physical identity that they themselves faced (see Levitt 2002). Deepa sums up a widespread viewpoint:

> I don't think I know enough about [Indian culture] right now. I don't want my kids to not know anything about it. The thing is, in terms of religion, . . . my mom or my grandma knows what's happening and they tell me what's happening, [but] I don't know it for myself. When it's my time, I wouldn't know what to tell my kids. That's who I am. That's who my kids will be too. I think it's important that they know who they are (1999).

Searching for Religion Apart from Temples

Despite some assimilation, the second generation does not want to create a new style of Hinduism, one based simply on connections to family or culture broadly. Instead, actors seek an authentic version, with a clearer understanding of religious texts, rituals, myths and stories, the major holidays, etc. (McDermott 2000). Yet, parents alone could not explain enough about the religion since, while practitioners of it, they were not necessarily experts. Counting on parents is especially difficult for those who live away from them. So, interviewees have sought a deeper appreciation of Hinduism, but ironically, as they seek this, they rarely turn to the temples because these organizations are *too* authentic. My second generation informants went to temples once every few months, mostly for major festivities, if at all.

Institutions serve as a fourth factor (along with external labelings, cultural ties, and interests) that encourages individuals to claim group boundaries. While religion itself is an institution, it is similarly useful to consider temples as religious institutions. As such, they supply opportunities for individuals to learn of and practice the religion within a community atmosphere, which in turn furthers people's conception of the group boundary. While the other factors that promote group boundaries could link generations within an ethnic/religious community, we see below that this final factor threatens to divide it at the local level. What are some of the underlying reasons for this lack of interest in what would appear to be the core religious institution of the Hindu community?

Some community leaders assumed that the low attendance of the adult second generation stemmed from a disinterest in religion due to failures by either parents or themselves. Mehta represented the former perspective; when asked about how many in the adult second generation attended the Metroplex temple, he replied,

> Zero. Zero. The thing that we are missing is [age] sixteen to forty. I divided into two parts—sixteen to twenty is the youth, twenty and on is young adults, professionals—that we are missing. They will only come four or five times a year. Let me tell you, it is not the temple. . . . It's the parents—if the parents don't bring, how can they come (1999).

Maraj, on the other hand, represents the latter perspective, assigning the blame more to community leaders, particularly temple leaders. When I asked him how many second generation adults attended the temple, he gave a lengthy reply:

> A lot less than I would like to see . . . As much as we would like to transplant India here, sooner or later, unless [you] are going to try to make some changes and accommodations especially to our youth, we're going to lose them. Because the other culture out there is what they're exposed to most of the time. Very often it is [a] very attractive and very appealing alternative, much more easi[ly] accessible, much more comfortable in a lot of ways. I hope we can get our stubborn ones to see that light. . . . We have too many people who are first-generation Indians here and aren't awakened to the fact that some day or another, these kids are going to say "hey, I don't understand all this Hindu mumbo-jumbo stuff that you guys are doing. Leave me alone. Look, here's a simple way to go and worship something—here's a priest and a bible and I'll go home. Or [I'll] just forget religion totally" (1999).

The other Dallas temples had the same difficulties of drawing in the adult second generation. According to one member of the youth group at the Swaminarayan temple, "Between 25 and 40, that age group is not that big here" (1999). Yet, Maraj's concern that the second generation will decide to "forget religion entirely" is misplaced. The fact that they do not understand it has not led to an abandonment of "this Hindu mumbo-jumbo stuff" but instead to a desire to learn more.

Temple leaders had already tried some changes in order to appeal to acculturated youth. Leaders feel it necessary to conform to institutional Western, Christian norms (Warner 1993). The act of creating a temple is often meant, ironically, to help the second generation fit in with their Christian peers by giving them a "church" of their own with services on Sundays. This applies to non-Hindus as well. Jain explained the reason for the Jain temple's creation:

> For worship. My daughters in the third or fourth grade would come to me and ask, "Dad, my friends go to church. How come we don't?" That's another immigrant problem. You have to explain to children who are going to come into contact with those who have the same belief system (2000).

Yet, simply having temple services on a Sunday was still not enough to necessarily make the second generation comfortable with attending, despite informants' interest in a deeper understanding of religion. I now explain why not.

One problem was, as Maraj indicated, language. Interviewees' linguistic assimilation limits their ability to participate fully in the temple, even as they maintain an interest in authentic culture. It was not merely difficulty in understanding lectures, which could be translated into English, but the services themselves, which took place in Hindi, Gujurati, or Sanskrit. For instance, Meena comments on how the language barrier prevented her from attending a temple as much as her Christian friends attended church: "Part of the reason I feel like that is because I go to the temple, and the preacher there says everything in hard core Indian, and I don't understand it. I'm just there to be there. I'm just looking around. If some of it was in English, I would be a lot more into it and more willing to go a lot more regularly than I do right now" (1999). Similarly, Kithana worried about not belonging to the temple.

> I hate going to temple, but when I'm there I like it. Makes me feel more Indian. I'd like to try to maintain it and go more. I feel very uncomfortable there, that they will be able to tell that I don't belong there. . . . We go to the temple every now and then. As a kid you don't mind going, but as an adult you don't understand what they're saying so you get bored. So you don't follow up. I went to a lecture a while ago, and didn't understand a word of what was going on, and I was like, what's the point? (1999).

Some in the first generation also faced difficulty in following the rituals but had more familiarity with them while growing up, not only within families but in a supportive surrounding, which the second generation lacked. Also, with a minority religion, informants felt it necessary to be able to explain, and so defend, their practices, and so were not content with the performance alone. As a result, they felt like imposters who, as Meena said, simply "look around."

The second explanation is that second generation participants feel uncomfortable being the only young adults in the temple surrounded by the first generation. For instance, Rajat rarely attended the temple and explained, "Sometimes, I do feel a little bit awkward because I don't know what they're doing. What do we do with this? . . . Most people around the temple are from our parents generation or beyond that, [and] they still seem to think of us as kids. Most of us are now in our mid 20's or 30's. We are pretty much fully functioning adults" (1999). The second generation may visit temples on occasion to connect to a parents' homeland but did not feel ownership over it without peers present. Temple leaders recognized this lack of attendance and believed that classes for current youth would keep them from reproducing the trend of the adult second generation. But, leaders had no plan for making the current adults, many planning their own families, more religiously aware.

In effect, the temple leaders have misread the second generations' lack of attendance as a lack of interest. Rather than alter the language and intergenerational dynamics, the temple introduced non-religious events to attract the second generation. These were not meant as substitutes for or dilutions of religious aspects, but as additions to current offerings. As Maraj said,

> I think the fact is that we'll never lose [the second generation] in entirety. Let's face it, if you're Indian, there are a lot of things that attract you back to Hinduism. It doesn't have to be religion – it could be cultural programs. Dances, having dances for youth, and it doesn't have to be religious ones. ... We do have language classes, music classes, dance classes. We have religious classes, all at the temple (1999).

It is ironic that the temples were searching for mostly non-religious ways of bringing in the second generation just as informants sought a greater religious grounding so as to feel part of the main elements of the temples, that is the religious services. Participants often turned to their own efforts and organizations to be part of a religious community.

Guiding Themselves

Informants had always been interested in religion and gradually became focused on developing a more traditional appreciation of it due to categorizations, cultural ties, and interests. Yet even as participants' acculturation did not limit a quest for authenticity, it guided how they engaged with it. Many in the second generation have looked elsewhere than the temples to learn of religion. Some adopt an individual approach. One informant, for example, grew tired of simply going through the motions at her Hindu temple and started reading on her own a text on Hindu philosophy to comprehend the meaning of the practices. A few other informants turned to popular cultural expressions. Another relied on a video to educate himself on essential Hindu mythology.

In addition to these independent efforts, The Indian American Networking Association (IANA) has played an increasing role as a religious space. It demonstrates the effects that local organizations can have on defining individuals' group boundaries, especially in geographic areas with fewer co-ethnics. IANA, a secular organization created primarily by and for the second generation, offers individuals a chance to be part of a religious community in a comfortable fashion that speaks to their degree of acculturation in two distinct ways. At the unofficial level members have used IANA to form a reading group on Hindu philosophy, and they hope to bring in a representative of a temple or someone from the first generation to facilitate their training. This reading group was not a sponsored program of IANA, like its charity events, finance seminars, social parties, etc. Still, some members were turning to IANA as their major site for religious training given this unofficial program. For example, when I asked Sangeeta how she would like to see the Metroplex temple change, she turned the conversation to IANA.

> I would love to take a class on religion. My school didn't offer it, and I wish they did. There is a group here that has meetings once a month. I haven't been able to make one yet. I would say that 80 percent of them are IANA members. They talk about the religion and what it means to be Hindu. They have pot luck lunches once a month and that's very nice. I need to do it. I just haven't gotten around to it. But the fact that it is even there is cool (1999).

For Sangeeta, the IANA allowed members to develop a religiosity in a way that suited their acculturation by searching for a distinct meaning of Hinduism that one could then articulate to outsiders. Even as IANA members tried to link to the temples, some conceived of the former as an equally important space. IANA did not seek to compete with the temple or first generation associations as sites of cultural offerings—but it was gaining stature as such.

At the official level, IANA recently recognized cultural occasions and placed religion, namely Hinduism, within that framework. Gauruv, president of IANA in 2002, wanted cultural events to become a core focus. Part of the reason stemmed from the kinds of Indian Americans in Dallas and their interests. He commented that:

> Our Northeast cities are having better luck with [political interest] . . . A lot of them have their jobs in political organizations. Dallas is more in the high tech business . . . I think that one thing a lot of people don't have is the cultural

> learning. I think that is something that should be taught and is needed. It's a very rich culture, and as we get older we lose that history over here (2002).

According to Gauruv, IANA could serve as a stepping stone for the second generation to get involved in the major Indian American cultural associations in Dallas, run by immigrants.

The cultural events that IANA celebrates are secular, but not exclusively so. Among the secular celebrations are India's independence day and Gandhi's birthday, as well as Hindi films, plays, and music performances. However, while IANA is a secular organization, it does officially celebrate major Hindu religious occasions. It frames them as cultural rather than religious events. These efforts, in effect, commemorate religion in the same manner as members' adolescent understanding of it, despite their desires to change that. Events include celebrating Diwali and garba.[24]

As one example of such an effort, consider a Diwali dinner sponsored by the IANA in 1999. The invitation indicated that traditional Indian or dressy Western attire was appropriate, and about a quarter of the men and half of the women wore traditional clothes to the dinner. The invitation did not mention Hinduism or religion. The event took place at an Indian restaurant and also entailed a fund-raiser for Indians in India. Yet, the symbols of "traditional clothes" and food were the extent of the cultural recognition. No religious comments were publicly made at the dinner, and it was indistinguishable from a secular, formal dinner. Non-Hindus took part in the celebration as well as Hindus. Still, members increasingly found this peer-based group a comfortable way to practice religiosity. For instance, Lukshmi said, "I think IANA is a natural way to participate in holidays, just having someone around to share the things that are more Indian" (1999).

Events such as this give the second generation a strong sense of religious community. Yet, importantly they do not necessarily further people's appreciation of religion. IANA has taken on (not necessarily over) the role of the temple in this respect, becoming a local designator of religion.

Conclusion

The first generation of Indian Americans in Dallas built temples and promoted religion for children. The second generation has grown up with mixed degrees of involvement in temples, with many having a limited amount. Nonetheless, immigrant descendants continue to care about religion. Their degree of interest has remained strong or increased, but their interpretation of religion has shifted. Due to external and internal factors, in particular involving one's life course, informants want a deeper involvement in a religious community and appreciation of their religion. The religious conservatism of Texas makes religion an even more salient marker for Hindu Americans than it would be already, and brings the community together. Yet one factor—the role of institutions—drew them away from the first generation. Ironically, as the second generation sought an authentic notion of religion, it avoided temples because they were too authentic. This is despite the fact that temple leaders were looking for ways outside of the religious services to reach out to the second generation.

Instead, immigrant descendants turned to their own organization, the Indian American Networking Association, which provided a religious option suitable for their advanced degree of acculturation. In the process they are distancing themselves from the first generation. This will continue unless temples change or unless external and internal factors drive individuals back to the temple despite their reservations.

At a broader, theoretical level we see the need for a comprehensive approach to studying group boundaries. Acculturation is presented within assimilation theory as an end point or within constructionist theories as merely a temporary moment that can change based on circumstances. People's group boundaries do change due to external circumstances, and we must account for the effects of multiple variables (i.e., categorizations, cultures, interests, and institutions) on group boundary formations. So, religious acculturation does not represent an end to a group's interest in the nuances of faith. But, as seen here, acculturation still impacts how groups approach an identity, even after actors' understanding of it changes. A snapshot view of informants' current interests in religion would be unable to explain the appeal of IANA's popular approach given its incongruence with actors' current desires. A longitudinal approach to actors' group identities helps clarify how previous and current interpretations of identities both influence boundary formation. Acculturation, then, impacts groups' practices. In addition, local organizations and institutions offer the means to claim group boundaries. This is in contrast to only concentrating on the degree of people's commitments, on attitudes towards their background, or on macro forces that shape group options. Group adaptation takes place ultimately at the local level, even as it is influenced by other factors. However, these boundaries may diverge from strictly religious boundaries, towards more general cultural boundaries, as other than religious forces shape group options.

Notes

1. This analysis focuses on Hindus since practically all participants were such. This focus is not meant to privilege them over other Indian American religious groups in the U.S.

2. Members of the Asian American Hotel Owners' Association, mostly made up of mostly South Asian Americans, own over 50 percent of the hotels/motels in the U.S.

(http://www.newsindia-times.com/2002/05/10/tow18-top.html). The number of Asian American owners is actually even higher, since many are not members of the organization.

3. From the *1999 Audit of Anti-Asian Violence: Challenging the Invisibility of Hate.* Compiled by the National Asian Pacific American Legal Consortium and its affiliates, the Asian Pacific American Legal Center, the Asian American Legal Defense and Education Fund, and the Asian Law Caucus.

4. As one example, there was a temporary investigation of four Muslim American medical students who were driving to Florida and were erroneously accused (by someone sitting at a table near them at a diner) of plotting terrorism. As a result of this accusation, the students lost their admission to a university in Florida even though they had done nothing related to terrorism, and had not committed any crime.

5. *Dallas Business Journal*, Dec. 5, 2000.

6. Recently the former mayor of Dallas, Ron Kirk, was called the "business mayor," as a sign of his attempts to attract big business to Dallas (*Dallas Observer*, March 7, 2002).

7. Data extracted from Steven Ruggles and Matthew Sobek et al., Integrated Public Use Microdata Series: Version 2.0. Minneapolis: Historical Census Projects, University of Minnesota, 1997.

8. These data are from the Census 2000 Supplementary Survey Profile of Dallas—Fort Worth, TX CMSA (MSA/CMSA).

9.U.S. Bureau of the Census 2000.

10. These data are from Census 2000 Summary File 4, Dallas County. They refer to median household incomes in 1999.

11. http://www.dfwinternational.org/_content/media/immigrants/ NorthTexasImmigration Report2005.pdf p.24.

12. http://faculty.smu.edu/rkemper/anth_3346/Dallas_non-western_religions_1996.htm

13. One Korean American interviewee said that he moved here from San Francisco partly because it had a more public acceptance of religion.

14. http://www.adherents.com/rel_USA.html

15. http://www.harbornet.com/rights/texas.txt

16. Research was conducted on both Indian and Korean Americans in Dallas. This paper only contains data on Indian Americans.

17. I interviewed an equal number of men and women. I met some informants through membership lists of ethnic social organizations. Others were contacts from other participants who were less involved in their ethnic community. I had not previously met anyone that I interviewed.

18. The second generation interviewees, without intention, were mostly Hindu given their numerical dominance in the area and throughout the country, with a few Jains. I interviewed one Hare Krishna and one Sikh as well.

19. The group I spoke to were all male. Gender segregation is enforced in the temple, including the near prohibition of males and females talking directly to one another inside the temple.

20. Practically all the names have been changed to preserve confidentiality. If a name is not changed, it is because it is so common among a religious group that many persons following that religion share it.

21. IANA is a pseudonym for the organization. The Dallas organization is one of many such associations in major cities across the country. Membership is primarily second generation professionals, college-educated. Many join in order to meet a partner

and also for friendships and cultural and professional development. Most are single, although a growing number are married. Whether informants were members or not, almost all had heard of it. The association has monthly social events, charity events, professional development trainings, financial investment trainings, and cultural programs.

22. A "pooja" is a Hindu ritual of praying to religious deities, chanting, and offering deities food.

23. For instance, a California school at first prohibited Sikh American males from wearing a kirpan, which is a small dagger-shaped object considered a sacred element of the religion. Those who petitioned the ban see wearing the kirpan as protected under religious freedom. A federal appeals court ultimately allowed students to wear kirpans in the California schools. Sikhs had to turn to the courts in Canada as well. The Supreme Court there also ruled to allow the kirpan. http://www.boston.com/news/world/articles/2006/03/03/ canadas_high_court_ oks_sikh_daggers/. Accessed 3/4/06.

24. Garba refers to a traditionally Gujarati dance in honor of the Hindu goddess Amba. Women and men dance in a circle, clapping hands or sticks. The dance is performed annually during the fall festival of Navratri.

References

Alba, Richard, and Victor Nee. 2003. *Remaking the American Mainstream: Assimilation and Contemporary Immigration*. Cambridge, MA: Harvard University Press.

Bankston, Carl. 2000. "Sangha of the South: Laotian Buddhism and Social Adaptation in Rural Lousiana." In *Contemporary Asian America: A Multidisciplinary Reader*, edited by M. Zhou and J. Gatewood. New York: New York University Press.

———. 2003. "Immigrants in the New South: Introduction," *Sociological Spectrum* 23(2):123-128.

Brady, Marilyn Dell. 2004. *The Asian Texans*. College Station: Texas A&M University Press.

Chai, Karen. 1998. "Competing for the second generation: English-language ministry at a Korean Protestant church." In *Gatherings in Diaspora*, edited by S. Warner and J. Wittner. Philadelphia: Temple University Press.

Chan, Sucheng. 1991. *Asian Americans: An Interpretive History*. Boston: Twayne.

Chaves, Mark. 2002. "Abiding Faith." *Contexts* 1(2):19-26.

Chong, Kelly. 1998. "What it Means to be Christian: The Role of Religion in Construction of Ethnic Identity and Boundary among Second-generation Korean Americans." *Sociology of Religion* 59(3):259-286.

Cornell, Stephen, and Douglas Hartmann. 1997. *Ethnicity and Race*. Thousand Oaks, CA: Pine Forge Press.

Ebaugh, Helen Rose, and Janet Saltzman Chafetz. 2000. *Religion and the New Immigrants: Continuities and Adaptations in Immigrant Congregations*. Walnut Creek, CA: Altamira Press.

Eck, Diana. 2000. "Negotiating Hindu Identities in America." In *The South Asian Diaspora in Britain, Canada, and the United States*, edited by H. Coward, J. Hinnells, and R. Williams. Albany: State University of New York Press.

Espiritu, Yen Le. 1992. *Asian American Panethnicity*. Philadelphia: Temple University Press.

Gans, Herbert. 1962. *Urban Villagers*. New York: Free Press.

———. 1979. "Symbolic Ethnicity: The Future of Ethnic Groups and Cultures in America." *Ethnic and Racial Studies* 2:1-20.

George, Sheba. 1998. "Caroling with the Keralites: Negotiation of Gendered Space in an Indian Immigrant Church." In *Gatherings in Diaspora: Religious Communities and the New Immigration*, edited by S. Warner and J. Wittner. Philadelphia: Temple University Press.

Ghosh-Pandy, S. 1998. "Across Many Oceans: Asian Indians in the United States." In *The New Dallas: Immigrants, Ethnic Entrepreneurship, and Cultural Diversity. A Collection of Student Papers*, edited by S. Cordell and J. Elder. Dallas: William P. Clements Center for Southwest Studies, Southern Methodist University.

Gibson, Margaret. 1988. *Accommodation without Assimilation: Sikh Immigrants in an American High School*. Ithaca, NY: Cornell University Press.

Hazel, Michael. 1997. *Dallas*. Austin, TX: Texas State Historical Association.

Jenkins, Richard. 1994. "Rethinking Ethnicity: Identity, Categorization and Power." *Ethnic and Racial Studies* 17(2):197-219.

Kibria, Nazli. 2002. *Becoming Asian American: Second Generation Chinese and Korean American Identities*. Baltimore: Johns Hopkins University Press.

———. 2006. "South Asian Americans." In *Asian Americans: Contemporary Trends and Issues*, edited by P.G. Min. Beverly Hills, CA: Sage Publications.

Kurien, Prema. 2000. "'We Are Better Hindus Here': Religion and Ethnicity among Indian Americans." Pp. 99-120 in *Religions in Asian America*, edited by P. Min and J. Kim. Walnut Creek, CA: AltaMira Press.

Leonard, Karen. 1992. *Making Ethnic Choices*. Philadelphia: Temple University Press.

———. 1997. *The South Asian Americans*. Westport, CT: Greenwood Press.

Lessinger, Johanna. 1995. *From the Ganges to the Hudson: Indian Immigrants in New York City*. Needham Heights, MA: Allyn and Bacon.

Levitt, Peggy. 2002. "The Ties that Change: Relations to the Ancestral Home over the Life Cycle." Pp. 123-44 in *Religions in Asian America*, edited by P. Levitt and M. Waters. New York: Russell Sage Foundation.

Maira, Sunaina. 2002. *Desis in the House: Indian American Youth Culture in New York City*. Philadelphia: Temple University Press.

McDermott, Rachel. 2000. "New Age Hinduism, New Age Orientalism, and the Second Generation South Asian." *Journal of the American Academy of Religion* 68(4):721-731.

Min, Pyong Gap, and Rose Kim, editors. 1999. *Struggle for Ethnic Identity: Narratives by Asian American Professionals*. Walnut Creek, CA: AltaMira Press.

Okihiro, Gary. 1994. *Margins and Mainstreams: Asians in American History and Culture*. Seattle: University of Washington Press.

Portes, Alejandro, and Ruben G. Rumbaut. 2001. *Legacies: The Story of the Immigrant Second Generation*. Berkeley: University of California Press.

Prashad, Vijay. 2000. *The Karma of Brown Folk*. Minneapolis: University of Minnesota Press.

Rajagopal, Arvind. 1995. "Better Hindu than Black? Narratives of Asian Indian Identity." Presented at the annual meetings of the SSSR and RRA, St. Louis, Missouri. Referenced in Kurien, P. "'We Are Better Hindus Here': Religion and Ethnicity among Indian Americans."

Takaki, Ronald. 1989. *Strangers from a Different Shore: A History of Asian Americans*. New York: Penguin Books.

U.S. Bureau of the Census. 2000. Factfinder Webpage.

Warner, R. Stephen. 1993. "Work in Progress towards a New Paradigm for the Sociological Study of Religion in the United States." *American Journal of Sociology* 98:1044-93.

Warner, R. Stephen, and Judith Wittner. 1998. *Gatherings in Diaspora: Religious Communities and the New Immigration.* Philadelphia: Temple University Press.

Williams, Raymond Brady. 1988. *Religion and Immigrants from India and Pakistan.* Cambridge: Cambridge University Press.

———. 1998. "Asian Indian and Pakistani Religions in the United States," *The Annals of the American Academy of Political and Social Science* 558:178-195.

Wolfe, Alan. 2000. "Benign Multiculturalism." In *Multiculturalism in the United States,* edited by Peter Kivisto and Georganne Rundblad. Thousand Oaks, CA: Pine Forge Press.

Yang, Fenggang, and Helen Rose Ebaugh. 2001. "Transformations in New Immigrant Religions and Their Global Implications." *American Sociological Review* 66(2):269-88.

Zelinsky, Wilbur, and Barrett A. Lee. 1998. "Heterolocalism: An Alternative Model of the Sociospatial Behaviour of Immigrant Ethnic Communities." *International Journal of Population Geography* 4:281-298.

Zhou, Min, and Carl Bankston. 1998. *Growing up American: How Vietnamese Children Adapt to Life in the United States.* New York: Russell Sage Foundation.

Zhou, Min, Carl Bankston, and Rebecca Kim. 2002. "Rebuilding Spiritual Lives in the New Land: Religious Practices among Southeast Asian Refugees in the United States." Pp. 37-70 in *Religions in Asian America: Building Faith Communities,* edited by P. G. Min and J. Kim. Walnut Creek, CA: AltaMira Press.

Chapter 5

Spatial Disjunctures and Division in the New West: Latino Immigration to Leadville, Colorado

Nancy Hiemstra

> When I first arrived, my husband sent me to the store alone. The clerks didn't speak Spanish, and I got so nervous my knees were shaking! . . . I was so nervous because if they asked me something, "how are you," or something, I got scared. (Bonita Rivera, age 27)

Six years ago Bonita Rivera moved to Lake County, Colorado, from a small ranching and farming community in the state of Aguascalientes, Mexico. In Mexico her family's income came from harvesting *guava* fruit and making various products to sell, and they constantly struggled financially. Her husband Jorge's family had left the village years earlier for the United States, but still returned periodically for visits. Jorge and Bonita met on one of these visits and eventually married. They live in a trailer park several miles outside of the county's only town, Leadville. Jorge does construction work in Eagle County, an hour's drive away. During the day, he takes their only car to work, and Bonita remains in the trailer with their two small children. Her contact with native-born residents is primarily limited to trips to the store, occasional evening parent meetings at the school, and doctor's visits.

Lake County is located in a valley between the Sawatch and Mosquito mountain ranges, in west central Colorado (see Figure 5.1). Situated at over 10,000 feet, Leadville is the highest incorporated town in the U.S., and winter is the dominant season here. It is not a place that readily comes to mind as a destination for new Latino immigrants. However, Bonita and Jorge are among the many immigrants, primarily Mexicans, who have moved to this area since the mid-1980s. According to the U.S. Census Bureau, by 2000 over 36 percent of the total county population of 7,812 was Latino (U.S. Census Bureau, 2000a). A local 2002 estimate that included undocumented immigrants placed the number of Latinos at approximately 50 percent of the county's population.[1] For the 2004-2005 school year, 62 percent of students in the district were classed as "Hispanic" (Flores 2005).

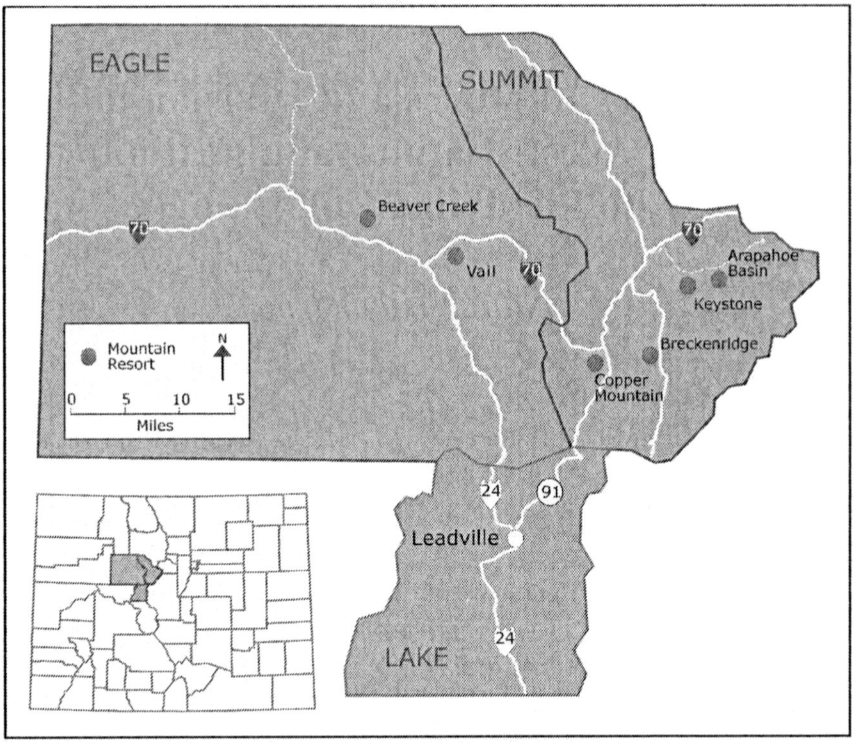

The local commercial landscape offers some scattered clues to the town's changing demographics (Berry 2004; Oberle 2004).[2] Among the Old West-style buildings on the main street (Figure 5.2), there are several stores and eateries catering to the growing Latino population. A few church signs now advertise services in Spanish, including one all-Spanish Evangelical church, the Iglesia Siloe (Siloe Church). Despite these subtle visual indicators, however, Bonita Rivera's experience of limited contact with native-born residents is not unusual. There is strikingly little Latino participation in the daily activities of the native-born community. Doug, a School Board member, underscores the lack of interaction from the perspective of non-Latino residents:

> Most people you stop on the street corner, and you say, "what's the breakdown of Lake County?" you know, Anglo to Hispanic, and they would not know that the school district is Anglo minority, they would not guess that.

Clearly, Latino immigrants' marginal presence in town does not accurately represent the county's demographic breakdown.

Figure 5.2 Leadville's Main Street

The numerous case studies in this volume as well as other recent studies attest to the growing geographic diversification of Latino immigration, beyond established destinations in large cities and border regions. Furthermore, whereas Latino workers have long been associated with migrant agricultural work, in the past two decades they have been incorporated into changing regional economies in year-round, often non-agricultural sectors of the labor market, such as the service sector, construction, and manufacturing. Ways in which communities are changing as a result of these patterns have been documented for many regions of the United States, including the Mid-West and Plains (Naples 1994; Cantú 1995; Stull et al. 1995; Driever 2004; Gouveia et al. 2005; Grey and Woodrick 2005); the South (Cravey 1997; Johnson-Webb 2002; Kandel and Parrado 2004; Donato et al. 2005; Griffith 2005; Hernández-León and Zúñiga 2005; Rich and

Miranda 2005); and the Northeast and Mid-Atlantic states (Price and Whitworth 2004; Dunn et al. 2005; Shutika 2005). The mountain resort industry of the West has recently emerged as a new Latino immigrant employer (Rothman 1998; Clifford 2002; Durand et al. 2005; Krug 2005). However, to date there has been very little research done on this new type of Latino destination.

My goal in this chapter is to contribute to the growing body of literature on new sites of immigration by providing an in-depth look at a region and industry in which Latino immigration has not yet received much attention. In addition to providing empirical data on the county's changing population, I explore spatial patterns and movement in an effort to better understand the changing cultural landscape. I also address the incongruity between the increasing Latino population and its minimal engagement in the community. In the next section, I provide the regional context for contemporary immigration to the region and describe salient characteristics of the Latino population in Lake County. Next, I identify two acute spatial disjunctures that severely limit interaction between native-born and Latino immigrant residents. Finally, I explore the interactions that do occur, focusing on the principal challenges to creation of productive, inclusive spaces in the community.

Regional Transition and Latino Immigration to Leadville

The early history of Leadville is that of a classic mining town. Lake County's somewhat harsh physical environment proved to be incredibly rich in minerals; gold was discovered in the 1860s, silver in the 1870s, and, in subsequent decades, lead, zinc, and molybdenum. For over a century, Lake County's economy and population mirrored the boom and bust of the mining industry. Proclamations that gold and silver had been found in Leadville were headlined in national newspapers and passed among prospective miners in the late 1800's (Dempsey and Fell 1986).[3]

The lure of wealth drew fortune seekers from many areas of the world, and immigrants were integral to the settling of early Leadville. Census data shows that from 1880 to 1920, at least a third of the county's population was foreign born (U.S. Census Bureau 1870-2000). At first, the largest immigrant group was Irish; other sizeable groups included Canadians, Cornish, French, Germans, Norwegians, and Swedes. In the next few decades, Italians and groups from the former Austro-Hungarian empire such as Austria, Croatia, Slovenia, and Yugoslavia came to dominate the new arrivals. Initial conflict between these immigrant groups in the early part of the twentieth century gradually subsided as their descendants became more identified as residents of Leadville than as members of distinct ethnic groups (Blair 1980).[4]

While a local Census in 1879 indicated that nine Mexicans were among the town's 5000 residents, local historians report that Latinos first settled in Lake

County in significant numbers in 1917 (Blair 1980; Voynick et al. 2002).[5] Small numbers of Mexican and Mexican-American workers continued to come to the region to work in the mining industry throughout its operational years. A study by Nostrand (1992) suggests that "Hispanos," Spanish-speaking descendants of Spaniards, came to the area after 1940 from northern New Mexico and southern Colorado. According to Nostrand, these Hispanos were forced to leave their homeland in northern New Mexico and southern Colorado because of the declining availability of agricultural labor in combination with increased competition from Mexican immigrants. Mexican-Americans and Hispanos struggled for decades to gain acceptance by the majority population.[6] By the 1980s, however, these two "Latino" groups had largely blended into the general community, and no longer differentiated themselves from each other (Larsh and Nichols 1993; Voynick et al. 2002).

In 1982, dropping molybdenum prices on the world market forced the county's last major mine, Climax Molybdenum Mine, to close.[7] Within a period of eighteen months, the county's population dropped from 13,500 to 8,500, and the numbers of students and teachers in the schools were cut in half. Numerous stores closed, and three hundred houses were put up for sale for half of what they had been worth. The assessed value of Lake County went from $278 million in 1981 to under $39 million three years later. Some of the remaining Lake County residents found work in Summit and Eagle counties to the north. Before Climax closed, 2,000 out-of-county residents commuted to work *in* Lake County, but by 1987, 1,700 Lake County residents, approximately half of its workforce, commuted *out* of the county (Voynick 1996; Voynick et al. 2002).

As the extraction-based economy in Lake County crashed, the recreational economy took off in neighboring Summit and Eagle Counties in the early 1980's. Following Aspen's post-war example, numerous ski resorts opened in the area in subsequent decades: Breckenridge in 1961, Vail in 1962, Keystone in 1970, Copper Mountain in 1973, and Beaver Creek in 1980. This economic transition is representative of changes taking place throughout the U.S. West (Rothman 1998; Clifford 2002; Coleman 2004).

The demand for low-wage workers skyrocketed with the expanding labor needs of resorts, hotels, restaurants, construction companies, and related businesses. Faced with a dearth of workers, the resort industry has turned to an increasingly available and willing source: Latino immigrants. While many employers go through the established bureaucratic channels to ensure that their employees are legally permitted to work in the U.S., many others do not hesitate to employ undocumented workers.[8] Employers typically pay significantly lower wages to immigrant workers than to native-born workers, demand more hours, and do not provide them with the same degree of benefits.

Consequently, the size of the Latino population in the region increased significantly in the late 1980s and early 1990s (Rothman 1998; Clifford 2002), and by 2001, Aspen and Vail had more Latino employees than those of other backgrounds (McAllister and Lipsher 2001). Today, Latino immigrant labor is indispensable to central Colorado's mountain resort industry. According to an Associated Press story in 2000, "[Latino workers] have become a powerful force in resort country, where businesses struggle to find workers in an economy that boasts a 2 percent to 3 percent unemployment rate" (Banda 2000).

Affordable housing for the increasing numbers of laborers in the resort counties is insufficient, to say the least, both in quality and availability. The primary corporate strategy for profit has been to link skiing to real estate development, which drives up the value of property and property taxes in the surrounding area, as well as the general cost of living (Rothman 1998; Banda 2000; Clifford 2002).[9] As a result, low-wage workers have sought housing elsewhere, such as Lake County. Though housing costs in Lake County have gradually increased since the 1980s, they remain reasonable in comparison to those of the resort counties (U.S. Census Bureau 1970-2000). For example, a trailer home in Leadville's Mountain View Trailer Park costs one-third of the cheapest condos in Vail (Voynick et al. 2002). It is not surprising, therefore, that Latino immigrants began to make their way to Leadville within a few years of their arrival.

While financial reasons are certainly paramount to immigrants' decisions to live far from where they work, other factors come into play. Social networks are established that expand and solidify patterns of immigration to a specific location, such as Leadville. Migrants take advantage of connections with family and friends to facilitate movement and raise chances of success (Zahniser 1999; Mitchell 2000; Massey et al. 2002). It also appears that low-wage laborers, and in particular Latinos, may be seen as less desirable neighbors by resort owners. When Vail Associates bought a trailer park in 1995 to develop the land, the corporation forced out residents, the majority of whom were Latino workers. Most towed their trailers to cheaper lots in Lake County (Ring 1995b).

It is in this context that families like that of Bonita Rivera have been drawn to Lake County. While some immigrants to Leadville lived in other areas before coming to the region, such as California or Texas, today Lake County is often their first destination after they cross the U.S. border. The immigrant population in Lake County has followed typical patterns in that at first it consisted largely of young males. With time, however, more and more immigrant families have settled in this small county. Though remittances are sent out of country by some individuals, anecdotal evidence suggests that immigrants in Lake generally use incomes to improve their family's situation within the U.S.

It would be incorrect to assume that "Latinos" in Leadville constitute a singular, unified group (Arreola 2004; Zúñiga and Hernández-León 2005). Arreola (2004) writes, "Hispanic/Latino Americans are not one group, but many" (1). In Lake County, "Latinos" are Mexican-Americans, Hispanos, and new immigrants. Research indicated that many non-immigrant Latinos look warily upon new immigrants, and numerous immigrants said the worst discriminatory treatment they had experienced came from non-immigrant Latinos. Other studies have documented the conflict that can occur between second- and third-generation Latinos and new arrivals (Rodríguez and Nuñez 1986; Driever 2004). I took this separation into consideration when making choices about terminology used in this chapter; I group non-immigrant Latinos (Mexican-Americans and Hispanos) into the category of "native-born" or "long-term" residents.

There is also significant diversity *within* the new immigrant community. Almost all contemporary Latino immigrants to Lake County today are Mexican (there are a few Honduran and Guatemalan families). They hail from a wide range of Mexican states, the most common of which are Chihuahua, Zacatecas, Aguascalientes, and Durango. Recent immigrants have brought with them a variety of religions, traditions, and cultural expectations, and my research suggests that rivalries sometimes exist between individuals from different Mexican states. Immigrants generally socialize with family members and in small groups based on, for example, religious or sports-related affiliations. With the exception of these groups, as yet there are few indications of the formation of a singular, unified Latino immigrant community that acts as a counterpart to the pre-existing native-born social landscape.

Research Framework and Methodology

This research is grounded in the idea that interactions between immigrants and native-born residents in new sites of immigration both affect and reflect the ways in which all residents negotiate the rapidly changing demographics. Economic restructuring reshapes opportunities for interaction by bringing groups of people into contact in new ways. Bach et al. (1993, 47) found, "Even in intimate, leisurely encounters, possibilities for change exist along with separation and distance." While shared spaces can become sites of mutual understanding and appreciation, they can also become sites for the representation and reinforcement of difference. Research in Lake County sought to first identify where interactions occurred, and then to assess the character and quality of these interactions.

I first became aware of and interested in Latino immigration and community change when I lived in Leadville from August 2001 to June 2003, working as a high school Spanish teacher. As a resident, I participated in various social, educational, and political activities and spaces. Additional data was collected during four weeks in August and September of 2004. Participants were contacted through local businesses, community programs working with immigrants, and English as a Second Language classes, or were contacted because of their role in the school district or local government. Immigrant participants interested in taking part in the study were given three options: complete a short personal background survey, participate in a semi-structured interview, or attend a focus group. As a result, twenty-five surveys were collected, eighteen immigrants were interviewed, and fifteen immigrants participated in focus groups. Twenty-four semi-structured interviews were conducted of native-born residents. Also, I reviewed two local newspapers, the *Herald Democrat* and the *Leadville Chronicle*, from September, 2001 to April, 2005, to keep abreast of local events and opinions.

Spatial Disjunctures

Leadville is a small mountain town with a limited number of public spaces, which I define here as places accessible to all residents as they move through their daily routines. There is one major grocery store (a Safeway), one drug store and pharmacy, one hospital, a county courthouse, city hall, four schools in the school district, and various stores, restaurants, offices, and hotels. When immigrant and native-born residents were asked where they interact with each other, their answers were not surprising, including the range of public spaces just listed. However, numerous interviewees listed various locations, then, unprompted, added a comment doubting whether it was really 'interaction' or simply being in the same physical location. Bonita said, "Almost never. When I need to go to the store. When I go shopping, that's the only time I talk to them."[10] Francisco, an immigrant resident, drew attention to the cursory nature of interaction in a store: "If you go to a store, you already know what you're going to buy; you grab the item and go to pay. So you don't really talk with the clerk, with customers." Sam, a native-born interviewee, commented that most interaction probably occurs in the schools, because they are "the only place it's forced." The response of Paul, a long-term resident, was very telling. He paused, then replied slowly, "I'm not sure there is any."

This stark *lack* of immigrant and native-born interaction is directly tied to the highly uneven effects of the changing regional economy. Two scales of spatial disjuncture immediately narrow opportunities for mutual engagement: the separation of home and work, and residential separation.

"Here in Leadville, I Only Come to Sleep"

Since the demise of the mining industry, Lake County has largely become a bedroom county for the prosperous mountain resort areas. The routes out of Leadville, Highway 24 or Highway 91 (passing by the now defunct Climax Mine), to mountain resorts and surrounding towns have glibly been called the "Leadville Indy-500" by locals (Ring 1995a). Commuters go back and forth over the high mountain passes, often snow-covered and treacherous in winter, to either Summit or Eagle County.[11] See Figure 5.1.

Like Bonita Rivera's husband Jorge, most Latino immigrants living in Lake work in neighboring counties. A significantly higher percentage of Latino workers than white workers commute: according to the 2000 Census, 70 percent of the Hispanic/Latino population, and 48 percent of the White population (U.S. Census Bureau 2000b). Furthermore, this research indicates that the inclusion of undocumented residents (not necessarily included in the Census) as well as immigration to Lake County since 2000 increases the Latino percentage considerably. In addition to spending forty to ninety minutes traveling each way to and from work, the low-wage positions occupied by immigrants typically demand overtime hours. Many immigrants work at least six days a week. Also, in an effort to supplement their low wages, immigrants often hold two or even three jobs. Martín, the pastor of a Spanish-speaking church, said:

> The people don't work here in Leadville. They work in Vail, in Eagle, Gypsum. In short, in other places. So, people leave early, and get home late. Especially women, they come home to cook, bathe the kids, and then sleep. . . . And the next morning, once again they get up early.

These factors create a greater disjuncture between home and work for immigrant workers than for native-born workers. Consequently, immigrants' opportunities for interaction where their families reside are heavily impacted, both in energy and time. Manuel, an immigrant employed in Eagle County admits, "Here in Leadville, I only come to sleep, practically."

This time away from home also negatively affects the opportunities of the children of commuting immigrants. School administrators and teachers report feeling frustrated by the lack of parental involvement in the schools and in their children's education. Amy, a teacher, said:

> [I]t's really hard to get in touch with parents, the ones who work over the hill, because they're leaving so early in the morning, getting back so late at night that it's difficult for them to be involved in their child's education because they're just trying to get by. And there's not really time.

Local law enforcement officials as well as leaders in the Latino community believe that immigrant parents' absence from home also contributes to juvenile delinquency.

Finally, this home-work disjuncture leads to a temporal separation of public spaces most commonly used by all residents, such as stores. For example, because of their work schedules, Latino immigrants tend to do their grocery shopping later in the evening. It is not unusual for immigrant shoppers to far outnumber native-born shoppers in Safeway after 9 p.m. So, while immigrant and native-born residents do move through some of the same public spaces, they do so at different times.

"I Think They're Pretty Isolated Out There"

The second spatial disjuncture evident in Lake County is a high degree of residential separation between immigrant and native-born residents. Although the county average is 36 percent Latino, this percentage rises to almost 80 percent in the census block comprising the northwest quadrant of the county (U.S. Census Bureau 2000a). The county's largest trailer park is located in this area. Immigrants easily make up the bulk of residents in this and other smaller trailer parks (Figure 5.3). Native-born residents typically live in town, where immigrant residents are a minority. Immigrants who do live in town typically rent low-cost, sometimes subsidized apartments, and very few own homes. This pattern is certainly not unique to this particular immigrant destination; the degree of residential separation is frequently used as an indicator of immigrant accommodation (Bach et al. 1993; Allen and Turner 1996; Johnson et al. 1999; Johnston et al. 2003). While immigrants' success should not be measured solely according to their ability to blend into the "mainstream" residentially (Ellis et al. 2004), residential distance does influence opportunities for interaction (Bach et al. 1993).

In Lake County, a variety of factors converge to funnel immigrants into the trailer parks. Newcomers often hear about openings in the trailer parks from friends or family already living there. María recently moved from Eagle, and she explains how they chose their new trailer home, "We're here because my husband was asking around for a place to live. And, obviously, it was only other Spanish-speakers that he could talk to, and fully explain everything." Discrimination in the rental and housing market also plays a role. Reid, a local law enforcement officer, noted, "There are certain, sad to say, there are still people in this community, as is nation-wide, that own property, that rent property, that will not rent to somebody that doesn't speak much English." Diego, a recently naturalized immigrant, applied to purchase a home in a new neighborhood under construction. He said in frustration, "I sent in my application, and I included all the necessary papers, and ask me if I have received an answer from them!" Immigrants may have negative experiences when they do try to live in native-born areas. Two immigrant families that rented homes in town had neighbors that refused to acknowledge them, even ignoring personal greetings called out on the street. Such interactions undoubtedly make a lasting impression and discourage others from living in town.

Despite the desire of many immigrants to buy a house, there are fundamental political and economic realities that make it difficult. Drawn to the region by the availability of low-wage employment, many immigrants do not have the necessary financial resources. Bonita Rivera confessed, "I don't like my home, because, as it's a trailer, the air comes in everywhere!" However, she explains, "We don't have the money to buy a house. And bank financing is so expensive, and we don't have enough. The truck is financed . . . and having small children costs so much." The impact of legal status on residential patterns is profound.

While buying property is not contingent on "legality," most low-wage earners do not have sufficient cash to buy a house, and getting a mortgage is nearly impossible for undocumented immigrants. Mortgage lenders use social security numbers to check credit history, and many immigrants in the region do not have either the valid number or a credit history (Webb 2005). Trailers, in contrast, are purchased directly from the trailer park owner, who sets up a monthly payment system with the buyer.

Figure 5.3 Mexicans Residing in a Leadville Trailer Park in Winter

Incorrect assumptions and a lack of information about "the system" and available opportunities affect immigrants' residential choices. Low-wage employment certainly limits housing opportunities, and Latinos are undoubtedly aware of the fact that they typically earn less than native-born residents. However, there are some native-born residents who are low-wage workers, and most of those living in Lake County do live in town; this suggests that some in-town housing opportunities exist that would be economically feasible for Latino immigrants. By assuming that they cannot afford to live where native-born residents do, immigrants may preemptively exclude themselves from these housing opportunities. Daniela, an employee of a local non-profit working with immigrants, stated:

> [S]ome that do have a legal status, they don't know that they can go out, apply and get a home loan. You know, so to a lot of them it's easier, because in the trailer park, the man there does the finances for them. It's easier to just go, and

give him their money and have a home, and be paying for it and in three years it's theirs.

There are few resources available for immigrants who do have the required documentation, and they find navigation of the U.S. system of home ownership confusing and intimidating. One local bank told the author that the bank's policy was to deny loans to non-citizens, regardless of residency status. Such a policy was denied by the regional manager, who said that the issue was the social security number. This mix-up offers additional proof that the process of obtaining a mortgage is difficult and confusing for immigrants regardless of their legal status.

The sense of separation between immigrant and native-born residents created by the physical distance of the trailer parks from town is deepened by issues of transportation. With the exception of buses provided by some resort employers for employees, there is no public transportation in Lake County. Residents must therefore get around in personal vehicles or on foot, and most immigrant families do not own more than one car (if that). The various trailer parks range from three to five miles outside of town. This distance can be especially difficult for women who stay at home while husbands leave in the car for work during the day. Millie, who works with a social service program, explains the challenges for some of her clients to get into town, "I think they're pretty isolated out there. And if their husbands don't bring them, sometimes they don't get out." Such distances are difficult to travel by foot for parents with small children, and prohibitive in cold and icy conditions. There are no sidewalks or paths along the highways between trailer parks and town, and road shoulders are often piled with plowed snow during the extended winter months.

Spaces of Interaction

Other studies on new sites of immigration have found a range of responses by long-term residents, from welcoming accommodation to outright hostility (Bach et al. 1993; Rich and Miranda 2005; Shutika 2005). This range certainly exists in Leadville. While anti-immigrant feelings are certainly not the rule for native-born residents in Leadville, some are obviously reluctant to welcome immigrant newcomers. National nativist discourses that blame "illegals" for taking jobs and abusing services are repeated in Lake County. Place-specific variables also come into play, as the general lack of interaction enables the perpetuation of stereotypes and spreading of misinformation. Furthermore, the mining bust and the rise in the Latino population occurred close enough in time that lines of causation have been blurred for some native-born residents, and they hold immigrants responsible for subsequent changes in the county.

However limited they may be, interactions between immigrant and native-born residents do occur in Lake County, and spaces of interaction can be marked by confusion, anxiety, and even conflict. One non-profit organization periodically organizes potlucks that include all residents, and "even then, it's not a friendly atmosphere. It's really tense" (Daniela). While many immigrant interviewees had few personal stories of negative interactions with native-born residents, even isolated negative experiences have a profound effect. Yesenia reflected that: "Negative experiences, racist ones, like that person that said, 'Why are the Mexicans coming, what are they doing here?' That, like how you're thought about, it brings you down, crushes you."

Such experiences can make a lasting impression and shape future interactions. My research identified three principal barriers to the formation of unmarked, welcoming spaces of interaction in Leadville. First, the structurally entrenched socioeconomic hierarchy constantly places immigrants at a disadvantage in shared spaces. Second, immigrants often struggle to negotiate local cultural expectations. Third, the legal condition of being undocumented profoundly shapes many immigrants' lives, including distorting opportunities for engagement in the community. Clearly, these obstacles are complicated by the spatial disjunctures already discussed.

"The People That Live Here Have a Lot of Power"

The economic and political forces that drive immigration pervade local interactions. As low-wage workers, Latino immigrants immediately occupy a lower position in the region's labor and income hierarchy than do most native-born workers (U.S. Census Bureau 2000c). Having fewer financial resources makes it more difficult for immigrants to engage in the larger community. As a school board member, Doug, points out, "If you're worried about dinner on the table, it's hard to think about taking time and doing public service." Also, this hierarchical placement conceptually places immigrants in a lower social class than native-born residents and creates an imbalanced power dynamic in many places where immigrants and native-born residents interact. For example, a local motel owner stated that his only contact with immigrants occurred when they came to his office in need of employment. Diego highlights this characteristic of relationships: "The people that live here have a lot of power . . . for example, in matters of the police, judges, people that work with the government, because automatically they are the first people that we have to turn to."

Many immigrants cited social service offices as typical locations for interaction with native-born residents, and as Greg, an employee of the county's social service department, noted, "Well, social services are generally not positive. A lot of times we have to tell immigrants that they can't have benefits." Such limited contact simultaneously skews native-born perceptions of immigrants. Laura, a non-profit employee, commented, "If [people] do see each other, it's in a crisis mode. It's using services, so then the perception is that's all people do, is using services."

Additionally, the life experiences of most immigrants are resoundingly different from those of native-born residents who are retired miners, local civil servants, educators, students at the community college, "ski bums," business owners, etc. Before coming to the United States, most immigrants in Lake County worked as ranchers, farmers, or in *maquiladora* factories. Almost all immigrant interviewees decided to immigrate because of the severe economic hardships they faced in their home country as wages in these industries decreased. New immigrants typically have no more than a middle school education, and some exhibit a limited level of literacy. Bonita Rivera observed, "Almost everyone that comes here as an immigrant, it's because he didn't study in his country, and because of that he has to come here to look for a better life."

Immigrants may not have enough information and cultural understanding to see education as a tool to ascend the socioeconomic ladder. Laura, a non-profit organization employee, reflects on immigrant students' futures:

> There's very little motivation to graduate from college because you can get a construction job without having a high school diploma, at this point in the economy. Or housekeeping job or whatever. . . . And so for families needing another breadwinner in the family to contribute economically, [immigrant children] aren't really motivated to get a diploma. And yet, in our culture, it will make the difference between a high level of success and not.

Amy, director of a program that works to involve parents in their children's education, maintains that most immigrant parents don't understand American expectations of parental involvement in schools. She said, "...people who haven't had a lot of education are not really aware of what's expected of them and how much it can affect their children's future." Unwittingly, immigrant parents may limit their children's opportunities to the scope of their own.

"But I Don't Know English, and That's My Problem"

Immigrants must negotiate a new set of customs in order to engage in the preexisting social landscape. For instance, several interviewees expressed their initial surprise at the U.S. custom of shaking hands because in their home town, physical contact in greetings was only the norm between women. Pedro, a recent immigrant from Mexico, offered this anecdote:

> There's always the little problem that we don't understand each other. But... They're very friendly. [My wife], in the beginning, everyone always greeted her, "hi!" Well, I answered them, but she didn't. [I said] "Answer them, answer

them, they're talking to you, answer them." And now, she knows to answer them. Because here they greet you a lot.

There were also numerous examples of cultural differences which caused conflict and tension. Latino residents' practice of playing music loudly from cars has angered some white residents, and ignited a local effort to make noise regulations more strict. A native-born interviewee, Tom, commented angrily on the tendency of Mexican men to call out flirtations to women on the street, ". . . the way they treat our young ladies and what have you . . . I just don't like them."

Cultural differences are compounded by economic resources (or lack thereof). For example, immigrant mothers often bring their children with them wherever they go. They do so out of custom and because it is difficult to hire childcare. This practice has evoked some sharp comments from long-term residents at school meetings and in stores, regarding appropriateness as well as the amount of noise Latinos allow their children to make. Latina mothers, in turn, were stung by some native-born residents' reactions, and expressed that they seem to have different ideas of how children should behave in public. One remarked, "Clerks at Safeway and Family Dollar, they are always telling our kids to be quiet. They seem to think that children are totally quiet."

Language has been described as "the great divider" (Bach et al. 1993, 36) in relations between immigrant and native-born residents. As in most new sites of immigration in the U.S., new Latino immigrants in Lake County usually have very limited English language skills, and the majority of native-born residents do not speak Spanish. All residents may feel frustration or anxiety when they don't understand what is being spoken around them. Sandra, a bilingual non-profit employee, put it this way: "Whenever there's a language barrier, you'll have people that are like, 'what are they saying? They're dishonest,' and they're just talking about the selection of fruit that's out on the table, same thing as we are, but it's just the misunderstanding of language."

Immigrants' lower position in the local social hierarchy leads to assumptions that immigrants must learn English. Some native-born residents interpret immigrants' lack of English language skills as unwillingness to "fit in." Martín, a pastor, told of being invited to a meeting as a liaison to the Latino community: "They asked me this question: 'Why are the Mexicans arrogant, conceited, don't talk [to us]?' [I responded:] Why? Because they don't know the language! They're afraid to talk."

For immigrants, difficulty expressing oneself can result in embarrassment and shame. Bonita Rivera's quotation, that opens this chapter, illustrates the fear created by not being able to respond verbally in the most basic of daily interactions. Such feelings contribute to an overall hesitation to engage with English speakers.

The spatial disjunctures that exist limit opportunities for the acquisition of language and cultural skills. For example, while immigrant interviewees repeatedly acknowledged the importance of learning English, they were challenged to make it happen. Juanita, a recent immigrant, recognized that there are few opportunities for job advancement without knowing the language.[12] She observed "As for me, I tell you, I really need to learn English. Because, with English, I could get a better job, meet more people, and they would help me and I'd help other people. But I don't know English, and that's my problem."

However, while free English as a Second Language classes are offered by the local community college in the evening as well as during the day, the long work hours and commute leave many immigrants exhausted.[13] Daniela, a nonprofit employee, explained: "[E]ven though they wish to take classes, they can't because of their work. And others . . . they spend so much time away from their family already, having to come home and go somewhere else, it's so hard."

Some immigrants report learning English, trial-by-fire style, at work, but sometimes this workplace English is restricted to the vocabulary necessary to simply get the job done. Full-time homemakers, often isolated in trailer parks, have even fewer opportunities to interact with English speakers. Furthermore, several interviewees reported that instead of practicing their own language skills, they relied on their children as they learned English.

Students whose parents do not speak English may have a harder time in school than students with English-speaking parents.[14] Some parents hesitate to get involved as school volunteers if they don't speak English. Also, Pam, a school administrator, noted that language was a source of frustration for teachers in the public schools: "About 35 to 40 percent of the parents any teacher communicates with will not be able to speak English. So right there, you count on parents assisting their kids in some way. The most successful kids have parents who are also very in tune with what the school is doing." Therefore, immigrant parents' difficulty learning English may further contribute to maintaining their children's future position in the local labor hierarchy.

"My Baby's Been Out of Milk Since Yesterday, and I'm Scared to Go to the Store"

In May of 2004, the Lake County sheriff's office, in cooperation with several federal and state agencies, completed an eight month-long undercover narcotics operation. The operation concluded with the arrests of around a dozen locals, including a number of Mexican nationals living in the county's trailer parks. Though the operation only targeted those involved in drug trafficking, all undocumented immigrants in the area were terrified. Many went to stay with relatives outside the county, or didn't leave their homes. The schools noticed a significant drop in attendance, and businesses serving immigrants reported fewer sales. Frank, a local law enforcement officer who serves as a liaison with the Latino community recounted: "You know, in Safeway, there was not one Mexican in there. You'd go places, they weren't around. . . . A lady called, I felt sorry for her, she said, 'Are they going to pick us up? My baby's been out of milk since yesterday, and I'm scared to go to the store.' . . . I'm not kidding you, for two days, they disappeared."

This vignette illustrates that undocumented immigrants are constantly aware of the risk generated by their uncertain status, and vigilant because of it. While political categorization by legal status (or lack thereof) determines access to certain economic and political privileges, such as acquiring a home mortgage, being able to vote, and obtaining a driver's license, it also profoundly shapes the lived experiences of many immigrants (Chavez 1998; Bailey et al. 2002; Nevins 2002). Several undocumented interviewees revealed that they constantly worry about their family being split up through deportation. The undercurrent of fear and vulnerability punctuates the daily life of undocumented immigrants. María confessed: "I tell you that at the beginning, I didn't go out, because I said, 'it isn't my place, it isn't my people, I am here without permission.' It felt like it said here on my forehead 'illegal.' So, I was very afraid to go out."

Obviously, the feeling of being physically marked by legal status severely curbs willingness to engage in the community. Native-born resident Sandra explains how the desire for invisibility is another factor in residential separation: "[They] are scared of being messed with, because they probably don't have documentation. So, it's almost like you establish a safe little nesting area that is welcoming to people who cannot prove that they're here legally." Immigrants prefer, therefore, to remain in places where they don't feel conspicuous.

Being "illegal" entails a large amount of uncertainty about the future, which heightens immigrant reluctance to engage in the community. Bailey et al. (2002) coined the phrase "permanent temporariness" to describe the situation of Salvadoran immigrants that resulted after living in the U.S. for years under "Temporary Protective Status." This term conveys a sense of never-ending, helpless impermanence that can be applied to the situation of undocumented immigrants. Immigrant interviewees conveyed a sense of reluctance to plan for a future that may never come to pass.

It is also very difficult for undocumented workers to improve their socioeconomic situation. First of all, whether an immigrant is working on a legitimate permit or not, his or her non-citizen status ensures that the employer maintains the upper hand in the employer-employee relationship. Employers have the power to fire immigrants at any time and they may report undocumented employees to the U.S. Immigration and Customs Enforcement (ICE). This power deters immigrants from taking action to better their situation. Pastor Martín tells of trying to organize Latinos: "Several times we have called to make our voice heard. But they don't cooperate. They don't cooperate because they are afraid of losing their jobs, afraid of being put in jail, of being deported."

Being "illegal" also takes away immigrants' ability to defend themselves, and leaves them feeling vulnerable and helpless. One immigrant spoke of his frustration at what he considered discriminatory treatment by his trailer park manager, "He knows very well that if he gives us an eviction order—what can we do?"

Advancement through education is disrupted by "illegal" status as well. For example, while all students in Colorado are entitled to public education through high school, undocumented students are not eligible for in-state tuition in state and community higher education programs. Undocumented parents may be hesitant to participate in their children's schools, the negative effects of which have already been discussed. Faulty assumptions also prevent immigrants from accessing available services. Sue, a school administrator, disclosed:

> [T]hey're so concerned, many times, if they don't have appropriate documentation, they're very fearful about privacy and confidentiality. And they come in, like, I don't know how much I can tell you, I don't want to get in trouble, and that sort of thing. But my child really needs medical care, they need dental care . . . so they finally come in, spilling it all.

Before a non-profit worker made efforts to take Latina immigrants to the public library, these women assumed the library was off limits to them because of their "illegal" status. Some immigrants expressed that they were hesitant to register for free English classes because they were afraid that a social security card and address would have to be provided.[15]

The social contradictions inherent in the demand for their labor at the same time they are categorized and treated as "illegals" is clearly not lost on immigrants. While employers face little to no retribution for their hiring practices, undocumented immigrants are frequently punished for the "illegal" behavior in which they must engage simply to survive. Dora, a housekeeper in Eagle County, expressed her bewilderment at the government's treatment of Mexican workers: "You come to work, for a better life . . . You don't come to commit crimes, like robbery and other things. You come only with the goal of working. And when you hear, 'La Migra!' it makes you afraid."

One immigrant observed that immigrants aren't asked for their papers when they buy lottery tickets, but they certainly would be if it came time to collect on a win. Another pointed out that as soon as Latino immigrants finished constructing the homes of millionaires in Summit and Eagle counties, they were suddenly unwelcome. These inconsistencies cause many undocumented immigrants to become angry and frustrated with the laws in their new home, and can stifle interest in community involvement.

Conclusion

In the last twenty years, two developments in particular prompted Latino immigration to Lake County. First, as a result of the collapse of the mining industry, housing costs are significantly lower than in neighboring counties. Second, the nearby mountain resort industry is increasingly dependent on Latino immigrants for the low-wage labor they provide. Paradoxically, the very conditions under which immigrants have come to the region create two spatial disjunctures: between home and work, and residential segregation. By reinforcing immigrant apartness, these disjunctures limit opportunities for interaction and inhibit cultural understanding. What's more, many of the interactions that do occur take place in public spaces stratified by markers of difference, particularly dissimilar socioeconomic backgrounds, language and culture barriers, and disparate legal status. Clearly, the region's economic dependence on Latino immigrant workers does not translate to acceptance and belonging at the local level.

This chapter in no way identifies all elements of interaction in Leadville. Here, I outline three areas that beg for additional study. First, the socioeconomic hierarchy in Lake County and the mountain resort industry obviously corresponds with differences constructed on the basis of race. Bach et al. (1993, 31) found, "Like residential or occupational segregation, racial and ethnic inequality is a force of its own in shaping opportunities for newcomers to interact with established residents," The social and political processes at work in the development and maintenance of racialized social landscapes demand further investigation. Second, numerous immigrant interviewees said the majority of their interactions with native-born residents took place at work. Several studies have found that the employer's role is critical in determining what form local immigrant incorporation takes (Bach et al. 1993; Donato et al. 2005). Employers who recognize the vital economic role immigrants play can act as their champions in the community (Studstill and Nieto-Studstill 2001; Grey and Woodrick 2005). Future research in this region must explore employer-immigrant relationships. Finally, it is important to remember that neither native-born nor immigrant groups are homogenous and of one mind (Zúñiga and Hernández-León 2005). There is a broad range of opinions regarding new immigration among both white and Latino native-born residents. Also, it is interesting that though new Latino immigrants have not been embraced by the native-born community, they have not yet formed an alternative social framework of their own. The dynamics of these intra- and inter-group relationships and opinions invite more focused inquiry.

The residents of Lake County are still in the process of negotiating changing relationships. Structurally entrenched imbalances threaten to confine Latinos to their current position in the socioeconomic hierarchy. The condition of illegality, in particular, has the potential to create permanent divisions. Differences in language and culture may subside, but conceptual scars could remain as a result of initial treatment of immigrants based on legal status. As a theoretical concept, citizenship includes the daily practices of inclusion and exclusion, such as who participates in local political decisions or who uses and feels comfortable in public spaces (Fraser 1990; Staeheli and Cope 1994; Kofman 1995; Painter and Philo 1995; Yuval-Davis 1997). Feeling uncomfortable or unwelcome in shared spaces today could problematize future understandings and practices of citizenship for these immigrants. In this scenario, the naturalized children of undocumented immigrants will remain trapped in the lower echelon of local society, not empowered to improve their position.

However, the tangible divisions that exist today could dissolve, allowing the formation of a more singular group (still with diverse elements, but composed of individuals who envision themselves to be equal members of the community). In this more optimistic scenario, the dynamics of interaction would shift for both immigrant and native-born residents in places such as Lake County as more interaction occurs and immigrant participation increases. Indeed, there are numerous indications that productive interaction is increasing in Lake County. Many community leaders in Leadville are making important efforts to bring immigrants into shared public space and to include them in local events and daily life. A local non-profit organization applied for and received a grant to foster integration, and it is in the early stages of planning how to use the money.[16] The lead applicant for the grant reported, "I do feel in the last year that there is a different level of readiness to embrace our new population of people."

In conclusion, this research in Leadville emphasizes the importance of early interactions between immigrants and native-born residents. The behaviors practiced and relationships formed as new patterns of immigration are established set the tone for the evolution of communities across the country. In emerging immigrant destinations, broader socioeconomic and political forces coalesce with specific local dynamics and history. Understanding ways in which this interface affects immigrant and native-born interaction is essential to anticipating challenges, taking advantage of opportunities, and creating productive and inclusive spaces.

Acknowledgments

The research for this article was funded by a Margaret Trussell Graduate Student Scholarship from the Association of Pacific Coast Geographers, a Graduate Summer Research Scholarship from the University of Oregon's Center on Diversity and Community, and a Graduate Summer Research Grant from the University of Oregon Department of Geography. I would like to thank Lise Nelson and Roger Hiemstra for their insightful comments on drafts of this chapter.

Notes

1. County officials estimated that if undocumented immigrants were included, the total county population would be around 10,000. Undocumented immigrants were significantly undercounted in the Census, officials believe, because of their hesitation in participating.

2. A cursory review of local residential areas (both in the town of Leadville and in surrounding trailer parks) showed that there is little evidence of proven indicators of Latino occupation, such as bright paints, religious shrines, and flags (Arreola 1988; Benedict and Kent 2004).

3. There is a wealth of information on the colorful history of early Leadville. See Blair 1980; Smith 1982; Dempsey and Fell 1986; Larsh and Nichols 1993; Fitzsimmons 2000.

4. For further discussion of the role of the mines as an equalizer among distinct groups, see Larsh and Nichols 1993; Voynick et al. 2002.

5. Climax Mine opened in 1917. Around this time, several factors converged to encourage greater movement across the U.S.-Mexico border and to Colorado. Restrictive immigration laws slowed Mexican migration to a trickle until the early 1900s. Then, agricultural employers in western states successfully lobbied to allow Mexicans into the country for farm labor. Also, at this time many Mexicans came to Colorado specifically for mining-related employment. Finally, from 1910-1920, the Mexican Revolution created economic and political chaos in Mexico. It is likely that some of the resulting immigrants made their way to Leadville. For a more thorough discussion, see Kulkosky 1998.

6. Census categories make it nearly impossible to differentiate Mexican-Americans from Hispanos in population counts. It is also very difficult to estimate what percentage of the current "Latino" population is made up of Mexican-Americans and Hispanos who were already in Leadville before new patterns of Latino immigration began; I estimate that it was roughly 10-15 percent of Lake County's total population.

7. The Asarco Black Cloud Mine, which produced lead, zinc, silver, and gold, remained open until 1999. Employment gradually decreased until its closure, when it employed 105 miners (Quillen 1999).

8. In the resort counties, some employers obtain H2-B temporary visas for workers. However, the national yearly allotment of H2-Bs is far less than the demand. Through these visas, residency is contingent upon employment with the designated employer sponsor.

9. For a thorough analysis and critique of the wide-ranging impacts of the mountain resort industry, see Rothman 1998 and Clifford 2002.

10. All quotes originally in Spanish were translated by the author. All interviewee names are pseudonyms.

11. According to the 2000 Census, 52 percent of all Lake County workers commute out of county. 26 percent commute to Eagle County, and 24 percent commute to Summit County. The work destinations of the remaining 2 percent are varied.

12. For the period during which local newspapers were reviewed (September 2001 –April 2005) the *Leadville Chronicle*'s classified section typically featured numerous ads for low-wage jobs in Summit and Eagle counties, such as housekeepers, hotel maids, construction workers, and babysitters. These ads frequently require English skills. Interestingly, bilingual employees are increasingly sought, usually for management positions.

13. The school district has worked together with the community college to provide free English as a Second Language classes for adults since 2003, and each year more teachers and classes have been added to fill demand.

14. For a discussion of additional challenges facing immigrant parents, see Valdés 1996.

15. While the registration form does ask for this information, filling it out is not required for enrollment.

16. The Colorado Trust awarded a number of "Immigrant Integration Grants" to communities throughout the state in August 2004. The Trust dispenses $75,000 each year for four years.

References

Allen, James P., and Eugene Turner. 1996. "Spatial Patterns of Immigrant Assimilation." *Professional Geographer* 48(2):140-155.

Arreola, Daniel D. 1988. "Mexican American Housescapes." *Geographical Review* 78 (3):299-315.

———. 2004. "Introduction." Pp. 1-12 in *Hispanic Spaces, Latino Places*, edited by D. D. Arreola. Austin: University of Texas Press.

Bach, Robert, Rodolfo de la Garza, Karen Ito, Louise Lamphere, and Niara Sudarkasa. 1993. *Changing Relations: Newcomers and Established Residents in U.S. Communities*. New York: Ford Foundation.

Bailey, Adrian J., Richard A. Wright, Alison Mountz, and Inés M. Miyares. 2002. "(Re)producing Salvadoran Transnational Geographies." *Annals of the Association of American Geographers* 92(1):125-144.

Banda, P. Soloman. 2000. "Ski Towns Protective of Menial Workers." *Associated Press State* and *Local Wire*. November 17.

Benedict, Albert, and Robert B. Kent. 2004. "The Cultural Landscape of a Puerto Rican Neighborhood in Cleveland, Ohio." Pp. 187-205 in *Hispanic Spaces, Latino Places*, edited by Daniel D. Arreola. Austin: University of Texas Press.

Berry, Kate A. 2004. "Latino Commerce in Northern Nevada." Pp. 225-38 in *Hispanic Spaces, Latino Places*, edited by Daniel D. Areola. Austin: University of Texas Press.

Blair, Edward. 1980. *Leadville: Colorado's Magic City*. Boulder, CO: Pruett Publishing Company.

Cantú, Lionel. 1995. "The Peripheralization of Rural America: A Case Study of Latino Migrants in America's Heartland." *Sociological Perspectives* 38(3):399-414.

Chavez, Leo. 1998. *Shadowed Lives: Undocumented Immigrants in American Society*. Fort Worth: Harcourt Brace Publishers.

Clifford, Hal. 2002. *Downhill Slide: Why the Corporate Ski Industry Is Bad for Skiing, Ski Towns, and the Environment*. San Francisco: Sierra Club Books.

Coleman, Annie Gilbert. 2004. *Ski Style: Sport and Culture in the Rockies*. Lawrence: University Press of Kansas.

Cravey, Altha J. 1997. "Latino Labor and Poultry Production in Rural North Carolina." *Southeastern Geographer* 37(2):295-300.

Dempsey, Stanley, and James E. Fell. 1986. *Mining the Summit: Colorado's Ten Mile District, 1860-1960*. Norman: University of Oklahoma Press.

Donato, Katharine M., Melissa Stainback, and Carl L. Bankston III. 2005. "The Economic Incorporation of Mexican Immigrants in Southern Louisiana: A Tale of Two Cities." Pp. 76-100 in *New Destinations*, edited by Victor Zúñiga and Rubén Hernández-León. New York: Russell Sage Foundation.

Driever, Steven L. 2004. "Latinos in Polynucleated Kansas City." Pp. 207-23 in *Hispanic Spaces, Latino Places*, edited by Daniel D. Arreola. Austin: University of Austin Press.

Dunn, Timothy J., Anna María Aragonés, and George Shivers. 2005. "Recent Mexican Migration in the Rural Delmarva Peninsula: Human Rights versus Citizenship Rights in a Local Context. Pp. 155-83 in *New Destinations*, edited by Victor Zúñiga and Rubén Hernández-León. New York: Russell Sage Foundation.

Durand, Jorge, Douglas S. Massey, and Chiara Capoferro. 2005. "The New Geography of Mexican Immigration." Pp. 1-20 in *New Destinations*, edited by Victor Zúñiga and Rubén Hernández-León. New York: Russell Sage Foundation.

Ellis, Mark, Richard Wright, and Virginia Parks. 2004. "Work Together, Live Apart? Geographies of Racial and Ethnic Segregation at Home and at Work." *Annals of the Association of American Geographers* 94 (3):620-637.

Fitzsimmons, Kathleen. 2000. "Silver City." *American Heritage* 51 (2):70-77.

Flores, Noreen (Lake County School District Administrative Assistant). 2005. *Email correspondence with Nancy Hiemstra.* February 26, Leadville, CO.

Fraser, Nancy. 1990. "Rethinking the Public Sphere: A Contribution to the Critique of Actually Existing Democracy." *Social Text* 25/26:56-80.

Gouveia, Lourdes, Miguel A. Carranza, and Jasney Cogua. 2005. "The Great Plains Migration: Mexicanos and Latinos in Nebraska." Pp. 23-49 in *New Destinations*, edited by Victor Zúñiga and Rubén Hernández-León. New York: Russell Sage Foundation.

Grey, Mark A., and Anne C. Woodrick. 2005. "'Latinos Have Revitalized Our Community': Mexican Migration and Anglo Responses in Marshalltown, Iowa." Pp. 133-53 in *New Destinations*, edited by Victor Zúñiga and Rubén Hernández-León. New York: Russell Sage Foundation.

Griffith, David C. 2005. "Rural Industry and Mexican Immigration and Settlement in North Carolina." Pp. 50-75 in *New Destinations*, edited by Victor Zúñiga and Rubén Hernández-León. New York: Russell Sage Foundation.

Hernández-León, Rubén, and Victor Zúñiga. 2005. "Appalachia Meets Aztlán: Mexican Immigration and Intergroup Relations in Dalton, Georgia." Pp. 244-73 in *New Destinations*, edited by Victor Zúñiga and Rubén Hernández-León. New York: Russell Sage Foundation.

Johnson, James H., Karen D. Johnson-Webb, and Walter C. Farrell. 1999. "Newly Emerging Hispanic Communities in the United States: A Spatial Analysis of Settlement Patterns, In-Migration Fields, and Social Receptivity." Pp. 263-310 in *Immigration and Opportunity: Race, Ethnicity, and Employment in the United States*, edited by Frank D. Bean and Stephanie Bell-Rose. New York: Russell Sage Foundation.

Johnson-Webb, Karen D. 2002. "Employer Recruitment and Hispanic Labor Migration: North Carolina Urban Areas at the End of the Millennium." *The Professional Geographer* 54 (3):406-421.

Johnston, Ron, Michael Poulsen, and James Forrest. 2003. "Ethnic Residential Concentration and a 'New Spatial Order?' Exploratory Analyses of Four United States Metropolitan Areas, 1980-2000." *International Journal of Population Geography* 9:39-56.

Kandel, William, and Emilio A. Parrado. 2004. "Hispanics in the American South and the Transformation of the Poultry Industry." Pp. 255-76 in *Hispanic Spaces, Latino Places*, edited by Daniel D. Arreola. Austin: University of Texas Press.

Kofman, Eleonore. 1995. "Citizenship For Some But Not For Others: Spaces of Citizenship in Contemporary Europe." *Political Geography* 14 (2):121-137.

Krug, Steve. 2005. *Magnitudes and Characteristics of the Circulation of Foreign Workers in the Western U.S. Ski Resorts.* Paper presented at Annual Meeting of the Association of Pacific Coast Geographers, Phoenix.

Kulkosky, Tanya W. 1998. "Mexican Migrant Workers in Depression-era Colorado." Pp. 121-33 in *La Gente: Hispano History and Life in Colorado*, edited by Vincent C. de Baca. Denver: Colorado Historical Society.

Larsh, Ed B., and Robert Nichols. 1993. *Leadville U.S.A.* Boulder, CO: Johnson Books.

Massey, Douglas S., Jorge Durand, and Nolan J. Malone. 2002. *Beyond Smoke and Mirrors: Mexican Migration in an Era of Economic Integration*. New York: Russell Sage Foundation.

McAllister, Bill and Steve Lipsher. 2001. "Rural Areas Seeing More Immigrants: 5 Colorado Counties Among 'the New Ellis Islands'." *Denver Post*. October 4.

Mitchell, Kathryne 2000. "Networks of Ethnicity." Pp. 392-407 in *A Companion to Economic Geography*, edited by Eric Sheppard and T. J. Barnes. London: Blackwell Publishers.

Naples, Nancy 1994. "Contradictions in Agrarian Ideology: Restructuring Gender, Race-Ethnicity, and Class in Rural Iowa." *Rural Sociology* 59 (1):110-135.

Nevins, Joseph 2002. *Operation Gatekeeper: The Rise of the "Illegal Alien" and the Making of the U.S.-Mexico Boundary*. New York: Routledge.

Nostrand, Richard L. 1992. *The Hispano Homeland*. Norman: University of Oklahoma Press.

Oberle, Alex. 2004. "Se Venden Aquí: Latino Commercial Landscapes in Phoenix, Arizona." Pp. 239-54 in *Hispanic Spaces, Latino Places*, edited by Daniel D. Arreola. Austin: University of Texas Press.

Painter, Joe, and Chris Philo. 1995. "Spaces of Citizenship: An Introduction." *Political Geography* 14(2):107-120.

Price, Marie, and Courtney Whitworth. 2004. "Soccer and Latino Cultural Space: Metropolitan Washington *Futból* Leagues." Pp. 167-86 in *Hispanic Spaces, Latino Places*, ed. Daniel D. Arreola. Austin: University of Texas Press.

Quillen, Ed 1999. "The Last Mine Closes In Leadville." *High Country News*, February 15.

Rich, Brian L., and Marta Miranda. 2005. "The Sociopolitical Dynamics of Mexican Immigration in Lexington, Kentucky, 1997 to 2002: An Ambivalent Community Responds." Pp. 187-219 in *New Destinations*, edited by Victor Zúñiga and Rubén Hernández-León. New York: Russell Sage Foundation.

Ring, Ray. 1995a. "The Leadville-Indy 500." *High Country News*, April 17.

Ring, Ray. 1995b. "Pedro Lopez, Entrepreneur." *High Country News*, April 17.

Rodríguez, Nestor, and Rogelio T. Nuñez. 1986. "An Exploration of Factors that Contribute to Differentiations Between Chicanos and Indocumentados." Pp. 138-56 in *Mexican Immigrants and Mexican Americans: An Evolving Relation*, edited by H. L. Browning and R. O. de la Garza. Austin: Center for Mexican American Studies.

Rothman, Hal K. 1998. *Devil's Bargains: Tourism in the Twentieth Century American West*. Lawrence: University of Kansas Press.

Shutika, Debra L. 2005. "Bridging the Community: Nativism, Activism, and the Politics of Inclusion in a Mexican Settlement in Pennsylvania." Pp. 103-32 in *New Destinations*, edited by Victor Zúñiga and Rubén Hernández-León. New York: Russell Sage Foundation.

Smith, Duane A. 1982. "Boom to Bust and Back Again: Mining in the Central Rockies, 1920-1981." *Journal of the West* 21(4):3-10.

Staeheli, Lynn A., and Meghan S. Cope. 1994. "Empowering Women's Citizenship." *Political Geography* 13(5):443-460.

Studstill, John D., and Laura Nieto-Studstill. 2001. "Hospitality and Hostility: Latin Immigrants in Southern Georgia." Pp. 68-81 in *Latino Workers in the Contemporary South*, edited by A. D. Murphy, et al. Athens: The University of Georgia Press.

Stull, Donald D., Michael J. Broadway, and David Griffith. 1995. *Any Way You Cut It: Meat Processing and Small-Town America*. Lawrence: University Press of Kansas.

United States Census Bureau. 1870-2000. *Censuses of Population.* Washington, DC: Census Bureau.

United States Census Bureau. 1970-2000. *Censuses of Population.* Washington, DC: Census Bureau.

United States Census Bureau. 2000a. *Summary File 1.* Washington, DC: Census Bureau.

United States Census Bureau. 2000b. *Summary File 3.* Washington, DC: Census Bureau.

United States Census Bureau. 2000c. *Summary File 4.* Washington, DC: Census Bureau.

Valdés, Guadalupe. 1996. *Con Respeto: Bridging the Distances Between Culturally Diverse Families and Schools.* New York: Teachers' College Press.

Voynick, Steve. 1996. *Climax: The History of Colorado's Climax Molybdenum Mine.* Missoula: Mountain Press Publishing Company.

Voynick, Steve, Ray Ring and Hal Clifford. 2002. "In Search of the Glory Days." *High Country News,* December 23.

Webb, Dennis. 2005. "A home of their own." *Vail Daily.* April 21. http://www.vaildaily.com/article/20050421/NEWS/104210029/0/ARCHIVES.

Yuval-Davis, Nira. 1997. "Women, Citizenship and Difference." *Feminist Review* 57:4-27.

Zahniser, Steven S. 1999. *Mexican Migration to the United States: The Role of Migration Networks and Human Capital Accumulation.* New York: Garland Publishing Inc.

Zúñiga, Victor, and Rubén Hernández-León. 2005. "Introduction." Pp. xi-xxix in *New Destinations,* edited by Victor Zúñiga and Rubén Hernández-León. New York: Russell Sage Foundation.

Chapter 6

Meatpacking and Mexicans on the High Plains: From Minority to Majority in Garden City, Kansas

Donald Stull and Michael Broadway

Garden City, Kansas, would appear at first glance to be an unlikely spot for a majority-minority community and an exemplar for twenty-first century America. Rising out of short grass and sandsage prairie, Garden City sits quite literally in the middle of America—1,640 miles from the Atlantic Ocean and 1,625 from the Pacific (Mares 1986). A trade and service center for small towns, unincorporated rural hamlets, and isolated farms and ranches in this sparsely populated region of the central High Plains, Garden City is also, as many of its residents will tell you, in the middle of nowhere. The nearest major cities are three hours away—Wichita to the east and Amarillo to the southwest—while the nearest metropolitan center, Denver, is five hours to the northwest.

Founded in 1879 amid hopes of diverting water from the Arkansas River, an average rainfall of eighteen inches a year and periodic droughts belie the town's optimistic name. Even so, irrigation was responsible for Garden City's first boom in the 1880s (Miner 1986), and beginning in the 1960s it gave birth to an even bigger boom, when the adoption of deep-well turbine pumps enabled farmers to tap the Ogallala Aquifer, a vast underground "reservoir" that extends from the Texas Panhandle to Nebraska. Center-pivot irrigation systems allowed farmers whose fields lay atop the aquifer to transform barren stretches of sagebrush into fecund "circles" of feed grains (Fund and Clement 1982; Stull 1990, 307). This abundance of feed spawned a cattle feeding industry, and by 1980, two million cattle were being "finished" within 150 miles of Garden City (Stull and Broadway 2004, 99).

In 1980, Garden City, like small towns throughout the Plains, was predominantly Anglo (82 percent). Mexican Americans, whose parents and grandparents were recruited in the early 1900s to work in the sugar beet fields, were the only sizeable minority (16 percent; Stull 1990). But the 1980s brought rapid change to Garden City and surrounding Finney County. By the end of the decade, Finney County's minority population had grown faster than all but five of the 3,137 counties in the United States (Garden City Telegram 1991). The catalyst for this growth was the opening, in December 1980, of the world's largest beef-processing facility in Holcomb, ten miles west of Garden City. The plant was owned by IBP but in 2001 the company was acquired by Tyson Foods, Inc. Three years later, an idle packing plant on Garden City's eastern edge reopened and expanded. By 1985, these two plants were running two shifts a day, six days a week, and employing over 4,000 persons. The local labor force could not begin to meet the demand for so many new jobs, and Garden City became a magnet for labor migrants from far and wide. Most of those drawn to the kill-floors and processing lines of Garden City's new beef plants are immigrants and refugees from Mexico, Central America, and Southeast Asia.

Between 1980 and 2000, Garden City and Finney County's official population shot up over 50 percent, while the proportion of foreign-born population soared from less than 4 to over 22 percent (Table 6.1). In 2000, only 60 other counties in the United States could also claim more than 20 percent of their population as foreign born—and two of these were also in southwest Kansas (Ford [22.5 percent] and Seward [27.4 percent]; Mathis 2003, 1B). All three counties share one common denominator—the meatpacking industry.

The sudden transformation of Garden City into a multicultural mecca on the High Plains is part of a much larger change in the composition of the U.S. population. The 1965 amendments to the Immigration and Nationality Act abolished the quota system of immigration that favored West European immigrants since the 1920s. They raised the ceiling on numbers of immigrants, revised geographic and national limits, established a preference system for admission based largely on family reunification, and made special provisions for admitting refugees (Lamphere 1992, 7). The 1965 amendments and the subsequent Indochina Immigration and Resettlement Act, the Refugee Act of 1980, and the Immigration Control and Reform Act of 1986 have all contributed to an increase in United States immigration.

By the mid-1980s, Latin America and Asia had become the primary source of U.S. immigrants. Accompanying this change in origins, immigrant destinations became more diverse. Throughout most of the twentieth century, the availability of jobs and social support networks meant that immigration was largely confined to urban areas in California, New York, Illinois, Florida, and Texas. But between 1990 and 2000 the proportion of foreign-born residents settling in these five states dropped from 75 to 66 percent. At the same time, the foreign-born population of Arkansas, Colorado, Georgia, Nevada, North Carolina, Tennessee, and Utah doubled (Martin and Midgley 2003).

Table 6.1 Demographic Changes, Finney County and Garden City: 1980, 1990, 2000

	Area	1980	1990	2000
Population	Finney Co.	23,825	33,070	40,253
	Garden City	18,256	24,097	28,060
% Foreign Born	Finney Co.	3.2	9.9	22.7
	Garden City	3.8	9.8	22.8

Sources: U.S. Census Bureau 2000 Census of Population and Housing. *Summary Social Economic & Housing Characteristics PHC*; U.S. Census Bureau 1990 Census of Population and Housing. *Social & Economic Characteristics CP-2-18, Kansas*. Washington, D.C.; U.S. Census Bureau 1980 Census of Population and Housing. *General Social and Economic Characteristics PC80-1-C18, Kansas*, Washington, D.C.

Midwestern farm states have also been affected by these changes. The number of foreign-born residents in Kansas jumped from 62,840 in 1990 to 134,735 in 2000 (U.S. Census Bureau 1990, 2000). Iowa's large increase in its foreign-born population has been attributed to the "lure" of jobs in food processing and the region's "progressive traditions and liberal social programs" (Cantu 1995, 401). But a more detailed analysis indicates that food-processing industries have recruited immigrants as part of a broader restructuring of the U.S. economy, which is characterized by the increasing substitution of machinery for labor in manufacturing and agriculture, the emergence of oligopolies in most sectors of the economy, the redeployment of capital in a continual search for cheaper production sites, and increases in low-wage, low-skilled jobs, heavily reliant on women, minorities, and immigrants (Knox and Agnew 1989; Sassen 1990).

Meatpacking not only exemplifies these trends, it has been at their forefront. In the last quarter of the twentieth century, white middle-class meat cutters were replaced by immigrant and refugee line workers from developing countries, as meatpacking was transformed from a unionized, urban industry, paying well above the manufacturing average, to a nonunion, rural industry, paying well below it (Broadway 1995). This changeover altered the social and demographic fabric of many rural communities, beginning in the Midwest in the 1980s and spreading through the South in the 1990s to towns with poultry plants and other industries with harsh working conditions and relatively low pay (Stull, Broadway, and Griffith 1995; Stull and Broadway 2004; Fink 2003). Within less than a decade many small towns have been transformed into multicultural communities (Kandel and Parrado 2004; Striffler 2005), and "*barrios norteños*" are no longer confined to cities such as Chicago, Kansas City, or St. Paul (Valdés 2000). In what has been called the Nuevo New South (Fink 2003), Latinos are dramatically increasing in the cities and countryside alike. Haverluk (2004) describes the "Hispanization" of Hereford, Texas—the site of several meat processing facilities—by noting the growth of Hispanic businesses in the downtown area, the increasing role of Latinos in the town's political life, and the lessening of residential segregation within the community. In some communities the influx of newcomers has not always been welcomed, and long-term Anglo residents have responded by moving elsewhere or withdrawing their children from public schools (Engstrom 2001).

This chapter analyzes the social and economic changes in Garden City since the early 1980s and focuses on how the presence of Mexican and other Latin American immigrants has altered the cultural landscape. Before proceeding, we offer an overview of the role of immigrants in the meat industry and how communities can accommodate newcomers.

New Packing Plants, New Immigrants, and the Context of Reception

High employee turnover, dangerous working conditions, and low wages make meatpacking jobs unattractive to many Americans, so packers have turned to immigrants and refugees for their staffing needs. When a new plant starts up, yearly turnover among line workers often reaches 200 percent or more before it drops to the industry average of 72-98 percent (Stull and Broadway 1995). Thus, Tyson's Finney County plant must replace approximately 1,600-2,200 workers a year. The industry's insatiable appetite for workers means that local labor pools are soon exhausted and plants must recruit from farther and farther afield. Current employees are frequently paid bonuses of $150-200 for recruiting new workers if they remain on the job past the probationary period of 90-120 days (Human Rights Watch 2004). This practice, in turn, fosters chain migration and the emergence of immigrant enclaves in packing towns, often from specific sending communities (see Grey and Woodrick 2002; Fink 2003).

Labor migrants' decisions about whether to move to a new community are influenced by social networks that provide information about employment opportunities, working conditions, and housing (Boyd 1989). Once established, these networks promote migration long after the structural factors that induced the initial migration have changed (Massey et al. 1987; Portes 1985).

Alejandro Portes and Jòzsef Börörcz (1989) argue that immigrant assimilation is a function of the social class of the migrants, their conditions of exit, and the context of reception in host communities. Migrants' social class and the circumstances surrounding their decision to leave their homeland are beyond the control of host communities. But the reception provided to migrants is not. It is determined by government policy, the attitudes of employers and local people, and the presence or absence of ethnic communities.

Line work in a packinghouse does not require preexisting job skills or knowledge of English, and the industry has a long history of hiring immigrants, many believed to be here illegally. In the 1990s, the Immigration and Naturalization Services (INS) targeted undocumented (illegal) workers in a number of highly publicized raids on Midwestern meatpacking plants. These raids proved costly to the industry when lines were temporarily shut down and undocumented workers were either deported or fled. For example, at Excel's Schuyler, Nebraska, plant over 8 percent of the labor force left and production dropped by nearly 20 percent (Hord 1999).

In January 2004, President Bush proposed allowing illegal immigrants to apply for a three-year work permit, renewable for an additional three years, to alleviate labor shortages among U.S. employers and improve working conditions for illegal immigrants. Critics charge that such a program would give employers too much power, since the permit would only apply to a single employer, while others argue that such guest workers will take jobs away from native-born workers (Wood 2004).

Local communities clearly have no control over immigration policy or how it is enforced. Nor can they influence the meatpacking industry's working conditions, wages, or recruitment policies. But local leaders can influence public opinion and provide immigrants with a positive context of reception. The remainder of this chapter documents Garden City's transformation from a majority Anglo community to a majority-minority community and the impact the Mexican and Central American population has had upon the cultural landscape.

Mexican Migration to Garden City

The Early Years

There have been two distinct migrations of Mexicans to Garden City. The first wave began about 1905 and ended with the Great Depression, when many immigrants returned to Mexico. The state legislature promoted the sugar beet industry in southwest Kansas by subsidizing beet production. In 1906, a sugar beet factory was constructed in Garden City, and since not many locals were willing to thin, weed, and harvest the crop in the hot Kansas sun, Mexicans were recruited as field hands. In 1915 the state census counted eighty-four Mexicans living in

Garden City (Ávila 1997)—most south of the railroad tracks along present-day Maple Street, which remains the center of the barrio.

Mexican economic advancement in Garden City was "effectively thwarted by racial discrimination" and job availability (Ávila 1997, 29). In 1922, the town opened the "world's largest free outdoor concrete municipal swimming pool" on the edge of the barrio, but barred Mexicans and African Americans from swimming in it.

When the sugar beet season started, Mexican families moved out into the countryside to be near the fields and took their children with them, ensuring that many never obtained a high school education. In fact, the first Mexican American male did not graduate from Garden City High School until 1950.

In 1930 the southwest regional director of President Hoover's Emergency Committee on Unemployment wrote to the Kansas governor asking employers not to hire Mexicans, who he blamed for high unemployment. Some employers resisted these demands, but many Mexicans feared for their jobs and returned home. Finney County's Mexican population actually declined by 71 percent from 1930 to 1940 (Ávila 1997).

The arrival of the beef plants in the early 1980s precipitated the second wave of Mexican migration to Garden City, which continues to the present.

Recent Migration

In 1979, the year before IBP opened its plant west of Garden City, unemployment in Finney County averaged only 400 persons. But this plant, the world's largest, would require more than 2,000 workers before it would become fully operational in 1982; a year later, what would become the ConAgra plant opened. By the year 2000, these two plants combined to employ 5,300, of whom 90 percent were hourly employees. The need to fill so many jobs, coupled with employee turnover that exceeded 100 percent in 1990 (Cultural Relations Board 2001, 14), forced meatpacking plants to recruit far and wide.

A major source of employees during IBP's first few years was Wichita, 210 miles east of Garden City. Wichita had Kansas's largest population of Southeast Asian refugees, but layoffs in its meatpacking and aircraft plants, a national recession, and a federal policy that promoted refugee self-sufficiency combined to "push" many Vietnamese and Laotians from Wichita to Garden City, where most went to work at IBP. Before long, chain migration and recruiting incentives attracted Southeast Asians from as far away as Alaska and Hawaii (Broadway 1985). By the mid-1980s, more than 2,000 Southeast Asians, primarily Vietnamese, had settled in Garden City. But their numbers have dwindled as fewer and fewer refugees arrived from Southeast Asia, and as more and more moved away to seek climates more akin to their homeland; to take jobs or start new businesses elsewhere with money saved from their jobs in the beef plants; and to follow their children when they went away to college. Estimates by knowledgeable community members place the current Southeast Asian population in Garden City at under 1,000 (WenDee LaPlant interview, July 3, 2005). In keeping with the industry's long-standing recruitment policy, once the Southeast Asian labor source had been tapped out, businesses turned to another source, Mexican labor.

By the late 1980s, IBP recruiters were already traveling to Texas and New Mexico in search of workers, which helped boost Garden City's Hispanic population. But it was during the 1990s that Mexican immigration to Garden City surged. The company had always recruited in border cities by advertising on radio stations that could be heard in Mexico. But beginning in the mid-1990s, IBP, with the blessing of the INS, established a labor office in Mexico City, even offering to pay recruits' bus fares to the United States (Cohen 1998).

Many newcomers were not formally recruited; instead they learned about employment opportunities through friends and relatives. Angelica came to Garden City in 1988 from Chihuahua. Her father was an accountant, and after twenty-five years with the same firm he was told to quit or be demoted. He had friends in southwest Kansas, and he came to Liberal, where he then heard of a job at IBP in Garden City. He and his wife left their children with their grandparents for three months until they got established. Angelica did not want to leave Chihuahua, but now she is glad they did. Both her parents still work at IBP—her mother with *cuchillos* (knives), doing something with heads and tongues—Angelica isn't sure, and her father in maintenance. As a child of packinghouse workers, Angelica has heard many stories about the plants, but she has never set foot inside of one. She has been spared from such work by parents who have sacrificed much to make a better life for their children.

Angelica's parents are American citizens now, and she became one in November 2004. That same month she married Jeremy, an Anglo. Her grandparents were unable to obtain a visa to attend her wedding, thanks to restrictions put in place after September 11, 2001 (author's fieldnotes 2004).

Between 1990 and 2000, the Hispanic share of IBP's labor force rose from 58 to 77 percent, while at ConAgra the equivalent figures are 56 and 88 percent (Cultural Relations Board 2001). Not surprisingly, the Hispanic share of Garden City's population rose from 25.0 percent in 1990 to 43.9 percent in 2000, while non-Hispanic whites fell from 68.7 to 49.8 percent (Table 6.2).

Broad census categories, such as Hispanic, mask the human tapestry that Garden City has become. The Hispanics enumerated in 1980 were Mexican Americans, with a deep history in the town (Ávila 1997). By 2000, the label "Hispanic" encompassed not only these established residents, but new immigrants from Mexico, El Salvador, and Guatemala.

Although they remain the largest census category in Garden City, non-Hispanic whites no longer are a majority. Nor are they uniform in language and culture—Low-German-speaking Mennonites have been emigrating in significant numbers from Chihuahua, Mexico, to southwest Kansas over the past decade. Drought and economic desperation spawned their exodus from Mexico in the 1990s. Most live outside the town, where the men find work on large farms and feed yards. Their children do attend the public schools, and the distinctive dress of their women makes them readily observable when they venture into Garden City to shop, eat out in local restaurants, or seek medical care at the Mexican-American Ministries Care Centers and Clinic.

Table 6.2 Garden City Racial Composition: 1980, 1990, 2000

	1980		1990		2000	
	#	%	#	%	#	%
Non Hispanic White	14,920	81.7	16,548	68.7	14,169	49.8
Hispanic	2,968	16.2	6,018	25.0	12,492	43.9
Black	182	1.0	435	1.9	425	1.5
Others	186	1.1	1,096	4.4	1,365	4.8
Total	18,256	100.0	24,097	100.0	28,451	100.0

Sources: U.S. Census Bureau. 2000. *Census of Population PHC 1-18 Kansas*. Washington, D.C.; U.S. Census Bureau. 1990. *Census of Population Social and Economic Characteristics*, CP-2-18, Kansas. Washington, D.C.; U.S. Census Bureau. 1980. *General Population Characteristics, Part 18, Kansas*, PC80–1–B18. Washington, D.C.

Garden City's Boom and Bust

Between 1979 and 2000, Finney County[1] added over 12,000 nonfarm jobs. Nearly 5,000 of these new jobs were in manufacturing, almost all in meatpacking. The other sectors showing substantial growth were services, government, and retail trade. Many of these new jobs, such as those in retailing and food services, pay poorly and provide only part-time employment. As a result, the average wage per job in Finney County fell from 92 percent of the Kansas average in 1980 to 83 percent in 2000. Per capita income fell even more (Table 6.3).

Declines in relative income levels are only part of the story. The percentage of people officially living in poverty has risen from 8.5 percent of Garden City's population in 1980 to 14.3 percent in 2000. The number of persons lacking a high school education has increased along with the number of persons who do not speak English, but many of the area's newly created jobs—whether in the packinghouses or in immigrant-owned businesses—do not require knowledge of English (Table 6.4).

Table 6.3 Finney County Selected Economic Indicators: 1980, 1990 and 2000

Year	Average Wage Per Job	% of Kansas average	Per Capita Income	% of Kansas per capita income
1980	11,752	92.5	9,415	93.8
1990	17,150	86.6	15,593	85.8
2000	23,956	83.5	20,927	76.4

Source: Kansas Center for Community Economic Development 2003. *Kansas County Profile Report: Finney County*. Policy Research Institute, University of Kansas, Lawrence.

Throughout the 1980s and 1990s, Garden City's population and economy grew. But this growth came to an abrupt end on Christmas night 2000, when a fire, blamed on spontaneous combustion, gutted the ConAgra beef plant. The next morning, most of ConAgra's 2,300 workers found themselves out of a job. Single workers left soon after the fire, but those with families remained in Garden City, hoping the plant would reopen. Some workers who left for packinghouse jobs in neighboring states returned, disappointed in these new communities and their schools. Others left families behind so their children could finish out the school year. Still others found jobs in town or commuted to packinghouse jobs in Dodge City, Liberal, and even in Guymon, Oklahoma, 100 miles to the south.

Less than a year after the fire the nation suffered the horrific events of September 11, 2001, which exacerbated the city's economic slump. Then, on December 23, 2003, Secretary of Agriculture Ann Veneman announced that a dairy cow slaughtered two weeks earlier in Washington State had tentatively tested positive for bovine spongiform encephalopathy (BSE). Cattle prices, which had been at record highs, went into free fall; Japan, Mexico, South Korea, and a host of other countries blocked U.S. beef imports. On Christmas day, a laboratory in England confirmed the first case of so-called mad cow disease in the United States.

Tyson reduced its hours in the wake of export bans. By the following summer, when the plant usually runs six days a week and workers can get all the overtime they want, Tyson cut line workers' weekly hours to thirty-two, and early in fall 2004 they were slashed to twenty-four. The resulting drop in take-home pay combined with the job losses to increase the demand for social services (Kansas Department of Social and Rehabilitation Services n.d.)

Table 6.4 Garden City, Selected Social Characteristics: 1980, 1990, 2000

	1980		1990		2000	
Indicator	#	%	#	%	#	%
Persons 25 years or older with less than a grade-9 education	1,651	17.0	1,811	13.5	2,927	18.8
Persons 5 & older who speak only English	13,691	83.4	16,859	77.5	15,260	60.4
Spanish speakers 5 & older who speak English not well or not at all	n.d	n.d	836	22.2	3,124	35.1
Persons below the Poverty Level	1,516	8.5	2,181	9.3	3,927	14.3

Sources: see Table 6.1. n.d. refers to no data

December 25, 2000. September 11, 2001. December 23, 2003. Three years—three devastating blows to Garden City's economy. By 2004 total job losses since the fire amounted to 2,542 (Whitham 2005). It isn't down and out, but as one prominent public figure put it: "Garden City has lost its swagger."

The town's changing fortunes and demography can be seen through the lens of the challenges confronting the local school district. Enrollment in Garden City public schools (USD 457) increased throughout the 1990s, peaking in 2000 at 7,864 students. Hispanic enrollment, as well as its share of the total student body, climbed steadily from 31 percent in 1990 to 61 percent in 2002. Since then Hispanic numbers have fallen and teacher layoffs have followed. Paralleling these enrollment changes the demand for free and reduced-price school lunches has increased from 37 percent of the student body in 1995 to 58 percent in 2004, reflecting the declining income of many of the town's residents (Kansas State Board of Education n.d.).

Yet Garden City remains a magnet for migrants from Mexico, El Salvador, and Guatemala. Most have limited knowledge of English; some are illiterate in their native language. The school district established a Newcomer Center to deal with this challenge. The center provides adult basic education, English-as-a-second-language, and survival English instruction for adults and students in grades 5-12, as well as community information on housing, health care, and education.

Mexican Immigrant Settlement and Assimilation

Garden City was bursting at the seams during the 1980s, as it strained to accommodate the rapid influx of culturally and linguistically diverse newcomers looking for work in the beef plants. A severe housing shortage forced IBP to delay start-up of its second shift. Arguing that some of its workers were sleeping in motels, cars, even under the Arkansas River bridge south of town, IBP pressured local officials to approve a rezoning request for a mobile home park on the town's eastern edge. Occupied mostly by Southeast Asians and Hispanics who worked in the beef plants, by 1988 East Garden Village contained 465 occupied lots—about a tenth of the town's population (Benson 1990). Eight other mobile home parks were scattered around town, which helped disperse newcomers throughout the community (Broadway 1990).

In a town where students are not bused to maintain a racial balance, elementary school enrollments serve as a valid proxy for residential patterns. Comparing USD 457 enrollment records for 1989 and 2004 in Figure 6.1, we see that Hispanics have dramatically increased in all the district's elementary schools. In the late 1980s, the largest Hispanic populations surrounded the old downtown area in the Buffalo Jones, Alta Brown, and Garfield schools. Fifteen years later, Hispanics are the majority in all but two of Garden City's elementary schools. But even in these two schools, both in the town's northeast quadrant, the proportion of Hispanics exceeds 45 percent.

Since the late 1980s, Garden City has regularly elected Hispanics to its city council, and several have served as mayor. Two of five council seats presently are held by Hispanics. The mayor is Latina, the first in the city's history. Juana "Janie" Perkins "moved to Garden City from San Antonio de Aceves in the state of Guanajuato, Mexico, at the age of 10" (Tietgen 2005:A1). When not serving as mayor, Janie is the public school district's migrant community resource coordinator. In 2005 she was named to the Kansas State Board of Regents. And Angelica is now the director of public relations, marketing, and membership for the Garden City Chamber of Commerce.

The changing demographics of the public schools have been accepted and even applauded by an increasingly progressive school board, administration, and faculty. Intramural sports, especially soccer and basketball, have been instrumental in making immigrant students feel more involved with the schools. The high school has an Asian club and Latin Lingo, a modern dance group that focuses on salsa and other contemporary dances rather than the more traditional *ballet folklórico* (some non-Hispanics belong to this club). In 2004, the high school held its first Latino dance, which drew 250: 60 percent were ESL students, and most had never been to a dance before. There were no Anglos at the dance, however, and high school students segregate themselves by ethnicity in the cafeteria and most other activities. Even so, the changing face of Garden City is also reflected in the high school's first Hispanic principal, who is now in his third year.

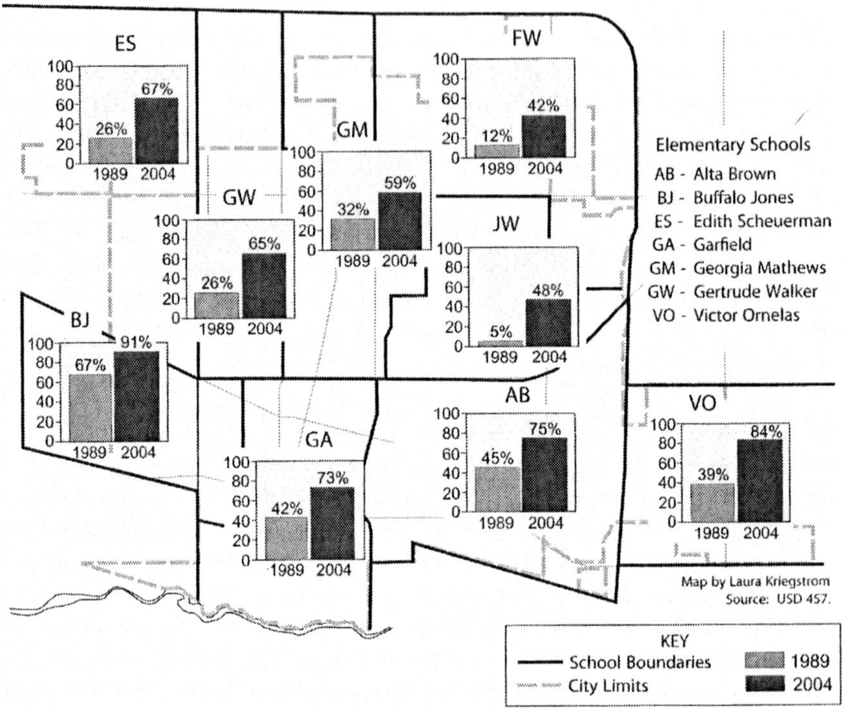

Figure 6.1 Percent Hispanic in Elementary Schools of Garden City, Kansas, 1989-2004

Twelve languages are now spoken in Garden City schools, and the district tries hard to recruit minority and bilingual teachers. Teachers are paid a $1,500 bonus if they can pass a proficiency test in Spanish. The district has had a "grow-our-own" program since the late 1980s; however, only nine Garden City High School graduates now teach in the school district, and not all of them are minorities. A natural pool of foreign language speakers comes from the paraprofessionals, who regularly serve as assistants in the classroom. Paras are eligible for release time during the day to take one course per semester at Garden City Community College or Ft. Hays State University. Despite efforts to deal with rapid change and increase Hispanic students' involvement in school activities, they are significantly underrepresented in high school honors classes and overrepresented among students who drop out and who have disciplinary problems (author's fieldnotes 2004). Yet it is vital for the community's future that this human capital be fully harnessed.

The Mexican Cultural Landscape

Visible evidence of the Mexican American presence in Garden City pervades the residential and commercial landscape. Arreola (1988) identified three characteristic traits of Mexican American neighborhoods in borderland cities; the presence of fences, bright exterior colors, and religious shrines. Many homes in the old barrio south of the railroad tracks share these features and other examples can be found in the neighborhood surrounding Buffalo Jones Elementary School on the town's west side.

Among area employers with ten or more workers listed by the chamber of commerce in 1994, not a single one was identifiably minority owned, though many employed significant numbers of minorities and immigrants. In that same year, however, the chamber identified sixty-one minority businesses and initiated an "inclusion committee" to develop leadership programs for Hispanics (Stewart 1994). Ten years later, the chamber of commerce listed 100 Hispanic- and sixteen Asian-owned businesses, of which twenty belonged to the chamber. At least 10 percent of the Hispanic businesses are owned by Guatemalans and Salvadorans, and there is now a Spanish-language radio station, KSSA, serving southwest Kansas. The most common businesses are restaurants.

Nearly all Hispanic businesses are west of Main Street or along Fulton Street and its extension, US Highway 51. Small family-owned stores, including bakeries, clothing stores, a shoe shop, and restaurants are found up and down 8th Street (Figure 6.2). The largest concentration of Hispanic-owned stores is in the vicinity of Five Points, a major intersection near the town's western edge. Within a stone's throw of this intersection are more than 20 Mexican businesses—auto repair shops, car dealerships, bars, liquor shops, a Christian book store, and particularly restaurants (Figure 6.2). A strip mall and several big box stores, including a Home Depot, Target, and Wal-Mart, are on the other end of town on East Kansas Avenue.

Most minority businesses are small, but they constitute a robust sector of Garden City's economy. For example, a businessman who opened a Mexican grocery in 1983 now also owns a bus line that employs eighty drivers and regularly runs from Garden City to El Paso, Texas, and through to Juarez and Santa Rosa, Mexico. Its routes also extend to other cities in Kansas, as well as to Los Angeles and Denver (Tietgen 2004).

Based on interviews carried out as part of our team's original research in 1988-1989, Campa (1990, 357) concluded that interaction between immigrant Latinos and established Mexican Americans was very limited: "Many of the local Mexican Americans may conduct their daily business without ever speaking with or seeing an immigrant except in stores, perhaps in church, and less frequently in the workplace. . . . Local Hispanics have acculturated in varying degrees into community life and class differences further isolate the native from the newcomer Hispanics." Although still distinct culturally and linguistically, interaction between native-born and immigrant Hispanics—and Anglo and Asian Americans for that matter—is much more common. Not only

Figure 6.2 Mexican Taqueria in Five Points Area, Garden City

are immigrant Hispanics far more numerous than they were in the 1980s, but they are also far more intertwined within the social, economic, and political fabric of the community than they were when we began studying Garden City two decades ago.

Conclusions

In 1906, three Mexicans lived in Garden City; a century later half the town's population is Hispanic. Recent surveys show that nearly half the Mexican population has relatives living in the U.S., which will ensure continued movement back and forth across the border (Massey and Espinosa 1997). Present levels of immigration from Mexico and elsewhere in Latin America are likely to continue, in large part because the "push factors" of low incomes, unemployment, and poverty persist south of the border. Unless the economic situation dramatically improves in Mexico and elsewhere in Latin America, the lure of jobs and the knowledge of opportunities provided by family and friends will remain strong, and Garden City's Hispanic population will continue to increase.

Meatpackers have depended upon immigrants for their labor for over a hundred years. In the past, when plants were located in urban areas, labor supplies were plentiful. But since the shift in plants to small towns in rural areas, the packers have recruited immigrants to these new locations. Communities are powerless to alter the meat processing industry's recruiting practices and operating procedures, instead they must deal with the human consequences of an industry that thrives on low-cost immigrant labor (Stull and Broadway 2001; Broadway 2000). For Garden City this has meant that for the past twenty-five years it has dealt with the challenges of sudden population growth, cultural change and service provision to an increasingly impoverished population. The town has met head on many of the challenges that have accompanied its transition from a predominantly Anglo community to a majority-minority one. Its citizens have taken on the hidden costs of "economic development" with few complaints, schools have retrained teachers in bilingual education, and volunteers have provided money and time to assist newcomers. Indeed the Kansas Advisory Committee to the U.S. Civil Rights Commission (1987) concluded that despite the large numbers of immigrants that descended upon Garden City in the 1980s, there had been no major examples of discrimination in employment, housing, public accommodations, or administration of justice. The financial, as well as the social, costs of the town's boom in the last two decades of the twentieth century and its bust in the first decade of the twenty-first can be placed at the feet of an industry that enjoys billions of dollars in sales, hundreds of millions in profits, millions in tax incentives, and shows little consideration for the communities its plants and employees call home.

In a widely cited article called "The Hispanic Challenge," Samuel Huntington (2004, 2) argues that "the single most immediate and most serious challenge to America's traditional identity comes from the immense and continuing immigration from Latin America, especially from Mexico." Huntington maintains that this current wave of immigration from Latin America is fundamentally different from previous waves, and past "assimilation successes" are not likely to be duplicated. He believes this massive and prolonged Hispanic immigration will affect the United States in two significant ways: 1) important portions of the country will become predominantly Hispanic in language and culture; and 2) the nation as a whole will become bilingual and bicultural. If present trends continue, he fears, "the cultural division between Hispanics and Anglos could replace the racial division between blacks and whites as the most serious cleavage in U.S. society" ((Huntington 2004, 40). For Huntington (2000, 22), "Mexican immigration looms as a unique and disturbing challenge to our cultural integrity, our national identity, and potentially to our future as a country."

Garden City offers an ideal laboratory to explore Huntington's assertions. We first went to Garden City in 1985 and there is no doubt that over the ensuing two decades Garden City has come to look, sound, and taste more and more like South Texas. It has become a decidedly different place—ethnically, linguistically, culturally—before our very eyes. And it differs dramatically from Kansas as a whole, which is 86 percent non-Hispanic white, 7 percent Hispanic, and only 1 percent Asian (Associated Press 2004). So-called minorities comprised just over 50 percent of Garden City's population in 2000, and more than 4 of every 10 Garden Citians were Hispanic. Public signs are regularly posted in English and Spanish and signs in Vietnamese, Lao, even Low German, are commonly found in the schools, the Post Office, social and health service agencies.

On our last research trip to southwest Kansas in October 2004, we spent an evening with José, an old friend and an immigrant from Zacatecas. After getting out of the service, José moved to Dodge City from California to work at Excel, and for five years he was the union representative for United Food and Commercial Workers (UFCW) in southwest Kansas. Since then he has been a real estate agent, a shoe store owner, a bank representative, and an outreach worker for Mexican-American Ministries, the primary provider of health care for the poor in southwest Kansas.

José, who owns the Windmill Restaurant in Spearville, had recently opened a bar called Cowboys and Vaqueros on Wyatt Earp Boulevard in Dodge City. Joining us at Jose's table were Brad, an Anglo wheat farmer and José's former real estate partner; Albert, a Puerto Rican who owns an auto repair shop; Miguel, another old friend who is a mental health professional and an immigrant from Chihuahua. Miguel drove up from Liberal with Suhail, an orthopaedic surgeon from India. A Mexican immigrant and two Anglos worked the bar. Across the room Mexicans, Vietnamese, and Anglos played pool and billiards, while we drank beer, ate *cueritos*, and talked about basketball, work, and family. José spoke proudly of his oldest son, who recently graduated from Wichita State University and wants to be a chiropractor, and he worried about his next oldest who had just reenlisted in the army (Special Forces) and was waiting to ship out to Afghanistan.

So, is Huntington right? Do José, Angélica, and the many thousands they represent pose a "challenge to our cultural integrity, our national identity, and potentially to our future as a country"? We think not.

Garden City's newcomers reaffirm America's faith in the immigrant dream–to make a new life in a new land where their children can pursue their own dreams. Immigrants come seeking work; some stay to become citizens and raise the next generation of Americans. As Janie said when she was sworn in as Garden City's first new-immigrant and first Latina mayor on April 14, 2005: "I am living proof that [the American dream] is not only possible, but alive and well. . . . I feel like Laura Ingalls of the 21st century. Forty-two years ago, I was born in a small village with no electricity, plumbing or a place to get primary education. . . . I want to thank my parents for having the courage to seek a better life for their children" (Tietgen 2005, A1).

We do believe, however, that the cultural integrity of our state and nation, and the values we espouse, are challenged by the xenophobia that Huntington and others like him foment. Garden City was founded by immigrants, and it has always attracted them—some stay, others don't. Garden City's fortunes in the decades to come will depend in no small measure on its emerging majority of Hispanic citizens. And we are confident that Garden City is in good hands.

Note

1. Kansas' Finney County is the unit for this analysis since Garden City accounts for 75 percent of the county's population and many its residents are employed outside the town.

References

Arreola, Daniel D. 1988. "Mexican American Landscapes." *The Geographical Review* 78 (3):299-315.

Associated Press. 2004. "Kansas Growing in its Diversity." *Garden City Telegram*, January 2.

Ávila, Henry J. 1997. "The Mexican American Community in Garden City, Kansas, 1900-1950." *Kansas History* 20:23-37.

Benson, Janet E. 1990. "Good Neighbors: Ethnic Relations in Garden City Trailer Courts." *Urban Anthropology* 19 (4):361-386.

Boyd, Monica. 1989. "Family and Personal Networks in International Migration: Recent Developments and New Agendas." *International Migration Review* 23 (3):638-670.

Broadway, Michael J. 1985. "The Characteristics of Southeast Asian Refugees Residing in Garden City, Kansas." *The Kansas Geographer* 19:5-18.

———. 1990. "Settlement and Mobility Among Newcomers to Garden City, Kansas in the 1980s." *Journal of Cultural Geography* 10 (1):51-62.

———. 1995. "From City to Countryside: Recent Changes in the Structure and Location of the Meat and Fish Processing Industries." Pp. 17-40 in *Any Way You Cut It: Meat Processing and Small Town America,* edited by Donald D. Stull, Michael J. Broadway, and David Griffith. Lawrence: University Press of Kansas.

———. 2000. "Planning for Change in Small Towns or Trying to Avoid the Slaughterhouse Blues." *Journal of Rural Studies* 16:37-46.

Campa, Arthur. 1990. "Immigrant Latinos and Resident Mexican Americans in Garden City, Kansas: Ethnicity and Ethnic Relations." *Urban Anthropology* 19:345-360.

Cantu, Lionel 1995. "The Peripheralization of Rural America: A Case Study of Latino Migrants in America's Heartland." *Sociological Perspectives* 38 (3):399-414.

Cohen, Laurie P. 1998. "Meatpacker Taps Mexican Labor Force. Thanks to Help from an INS Program." *Wall Street Journal*, October 15, 1998.

Cultural Relations Board, City of Garden City, Kansas. 2001. "Changing Relations: Newcomers and Established Residents in Garden City, Kansas, 1990-2000." Typescript manuscript, 34 pp.

Engstrom, James D. 2001. "Industry and Immigration in Dalton, Georgia." Pp. 44-56 in *Latino Workers in the Contemporary South,* edited by Arthur D. Murphy, Colleen Blanchard, and Jennifer A. Hill. Athens: University of Georgia Press.

Fink, Leon. 2003. *The Maya of Morgantown: Work and Community in the Nuevo New South.* Chapel Hill: University of North Carolina Press.

Fund, Mary, and Elice Watkins Clement. 1982. *Distribution of Land and Water Ownership in Southwest Kansas.* Whiting: Kansas Rural Center.

Garden City Telegram. 1991. Ethnic Diversity in Finney County. August 19.

Grey, Mark A., and Anne C. Woodrick. 2002. "Unofficial Sister Cities: Meatpacking Labor Migration Between Villachuato, Mexico, and Marshalltown, Iowa." *Human Organization* 61:364-376.

Haverluk, Terrence W. 2004. "Hispanization of Hereford, Texas." Pp. 277-91 in *Hispanic Spaces: Latino Places,* edited by Daniel D. Arreola. Austin: University of Texas Press.

Hord, Bill 1999. "Nebraska Cattle Industry Finds INS Operation Causing Havoc." *Omaha World-Herald,* May 12.

Human Rights Watch. 2004. *Blood, Sweat, and Fear: Workers' Rights in U.S. Meat and Poultry Plants.* New York: Human Rights Watch.

Huntington, Samuel P. 2000. "Why Mexico is a Problem." *The American Enterprise*, December, 20-22.

———. 2004. "The Hispanic Challenge." *Foreign Policy*, March/April: 30-45.

Kandel, William, and Emilio A. Parrado. 2004. "Hispanics in the American South and the Transformation of the Poultry Industry." Pp. 255-76 in *Hispanic Spaces: Latino Places,* edited by Daniel D. Arreola. Austin: University of Texas Press.

Kansas Advisory Committee to the U.S. Civil Rights Commission. 1987. "Committee Forum on the Status of Civil Rights in Garden City and Finney County, Kansas: A Briefing Report." 22 pp.

Kansas Department of Social and Rehabilitation Services. 2005. "Program Statistics." http://www.srskansas.org/admin/mapprogram.html accessed 2/14/2005.

Kansas State Department of Education 2005. "K-12 School Reports." www.ksde.org/k12/k12.html; accessed 2/14/2005.

Knox, Paul, and John Agnew. 1989. *The Geography of the World Economy.* London: Edward Arnold.

Lamphere, Louise. 1992. "Introduction: The Shaping of Diversity." Pp. 1-34 in *Structuring Diversity: Ethnographic Perspectives on the New Immigration,* edited by Louise Lamphere. Chicago: The University of Chicago Press.

Mares, F. 1986. "Southeast Asians Flock to Garden City." *Kansas City Times*, May 24.

Martin, Philip and Elizabeth Midgley. 2003. "Immigration: Shaping and Reshaping America." *Population Bulletin* 58 no. 2.

Massey, Douglas S. and Kristin E. Espinosa. 1997. "What's Driving Mexico—U.S. Migration? A Theoretical, Empirical and Policy Analysis." *American Journal of Sociology* 102:939-999.

Massey, Douglas S., Rafael Alarcón, Jorge Durand, and Humberto González. 1987. *Return to Aztlan: The Social Process of International Migration from Western Mexico.* Berkeley: University of California Press.

Mathis, Joel. 2003. "Kansas' Foreign Born Population Booms during the 1990s." *Lawrence Journal World,* December 24: 1B, 5B.

Miner, Craig. 1986. *West of Wichita: Settling the High Plains of Kansas 1865-1890.* Lawrence: University Press of Kansas.

Portes, Alejandro. 1985. "Urbanization, Migration and Models of Development in Latin America." Pp. 109-125 in *Capital and Labour in the Urbanized World,* edited by John Walton. London: Sage Publications.

Portes, Alejandro, and Jòzsef Böröcz. 1989. "Contemporary Immigration: Theoretical Perspectives on its Determinants and Modes of Incorporation." *International Migration Review* 23 (3):606-630.

Sassen, Saskia 1990. Economic Restructuring and the American City. *Annual Review of Sociology* 16:465-490.

Stewart, Itzel. 1994. "Hispanics Eye Chamber." *Garden City Telegram*, August 20.

Striffler, Steve 2005. *Chicken: The Dangerous Transformation of America's Food.* New Haven, CT: Yale University Press.

Stull, Donald D. 1990. "'I Come to the Garden:' Changing Ethnic Relations in Garden City, Kansas." *Urban Anthropology* 19 (4):303-320.

Stull, Donald D., and Michael J. Broadway. 1995. "Killing Them Softly: Work in Meatpacking Plants and What It Does to Workers." Pp. 61-83 in *Any Way You Cut It: Meat Processing and Small Town America*, edited by Donald D. Stull, Michael J. Broadway, and David Griffith. Lawrence: University Press of Kansas.

———. 2001. "'We Come to the Garden' . . . Again: Garden City, Kansas 1990-2000." *Urban Anthropology* 30 (4):269-300.

———. 2004. *Slaughterhouse Blues: The Meat and Poultry Industry in North America.* Belmont, CA: Wadsworth.

Stull, Donald D., Michael J. Broadway, and David Griffith, eds. 1995. *Any Way You Cut It: Meat Processing and Small Town America.* Lawrence: University Press of Kansas.

Tietgen, Gwen. 2004. "Business Owner: Working with City a Good Experience." *Garden City Telegram*, June 16.

———. 2005. "Perkins Makes City History." *Garden City Telegram*, April 15.

U.S. Census Bureau. 1993. *1990 Census of Population and Housing, Social and Economic Characteristics CP-2-18, Kansas.* Washington, DC.

———. 2003. *2000 Census of Population and Housing, Summary Social, Economic & Housing Characteristics PHC-2-18 Kansas.* Washington, DC.

Valdés, Dennis N. 2000. *Barrios Norteños: St. Paul and Midwestern Mexican Communities in the Twentieth Century.* Austin: University of Texas Press.

Whitham, Jeff. 2005. "Mayor Looks at 'State of the City.' *Garden City Telegram*, May 1.

Wood, Daniel B. 2004. "Do Citizens Really Want These Jobs?" *The Christian Science Monitor*, January 13.

Chapter 7

Cultural Retrenchment and Economic Marginality: Mexican Immigrants in San Antonio

Richard C. Jones

San Antonio is a continuous immigration gateway city with a surprisingly diverse immigration history. Its small Spanish-origin population (4000 at its independence in 1835) was built upon by immigrating Germans and Anglo-Celts in the middle 1800s, Mexicans beginning in the late 1800s, Polish and Italians in the early 1900s, and since 1965 by various Asian groups. The Mexican-origin population alone is now over half that of Bexar County (the central city county), or 728,000 out of 1.4 million, which together with a large non-Hispanic white minority, are responsible for the city's "bicultural" label. This is not really accurate for two reasons: first, the non-Hispanic group is culturally very diverse; and second, the "Tejano" subculture of the city's established Mexican-origin population is notably different from that of its approximately 100,000 first generation Mexican residents.

This chapter focuses on the economic and cultural adjustment of first generation Mexicans in San Antonio, which is in some ways emblematic of their situation nationwide, and in others unique to the Southwest and South Texas. It comes as an unexpected surprise that Mexicans' shared roots with Mexican Americans make their adjustment in San Antonio no easier, and in some ways more difficult, owing in part to the historical and political "baggage" between Mexico and the United States (Riding 1985). I begin with a discussion of national and regional patterns and trends in the Mexican origin population, including indicators for their integration and acculturation. Then I summarize the history and patterns of Mexican immigrants in San Antonio, leading into an analysis of the integration and acculturation of a sample of first generation Mexicans living in the city. I conclude with policy implications and suggestions.

A Profile of the Mexican Origin Population of the United States

Rapid growth in the Mexican-origin population of the United States is suggested by its increase from 8.7 million in 1980 to 20.9 million in 2000 to perhaps 25 million today (Pollard and O'Hare 1999; Ramirez 2005). Their numbers now outnumber those of Blacks, are twice those of all Asian groups combined, and almost twice those of all other Hispanic groups combined. If we consider the 68 million immigrants that have come to the U.S. over the past 180 years, 10 percent have been Mexican, more than any other nationality except Germans—a situation likely to change in less than a decade (*New York Times Almanac* 2004, 295). Geography and economics help explain this dramatic increase: the United States and Mexico share a 2000-mile land border and a per capita income differential of more than 4 to 1 that has been even higher in the past. History has also played an important role. Over the past century immigration from Mexico has been propelled by political push forces during the Mexican Revolution and its aftermath (1910-1930); economic pull factors in the U.S., including the war and post-war boom (1930-70); and economic push factors in Mexico including a series of depressions precipitated by global forces and Mexico's response to them (1970+).

This rapid growth has been accompanied in recent years by a geographical dispersion from the Southwest into the far reaches of the country, as documented by a growing literature (Massey et al. 2002; Arreola 2004; Zúñiga and Hernández-León 2005). Census data clearly reflect these trends (Table 7.1). In 2000, the Southwest region had over three-fourths (77 percent) of the country's Mexican-origin population—with two thirds (66 percent) in only two states, California and Texas; however, a comparison of immigrants with total Mexican-origin persons is very revealing. In every other region besides the Southwest, the percent of Mexican foreign-born exceeds the percent of the total Mexican-origin population (Table 7.1). Thus, immigrants are the vanguard of new generations of Mexican Americans outside the Southwest. This is not simply a process of contagious diffusion, but a specific response to new "points of light" (or shadow, depending on your point of view) in the restructuring U.S. economy. Agribusiness and the growth of new gateway cities have created unprecedented low-wage job opportunities for Mexican migrants in states such as Georgia, North Carolina, Kentucky, Kansas, and Nebraska. We are seeing a cultural transformation of the U.S. heartland as a result. Hidden by these trends is the inflow of immigrants into parts of Southwestern states with a traditionally low Mexican presence, e.g., the Texas High Plains, the retirement communities of Arizona, and the tourist resorts of Colorado.

Table 7.1 Geographic and Demographic Profile of the Mexican Origin Population, United States, 2000

Geographical Entity	Populations, 1000s			Percentage Distribution of Populations		
	U.S. Population	Mexican-origin Population	Foreign-born Mexican-origin Population	Total Population	Mexican-origin Population	Foreign-born Mexican-origin Population
U.S. total	281,422	20,900	8,549	100.0	100.0	100.0
Northeast[a]	60,427	521	289	21.4	2.5	3.4
Midwest[b]	64,393	2,204	950	22.9	10.5	11.1
Northwest[c]	12,632	674	281	4.5	3.2	3.3
Southeast[d]	72,733	1,391	762	25.8	6.7	8.9
Southwest[e]	71,417	16,111	6,266	25.4	77.1	73.3
California	33,872	8,601	3,642	12.0	41.2	42.6
Texas	20,852	5,180	1,744	7.4	24.8	20.4
San Antonio[f]	1,392	545	96	0.5	2.6	1.1

[a] CN, DC, DE, ME, MD, MA, NH, NJ, NY, PA, RI, VT
[b] IL, IN, IA, KS, MI, MN, MO, NE, ND, OH, SD, WI
[c] AK, ID, MT, OR, WA, WY
[d] AL, AR, FL, GA, KY, LA, MS, NC, OK, SC, TN, VA, WV
[e] AZ, CA, CO, NV, NM, TX, UT, HA
[f] Bexar County, Texas

Source: U.S. Bureau of the Census, Summary File 4 (SF4), 2000.

Mexican Immigrants in a Position of Sustained Marginality

Mexican immigrants frequently perform 3-D jobs (dirty, dangerous, and dead-end). Meatpacking in the Upper Midwest (Stull 1990; Stull and Broadway 2004) and tobacco, textile, forestry, and poultry operations in the Southeast (Murphy et al. 2001)are industries that could not exist without Mexican labor. However, the low pay and benefits they receive place Mexicans at the margins of U.S. society, and their undocumented status reinforces this marginality. The influx of Mexican families has often been accompanied by social rejection by host populations in homogenous rural communities of the Midwest and traditionally bi-cultural towns of the Southeast (S. Simon 1999; Campo-Flores 2001; Foust et al. 2002). The situation of

Mexicans in large cities is equally problematical (Ortiz 1996; Vigil 1997; Smith 2001; Public Broadcasting System 2004).

Unfortunately, there is little evidence of improvement in the condition of immigrant Mexicans with time in the United States. Economic integration among the first generation is for practical purposes nonexistent, whether we measure this in terms of occupational mobility (Smith 2001) or earnings (Ortiz 1996). Furthermore, the longer a Latino (as opposed to an Asian or European) immigrant has been in the U.S., the more public assistance he/she uses (Pastor 1999). Nor is there significant acculturation. Improvement in English-speaking ability among Mexicans (as among Dominicans or Salvadorans) is inconsequential—in contrast to that among Chinese, Koreans, and Vietnamese (Lopez 1996; Alba and Nee 2003, 223).

In the Southwest, Mexican immigrants do not have to face the same problems as elsewhere in the country—or at least so it would seem—because a mediating culture already exists there: that of Mexican Americans. Some argue that a single "composite culture" of Mexicans and Mexican Americans exists in the Southwest, and that this culture represents the interests of both long-term and newly-arrived coethnics. Daniel Arreola's book *Tejano South Texas* (2002) represents this point of view; it documents a new cultural province defined by foods, music, fiestas, language and political organizations. Arreola argues that South Texas is a "Mexican American homeland," and San Antonio, "the cradle of Texas Mexican identity." (Arreola 2002, 6-7). Further support of this unified view is found in recent reports suggesting that Hispanic residential segregation is declining in the Southwest even as it increases elsewhere in the country (Fields and Herndon 2001). Mexican Americans and Mexicans are living closer to Anglos and blacks, and to each other.

Other research suggests an adversarial relationship between Mexicans and Mexican Americans, particularly in the Southwest. This relationship at its roots is based on a less than cordial binational history between the U.S. and Mexico—a history played out in the Border Southwest. At different times in the past century and a half, the U.S. has usurped half of Mexico's territory; supported the Mexican dictator Porfirio Diaz; invaded Mexican territory (during the Mexican Revolution) (Riding 1985, 316-39); and often treated Mexico with condescension in regards to water policy, drug policy, immigration, and trade issues. For its part, Mexico has frequently taken anti-U.S. political stances (supporting Cuba and opposing the war in Iraq, for example), tightened entry requirements for Americans, and refused U.S. foreign aid or official U.S. assistance in times of natural disasters. This historical record of disagreement and mistrust cannot but have an effect on how Americans (including Mexican Americans) and Mexicans treat each other in the most mundane of encounters. In other words, *emotional nationalism* (Riding 1985, 317) regularly governs relations between Mexicans and Americans.

The immigration literature reflects upon reciprocal stereotypes that fuel (and are fueled by) this emotional nationalism. Mexicans, particularly those from the nationalistic central parts of the country, hold disdain for the "pachuco" (Mexican American) who has abandoned his roots and country and when he returns to visit, brings both contempt for his homeland, and corrupted moral values (López-Castro 1986). For their part, Mexican Americans denigrate the Mexican migrant who (in their view) clings to his culture, refuses to accept U.S. cultural and social institutions, and taxes the social system because of his low educational level and poverty. In addition, Mexican Americans may accuse Mexicans of machismo, rigidity to change, oversensitivity to questions of honor, resorting to violence to settle scores, etc. (Shain 1999/2000). Interestingly, the majority culture of both countries looks down on Mexican Americans, identifying them with the vices of the other country. Arguably, this mutual estrangement has contributed to the emergence of the Tejano cultural region.

As Mexican Americans become more mainstream through economic and political advancement—i.e., better integrated with the dominant Anglo majority—there is evidence that they become less concerned about discrimination against immigrants of their own ethnic group. Hispanic support for immigrants in the middle 1990s (Rosales et al. 2001) was compelled by issues such as Proposition 187 in California and IRIRA (The Immigration Reform and Immigrant Responsibility Act of 1996) nationwide. However, this support declined as Hispanics advanced economically in the late 1990s, and the Hispanic political agenda shifted to emphasize other issues, among which crime, gangs, drugs, poor political representation, and low education were paramount (Lee et al. 2001; Michelson 2001; Michelson and Pallares 2001; Ono 2002). Not only were immigrant rights downplayed on this agenda, but immigration was viewed by many Mexican Americans as contributing to these problems.

Clearly, Mexican problems in adjusting to the U.S. Southwest involve discrimination and stereotyping by Anglos as well as Mexican Americans. These are well-documented (Meinig 1969; Jordan 1993; Ortiz 1996; Ramos 2002, 29).

In summary, Mexican immigrants in the Southwest have to adjust to two different societies—that of Anglos and that of Mexican Americans. The emotional prism through which Mexico and the U.S. see each other makes easy adjustment difficult. Mexican Americans are expected to prove their "Americanness" in a myriad of ways, from speaking good English, to following Anglo conventions about time and work, to pursuing professional careers, to supporting U.S. foreign policy, to decrying Mexican crime, corruption, poverty, and politics, etc. These pressures over time and generations have helped create an emotional gulf between Mexican Americans and newly arrived Mexican immigrants (see also Driever 2004, 220-221), who tend to be relatively poor and uneducated.

Mexican Integration and Acculturation: a Statistical View

In an effort to address the question of Mexican adjustment more directly, I present comparative statistics calculated from the 2000 Census. The literature recognizes two separate processes of immigrant adjustment. *Integration* involves the social and economic incorporation of immigrants into the host society. In *social integration*, the immigrant establishes contacts with members of the dominant ethnic group(s) as neighbors, friends, club or society members (Berry 1990; Marger 1994, 118). In *economic integration*, the immigrant moves toward parity with the host society in occupational status, income, and education (Marger 1994, 118-20). *Acculturation*, on the other hand, involves adoption of host-society cultural traits such as language, religious beliefs, preferences for food, etc. (Marger 1994, 117-18). These two processes may work together or not, as illustrated in Chapter 1. High-status Asian or Latino immigrants may be highly integrated but not acculturated, for example. For lower status groups like Mexicans, poor integration and low assimilation appear to go hand in hand.

Table 7.2 considers two inverse indicators of integration and acculturation: (1) the percentage of the population living below poverty level in 2000 (economic integration); and (2) the percentage of the population five years and older who speak English "not well" or "not at all" (acculturation). These indicators are compared across major U.S. regions for three population subgroups: those of non-Mexican origin; those native-born of Mexican origin; and those born in Mexico. First, note that the "Mexican-American" population (native born of Mexican origin) is approximately twice as likely to live in poverty as the "non-Mexican" population, and the immigrant population is even more likely—a gap that has been noted by several authors (Ortiz 1996; Smith 2001). However, Mexican immigrants (just as Mexican Americans) are relatively better off in the Southwest than elsewhere, perhaps owing to their greater vintage there and the likelihood they have residency or citizenship status. San Antonio's immigrant population is even better off (see table), and it does exhibit lengthy vintage: a 1992 survey of San Antonio's Mexican-surname households found that over three-fourths of their Mexican-born members entered the U.S. before 1970 (Jones 1996). Mexican immigrants are best off in the Midwest, likely due to their employment in the relatively high-paying manufacturing sector (meat and poultry processing in particular). Despite their lower poverty rates, it is interesting that Mexicans exhibit larger poverty gaps with Mexican Americans in the Southwest than in most other regions (see ratio in column d). San Antonio exemplifies this trend.

There are even larger gaps in the English-speaking ability among the groups (Table 7.2), especially indicating a rapid acquisition of English between the first and later generations of Mexican Americans. Mexican immigrants' English is marginally better, again, in the Southwest and Midwest, with San Antonio sharing notably in this trend. This suggests a relationship between acculturation and integration. In fact, bivariate correlations with state as the unit of analysis indicate that for the Mexican-born population, speaking English poorly is directly related to poverty ($r_p = 0.597$); a similar relationship is found for the native-born Mexican-origin population ($r_p = 0.521$).

Table 7.2 Poverty and English-Speaking Ability among Different Populations in the U.S., 2000

	% of Population Living Below Poverty Level				% of Population (5 yrs+) Who Speak English "not well" or "not at all"			
	(a) Non-Mexican-origin Population	(b) U.S.-born Mexican-origin Population	(c) Foreign-born Mexican-origin Population	(d) Ratio, c/b	(e) Non-Mexican origin Population	(f) U.S.-born Mexican-origin Population	(g) Foreign-born Mexican-origin Population	(h) Ratio, g/f
U.S. total	11.48	21.61	26.14	1.21	2.52	5.85	50.00	8.55
Northeast[a]	11.05	24.15	27.00	1.12	3.74	6.79	54.55	8.03
Midwest[b]	9.87	16.93	19.50	1.15	1.11	5.37	49.26	9.17
Northwest[c]	10.45	23.08	28.83	1.25	1.54	4.62	50.00	10.82
Southeast[d]	13.67	24.44	28.20	1.15	1.85	6.14	57.27	9.33
Southwest[e]	11.15	21.91	26.73	1.22	3.84	5.91	49.01	8.29
California	11.32	20.75	24.93	1.20	5.78	5.62	48.39	10.27
Texas	11.81	24.05	29.74	1.24	2.44	6.86	50.25	7.33
San Antonio[f]	12.38	20.17	25.79	1.28	2.56	4.61	42.65	9.25

[a] CN, DC, DE, ME, MD, MA, NH, NJ, NY, PA, RI, VT
[b] IL, IN, IA, KS, MI, MN, MO, NE, ND, OH, SD, WI
[c] AK, ID, MT, OR, WA, WY
[d] AL, AR, FL, GA, KY, LA, MS, NC, OK, SC, TN, VA, WV
[e] AZ, CA, CO, NV, NM, TX, UT, HA
[f] Bexar County, Texas

Source: U.S. Bureau of the Census, Summary File 4 (SF4), 2000.

In summary, Table 7.2 provides relatively little support for the argument that a long Mexican American history benefits recent immigrants to the Southwest, or that it hinders them. On the one hand, Mexican immigrants in the Southwest and San Antonio exhibit lower poverty rates and better English skills than in other areas. However, this is apparently not due to their relationships with Mexican Americans, but to their longer residence time and residency status. In addition, relatively large gaps remain between the two groups regarding both poverty and English ability, implying that they are following different cultural and economic paths.

A Historical/Spatial Sketch of Mexicans in San Antonio

In San Antonio the Spanish found an ideal site and situation for establishment of their missions and civil settlement in the early 1700s. The city's Hispanic stock population (as New Mexico's) traces its roots back many generations. San Antonio became (and is) the primate city of South Texas—a cultural province quite different from the "Upper Southern" settlements to the north (Meinig 1969, Chapter 1). Its downtown still reflects Spanish influence in its Alamo and Military Plazas, the Alamo, San Fernando Cathedral, and La Villita. After Texas independence and statehood in the middle 1800s, this Spanish influence was ecclipsed by Upper Southern and Northern European migration to the city, and by 1900 San Antonio's business and political elite was decidedly "Anglo." "Mexicans," a term including those who had lived in the city for generations, held the working-class jobs in manufacturing and the services. They were second-class citizens with little political power, living in poverty on the south and west sides. This situation prevailed until the middle of the twentieth century.

Accelerating demographic growth stimulated by migration from Mexico, coupled with advances in Hispanic civil rights, reversed these trends in the 1960s and 1970s. San Antonio became the epicenter of Hispanic-serving organizations such as Communities Organized for Public Service, the Mexican-American Legal Defense and Education Fund, the Southwest Voters' Registration Project, the Hispanic Association of Colleges and Universities, and others. Hispanic representation in city government, school boards, and the upper echelons of business improved markedly—and with it, Hispanic political power and quality of life, in addition to jobs in middle-level services, retail trade, and government. This is reflected in statistics of Table 7.2. Nevertheless, many young Hispanics must move elsewhere to obtain good jobs in industry, finance, law, medicine, and the sciences. San Antonio has never been an industrial city, and its military sector—while well-paying and equal-opportunity—has been declining numerically for decades. Instead, San Antonio's economy has been driven by personal services and tourism. For all these reasons, San Antonio's population growth has seldom rivaled that of other large metropolitan areas in Texas.

One effect of San Antonio's long Hispanic history and relatively slow population growth is that its Hispanic foreign-born are a small proportion of its total Hispanic population (15 percent—compared to 33 percent for the state of Texas, 43 percent for California, and 70 percent for Georgia). The immigrant presence on the landscape is thus muted and hidden by the much larger and more politically-established Mexican American population. The city's population in 2000 was 59 percent Hispanic or Latino, of which 90 percent were of Mexican origin.

Latino immigrants in San Antonio (Bexar County) as of 2000 were concentrated in the southwest quadrant of the city, as shown in Figure 7.1. Approximately three-fourths of them live within Interstate Loop 410—San Antonio's "inner city." These immigrants are interspersed among the Mexican American population, whose pattern although not shown is quite similar to Figure 7.1. Latino immigrants in San Antonio exhibit a residential segregation index—i.e., residential clustering—higher than that of most other groups, including blacks, Asians, and non-Hispanic whites (Jones 2003; Jones and Crum 2004). Several reasons for this clustering may be offered. First, southwest of the CBD (the enclosed "bull's-eye" at the center of the figure) are remnants of San Antonio's labor-intensive assembly and manufacturing economy, in which Mexicans were historically heavily employed. This economy includes meat packing, apparel, produce, stockyards, warehouses, mechanical and repair shops, construction businesses, and transportation firms (Valdez and Jones 1984; Jones 1996 2006). Second, San Antonio's downtown, a tourist mecca just across I10W/I35S from the Hispanic westside, attracts Mexicans as cooks, busboys, waiters, janitors, maids, clerks, and salespeople. Third, reasonable housing and apartment prices and a familiar Spanish-speaking milieu characterize the near westside. The area is close enough to construction jobs in the booming "Great Northwest" (outside Loop 410 towards FM ["farm-to-market"] 1604) that Mexican workers can live downtown and commute daily to these jobs. Many Mexican Americans, in addition to inner city Anglos and blacks, are moving from their traditional neighborhoods to the suburbs, and Mexican immigrants are taking their place. As evidence, consider census tract data (Jones and Crum 2004) indicating that over half of the 1990-2000 increase in Latino immigrants was in the inner city—compared to only one fourth of Mexican American growth and one-twentieth of overall population growth in San Antonio. In relative terms, Latino immigrants were being substituted for other groups in the inner city.

Mexican Cultural Landscape Features

The foregoing sketch of spatial patterns at the tract level obscures what is happening at the street and block levels. There, to the educated eye, appears sporadic evidence for a *Mexican cultural landscape* of distinctive homes, yards, and street activity.

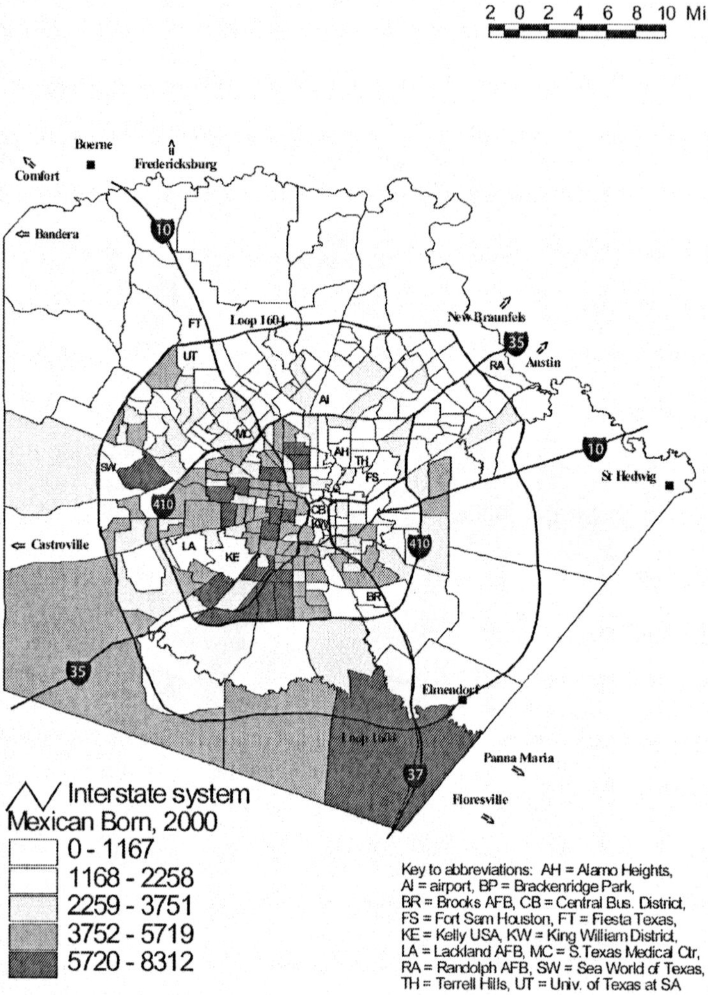

Figure 7.1 Mexican Immigrants by Census Tract, San Antonio (Bexar County), 2000

Mexican homes often border upon disamenity features such as creek beds, railroad tracts, urban arterials, or manufacturing and warehousing districts—the lowest-rent parcels. Just as often, Mexican families live in apartment complexes and homes (including old mansions) or converted garages in the inner city (Fig. 7.2). Mexican homes often exhibit features noted by Arreola (1988): colorful wood trim, yard statuary, small shrines to the Virgin of Guadalupe (Mexico's partron saint), frontyard gardens, and maguey and prickly pear cactus (Fig. 7.3). Another distinctively Mexican feature is a high level of outdoor neighborhood activity. It is not uncommon on weekends to see fifty or a hundred people packing a front or back yard for a quinceañera (debutante celebration for a girl on her fifteenth birthday), church confirmation, wedding reception, or birthday. These celebrations include picnics with piñatas, music, clowns or face-painters, singing and dancing and communing with friends for as long as people wish to stay.

Figure 7.2 Former Mansion converted to Apartments for Mexican Immigrants, Near Downtown San Antonio

The Integration and Acculturation of Mexican Immigrants in San Antonio: Results of an Interview Survey

Survey Design

These survey results derive from a questionnaire that I developed and administered in San Antonio between February 2004 and February 2005, with the help of Maria Maya Jones (my wife), who is from Mexico. Interviews were carried out in eight different neighborhoods in the San Antonio urban area, in census tracts that experienced rapid growth in Latino foreign-born persons between 1990 and 2000. Within these neighborhoods, households were selected randomly. Only households with a Mexican immigrant who moved to the U.S. in the last thirty years were interviewed.

Interviews were conducted face-to-face with heads of household or their spouses. Thirty-two, or 71 percent of the interviews were in the inner city (inside Loop 410: Fig. 7.1). This figure compares favorably with the proportion of Mexican immigrants living in San Antonio's inner city according to the Census: 75 percent. The neighborhoods were diverse in terms of housing density, types of housing, and distance from the city center. The questionnaire included forty closed questions on family background and living conditions, contacts, cultural preferences, and perception of discrimination. Two open-ended questions asked for the respondent's personal experiences regarding lifestyle changes and prejudice. Forty-five questionnaires were completed.

Figure 7.3 Mexican Home with Distinctive Yard Features, Southside of San Antonio

Demographic Status

Demographically, as presented in Table 7.3, our sample exhibits a low educational and job profile in San Antonio despite their having been in the U.S. for an average of almost twenty years. The proportion female was relatively high (over one-third), and the median immigrant first arrived in the U.S. when he/she was twenty-two years old. The median schooling is only eight years, and at the time of the interview the average immigrant household earned only $16,400.

Table 7.3 Demographic Characteristics of Sample: Mexican Immigrants in San Antonio, 2004-2005 (n=45)

Percentage female	35.6
Percentage married	57.8
Median year first arrived in U.S.	1986
Median age upon first arrival in U.S.	22
Median school years completed in Mexico	6
Median school years completed, total	8
Median household income, in $	16,400
Males, job in San Antonio: Carpentry (%)	40.7
Restaurant (%)	18.5
Other (%)	40.8
Total	100.0
Females, job in San Antonio: Manufacturing (%)	20.0
Grocery store (%)	20.0
Professional (%)	20.0
Other (%)	40.0
Total	100.0
Arrival in U.S. by period (%): before 1975	15.4
1974 – 1984	20.1
1985 – 1994	46.8
1995 and later	17.7
Total	100.0
Percentage born in metropolitan area in Mexico	64.4
Mexican state of birth (%): Border state[a]	61.8
North-central state[b]	28.5
Southern state[c]	9.7
Western state[d]	0.0
Total	100.0

[a] Tamaulipas, Nuevo Leon, Coahuila, Chihuahua, Sonora, Baja California Sur.

[b] San Luis Potosi, Guanajuato, Zacatecas, Jalisco, Durango.

[c] D.F., Morelos, Mexico, Hidalgo, Queretaro, Tlaxcala, Puebla, Michoacan, Colima, Guerrero, Oaxaca, Chiapas, Tabasco, Quintana Roo, Merida, Campeche.

[d] Baja California Sur, Sinaloa, Nayarit.

Source: Survey by author.

Secondary labor market jobs in construction, manufacturing, and personal services occupy the great majority of our heads of household. The sample reveals a noticeable surge in immigration between 1985 and 1994, between the passage of IRCA (the Immigration Reform and Control Act of 1986) and the 1994 border fortification known as "Operation Gatekeeper" (Massey et al. 2002, 94). Undocumented migrants were trying to get in "under the wire" or establish residency before the gates closed. Based on their Mexican origins, our sample is a diverse and relatively cosmopolitan group. An unusually large proportion of the sample (two-thirds) come from metropolitan areas in Mexico, suggesting that that country's economic problems and the government's neoliberal response to the problems affected people from all walks of life—not just rural and small town dwellers. A majority of the immigrants (three-fifths) were born in border states in Mexico and another substantial number (three-tenths) in north central states, duplicating the profile of Mexican immigration to San Antonio found in earlier studies (Cardenas and Flores 1978; Jones 1996).

Economic Integration

Census data indicate that in 2000, the median household household income of Non-Hispanic whites was $49,200 and that of Hispanics, $31,200. Our sample's median household income of $16,400 was scarcely one-half that of Hispanics in the city, in the 2000 census. Furthermore, only 8 percent of our sample were engaged in professional occupations (teachers, business-owners), slightly over one-third the rate of Hispanics (22 percent) as revealed in the Census. Most immigrants in our sample (almost two-thirds) work in jobs where their co-workers are principally Mexican (see below).

It is important to note that although the immigrants' economic situation places them at the margins of society, the jobs that they perform are central to San Antonio's economic base and quality of life. Those who work downtown provide a variety of high-touch services for tourists (such as waiter, cook, bartender, janitor, maid), or they work in manufacturing industries that provide low-cost goods for San Antonio consumers (clothing, meat, tortillas, building materials). Those who work in the northern suburbs are employed in the construction of roads, shopping centers, theme parks, and homes. As craftsmen many of them add those large and small touches that make homes comfortable or luxurious at low cost—new rooms, cabinets, tile, kitchen counters, air conditioning, painting, landscaping. This craftsmanship is everywhere to be seen but seldom acknowledged. Abel, one of our informants, noted that:

> The Mexican has constructed buildings, has constructed houses, has done many things, but the American does not see them; he zips about here and there, and when he doesn't need us any longer, he has la migra cast us back into Mexico.

Social Integration (in the Context of Economic Integration)

Table 7.4 reveals that limited social integration has taken place among our immigrant sample. Friends are principally (59 percent) Mexican. None of our sample have principally Anglo friends, and only one-fourth (24 percent) have Mexican

American friends—despite that fact that almost half (48 percent) have Mexican neighbors and most (as we saw earlier) live in neighborhoods where the population is predominantly Mexican American. These findings imply that Mexicans are not close socially to either Anglos or to Mexican Americans. This may be attributed in part to their limited contacts with Anglos and Mexican Americans as co-workers. Fellow workers are mainly Mexican (63 percent), less than one-fourth (23 percent) Mexican American and scarcely one-twentieth (6 percent) Anglo. The prevalence of Anglo and Mexican American supervisors and owners are higher but less likely to assist in social integration than are friends and neighbors, due to boss/worker social distancing (see below).

Table 7.4 Social Integration: Interaction of Mexican Immigrants with Other Ethnic Groups (n = 45)

Indicator	American (Anglo)	Mexican-American	Mexican	Other (or no principal group)	Total
Friends are principally:	0	24.4	58.5	17.1	100.0
Neighbors are principally:	7.1	47.6	40.5	4.8	100.0
Fellow workers are principally:	5.7	22.9	62.9	8.6	100.0
Job supervisor is:	34.4	31.3	25.0	9.4	100.0
Owner of establishment where you work is:	50.0	26.7	20.0	3.3	100.0

Source: Survey by author.

The survey results also add credence to the pessimistic conclusions about Mexican integration (both economic and social) reached by Smith (2001), Pastor (1999), and Ortiz (1996). In Table 7.5, I have divided the sample into two cohorts—those who first arrived in the U.S. after 1986 (short-term residents); and those who arrived in 1986 and before (long-term residents).

Setting aside for the moment our concerns about small sample size, the results across various indicators are reasonably consistent: *the longer time an immigrant has been in the U.S., the less economic integration and the more social integration he/she has experienced.* Whereas short-term residents earn $17,500 per year, this figure actually drops to $12,500 per year for longer-term residents. Closer inspection of the data helps explain this: the long-term residents worked in lower-paying salaried jobs (restaurant work, housecleaning, manufacturing), as opposed to the more skilled crafts jobs, construction, and shop management positions held by the short-term residents. The short-term residents have more schooling, but only by one year (nine vs. eight years)—not large enough to account for the income differential. A final example of poor economic integration is that the long-termers were more dependent than short-termers on public assistance (by 43.2 percent to 33.5 percent), supporting Pastor (1999).

Table 7.5 Economic and Social Integration of Mexican Immigrants: Differences by Arrival Cohort

		First entered U.S.:	
Indicator	Overall (n=45)	After 1986: *Short-term* (n=22)	1986 & Before: *Long-term* (n=23)
Economic Integration:			
Median household income, in $	16,400	17,500	12,500
% labor force in professional occupations	8.1	10.5	5.6
% of families using some form of public assistance	38.8	33.5	43.2
Education: Median school years completed	8	9	8
Social Integration (%):			
Friends are principally Mexican	58.5	50.0	66.7
Friends are principally Mexican American	24.4	20.0	28.6
Friends are principally Anglo	0.0	0.0	0.0
Other	17.1	30.0	4.7
Total	100.0	100.0	100.0
Neighbors are principally Mexican	40.5	47.4	34.8
Neighbors are principally Mexican American	47.6	36.8	56.5
Neighbors are principally Anglo	7.1	10.5	4.3
Other	4.8	5.3	4.4
Total	100.0	100.0	100.0
Fellow workers are principally Mexican	62.9	58.8	66.7
Fellow workers are principally Mexican American	22.9	29.4	16.7
Fellow workers are principally Anglo	5.7	5.9	5.6
Other	8.5	5.9	11.0
Total	100.0	100.0	100.0
Job supervisor is Mexican	25.0	33.3	17.6
Job supervisor is Mexican American	31.3	13.3	47.1
Job supervisor is Anglo	34.4	33.3	35.3
Other	9.3	20.1	0.0
Total	100.0	100.0	100.0

Ironically, this deterioration in economic integration is accompanied by greater social integration, specifically with Mexican Americans. Table 7.5 makes this clear. No one in our sample has principally Anglo friends, and few have mainly Anglo neighbors. However, long-term residents do have more Mexican American friends, neighbors, and job supervisors than short-term ones—despite the fact that fellow workers are increasingly Mexican.

The juxtaposition of social integration with Mexican Americans accompanied with economic disintegration suggests that Mexican immigrants may be subject to exploitative effects of San Antonio's Hispanic *ethnic enclave*. An ethnic enclave normally provides ready job opportunities for immigrants. However, it limits their mobility by creating class boundaries in favor of the ethnic elite (Muller 1993; White and Glick 1999; Wilson 1999)—here, Mexican Americans . As Jesús, one of our informants, put it:

> Mexican Americans are better educated, but Mexicans know how to work better. Still, Mexican Americans are the jefes. They are always bossing the Mexican around.

Acculturation

Acculturation of our sample has been minimal, supporting the observations of Alba and Nee (2003) and Lopez (1996). Table 7.6 reveals that some acculturation is taking place: ties with Mexico are less over time with the exception of visitation to Mexico, whose increase is probably due to regularization of legal status. Likewise, there is an increase in adoption of English by both immigrants and their children. What is striking about these latter figures, however, is their low levels—fewer than one-tenth of immigrants and c. one-third of their children use English as much as Spanish.

On other measures of acculturation presented in Table 7.6, it appears that our sample is becoming less rather than more Americanized. The long-term residents show less of a tendency to watch TV or listen to radio in English, and less of a preference for "American" food and music. A key question, however, is whether they are becoming more "Mexican-Americanized." The answer appears to be no. Although almost half of the sample have used such typical "Tex-Mex" expressions as "jonke" (junk, as in a car junkyard), "te llamo para atrás" ("I'll call you back," in lieu of proper Spanish "te llamo mas tarde"), the use of these and other expressions is less for long-term residents. Long-term residents prefer Mexican American music less—but Tejano cooking more—than short-term ones. One might argue that Tejano food has become so mainstream in San Antonio that it is just as much American as Mexican American. Nonetheless, almost 80 percent of our sample prefer Mexican cooking to either Tejano or "American."

Table 7.6 Acculturation of Mexican Immigrants by Arrival Cohort

Indicator	Overall (n=45)	First entered U.S.: After 1986: *Short-term* (n=22)	1986 & Before: *Long-term* (n=23)
Maintenance of Ties with Mexico:			
Participates in celebration of Sept.16 (%)	27.3	38.1	17.4
Has visited Mexico in past 5 years (%)	45.5	33.3	56.5
Prefers vacationing in Mexico vs. USA (%)	79.5	81.0	78.3
Adoption of English:			
Speaks English, or English and Spanish equally (%)	6.7	4.5	8.7
Children speak more English than Spanish (%)	28.9	23.5	33.5
Preference for English and "American" Lifeways:			
Watches more TV in English than Spanish (%)	22.7	31.8	13.6
Listens to radio in English more than Spanish (%)	4.7	4.8	4.5
Prepares "American" meals most frequently (%)	4.5	4.8	4.3
Prefers "American" music (%)	2.3	4.8	0
Attends church service in English vs. Spanish (%)	36.6	38.1	35.0
Adoption of "Tex-Mex" or Tejano Spanish:			
Has ever used the phrase: "Jonke" (%)	51.1	54.5	47.8
"Te llamo para atras" (%)	44.4	45.5	43.5
"Watchale" (%)	26.7	27.3	26.1
"Washateria" (%)	8.9	9.1	8.7
Preference for Mexican-American Lifeways:			
Prepares Mexican-American meals most freq. (%)	13.6	9.5	17.4
Prefers Mexican-American music (%)	9.1	9.5	8.7
Self-identification: prefers to be identified in US as:			
"American" (%)	2.3	4.8	0.0
"Hispanic, Latino, Mexican American" (%)	29.6	33.4	26.1
"Mexican, Mexicano" (%)	68.1	61.8	73.9
Total	100.0	100.0	100.0
Self-identification: prefers to be identified in Mexico as:			
"American" (%)	4.6	0	8.6
"Hispanic, Latino, Mexican American" (%)	6.9	4.8	8.6
"Mexican, Mexicano" (%)	88.5	95.2	82.8
Total	100.0	100.0	100.0

What are the reasons for this persistent adherence to Mexican culture? Several of our respondents saw their culture as a necessary retreat from the hurry, stress, impatience, and aloofness of Americans and American life. For example, a respondent, Juan, comments:

> Here (in the U.S.) there is so much stress and pressure. Life is more rapid. People don't talk to their neighbors. My American neighbors called the police instead of telling us our music was too loud. . . . I go some weekends [to his home town in Nuevo León state] and come back refreshed. All is healed.

Two-thirds of our sample prefers to be identified as "Mexican" in the United States. A common refrain is that of our informant Lupe, who stated: "In my heart, I am Mexican, one hundred percent Mexican." The rest of our sample prefer "Hispanic," "Latino," or "Mexican American"; none prefer "American." In other words, our sample exhibits low *psychological assimilation* (Marger 1994, 120-21). Significantly, the proportion preferring Hispanic or Latino drops from one-third for short-term residents, to one-fourth for long-term residents.

These results and quotes signify *cultural retrenchment*—the reinforcing rather than dimunition of Mexican Spanish, Mexican lifeways, and Mexican self-identification over time in the United States. In addition to a refuge from the stresses of American life, this retrenchment may be a direct response to the rejection of Mexico, Spanish, and Mexican immigrants by the host society—particularly, by Mexican Americans—as indicated by the following three respondents:

> When (Mexicans or Mexican Americans) get their papers, and want to succeed, they identify themselves as Americans. Their children don't accept their Mexican origins and they want to forget their Spanish (Maria).

> In Walmart, a Mexican American woman was speaking Spanish to another Mexican American. I spoke to her in Spanish and she got very upset. Mexican Americans don't want to accept their Mexican roots because they're afraid they'll be mistreated or put down (Dagoberto).

> Mexican Americans deny their own roots. I realize why they don't want to speak Spanish (Mario).

Discrimination

There is clearly a perception by our sample that discrimination against them occurs because they are Mexican. We asked for their perception of three types of discrimination—on the job, in the schools, and in the receipt of public services. Their responses are summarized in Table 7.7.

Table 7.7 Discrimination against Mexican Immigrants: Selected Indicators and Differences by Arrival Cohort

Indicator	Overall (n=45)	First entered U.S.: After 1986: *Short-term* (n=22)	1986 & Before: *Long-term* (n=23)
Feels American bosses mistreat Mexican workers (%)	45.2	35.0	54.5
Feels Mex-Amer. Bosses mistreat Mex. Workers (%)	57.9	50.0	63.6
Feels American teachers neglect Mex. students (%)	32.5	10.0	55.0
Feels Mex-Amer. teachers neglect Mex. students (%)	21.1	10.5	31.6
Feels American public servants help Mexicans less (%)	46.5	30.0	60.9
Feels Mex-Amer. public servants help Mexicans less (%)	62.5	55.0	70.0
Feels more discrimination exists in US than Mex (%)	68.4	65.0	72.2

Source: Survey by author.

Around one-half feel that bosses and public servants discriminate. It is particularly interesting that in these two arenas, discrimination from Mexican Americans is seen as more prevalent than discrimination from "Americans" (Anglos). The perception of neglect of Mexican students in the schools is considerably less, and MexicanAmerican teachers are seen as less likely to neglect Mexican students—a clear indication of the importance of language in a teacher's effectiveness in helping these students. Finally, note in the table that almost two-thirds of our sample felt there is more discrimination (in general) in the U.S. than in Mexico. The statements of three respondents are given below:

> The Mexican American bosses pay less, treat us worse (Daniel).
>
> At the doctor's office, they made my wife wait one hour. Anglo and Mexican American kids went in ahead of us. Both Mexican American and American nurses were sarcastic and assumed she knew no English (Rosita).
>
> In the 4th grade in San Antonio, although the teacher wanted to help me, he couldn't because he didn't know Spanish. Now, all is changed . . . signs in Spanish, bilingual classes (Lupe).

In light of our findings on integration and acculturation for different arrival cohorts, it is intriguing although not surprising that perception of discrimination is significantly greater for long-term residents. This may be observed in Table 7.7—in all three discrimination arenas, from both Anglos and Mexican Americans. Most notable is the increasing perception of discrimination from Anglo bosses, teachers, and public servants. Anglos are the ultimate "gatekeepers" in San Antonio society—a fact evidently impressed upon those who have been around longer.

The underlying causes of these perceptions are open to question. What is known is that after almost twenty years in the U.S. our long-term group exhibits very low—and declining—socioeconomic attainment on all criteria. A median income of $12,500 is bare survival for a family, even in San Antonio. Recent arrivals do better ($17,500) but this income is still at subsistence level. Nevertheless, these recent immigrants—young and idealistic—may discount their low incomes, believing the American dream is still realizable. Earlier arrivals, seeing that it is not, may conclude that there is discrimination against Mexicans in U.S. society.

Conclusions and Commentary on Immigrant Adjustment

In this chapter, I broadly survey Mexican immigration trends and patterns, and then employ multiple methods to examine the adjustment of Mexican immigrants in San Antonio since 1990. Census data and recent research reveal a dispersion of Mexican immigrants far beyond the U.S. Southwest over the 1990-2000 decade. Of course, the Mexican immigrant population continued to grow rapidly in the Southwest, too (in San Antonio, at twice the rate of the native Hispanic population: Jones and Crum 2004). Whether within or outside of the Southwest, however, the economic integration of Mexican immigrants is relatively low, and their acculturation, lower still.

My case study of San Antonio reveals a large influx of Mexican immigrants between 1990 and 2000, as well as the displacement of Mexican Americans, blacks, and non-Hispanic whites from the inner city. Field research has disclosed that Mexicans are blended residentially into Hispanic neighborhoods on the near southwest side of San Antonio. Their homes are distinguished by their bright colors, plants, statuary, etc.; as well as the level of street activity nearby.

An interview survey of a sample of forty-five Mexican households (2004-2005) in areas of rapid Latino immigrant growth in San Antonio uncovered a widespread lack of adjustment to the host society (whether Anglo or Mexican American) among these families. They have relatively few Mexican American or Anglo friends, tend to work alongside other Mexicans, prefer Mexican to Tejano lifeways, and are poorly integrated economically. On practically all of these indicators, those immigrants who have been in the U.S. longer are less well-adjusted, suggesting *cultural retrenchment* and worsening *economic marginality*. A notable finding is that our sample perceives considerable anti-Mexican discrimination on the job and among public servants—with Mexican American job supervisors and public servants judged more likely to discriminate than Anglos. This suggests class boundaries within the Hispanic community. Specifically, a Hispanic ethnic enclave appears to exist in the city, in which Mexican Americans hold the supervisory jobs and political power, and Mexicans are the laboring class.

There is a growing negativism in U.S. society towards Mexican immigration, as captured in a recent *Newsweek* article by Robert Samuelson (2005), who writes:

> The uncontrolled inflow of unskilled Latino workers into the United States is increasingly sabotaging the assimilation process. . . . Will immigration continue to foster national pride and strength or will it cause more weakness and anger?

Samuelson concentrates on the low level of economic advancement and the resultant cost of Mexican (particularly illegal) immigrants to U.S. society. These economic arguments and more extreme ones (Huntington 2004) have been refuted in an extensive literature on the value of low-pay, "high-touch" jobs to the U.S. economy. These jobs, along with the revitalization and demographic turnaround brought by immigration in declining communities, provide benefits that far exceed the costs of education and health care for such immigrants and their children (J. Simon 1999; Murphy et al. 2001; S. Simon 2002). However, it is the implied causes for this low advancement—and the feelings of "weakness and anger" that it engenders—that are the most disturbing parts of Samuelson's argument. He espouses what others have referred to as a "culture of poverty" position—blaming low education and the culture of immigrants, rather than structural and societal factors in the United States, such as discrimination. Alternatively, could the low economic integration of Mexican immigrants be, at least in part, a function of anti-Mexican discrimination and the difficulties of adjusting to American society? If so, the "anger" that people feel might more profitably be directed at themselves for behavior that creates a self-fulfilling prophecy?

The question of whether the low economic position of Mexican immigrants is more related to their own characteristics than to their treatment by U.S. society may be tested with indicators developed from our interview survey. Consider household income as an indicator of economic integration (dependent variable), and three head-of-household characteristics (independent variables) whose indicators are as follows: (1) number of years of schooling, (2) perceived discrimination (whether greater in the U.S. than Mexico); and (3) inferred legal status. Legal status was judged on the basis of formal and informal comments made by our respondents during the open part of the interviews. All indicators are dichotomized for bivariate crosstabular analyses.

Table 7.8 presents the results of this test. Education (immigrant characteristic) and perceived anti-Mexican discrimination in the U.S. (treatment by society) are of analagous importance in explaining income. The educated are 20 percent more likely to earn high income; those who believe that discrimination is less in the U.S. are 23 percent more likely to earn high income. More important than either of these indicators is legal status (a measure of societal treatment): legal immigrants are 60 percent more likely to earn high income than illegal migrants. Furthermore, legality is related to discrimination (illegals are more vulnerable to it), and to education (illegals tend to have less). As a result, an immigrant's legality works indirectly to intensify the effect of the other two variables.

Table 7.8 Economic Integration of Mexican Immigrants and Explanatory Indicators

Indicator	Percent of Respondents Earning ≥ $15,000/year, by Response to Indicator: Yes	No	Ratio, Yes/no
Total years of schooling: more than 8?	57.1	47.6	1.20
Perceive less discrimination in the U.S. than in Mexico?	66.7	54.2	1.23
Legal status in the U.S.?	61.5	37.5	1.64
n	22	23	—

In the second generation, we may speculate (beyond the data gathered for this study, but based on other research) that the adjustment of Mexican immigrants in San Antonio is more rapid. English is ingrained from primary school onward, cultural ties to Mexico are much less, legality is automatic, and despite low family resources this generation is part of San Antonio's powerful Mexican American majority. The ultimate elite is still Anglo, however, so that Mexican American acceptance by Anglos is a new hurdle that must be addressed by the second generation.

Despite the better adjustment of the second generation, the fact remains that Mexicans in San Antonio are increasing at twice the rate of Mexican Americans, four times the rate of blacks, and thirty times the rate of non-Hispanic whites. Assuming this differential continues, first generation Mexican immigrants will become a greater proportion of San Antonio's population, and their poor integration and acculturation into the city will become a more pressing issue. This issue will appear as increasing poverty, greater demands on social services, poor adjustment of children in school, antisocial behavior in the inner city, and friction between the Mexican and Mexican American communities.

The regularization of legal status for the large undocumented Mexican population of San Antonio (estimated at 5 percent of the city's total) offers one solution to this dilemma. This step would raise wages and relative economic integration of Mexican immigrants, and at the same time remove the basis for much of the formal discrimination against them. Unfortunately, the present national political climate does not offer much hope for congressional implementation of a new amnesty policy in the near future.

References

Alba, Richard, and Victor Nee. 2003. *Remaking the American Mainstream*. Cambridge, MA: Harvard University Press.

Arreola, Daniel D. 1988. "Mexican American Housescapes." *Geographical Review* 78:299-315.

———. 2002. *Tejano South Texas: a Mexican American Cultural Province*. Austin: University of Texas Press.

———. 2004. *Hispanic Spaces, Latino Places: Community and Cultural Diversity in Contemporary America*. Austin: University of Texas Press.

Berry, John W. 1990. "Acculturation and Adaptation: a General Framework." Pp. 90-102 in *Mental Health of Immigrants and Refugees*, edited by Wayne H. Holtzman and Thomas H. Bornemann. Austin: Hogg Foundation for Mental Health.

Campo-Flores, Arian. 2001. "A Town's Two Faces." *Newsweek* 137(23):34-35. June 4.

Cardenas, Gilbert, and Roy Flores. 1978. *A Study of the Demographic and Employment Characteristics of Undocumented Aliens in San Antonio, El Paso, and McAllen*. San Antonio: Southwestern Regional Office, U.S. Comission on Civil Rights.

Driever, Stephen L. 2004. "Latinos in Polynucleated Kansas City." Pp. 207-223 in *Hispanic Spaces, Latino Places: Community and Cultural Diversity in Contemporary America*, edited by Daniel D. Arreola. Austin: University of Texas Press.

Fields, Robin, and Ray Herndon. 2001. "Segregation of a New Sort Takes Shape: Census: In a Majority of Cities, Asians and Latinos have Become More Isolated from Other Racial Groups." *Los Angeles Times*, July 5.

Foust, Dean, Brian Grow, and Aixa Pascual. 2002. "The Changing Heartland: An Influx of Newcomers both Buoys and Burdens Small-town America." *Business Week*. September 9.

Huntington, Samuel P. 2004. "The Hispanic Challenge." *Foreign Policy*, March/April:1-17.

Jones, Richard C. 1996. "Spatial Origins of San Antonio's Mexican-Born Population." *Rio Bravo* 5(1):1-26.

———. 2003. "The Segregation of Ancestry Groups in San Antonio." *Social Science Journal* 40:213-232.

———. 2006. "Cultural Diversity in a 'Bi-cultural' City: Factors in the Location of Ancestry Groups in San Antonio." *Cultural Geography* 23(2):33-69.

Jones, Richard C., and Shannon Crum. 2004. "Changing Spatial Patterns of Ethnic and Immigrant Groups in San Antonio, 1990-2000." Paper presented at the 2004 Conference on Race, Ethnicity, and Place. Washington, DC: Howard University. September 16-18.

Jordan, Terry G. 1993. "The Anglo-Texan Homeland." *Journal of Cultural Geography* 13(2):75-86.

Lee, Yeuh-Ting, Victor Ottati, and Imtiaz Hussain. 2001. "Attitudes toward 'Illegal' Immigration into the United States: California Proposition 187." *Hispanic Journal of Behavioral Sciences* 23(4):430-443.

Lopez, David E. 1996. "Language: Diversity and Assimilation." Pp. 139-63 in *Ethnic Los Angeles*, edited by Roger Waldinger and Mehdi Bozorgmehr. New York: Russell Sage Foundation.

López-Castro, Gustavo. 1986. *La Casa Dividida: Un Estudio de Caso Sobre la Migración a Estados Unidos en un Pueblo Michoacano*. Zamora: El Colegio de Michoacán (Mexico).

Marger, Martin. 1994. *Race and Ethnic Relations: American and Global Perspectives*. Belmont, CA: Wadsworth.

Massey, Douglas S., Jorge Durand, and Nolan J. Malone. 2002. *Beyond Smoke and Mirrors: Mexican Immigration in an Era of Economic Integration*. New York: Russell Sage Foundation.

Meinig, Donald. 1969. *Imperial Texas: an Interpretative Essay in Cultural Geography*. Austin: University of Texas Press.

Michelson, Melissa R. 2001. "The Effect of National Mood on Mexican American Political Opinion." *Hispanic Journal of Behavioral Sciences* 23(1):57-70.

Michelson, Melissa R., and Amalia Pallares. 2001. "The Politicization of Chicago Mexican Americans: Naturalization, the Vote, and Perceptions of Discrimination." *Aztlan* 26(2):63-85.

Muller, Thomas. 1993. *Immigrants and the American City*. New York: New York University Press.

Murphy, Arthur, Colleen Blanchard, and Jennifer Hill, eds. 2001. *Latino Workers in the Contemporary South*. Athens: University of Georgia Press.

New York Times Almanac. 2004. New York: Penguin Reference Books.

Ono, Hiromi. 2002. "Assimilation, Ethinc Competition, and Ethnic Identities of U.S.-Born Persons of Mexican Origin." *International Migration Review* 36(3):726-745.

Ortiz, Vilma. 1996. "The Mexican-Origin Population: Permanent Working Class or Emerging Middle Class?" Pp. 247-77 in *Ethnic Los Angeles*, edited by Roger Waldinger and Mehdi Bozorgmehr. New York: Russell Sage Foundation.

Pastor, Manuel, Jr. 1999. "Economics and Ethnicity: Poverty, Race, and Immigration in Los Angeles County." Pp. 102-38 in *Asian and Latino Immigrants in a Restructuring Economy: the Metamorphosis of Southern California*, edited by Marta López-Garza and David R. Díaz. Stanford, CA: Stanford University Press.

Pollard, Kelvin M., and William P. O'Hare. 1999. "America's Racial and Ethnic Minorities," *Population Bulletin* 54(3).

Public Broadcasting System. 2004. "Point of View: Farmingville." Film broadcast June 22, 2004.

Ramirez, Roberto. 2005. *Nosotros: Hispanos en los Estados Unidos*. Washington, DC: U.S. Census Bureau, Indormes Especiales del Censo 2000.

Ramos, Jorge. 2002. *The Other Face of America: Chronicles of the Immigrants Shaping our Future*. New York: Harper-Collins.

Riding, Alan. 1985. *Distant Neighbors: a Portrait of the Mexicans*. New York: Vintage Books.

Rosales, Grace, Mona Devich Navarro, and Desdemona Cardosa. 2001. "Variation in Attitudes toward Immigrants Measured among Latino, African American, Asian, and Euro-American Students." Pp. 353-67 in *Asian and Latino Immigrants in a Restructuring Economy: the Metamorphosis of Southern California*, edited by Marta López-Garza and David R. Díaz. Stanford, CA: Stanford University Press.

Samuelson, Robert J. 2005. "The Hard Truth of Immigration." *Newsweek* August 13:64-5.

Shain, Yossi. 1999/2000. "The Mexican-American Diaspora's Impact on Mexico." *Political Science Quarterly* 114(4):661-691.

Simon, Julian. 1999. *The Economic Consequences of Immigration*. Ann Arbor: The University of Michigan Press.

Simon, Stephanie. 1999. "An Insular Iowa Town, a Jolt of Worldliness: A Torrent of Diversity Has Been a Shock to Tiny Postville, Iowa." *Los Angeles Times*. January 26.

Smith, Robert C. 2001. "Mexicans: Social, Educational, Economic, and Political Problems and Prospects in New York." Pp. 275-300 in *New Immigrants in New York*, edited by Nancy Foner. New York: Columbia University Press.

Stull, Donald, ed. 1990. "When the Packers Came to Town: Changing Ethnic Relations in Garden City, Kansas." *Urban Anthropology* (special issue) 19:303-427.

Stull, Donald, and Michael Broadway. 2004. *Slaughterhouse Blues: the Meat and Poultry Industry in North America*. Belmont, CA: Wadsworth.

U.S. Bureau of the Census. 2000. Summary File 4 (SF4). Washington, DC: U.S. Census Bureau, Public Information Office.

Valdez, Avelardo, and Richard C. Jones. 1984. "Geographical Patterns of Undocumented Mexicans and Chicanos in San Antonio, Texas: 1970 and 1980." Pp. 218-35 in *Patterns of Undocumented Migration: Mexico and the United States*, edited by Richard C. Jones. Totowa, NJ: Rowman and Allanheld.

Vigil, James Diego. 1997. *Personas Mexicanas: Chicano High Schoolers in a Changing Los Angeles*. Fort Worth: Harcourt Brace.

White, Michael J., and Jennifer E. Glick. 1999. "The Impact of Immigration on Residential Segregation." Pp. 345-72 in *Immigration and Opportunity: Race, Ethnicity, and Employment in the United States*, edited by Frank D. Bean and Stephanie Bell-Rose. New York: Russell Sage Foundation.

Wilson, Franklin D. 1999. "Ethnic Concentration and Labor-Market Opportunities." Pp. 106-40 in *Immigration and Opportunity: Race, Ethnicity, and Employment in the United States*, edited by Frank D. Bean and Stephanie Bell-Rose. New York: Russell Sage Foundation.

Zúñiga, Victor, and Rubén Hernández-León, eds. 2005. *New Destinations: Mexican Immigration in the United States*. New York: Russell Sage Foundation.

PART THREE

EASTERN UNITED STATES

Chapter 8

Spaces and Places of Adaptation in an Ethnic Vietnamese Cluster in New Orleans, Louisiana[1]

Christopher Airriess

Some thirty years have passed since the first wave of Vietnamese refugees arrived in the United States after the fall of Saigon in April 1975. With a substantial flow of refugees continuing throughout the 1980s and early 1990s, followed by immigration based on family reunification during the balance of the 1990s, and coupled with the growth of the second generation in the United States, the total population of ethnic Vietnamese in 2000 reached 1,122,528 individuals. While the two states of California (39.7 percent) and Texas (11.9 percent) account for the majority of ethnic-Vietnamese in the country, there are a significant number of substantial settlement concentrations in the eastern half of the country. One such concentration is the New Orleans Metropolitan Statistical Area (MSA) where the 1980 to 2000 ethnic Vietnamese population almost doubled in size from 7,751 to 14,868 respectively. Ranked as the 16th largest urban concentration in the country in 2000, ethnic-Vietnamese accounted for 52 percent of the MSA's Asian American population in 2000.

The ethnic Vietnamese community that is the focus of this chapter accounts for 30 percent of the MSA total and is comprised of two contiguous census tracts at the far eastern edge of New Orleans (Figure 8.1). This settlement concentration can be quantitatively classified as an ethnic enclave based on the work of Allen (2005) who defines an ethnic enclave as census tracts in which a particular ethnic group is found at five times their metropolitan proportion. With ethnic Vietnamese comprising 1.1 percent of the New Orleans MSA population, the two census tracts quantitatively qualify as an ethnic enclave because the proportion of ethnic Vietnamese in census tracts 17.42 and 17.41 in 2000 is 42.7 and 28.4 percent respectively. Waldinger (2001), however, qualitatively defines an "ethnic enclave" as a spatial concentration of an ethnic group resulting from forced segregation based on discrimination or housing affordability as opposed to a more affluent "ethnic community" where individuals settle by choice. Quantitatively, the ethnic Vietnamese settlement concentration under study is an enclave, but qualifies qualitatively as an ethnic community. A compromise position is offered by Pamuk (2004) who quantitatively defines an "immigrant cluster" as a group of spatially contiguous census tracts where the ethnic population in at least one of these tracts is at least 10 percent greater than the county's total population for that immigrant group and where the other census tracts are five percent greater. This definition clearly warrants the two census tracts under study as an ethnic cluster.

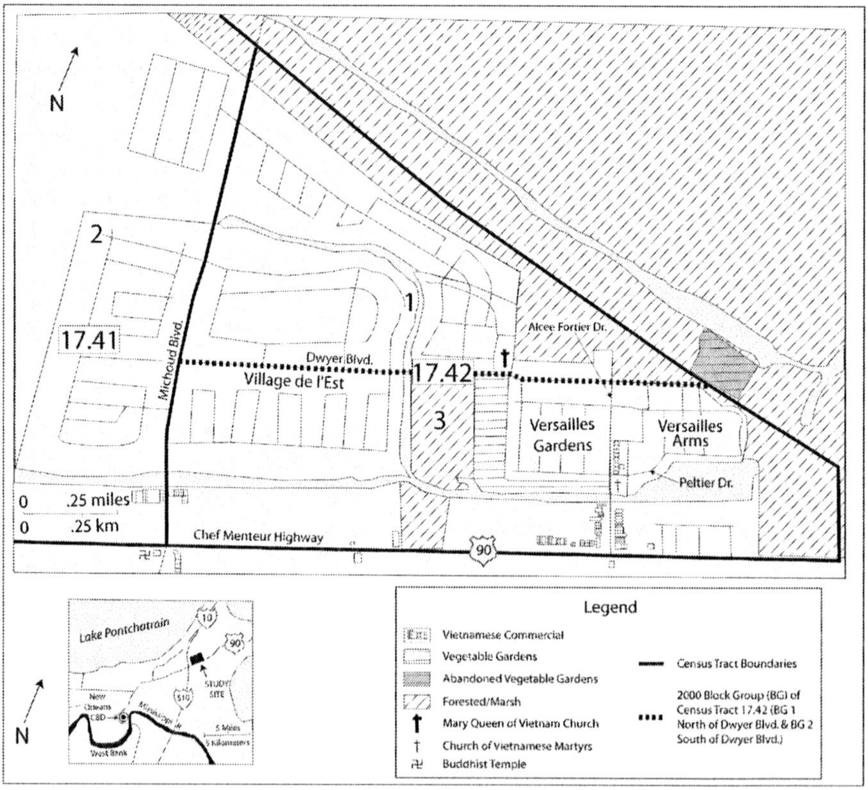

Figure 8.1 The Vietnamese Settlement Cluster of Versailles

The conceptual anchors to examine ethnic Vietnamese adaptation in this study are the terms space and place so central to understanding human geographical phenomena. While the term space can be applied to absolute space such as the geometrical and measurable locations on a map, the use of the term in the context of modern human geography is that space is constructed by humans in their everyday routinized lives (Dear 2000). Humans produce and reproduce many different spaces based on a variety of ever changing human relationships. There exist then gendered spaces, racialized spaces, ethnic spaces, public versus private spaces, and rural versus urban spaces to identify a few among many. Spaces can also be material and symbolic in nature, as well as possessing different scales from the global, regional, and local (Crang and Thrift, 2000). In the context of this study then, we can speak of spaces of adaptation and how these spaces are actively constructed as expressions of ethnic identity formation in a new destination country location. Spaces, however, possess subjective meanings to those individuals or groups that construct them. A term and concept harnessed to better understand the emotional attachment to space is "place" (Creswell 2004). As "sources of security and identity for individuals and for groups of people" (Relph 1976, 6) places are elemental aspects of human existence in that there exists a reinforcing relationship between individuals, community and place because it promotes a "collectively conditioned place consciousness" (Relph 1976, 34). Places can be real or material places as well as imaginary in nature as found in films and novels; in either case, they possess a sense of place (Creswell 2004).

Harnessing the concepts of space and place as they relate to an ethnic-immigrant community is certainly a worthwhile endeavor because when provided the opportunity, a newly arrived culture group attempts to "reproduce" albeit in modified form, the social environment of their home region. In a sense, "home is deconstructed on departure and then constantly reconstructed as the migrant experience and life cycle evolve" (Kershen 2004, 263). Similarly, immigrants "transform space into place by embedding culturally meaningful symbols into shared environments" (Armstrong 2004, 245). The significance of constructing space and place among Vietnamese refugees is amplified because while most immigrants migrate voluntarily for economic reasons, refugees are compelled to migrate based on fears of political and religious persecution (Freeman 1989). Indeed, the concept of place is central to understanding the experiences of refugees because they are a special population that are "out of place" based upon the strong attachment to the past and lost spaces and places of their homeland (Creswell 2004).

There exist three particular community spaces and places of this specific ethnic-Vietnamese community that are evocative of the adaptation process. The first is agricultural space because most of the first refugees were farmers and fisherfolk in their Vietnam homeland. The second is religious space as most refugees were Roman Catholic. Both are central to the community's shared sense of values and thus provide necessary anchors to the construction of a sociocultural continuity and stability of the past in the less secure present. While involving only a small number of refugees, the construction of commercial space is also critical to the community's adaptation process. Satisfying the basic needs of the co-ethnic population by providing familiar food, music, dress and other services, commercial spaces thus re-create, albeit in a modified form, a known sense of place. While it is recognized that no single ethnic space possesses the same meaning of place because of communally-based age and gender differentiation (Mitchell 2003; Johnston 1991), these three spaces are the most obvious expressions of shared values and belonging that defines a community (Agnew 1989).

Research Methodology

Research methodologies employed in this chapter include both quantitative and qualitative (ethnographic) techniques. For agricultural spaces, a combination of both techniques were used to quantify crop inventories and assemblages, in addition to better understand the subjective meanings of gardening to cultivators (Airriess and Clawson 1994). While this original research is dated, subsequent annual visits to the gardens provided a more current knowledge base of agricultural space. Sources of information to uncover the importance of religious faith and its material expressions in the community landscape were exclusively gained through unstructured interviews with church leaders and laypersons alike (Airriess 2002). For commercial space, both quantitative and qualitative information was generated during a one-month summer research period in 2004. Quantitative sources involved both phone surveys, structured interviews with half of the 93 store owners, as well as informal discussions with a handful of community leaders (Airriess 2006). Information on the impact of Hurricane Katrina is derived from a variety of newspaper sources as well as informal interviews conducted with Versailles residents during fieldwork conducted in early December 2005, and early February 2006. This fieldwork was funded by a National Science Foundation grant titled "Surviving Katrina and its Aftermath: A Comparative Analysis of Community Mobilization and Access to Emergency Relief by Vietnamese and African Americans in an Eastern New Orleans Suburb."

Origins, Migration, and Settlement Patterns

In the early 1990s, approximately 60 percent of the ethnic-Vietnamese adult population in Versailles originated from the Catholic diocese of Bui Chu south of Haiphong in former North Vietnam (Luong 1995). A substantial number of refugee adults also originated from the adjoining diocese of Phat Diem. Except for the diocese centered on the capital of Hanoi, Bui Chu and Phat Diem were the most Roman Catholic political administrative regions in the north. These two Red River Delta dioceses were characterized by many villages that were exclusively populated by Catholics whereby the church, priests, and missions organized and managed land clearance, welfare services, and education. These "closed villages" possessing an environment of social cohesion were referred to by the French as *chrétientés* (Hass and Nguyen 1971). The closed and independent character of the *chrétientés* solidified even more with the rise of the Communist-based Viet Minh government and their military conflict with the colonial French following World War II (Jamieson 1993). In 1954 the Viet Minh defeated the French and the Geneva Agreement was signed that same year dividing Vietnam into northern and southern halves. With assistance from Roman Catholic agencies abroad, the French government as well as the American seventh fleet, approximately 900,000 people were relocated to the south. Of that total, approximately 80 percent were Catholic and half of the Catholic population of Bui Chu and Phat Diem diocese were part of this exodus. The resettlement villages in the south were in many respects reconstructions of their northern Catholic villages, in addition to functioning as militarily strategic settlements to aid the anti-Communist cause.

The April 1975 Communist victory in South Viet Nam ushered in the large scale migration of Vietnamese overseas. Vietnamese migration to the United States encompassed four distinct waves of refugee movement. The 1975-1976 "first wave" refugees were primarily those better educated and urban inhabitants connected to the American war effort who feared political persecution, as well as Catholic fisherfolk and farmers fearing religious persecution. Some 60 percent of Versailles adults in the early 1990s were part of the "first wave."

The 1977-1979 "second wave" was primarily comprised of ethnic-Chinese and rural ethnic-Vietnamese forced to flee Vietnam as "boat people" who spent months and sometimes years in refugee camps in various Southeast Asian countries facing the South China Sea. These refugees were resettled and sponsored by church and other voluntary organizations throughout the United States. The "third wave" movement between 1979 and 1983 was anchored by the United Nations Orderly Departure Program coupled with the U.S. Refugee Act which raised the ceiling for refugees entering the country. The "fourth wave" began in the mid-1980s to the present and was comprised of primarily immigrants, rather than refugees. These immigrants gained entry in the United States based on the explicit government immigration policy of family reunification.

A brief exploration of the evolution of the study area that is informally known as Versailles is necessary to better understand the creation of ethnic space (Figure 8.1). Occupying reclaimed marsh and swamp, Versailles is the most eastern suburban residential subdivision of New Orleans MSA. The single family and duplex suburban residential developments of Versailles Gardens and Village de l'Est were developed in the 1960s as part of the general spatial decentralization of cities associated with improved intraurban transport and the dispersal of sources of employment to the urban periphery. Indeed, many of the original residents were Anglo employees at the newly established NASA rocket booster facility nearby. Opened in 1970, the Versailles Arms apartment complex functioned as part of federal government policy to scatter low income earners in the suburbs. While Versailles Arms was occupied by both Anglo and African-Americans working at a nearby NASA facility, the scaling back of NASA operations a few years before the arrival of Vietnamese refugees resulted in most Anglos from Versailles Gardens and Village de l'Est moving to new suburban developments elsewhere, and upwardly mobile middle-class African-Americans replacing Anglos. This process of neighborhood succession left the Versailles Arms apartment complex with low occupancy rates.

Neighborhood succession was restored when entire blocks of the Versailles Arms complex were rented to 1000 "first wave" refugees sponsored by the local Associated Catholic Charities. After a few years many upwardly mobile "first wave" refugees moved into Versailles Gardens and Village de l'Est by taking the place of most African-American families. Versailles Arms, however, continued to function as the "port of entry" for new arrivals, secondary migrants as well as a permanent home for lower income Vietnamese. Versailles Arms was designated as public assistance or "section eight" housing in 1976, and this attracted new refugee arrivals.

The study area has experienced both substantial population growth and the process of ethnic succession during the 1970-2000 period. In 1970, the study area possessed 4,945 inhabitants, but by 1980, the population more than doubled to 10,566 inhabitants as the city's eastern suburban frontier expanded. Since 1980, however, the population has stabilized. The study area in 1970 was almost exclusively white, but between 1980 and 2000, the percentage of whites dropped from 30.5 percent to 4.4 percent. By 1980, both blacks and Vietnamese became the majority populations with 34.8 and 31.7 percent respectively and their presence only increased by 1990. This succession trend continued throughout the 1990s with blacks increasing their share to 51.3 percent. The percentage of Vietnamese decreased slightly to 41.7 percent as some upwardly mobile families moved out of state or to other suburban locations in the New Orleans MSA. Some moved to a contiguous and more affluent and predominantly Black census tract (17.32) to the west where Vietnamese number 452 individuals or 5.5 percent of that tract's total population in 2000. This 1.3 percent decline of Vietnamese between 1990 and 2000 would have been substantially greater if 789 foreign born Vietnamese had not entered Versailles during the same period.

The spatio-demographic dynamics between 1990 and 2000 of the ethnic spaces of Vietnamese, blacks and whites in Versailles are not substantial, but sufficiently important enough to briefly discuss based on census block groups (Figure 8.1).[2]

In Zone 3, the Vietnamese population percentage decreased moderately from 51.8 percent in 1990 to 42.5 percent in 2000. Much of that decrease is explained by Vietnamese moving out of Versailles Arms into adjoining Versailles Gardens and Village d'lest. In the early 1990s approximately half of the population of Versailles Arms was Vietnamese, but in 2000 that decreased to 26.7 percent. Zone 1 has remained relatively stable between 1990 and 2000 with only a decline from 48.6 to 47.9 percent respectively. There was a corresponding increase of blacks from 40.7 percent in 1990 to 51.2 percent in 2000. Zone 2, however, witnessed a dramatic increase in Vietnamese residents. In part explained by Versailles Arms residents moving into single family dwellings, Vietnamese increased their share from 9.1 percent in 1990 to 29.4 percent in 2000. The black and white share of Zone 2 simultaneously decreased from 63.9 percent and 26.9 percent in 1990 to 52.4 percent and 13.7 percent respectively. In Zones 1 and 2 that comprise 90 percent of Vietnamese in the settlement cluster, 40 of the 59 census blocks possess a majority Vietnamese population.

Contours of Socioeconomic Adaptation

In part because of the common perception of the Versailles settlement cluster as a somewhat conservative and poor community, it is best that we examine some important social and economic variables to compare this community with others of greater geographical scale. At the outset, it is safe to make the generalization that the Versailles Vietnamese community relative to Vietnamese populations elsewhere has experienced a more difficult process of socioeconomic adaptation (Table 8.1).

Home ownership coupled with educational and occupational attainment also point to relatively low rates of socioeconomic mobility of Versailles Vietnamese when compared to Vietnamese at larger geographical scales. Home ownership increased from 1990 (37.3 percent) to 52.0 percent in 2000, but still remains marginally behind home ownership rates for Vietnamese in the New Orleans MSA and Jefferson Parish, as well as the New Orleans MSA as a whole. Despite much higher incomes, the depressed home ownership rates among Vietnamese nationally are explained by substantially higher real estate costs when compared to New Orleans. As expected, home ownership rates in Versailles vary; while Zone 1 (61 percent) and Zone 2 (70.3 percent) are above the settlement cluster average, Zone 3 home ownership is only 27.6 percent. Educational attainment measured as a percentage of the population twenty-five years or older possessing a bachelor's degree or higher is relatively low among Versailles Vietnamese when compared to Vietnamese in the New Orleans MSA, but substantially lower than Vietnamese in Jefferson Parish, the New Orleans MSA, and Vietnamese nationally. In Versailles, educational attainment in Zone 2 (20.6 percent) is almost three times greater than in Zone 1 (7.3 percent) and Zone 3 (7.4 percent).

Table 8.1 Socioeconomic Characteristics of Versailles Vietnamese Relative to Other Vietnamese Populations

Characteristic	Versailles Vietnamese	New Orleans MSA vietnamese	Jefferson Parish Vietnamese	New Orleans MSA	U.S. Vietnamese	U.S.
% in Poverty	31.3	24.5	17.7	18.3	24.2	12.3
Med. HH Income ($)	32,001	32,429	35,551	35,317	45,085	41,994
% Home Ownership	52.0	62.5	69.4	61.8	53.0	66.0
% with Bachelor's Degree (25 yrs.+)	11.8	14.5	17.9	19.4	19.4	26.0
% Professional/ Managerial Occups.	20.6	19.2	17.4	26.9	24.7	33.6

Source: U.S. Census 2000, SF 4, American FactFinder

As a result, only 20.6 percent of Versailles adults are employed in management, professional, and related occupations while most adults in Versailles are relegated to lower wage production (25.8 percent), service (18.8 percent), sales and office (18.7 percent) occupations. The percentage of Versailles adults in management, professional and related occupations is lower than the New Orleans MSA, Vietnamese in the U.S., and the U.S. as a whole, but is quantitatively similar to Vietnamese in both the New Orleans MSA and Jefferson Parish. Nevertheless, the slightly higher percentage of Versailles Vietnamese in management, professional, and related occupations when compared to Vietnamese in the New Orleans MSA and Jefferson Parish does not positively correlate to the balance of variables. Perhaps the production, service, and sales and office occupations in which the other two Vietnamese groups are engaged generate greater incomes.

Before leaving the subject of economic adaptation, it is important to point out that Vietnamese in Versailles and elsewhere in the New Orleans MSA have not constructed ethnic economies or "distinctive constellations of business ownership and/or employment of group members in certain economic sectors" (Logan, Alba and McNulty 1994, 691). Nevertheless, Vietnamese in the 1980s did possess a strong presence in the shrimp fishing industry of the central Gulf region. In 2003, some 275 individuals in Versailles owned fishing boats, were boat captains or vessel crewmen. These numbers are much lower when compared to the 1980s, after which many left the fishing industry because of increasingly low profit margins (Nguyen 2003). Many fishing families turned to operating convenience stores in low income neighborhoods in the city, as well as nail salons throughout the city.

This brief examination of these socioeconomic variables of Versailles Vietnamese informs us of the great diversity in socioeconomic attainment in the settlement cluster. While many experiencing greater socioeconomic mobility have moved out of Versailles into adjacent or distant middle and upper class suburbs, many have also decided to remain. Indeed, some experiencing upward mobility remain in the cluster and have built "trophy" homes in a neighborhood just northwest of Mary Queen of Vietnam Church. In these cases, children pool money to finance construction of the home to house a large extended family. Whether extended family or not, Pamuk (2004) has uncovered a similar phenomenon among some affluent ethnic Chinese and Filipinos in San Francisco who choose to reside in neighborhoods dominated by co-ethnics. An expression of adaptation in Versailles is derived from changed street names as a result of Vietnamese settlement. The older and earlier settled section of Versailles adjacent to Versailles Arms possesses a Saigon Drive that represents the past, but the newest section of Versailles where the "trophy" homes have been built, now supports a *My Viet* Drive, or Vietnamese American Drive.

Nevertheless, out-migration of some of the younger generation is common based on the relatively high percentage of foreign-born residing in the enclave between 1990 and 2000. In 1990, approximately 76.0 percent of the population was foreign born and this only declined to 67.7 percent by 2000. While arrivals from Vietnam contributed to this low decline of foreign born, it also is a reflection of younger couples with native born children who have migrated out of the settlement cluster. The out-migration of the socially and more economically mobile younger members of the population would also naturally inflate poverty levels. Lastly, we should not, however, give great explanatory power to residential concentration being the primary cause of relative poverty because as Viviani (1996) has pointed out among ethnic Vietnamese of Sydney, Australia, there are ethnic concentrations of middle class Vietnamese with none of the socioeconomic disadvantages associated with poverty found in much poorer ethnic Vietnamese residential clusters. Nevertheless, Versailles is commonly viewed by non-Vietnamese and Vietnamese alike as relatively disadvantaged economically, and culturally conservative.

Agricultural Spaces and Therapeutic Places

Perhaps the most conspicuous example of the ethnic-Vietnamese creation of space and place as expressions of adaptation throughout the 1980s and 1990s are vegetable gardens (Figure 8.1). Despite the relative disappearance of many vegetable plots beginning in the late 1990s, over twenty-five years of cultivation captured the attention of local newspapers and non-ethnic visitors to the community to the point that agricultural space seemed to possess iconic qualities for the community. Although agricultural space has significantly declined, attention to this disappearing agricultural space is certainly warranted because this too is a spatial expression of adaptation.

Plants cultivated in the mid-1990s included some thirty different leafy green vegetables, tubers, cucurbits, condiment and herbs, legumes, and medicinal plants not common to the Western diet (Airriess and Clawson 1994). The simplest explanation for the construction of agricultural space is land availability, a warm, humid climate regime, and that Vietnamese were "preadapted" to reproduce a version of their homeland agricultural system in a New World urban setting. While environmental factors as well as preadaptation are useful to explain the persistence of agricultural activity, other social, cultural and economic factors associated with adaptation play an equally decisive role in the constructing agricultural space.

Because gardeners are exclusively the elderly, more age specific explanations for the construction of agricultural space are warranted. Unlike younger members of the ethnic community, the elderly experience psychological adjustment problems because of the absence of employment opportunities, English language skills, and financial dependence upon children (Matsuoka 1990). As a result, the elderly population experiences a deep sense of powerlessness that engenders mental health problems (Rumbaut 1985). The physical act of gardening then is perceived as "hortitherapeutic" activity (Kaplan 1973) whereby "body and earth join to reproduce past spaces as well as empowerment spaces in the present associated with the orderly world of responsibility and commitment" (Airriess 2002, 241). A minority of the elderly then are perceived to be constructing rural spaces as "reminiscent place," a phenomenon often associated with the geographical experience of the elderly (Rowles 1980). Another aspect of psychological adaptation associated with gardening is that it allows for the persistence of traditional dietary habits (Kalcik 1984). Indeed, being connected to the body, food assists in anchoring ethnic identity through reconstructing a sense of place that is connected to home (Kershen 2004). This psychological connection to past place as expressed through urban gardening by elderly Vietnamese has been documented in suburban Australia as well (Head, Muir and Hampel 2004).

Economic explanations for constructing agricultural space must also be considered. Most elderly are economically marginalized and rely heavily on social security income and food stamps. Gardening then improves their economic position by selling vegetables to co-ethnic grocery stores and restaurants, as well as at the Saturday morning wet market. In addition, surplus produce helps reduce household food expenditures and are freely distributed to other low income elderly as an expression of mutual-aid relationships characteristic of peasant-based societies that have persisted in their new home (Rynearson and DeVoe 1984). Agricultural space can be classified, based upon both size and location, as backyard gardens or levee gardens (Airriess and Clawson 1994). Residents of Versailles Gardens have transformed their lawns to accommodate a wide variety of intensively cultivated vegetables (Figure 8.2). Because of the absence of space, homeowners have enlarged cultivation space to include the utility easement and reclaiming the canal bank. Although more space is needed, backyard gardeners have adhered to American suburban landscape tastes by not including the front yard as cultivation space. The segregation of backyard and front yard space with reference to vegetable cultivation is an important spatial expression of adaptation; the publicly exposed space of front yards is seen as Americanized space while the hidden cultivated backyards are more private and Vietnamese.

Because of a shortage of cultivation space in the more densely settled Versailles Arms apartment complex, the nearby owner of levee land agreed that residents could cultivate the unused space of the more level levee slope. With greater cultivation space, gardeners specialize in more space-consuming plants such as taro, sweet potato, ginger, eggplant and lemon grass. Not possessing the chain link fences of the backyard gardens to separate vegetable plots, levee gardens are often separated by individually constructed wooden stick fences.

With the levee visually separating the garden space from Versailles Arms, the exotic nature of agricultural space is certainly more apparent when compared to the backyard gardens. In part this is true because of the absence of younger ethnic Vietnamese in the levee gardens; possessing a future-looking and acculturated American identity, the gardens for this 1.5 and second generation are spaces symbolizing the past places of rural Vietnam with which they hold great ambivalence. Perhaps with the exception of some religious spaces, no other space in Versailles symbolically represents Vietnam as that of the gardens.

By 2005, the levee agricultural space has been largely depleted of gardeners. Walking distance to the gardens as well as the passing away of the elderly are the primary reasons for levee garden decline. Gardening does remain in most backyards, however. Many other houses without dedicated gardens do possess kitchen gardens providing basic herb and condiment needs, but with very few space-consuming vegetables. The general decline obviously relates to the passing away of the elderly, but larger and distant economic forces play an important role as well. In Houston, Texas home to the third largest urban Vietnamese community in the country, well-financed Vietnamese entrepreneurs now grow vegetables in all-season greenhouses. Produce is then trucked to wholesalers in New Orleans who then sell to restaurants and grocery stores in Versailles. In addition, vegetables are trucked to New Orleans wholesalers from southern California where Vietnamese owned mega-sized vegetable farms using Mexican agricultural labor are an additional source of fresh vegetables. Restaurants and grocery stores in Versailles have thus adapted to the larger economic structures common in the mainstream economy characterized by a geographic shift from the local to national scales in production and distribution patterns of food products.

Figure 8.2 A backyard garden supporting a wide variety of vegetables. Source: Author.

By 2005, the levee agricultural space has been largely depleted of gardeners. Walking distance to the gardens as well as the passing away of the elderly are the primary reasons for levee garden decline. Gardening does remain in most backyards, however. Many other houses without dedicated gardens do possess kitchen gardens providing basic herb and condiment needs, but with very few space-consuming vegetables. The general decline obviously relates to the passing away of the elderly, but larger and distant economic forces play an important role as well. In Houston, Texas home to the third largest urban Vietnamese community in the country, well-financed Vietnamese entrepreneurs now grow vegetables in all-season greenhouses. Produce is then trucked to wholesalers in New Orleans who then sell to restaurants and grocery stores in Versailles. In addition, vegetables are trucked to New Orleans wholesalers from southern California where Vietnamese owned mega-sized vegetable farms using Mexican agricultural labor are an additional source of fresh vegetables. Restaurants and grocery stores in Versailles have thus adapted to the larger economic structures common in the mainstream economy characterized by a geographic shift from the local to national scales in production and distribution patterns of food products.

Constructing Religious Spaces and Places

Attention given to the creation of religious space and place in Versailles is critical to understanding the adaptation process because of the context of the source region and migration experiences. While Vietnam is overwhelmingly a Buddhist/Confucianist country, some 25 percent of Vietnamese-born migrants in the United States were Roman Catholic. However, some 80 percent of Versailles Vietnamese were Roman Catholic in the early 1990s (Luong 1995). In fact, the first and only Vietnamese Catholic bishop in the United States was the pastor of the Versailles parish since its inception; Monsignor Dominic Luong was appointed the bishop of Orange in Orange County, California in 2003.

Much like a handful of regional or perhaps folk expressions of Roman Catholicism in the non-Western world, Vietnamese Catholicism possesses a rich vein of pietism anchored by the veneration of Mary, a suffering Christ, and a deep seated faith in family and country. In many respects then, Vietnamese Catholicism shares much with the conservative Catholic culture of south Louisiana (Nash 1992). The conservative character of Versailles Catholics is clearly connected to their minority status in Vietnam and is especially expressive of their refugee experiences. The original *chrétientés* village space of North Vietnam, Communist discrimination, and two forced migrations solidified their collective faith which became central to the adaptation process in a new country. These past experiences are not only expressed in the present construction of spiritual space and place as "spaces of memories" in Versailles, but take on new and perhaps more important meanings and forms when compared to their source regions as refugees adapt to new geographical contexts (Warner 1998).

The importance of religion in the community is evidenced by the multiple spaces and places possessing sacred significance. The first church was built three years after the first refugees arrived when a small prefabricated church named the Church of Vietnamese Martyrs adjacent to Versailles Arms was constructed (Figure. 8.1). The name is evocative of past experiential space as Vietnam in the mid-1990s ranked fourth in the world in the number of canonized saints, many of whom lost their lives during the anti-Western persecutions of the mid-1800s. Those that attend the 6:30 a.m. daily morning masses are primarily the elderly. A much larger second church, the 800-seat Mary Queen of Vietnam Church was constructed in 1986 and coincided with a newly created Vietnamese Catholic parish of the same name (Figures 8.1 and 8.3). Dedicated on Assumption Day, a day commemorating Mary's resurrection, the church is not architecturally distinctive. Plans called the construction of a pagoda-like structure that resembled the cathedral in Phat Diem, but the cost was beyond the financial means of the community. Perhaps the most sacred relic in the church is a statue of Mary that was smuggled out of South Vietnam in the days leading up to Saigon's fall. The statue was subsequently and appropriately named The Madonna of Refugees. Much like Our Lady of Charity, a Cuban Catholic Shrine in Miami for Cuban refugees (Tweed 1997), the Vietnamese Madonna embodies the homeland and thus a place that Vietnam-born adults who are pre-occupied with exile, were forced to flee. As a single site in the larger religious space of the church, the Madonna symbolizes an individual's interconnection with the experiential narratives of other older parish members (Entriken 1991). It is clear that The Madonna of Refugees is central to the adaptation process of the elderly.

Figure 8.3 Mary Queen of Vietnam Church. Source: Author.

Located on the front lawn of Mary Queen of Vietnam church are the South Vietnamese and American flags flanking the yellow and white flag of the Vatican. The centering of the Catholic Church flag is symbolic of the church's role in the adaptation process in that the church occupies a mediating function by accommodating the collective memory of past place with present place. In the more secular aspects of adaptation, the church maintains social support institutions for the community by providing mental health services critical to the adaptation of middle-age and elderly residents. The church operates a parochial day care center and nursery school. In both the spiritual and the practical worlds, the parish has constructed spaces to perpetuate homeland traditions while at the same time teaching life skills allowing refugee parishioners to acculturate into the dominant American society.

The obvious sacred and practical function that the church plays in community life illustrates how Mary Queen of Vietnam Church represents spaces of pastoral power (Dean 1999) inherent in Roman Catholicism. Because the church provides the only large scale space for community events, pastoral power in indirectly projected in seemingly non-religious community activities. Two recent events illustrate the nexus between the spaces of pastoral power, ethnic identity, politics, and adaptation. In February 2005 the church parking lot was the venue for a national and multi-Vietnamese community tour of an original boat used to escape by "boat people" from South Vietnam to the Philippines as part of a one day festival commemorating the 30 year anniversary of the fall of South Vietnam. Likewise, the community was able to convince the Louisiana legislature in 2003 to officially recognize the former South Vietnamese flag as the "heritage and freedom" flag of the community. In a sense, the flag symbolizes the space of a "free Vietnam" in the United States. That summer, and dovetailing with an educational award ceremony for ethnic Vietnamese high school students in New Orleans, a "heritage and freedom" flag celebration was held in the church parking lot with a handful of former South Vietnamese uniformed military officers in the crowd. While short lived, this event is an example of Soja's (1996) "thirdspace" in which space (in this case pastoral space) is appropriated for another purpose by those who have been marginalized in relation to their homeland to express their claim to being the "authentic" Vietnam.

An especially common form of sacred space and place are the many front yard statues of Jesus and the Virgin Mary. Common in other heavily ethnic-Catholic neighborhoods in the United States, statuary is of a votive nature in that they are erected as a promise to answered prayers in times of personal crisis (Arreola 1988; Manzo 1983). There exist many more statues of the Virgin Mary when compared to statues of Jesus. While common in Vietnam, Virgin Mary statues are indirectly an expression of the adaptation process. As true in Mexican folk Catholicism, the Virgin Mary is adored among Vietnamese Catholics (Nash 1992). As the symbolic mother of the community, the public display of Virgin Mary statues is thus a community affair.[3]

When coupled with a map of Vietnam, statues of the Virgin Mary take on added meaning. She assumes the function of being the mother of family, home and a new Vietnamese Catholic identity, and thus is a symbol for the warmth and nurturing of their homeland. As an expression of "geopiety" (Tuan 1976), statues of the Virgin Mary are a profession of one's reverence for the land, country and most importantly nation. As refugees, then, the statues of Virgin Mary can be in part perceived as an expression of religio-political "transnational" identities whereby individuals remain connected to past spaces and places as part of the adaptation process.

The construction of religious space and place described thus far is very much age specific in that it is expressive of the "inbetweenness" of the Vietnam-born population. The U.S.-born younger generation, however, often identify less with the place bound spiritual spaces that evoke past places with which their grandparents and parents identify. Part of the process of second generation religious adaptation is the attraction to a 2001 constructed Buddhist temple from an abandoned nursing home at the southwest corner of Chef Menteur Highway and Michoud Boulevard (Figure 8.1). Catering to Vietnamese Buddhists in the community, the temple has also attracted some Catholic second generation, sometimes married to Buddhist spouses. This process of religious adaptation can be interpreted in two interrelated ways. First, this adaptation process is simply expressive of religious change taking place within the larger dominant culture whereby non-denominational churches are experiencing dramatic growth in response to individuals desiring a less centralized and more lay person-centered religious environment. Second, perhaps some are not satisfied with the conservative culture of the Mary Queen of Vietnam Church that is very much oriented to foreign-born parishioners with experiences connected to transnational spaces and places. While the parish has done much to provide a wide range of recreational opportunities for the younger second generation, and has subsequently launched additional programs since the Buddhist Temple opened, such activities are still anchored to church spaces. In this sense, some of the second generation are indifferent to the spaces of pastoral power. Indeed, missing in Versailles is the secular space of a community center, for example, that would provide alternative community space for the second generation.

Old and New Commercial Spaces

Unlike religious and agricultural spaces and places, the commercial strips of Versailles are not spaces with which many of these formerly rural folk were intimately familiar before their arrival in the United States (Figure 8.1). The emergence of commercial space adjacent to a spatially clustered ethnic residential community is a common feature across ethnic spaces in the United States. At the most basic level, spatially clustered business activity enhances co-ethnic economic exchange. Space then, is conceptually perceived as a resource harnessed by entrepreneurs to capture commercial exchange from the co-ethnic residential population (Kaplan 1998). Commercial spaces are reflective of the adaptation process in two significant ways. First, ethnic-owned businesses provide a wide range of basic economic and cultural goods and services to lessen the sometimes traumatic experience of settling in a new country. Indeed, because food is one of the last ethnic behaviors to change in the adaptation process, close proximity of co-ethnic grocery stores is an important factor in residential choice among some immigrants (Donkin and Dowler 2002). Simultaneously, successful business owners over the long term do not want to remain captive to a local co-ethnic customer base, so the adaptive process also requires reaching out beyond this spatially captive market to include a non-Vietnamese as well as a distant co-ethnic clientele (Waldinger, McEvoy and Aldrich 1990). However, Relative to larger Vietnamese commercial spaces in Houston, Orange County in southern California, and San Jose, California, the limited amount of human capital of Versailles is a barrier to expanding the geographical scale of business. For example, only 25 percent of business owners possessed business experience in Vietnam because most of the earlier mid-1970s refugee residents were farmers and fisherfolk. Nevertheless, a small number of businesses have recently begun to expand their scale of commercial exchange beyond the local co-ethnic base, and are thus seen as adapting to a larger economy.

During the past thirty years, commercial space has dramatically expanded from forty businesses in 1990 to ninety-three businesses in 2003 (Airriess 2005; Airriess and Clawson 1991). Aside from three businesses established in the late 1970s and early 1980s along Chef Menteur Highway, the core of commercial space was developed at the west side of Alcee Fortier Boulevard and Chef Menteur Highway by the early 1980s, and the east side of the same intersection by the late 1980s (Figure 8.1). All of these businesses were new builds by store owners and often possess residential space on the second floor. The spread of commercial space during the 1990s includes rezoned apartments at the corner of Alcee Fortier Boulevard and Peltier Drive, the northeast corner of Michoud Boulevard and Chef Menteur Highway, as well as derelict commercial space at the Michoud Boulevard and Chef Menteur Highway intersection (Figure 8.1). These conversions represent what Loukaitou-Sideris (2002, 335) refers to as "ethnic gentrification" in that both residential and commercial space has been "reterritorialized" to suit the adaptation process of a newly arrived ethnic group. The reterritorialization process met with little resistence from the large African American residential population as few co-ethnic businesses existed. Thus the growth of ethnic-Vietnamese business in this process of occupational succession did not entail what might be referred to as "contested space."

Commercial space in Versailles is characterized as a "local ethnic market" (Aldrich and Waldinger 1990) in that businesses primarily serve a spatially contiguous ethnic customer base. These entrepreneurs have also been referred to as "internal shopkeepers." Indeed, some 41 percent of businesses rely on a local and co-ethnic customer base for 80 percent of their business and 68 percent of businesses rely exclusively on family members as a labor resource (Airriess 2005). The original and older commercial space is located at the corner of Chef Menteur Highway and Alcee Fortier where most of the local commercial exchange takes place. Although appearing later, the core also includes businesses located on the corner of Alcee Fortier Boulevard and Peltier Drive. Together, the core commercial space comprises forty-six businesses, or half the number of businesses in Versailles. Categorizing this core of commercial space as a "local ethnic market," is indeed justified as residents themselves commonly refer to this space as the "village." The balance of forty-seven businesses are oriented toward Chef Menteur Highway; they either line the highway or are located at the corner of Chef Menteur Highway and Michoud Boulevard (Figure 8.1). These businesses generally, but not exclusively, rely upon a greater proportion of non-local co-ethnic or non-Vietnamese business. More important for non-ethnic Vietnamese, grocery store and restaurant patrons feel more comfortable because they do not have to engage the strange or foreign spaces of the commercial core. There exists then commercial exchange that encompasses two geographical scales; one that is local in nature, and one requiring the capturing of greater geographical space. Although traditionally applied to globalized information networks, the term "space of flows" (Castells 1996) in this smaller geographical scale is certainly appropriate to describe these two, but sometimes overlapping customer hinterlands. The balance of this section on commercial space is based on a variety of observations that differentiate between these two geographical scales of businesses activity.

Indicative of the "local ethnic market" nature of commercial space, the fourteen food/grocery stores account for the greatest number (15 percent) of any business sector in Versailles and eight of the fourteen are found in the commercial core. Of the six oriented to the highway, one has re-occupied an abandoned Winn Dixie supermarket and counts 10 percent of its customer base as non-Vietnamese in search of "Asian foods." Two of the other six businesses are general convenience stores catering to the highway traffic and one is a seafood store relying on a similar traffic base.

Restaurants and cafes number eleven of the ninety-three businesses and comprise the second most common (12 percent) business types. Seven of the eleven restaurants and cafes are located in the commercial core. The cafes in particular are primarily populated by males as it is not socially acceptable for females to patronize such establishments. Of all the commercial spaces, cafes are then the most expressive of gendered space. The character of the four restaurants oriented to the highway is quite different from those in the commercial core. Two are ethnic-Chinese owned and possess the highest non-local co-ethnic as well as non-ethnic customer base in Versailles. Another is owned by a family from southern California who owns two other restaurants in the New Orleans area. The other restaurant is up-scale in nature attracting younger co-ethnic patrons from both Versailles and the larger New Orleans region. Unlike restaurants in the commercial core, two of these restaurants offer taped Vietnamese language entertainment shows from Orange County, California, production companies to attract a more affluent and acculturated co-ethnic clientele.

The third largest category of business is medical services and this is one of the business sectors locationally disposed to the commercial core. Only one of the ten health service businesses is oriented to the highway and that is the enclave's only chiropractic clinic. Health services are a basic service need, particularly among the settlement cluster's high proportion of elderly who require convenient pedestrian access. Spatial convenience is also important to the even poorer African American residential population who provide a substantial customer base. In addition, close spatial proximity of the four doctor's offices to the three pharmacies provide for agglomerative economies within the core. There are also nine beauty salons, but they are found in equal numbers in and outside of the core. More modern financial and professional service businesses are also locationally split with four in the core and five outside the core. Four of the five gold jewelry shops, however, are located in the core as these establishments so central to Vietnamese culture were some the first businesses in the core.

Additional observations concerning store location in or outside the core and the process of adaptation are also evident (Airriess 2005). First, while 70 percent of store owners in the commercial core live in the Versailles community, only 42 percent of business owners outside the commercial core reside in the local community. Second, professional services are dominated by second generation entrepreneurs who also tend to live outside of the Versailles community. Third, the names of businesses also possess locational and adaptative attributes because only 17 percent of the pre-1990 commercial core business possess names that are exclusively in English, while 44 percent of businesses outside the core possess names that are exclusively English.

Whether in the commercial core or not, Versailles commercial space is able to draw on a greater non-local customer base because it functions as a central place for a wider co-ethnic population in the New Orleans MSA as well as the substantial ethnic Vietnamese population located along the nearby Mississippi Gulf Coast. In this sense, the commercial enclave has become an ethnic specific regional shopping center. Its central place function beyond the local co-ethnic population is heightened by two attractions. One is Sunday mass at Mary Queen of Vietnam Church where families from distant neighborhoods dovetail mass with shopping activity. Indeed, Sunday is the busiest business day in Versailles. The second attraction promoting greater scales of commercial exchange is the Saturday morning wet market (Figure 8.4). Although locally grown vegetable production is much reduced, fresh seafood caught by Versailles fisherman attracts not only co-ethnics, but many other ethnic-Asians and Africans as well.

Improving opportunities to attract a greater distant co-ethnic and non-ethnic customer base is difficult for a number of reasons. Being located at the far eastern end of the New Orleans MSA is a major barrier to improving the geographical reach of Versailles businesses. First, Versailles occupies a geographical dead end in terms of through traffic because Interstate 10 has now usurped the far less traveled Chef Menteur Highway. Second, distant customers, whether co-ethnic or not, who seek things Vietnamese or "Asian" have an alternative in the now more populous and centrally located West Bank Vietnamese communities in Jefferson Parish (Figure 8.1). Growing from 672 in 1990 to 6,601 persons in 2000, there are an equal number of ethnic-Vietnamese businesses when compared to Versailles. Characterized by a population that is more educated with more urban experiences in Vietnam as well as a far more dispersed or "heterolocal" (Zelinsky and Lee 1998) residential settlement and business pattern, the West Bank Vietnamese community is perceived to be more progressive and willing to cater to non-Vietnamese customers.

Figure 8.4 Entrance to the Saturday morning wet market. Source: Author.

Hurricane Katrina's Impact and Recovery

Making landfall on the morning of August 29, 2005, near the Mississippi River delta, Hurricane Katrina made a third landfall along the Louisiana-Mississippi state line as a strong category 3 storm. With the storm eye passing approximately twenty miles east of Versailles, this very large storm possessed seventy-mile-an-hour winds and a storm surge of at least twenty feet. Unlike most other parts of New Orleans that were flooded as a result of levee breaches, Versailles was flooded by water overtopping the Intracoastal Waterway levee. With water depths reaching a maximum of six feet in some locations, but one to two feet in most homes, the waters had receded in Versailles to one to five feet by September 3, five days after the stormed passed. The water completely drained away two to three weeks after the storm. Over 90 percent of both Vietnamese and blacks evacuated before the storm's landfall with most making their way to Houston, Texas.

By early December, some 200 households or 20 percent of the total number of Vietnamese households had returned to Versailles to rebuild their houses. According to the pastor of Mary Queen of Vietnam Church, this number increased to 80 percent by July 2006. In terms of enclave businesses, 28 percent of businesses had re-opened by early February and by July almost 60 percent had returned. This percentage is more than double the percentage of business openings for eastern New Orleans as a whole. Blacks have not experienced similar rates of return in part because 40 percent of black residents lived in apartment complexes that by July 2005 showed no signs of rebuilding. Black homeowners, however, possess return rates in the 60-70 percent range.

The rapid return of Vietnamese to Versailles can be explained in part by their profound attachment to place. For most residents, Versailles has been their only home since leaving Vietnam and their spiritual connections to Mary Queen of Vietnam Church are very deep. The role of the church as the nexus for a variety of social networks at different geographical scales in the rebuilding process has been critical and multi-faceted (Chia-Chen Chen, Airriess, Keith et.al. 2006). At the local geographical scale, the church has been central in coordinating the delivery of building supplies and functioning as an arbiter between residents and insurance companies. The annual *Tet* or Lunar New Year festival sponsored by the church was held on church grounds in early February 2006 and was a critically important event to prove to the city government as well as former residents that the community was serious about rebuilding. The church also functioned as the organization that collected signatures from residents to convince the local utility company to provide power to the community as early as November 2005.

Realizing that successful rebuilding efforts would only materialize if more geographically broader and co-ethnic social networks were employed, the church reached out at a national scale. In this case, the scale of community was enlarged and redefined to include the national Vietnamese community. This included enlisting financial donations from co-ethnic contributors from around the country, through other Vietnamese Catholic churches, as well as various forms of co-ethnic media. Not only did the parish pastor travel to significant Vietnamese settlement concentrations in California to enlist the help of co-ethnic volunteers, but also received invaluable assistance from the National Alliance of Vietnamese American Service Agencies who sent a handful of young "fellows" who possessed the requisite academic background in community organization and activism. It was critical to obtain the help of co-ethnic outsiders because of the inward looking nature of the community and the control of the parish council by the elderly who possessed little experience in community activism. As a result, Katrina provided the "moment" or "conjuncture" for the community to become far more politically active in urban governance issues, and this is indeed a form of adaptation

It is obviously difficult to predict the post-Katrina future of Versailles. While it is true that few neighborhoods in eastern New Orleans have experienced as great of a percentage of evacuees return to rebuild, Versailles will be less populated than before. In addition, it is almost certain that Versailles will be less black because many were poor and renters. Much like blacks, some Vietnamese comprising the Katrina diaspora will remain in their relocation cities because employment and education opportunities for their children are appreciably better. In addition, while many Vietnamese evacuees have a very strong connection to the city and thus want to return, many will resettle in the West Bank communities where they possess ties with family and friends. We should not, however, underestimate the resiliency of Versailles Vietnamese and the importance of religious faith and a sense of community that functions as a magnet for rebuilding their 30 year home in the United States.

Conclusions

The Versailles Vietnamese settlement cluster and the community that constructed spaces and places since their arrival some thirty years ago is an example of one of many settlement concentrations that is not in a major U.S. metropolitan region. While the social and economic characteristics of Versailles are shared by other Vietnamese communities across the United States, it is in some respects distinctive based on the context of homeland as well as destination region experiences. The rural backgrounds and religious persecution of the first arrivals very much influenced the nature of space and place construction in the adaptation process. The locational situation of Versailles in the far eastern edge of the New Orleans MSA meant greater spatial isolation from larger social and economic interaction, which in turn afforded persistence of Vietnamese culture. In addition, the relatively poor New Orleans regional economy affords Versailles Vietnamese fewer opportunities for economic mobility. The impact of Hurricane Katrina has the potential to further isolate the community spatially, as well as provide fewer economic opportunities in which to experience socioeconomic mobility.

Although disappearing, gardening space, viewed from the mainstream perspective, possesses iconic qualities for the community as a whole. The construction of agricultural spaces by some of the community's elderly was only possible with a sufficient amount of open space afforded by Versailles being located on the suburban edge of the urban region. The specific dietary needs of the elderly as well as the opportunity to earn a modest income are important to understanding the construction of agricultural space. The intimate connection of the elderly to past agricultural space in Vietnam provides, however, a better explanation; the elderly were in a modified fashion reconstructing the spaces of home. In this sense then, both backyard and levee gardens are generational and therapeutic spaces critical to understanding adaptation. The passing away of the elderly coupled with the availability of fresh green vegetables from distant locations initiated a decline in agricultural space.

Perhaps more than agricultural or commercial spaces, the construction of religious spaces as expressions of ethnic identity formation is central to the adaptation process. Indeed, as Catholics in Vietnam, they were a religious minority. This magnified their experiences of difference and this difference was instrumental in constructing religious space in Versailles. It is with respect to religion that non-material spaces of the homeland are spiritually expressed through church naming, flags, and statues. Especially important are the statues of the Virgin Mary that are not only a material expressions of the motherland, but the traumatic experiences associated with the refugee migration process. The spaces of pastoral power that in part comprise church property are also spaces of remembrance for a country that is now lost space. In this sense, religious space intersects with political space. Nevertheless, a small second generation cohort has experienced religious adaptation by engaging the spaces of a local Buddhist temple. Both Catholic and Buddhist institutions are critical to re-building the post-Katrina community.

While historically not as familiar as agricultural and religious space, the commercial spaces constructed by Vietnamese entrepreneurs are also part of the adaptation process. Despite commercial space functioning as a local ethnic market, the number of businesses has more than doubled between 1990 and 2000, despite the growth of the co-ethnic population of Versailles remaining static. This growth in commercial space is a reflection of the adaptation process in that co-ethnic customer needs have changed through time, but also is expressive of an attempt to adapt to a distant co-ethnic and majority population customer base. While single businesses do not exclusively cater to the local versus a more distant customer base, these two spatial scales of commercial exchange are spatially manifested in store location being in the commercial core, or more oriented to highway traffic. Each location possesses a different space of flows. Adapting both business practices and diversity to capture a more distant space of flows is hampered by one, Versailles' peripheral location and two, competition from a more centrally located West Bank Vietnamese commercial community. Hurricane Katrina's negative impact on the commercial community threatens its ability to sustain, much less capture greater commercial traffic.

Notes

1. This chapter is a significantly revised version of Airriess 2002 and 2006. In addition, this chapter is an analysis of a Vietnamese-American community in New Orleans before the catastrophic events associated with the August 29, 2005, landfall of Hurricane Katrina. Before the conclusions section of this chapter, a brief description of Katrina's impact and resident' attempt to rebuild their community are discussed.

2. Between 1990 and 2000 Census tract boundaries for the study area changed. In 1990 the entire study area was encompassed by the single census tract 17.29 with the area

north of Dwyer Boulevard and east of Michoud Boulevard being block group 1, the area west of Michoud Boulevard being block group 2, and the area south of Dwyer Boulevard and east of Michoud Boulevard being block group 3. In 2000, new census tracts of 17.41 and 17.42 were created from the old 17.29 census tract. For census tract 17.42, block group 1 was formed from the old census tract 17.29 block group 1, and 17.42 block group 2 was formed from the old census tract 17.29 block group 3. The new census tract 17.41 was formed from the old census tract 17.29 block group 2.

3. As the Catholic missionaries in Mexico spiritually transformed the Aztec Mother Goddess into the much venerated Virgin of Guadalupe, French missionaries in Vietnam did the same with the Buddhist Goddess of Mercy. In Vietnamese, the Goddess of Mercy is *Phap Ba Quan Am* which is loosely translated as "the lady from on high worthy of veneration."

References

Agnew, John. 1989. "The Devaluation of Place in Social Science." Pp. 9-29 in *The Power of Place: Bringing Together Geographical and Sociological Imagination*, edited by John Agnew and James S. Duncan. Boston: Unwin and Hyman.

Airriess, Christopher A. 2006. "Scaling Central Place of an Ethnic-Vietnamese Commercial Enclave in New Orleans, Louisiana." Pp. 17-33 in *Landscapes of the Ethnic Economy*, edited by David. H. Kaplan and Wei Li. Lanham, MD: Rowman and Littlefield.

———. 2002. "Creating Vietnamese Landscapes and Place in New Orleans." In *Geographical Identities of Ethnic America: Race, Space, and Place*, edited by Kate A. Berry and Martha L. Henderson. Reno: University of Nevada Press.

Airriess, Christopher A., and David L. Clawson. 1994. "Vietnamese market gardens in New Orleans." *Geographical Review* 84 (1):16-31.

———. 1991. "Versailles: A Vietnamese Enclave in New Orleans, Louisiana." *Journal of Cultural Geography* 12 (1):1-13.

Aldrich, Howard E., and Roger Waldinger. 1990. Ethnicity and Entrepreneurship. *Annual Review of Sociology* 16:111-136.

Allen, James, and Eugene Turner, 2005. "Ethnic Residential Concentrations in United States Metropolitan Areas." *Geographical Review* 95(2):267-285.

Armstrong, Helen. 2004. "Making the Unfamiliar Familiar: Research Journeys towards Understanding Migration and Place." *Landscape Research* 29(3):237-260.

Arreola, Daniel. 1988. "Mexican American Housescapes." *Geographical Review* 78: 299-315.

Castells, Manuel. 1996. *The Rise of the Network Society*. Oxford: Blackwell.

Chia-Chen Chen, Angela, Christopher Airriess, Verna Keith, Wei Li, and Karen Leong. 2006. "Collective Efficacy and the Role of Community Networks in a New Orleans East Neighborhood before and after Katrina." Katrina Research Symposium: Social Science Research of the Katrina Aftermath, New Orleans, LA, November 3-4.

Crang, Michael, and Nigel Thrift. 2000. *Thinking Spaces*. London: Routledge.

Creswell, Timothy. 2004. *Place: A Short Introduction*. Malden, MA: Blackwell.

Dean, Mitchell. 1999. *Governmentality: Power and Rule in Modern Society*. Thousand Oaks, CA: Sage.

Dear, Michael. 2000. *The Postmodern Urban Condition*. Malden, MA: Blackwell.

Donkin, Angela, and Elizabeth Dowler. 2002. "Equal Access to Health Foods for Ethnic Minorities?" Pp. 199-213 in *Food and the Migrant Experience*, edited by Anne J. Kershen. Aldershot, UK: Ashgate.

Entriken, J. Nicholas. 1991. *The Betweenness of Place: Towards a Geography of Modernity*. Baltimore: The Johns Hopkins University Press.

Freeman, James. M. *1989. Hearts of Sorrow: Vietnamese American Lives*. Stanford, CA: Stanford University Press.

Haas, Harry, and Bao Luong Nguyen. 1971. *Vietnam: The Other Conflict*. London: Sheed and Ward.

Head, Lesley, Pat Muir, and Eva Hampel, 2004. "Australian Gardens and the Journey of Migration." *Geographical Review* 94(3):326-347.

Jamieson, Neil L. 1993. *Understanding Vietnam*. Berkeley: University of California Press.

Johnston, Ronald J. 1991. *A Question of Place: Exploring the Practice of Human Geography*. Oxford: Blackwell.

Kalcik, Susan. 1984. "Ethnic Foodways in America: Symbol and Performance of Identity." Pp. 37-65 in *Ethnic and Regional Foodways in the United States*, edited by Linda K. Brown and Kay Mussell. Knoxville: University of Tennessee Press.

Kaplan, David H. 1998. "The Spatial Structure of Urban Ethnic Economies." *Urban Geography* 19(6):489-501.

Kaplan, Rachael. 1973. "Some Psychological Benefits of Gardening." *Environment and Behavior* 5:145-162.

Kershen, Anne J. 2004. "The Construction of Home in a Spitalfields Landscape." *Landscape Research* 29(3):261-275.

Logan, John R., Alba, Richard D., and McNulty, Thomas L. 1994. "Ethnic Economies in Metropolitan Regions: Miami and Beyond. *Social Forces* 72(3):691-724.

Loukaitou-Sideris, Anastasia. 2002. "Regeneration of Urban Commercial Strips: Ethnicity and Space in Three Los Angeles Neighborhoods." *Journal of Architectural and Planning Research* 19(4):335-350.

Luong, Reverend Dominic. Personal communication, August 10, 1995.

Manzo, Joseph. T. 1983. "Italian-American Yard Shrines." *Journal of Cultural Geography* 4:119-125.

Matsuoka, Jon K. 1990. "Differential Acculturation among the Vietnamese." *Social Work* 35:341-345.

Mitchell, Katharyne. 2003. "Networks of Ethnicity." Pp. 392-407 in *A Companion to Economic Geography*, edited by Eric Sheppard and Trevor J. Barnes. Malden, MA: Blackwell.

Nash, Jesse W. 1992. *Vietnamese Catholicism*. Harvey, LA: Art Review Press.

Nguyen, Calvin. Personal Communication, August 28, 2003.

Pamuk, Ayse. 2004. "Geographies of Immigrant Clusters in Global Cities: A Case Study of San Francisco, 2000. *International Journal of Urban and Regional Research* 28(2):287-307.

Relph, Edward. 1976. *Place and Placelessness*. London: Pion.

Rowles, Graham. D. 1980. "Toward a Geography of Growing Old." Pp. 55-72 in *The Human Experience of Space and Place*, edited by Anne Buttimer and David Seamon. New York: St. Martin's.

Rumbaut, Ruben G. 1985. "Mental Health and the Refugee Experience: A Comparative Study of Southeast Asian Refugees." Pp. 433-86 in *Southeast Asian Mental Health*, edited by Tom C. Owan. Washington, D.C.: U.S. Department of Health and Human Services.

Rynearson, Anne M., and DeVoe, Pamela A. 1984. "Refugee Women in a Vertical Village: Lowland Laotians in St. Louis." *Social Thought* 10:33-48.
Soja, Edward. 1996. *Thirdspace*. Oxford: Blackwell.
Tuan, Yi-Fu. 1976. "Geopiety: A Theme in Man's Attachment to Nature and to Place." Pp. 11-39 in *Geographies of the Mind*, edited by David Lowenthal and Martyn J. Bowden. New York: Oxford.
Tweed, Thomas A. 1997. *Our Lady of the Exile: Diasporic Religion at a Cuban Catholic Shrine in Miami*. New York: Oxford University Press.
Viviani, Nancy. 1996. *The Indochinese in Australia, 1975-1995*. Melbourne: Oxford University Press.
Waldinger, Roger. 2001. "The Immigrant Niche in Global City-Regions: Concepts, Patterns, Controversy." Pp. 299-324 in *Global City-Regions: Trends, Theory, Policy*, edited by Allen Scott. Oxford: Oxford University Press.
Waldinger, Roger, David McEvoy, and Howard Aldrich. 1990. "Spatial Dimensions of Opportunity Structures." Pp. 106-30 in *Ethnic Entrepreneurs: Immigrant Business in Industrial Societies*, edited by Roger Waldinger, Howard Aldrich, and Robin Ward. Newbury Park, CA: Sage.
Warner R. Stephen. 1998. "Immigration and Religious Communities in the United States." Pp. 3-34 in *Gatherings in Diaspora: Religious Communities and the New Immigration*, edited by R. Stephen Warner and Judith G. Wittner. Philadelphia: Temple University Press.
Zelinsky, Wilbur, and Barrett A. Lee. 1998. "Heterolocalism: An Alternative Model of the Sociospatial Behavior of Immigrant Ethnic Communities." *International Journal of Population Geography* 4(4):281-298.

Chapter 9

The Quest for Home: Sheboygan's Hmong Population

Karl Byrand

Sheboygan, Wisconsin, sits alongside Lake Michigan halfway between Milwaukee and Green Bay. It has long called itself "the bratwurst capital of the United States," an identity linked directly to a predominantly German ancestry that extends back more than 150 years. In 1976, however, the city's ethnic composition began changing with the influx of Hmong individuals and families; by 2000, its Hmong population was the fourteenth highest in the nation, fifth in Wisconsin.

Because the Hmong culture is completely unlike any the vast majority of Sheboyganites have ever seen, with its most recent roots in the Laotian highlands and Thai refugee camps, it provides a good case study of both cultural landscape and social-cultural adaptation to host culture. In Sheboygan, as in the United States generally, the Hmong have been trapped between the conflicting goals of maintaining their own culture and integrating into U.S. society—goals made less accessible by the vast differences between the two cultures as well as the pressures placed upon them within U.S. society.

Overall, Sheboygan's Hmong have not generated an apparent and cohesive imprint on the city's cultural landscape. Although they constitute some 6 percent of the city's population according to 2000 Census figures (roughly 3000 out of a city population of 50,000), their residential pattern is dispersed and the resonance of their culture in Sheboygan is subtle and slight. In contrast, Hmong in Minneapolis-St. Paul, and Vietnamese in New Orleans, have clustered into definable neighborhoods, and have considerable cultural presence.

Associated with the above, perhaps directly related, are problems of cultural and social adaptation—in employment, educational obtainment, and health care. The latter is one of the most fascinating aspects of Hmong acculturation to examine, with Western medicine practices utilizing technology and delivery methods that run counter to their traditional practices and beliefs. As such, doctors have needed to learn how to be more sensitive and understanding of Hmong cultural beliefs, and the Hmong, to become more trusting and accepting of Western medicine. Adaptational difficulties have been magnified by significant language barriers, the hierarchical nature of authority within the Hmong family/clan, and the overall lower socioeconomic condition of the Hmong.

Despite such cultural conflicts, the Hmong have overcome many self-generated cultural barriers, as well as those generated by native Sheboyganites, and have increasingly become a more accepted part of the community. One particular example of this is the second-ever war memorial outside of Arlington National Cemetery to honor the Hmong who sacrificed their lives in support of the U.S. during the "Secret War" in Southeast Asia (1955-1974), the dedication of which took place in a popular Sheboygan lakeside park in July 2006. In addition to increased acceptance, the Hmong's imprint on the city's cultural landscape has also grown, as evidenced by businesses and cultural festivals.

Methodology

This study uses multiple data sources. U.S. Census data enable examination of increases in the U.S. and Sheboygan Hmong populations between 1990 and 2000 and provide a general idea of Hmong settlement patterns at the level of census tracts. Hmong residence data were also gathered from the Sheboygan phone directory, 2004-2005, for all residents who had Hmong clan names. Addresses were then recorded and mapped.

Most importantly for the discussion of adaptation and customs, information was obtained through interviews with Sheboygan's Hmong community leaders and prominent Hmong business persons and professionals. Non-Hmong individuals in Sheboygan who possess some close association with the Hmong in their professional lives were also interviewed. Information was gathered through open-ended interviews rather than relying on a pre-formed set of questions. While these findings are certainly more subjective in nature than the census and telephone directory data, they nonetheless provide a more human perspective that delves deeper into the lives of Sheboygan's Hmong population.

Hmong Migration History

Like many other refugees to the U.S. in recent decades, the Hmong (who have been in the U.S. since 1975), have a fascinating and poignant story to tell.

The Hmong come principally from the Laotian highlands, where their ancestors migrated to escape violent campaigns of genocide in China from the 17th to the 19th centuries. In Laos, the Hmong subsisted by using slash-and-burn agriculture on a tropical mountainous terrain. They typically kept to themselves in their adopted country, with some choosing to grow opium to trade with the French and Laotians during the French colonial period.

Later, with the Japanese occupying Laos from 1940 to 1945, many Hmong joined an organized militia of resistance. They became reputed for their martial skills and subsequently were sought as guerilla soldiers by various governments with interests in Indochina. This new vocation would have a tremendous influence on their future population geography.

During the early part of the Cold War (1945-1989) the U.S. found the Hmong to be valuable allies in U.S. efforts to implement anti-Communist agendas in Indochina. The Hmong were not only strategically located, but had intimate knowledge of the region. The CIA began recruiting, training, and funding a Hmong militia that established and protected mountain radar stations and air strips, rescued American pilots, and stopped the shipment of military supplies to the Communist Pathet Lao and North Vietnamese for sixteen years preceding the U.S. pullout in 1975. In their role, the Hmong protected countless numbers of Americans. Tens of thousands of Hmong were killed among a population of only 250,000 (Schofield 2005). The Hmong did not stop fighting until forced to by the U.S. withdrawal. In addition to the nearly 30,000 Hmong men and boys killed in action, many Hmong civilians died from direct fire and devastations caused by the war, and from other causes induced by the U.S. presence. Western diseases in camps established by the U.S. decimated men, women and children. Measles and malaria took a horrific toll, with the infant mortality rate reaching 70 percent at one point (Schofield 2005).

These sacrifices came with little reward. For their efforts, the Hmong soldiers were paid the equivalent of three dollars a month (Fadiman 1997, 128). Further, upon the U.S. withdrawal from Vietnam in 1973, the Hmong (despite promises to the contrary) were basically abandoned to their fate. The Communist Pathet Lao targeted the Hmong and Hill tribes of Laos for their resistance to the communists and loyalty to America. Many thousands of men, women and children were hunted down and exterminated (Schofield 2005).

In 1973, Hmong began fleeing to camps in Thailand; over the next two decades, Thailand's refugee camps would process some 350,000 Hmong refugees (Lo 2001). Insight on these terrible times was provided by Hmong students in several of the author's UW-Sheboygan geography classes. As part of written assignments, these students recorded the hardships they and their families weathered in their home country. These included crossing the Mekong into Thailand; escaping the murderous Viet Minh; and struggling to survive in refugee camps. Their stories included tales of poisoned food, starvation, and overcrowding, and are corroborated in other accounts (Fadiman 2001; Vang 2001; Yang 2005).

The Hmong in the Thailand camps could seek asylum in other countries, but many chose to remain in hopes that the communists in Laos would be overthrown and they could return home. Some participated in the Chao Fa, a resistance group, launching guerrilla attacks against the communists. Many, however, chose to emigrate to France, Australia, Canada, and particularly, to the

United States. The U.S. gave refugee status to them without reservation, in light of their precarious situation under the Geneva Convention. Beginning in 1975 the first Hmong refugees arrived in the United States and a steady stream continued to arrive until the 1990s, when refugee camps in Thailand were closed.

Hmong Population in the World, the United States, and Wisconsin

Estimates of how many Hmong there are in the world range from six million to more than eight million, with the vast majority residing in China's southern provinces (Foo 2002, Lai 2003, Miyares 1997, Pfaff 1995). Population estimates of Hmong living in Southeast Asia range from 500,000 to four million (Foo 2002, Lai 2003). These numbers far surpass the U.S. Hmong population of only some 170,000 (Table 9.1).

The Hmong Settlement Process in the U.S.

As shown in Table 9.1, the number of Hmong residing in the United in 2000 was approximately 170,000—2-3 percent of the total Hmong population worldwide. The U.S. Hmong population is growing quite rapidly. The factors cited below, in addition to the young age profile (in 1985, 49 percent were under fifteen) and high fertility rate of this population, led to a nearly 80 percent increase between 1990 and 2000 (Pfaff 1995, 67).

It will be noted that three states accounted for 83 percent of the total Hmong population in the U.S. in 2000. This is explained in part by the work of voluntary organizations (Volags)—secular and religious institutions that cooperated with the U.S. State Department to locate refugee families. This cooperation had a profound effect on the geography of the Hmong in the United States. Even though all of the four major U.S. regions—the Northeast, the South, the West, and the Midwest—saw a growth in their Hmong population, there was a significant shift in U.S. regional dominance from the West to the Midwest between 1990 and 2000.

The federal government, under the Refugee Act of 1980, sought to disperse the Southeast Asian refugees as much as possible to aid in their rapid assimilation while at the same time reducing the financial burden on local communities. The government first assigned the Hmong to fifty-three cities in twenty-five different states and stipulated that no more than 3,000 Hmong could be located in any one state. The policy was initially successful in that it generated a large number of geographically dispersed Hmong communities, so that in 1985, according to a U.S. Hmong resettlement study, thirty states were hosting seventy-two Hmong communities, most of which had Hmong populations less than one thousand people (Pfaff 1995).

Table 9.1 Top U.S. States in Hmong Population, U.S. Census

State	2000 Hmong Population	1990 Hmong Population	2000 Hmong Percentage of U.S.	1990 Hmong Percentage of U.S.
California	65,095	49,343	38.4%	52.2%
Minnesota	41,800	17,764	24.7%	18.8%
Wisconsin	33,791	16,980	19.9%	18.0%
Rest of U.S.	28,742	10,352	17.0%	11.0%
National Total	169,428	94,439	100%	100%

Source: Pfeifer 2001

Ultimately, however, the State Department's dispersal policy was a failure. Rapid secondary migration of newly arrived Hmong individuals and families to regions where they had clan affiliations reinforced "existing settlement patterns rather than distributing the refugees in a more even manner" (D.C. Everest Area Schools 2001). Furthermore, the "family reunification" clauses in U.S. immigration law tended to bring new migrants into established clusters as opposed to generating new beachheads of settlement. The large California Hmong community has grown in response to both of these factors. Finally, the Volags in states such as Minnesota and Wisconsin were more accepting and resourceful in drawing Hmong immigrants, thus creating preferred nuclei for Hmong community formation (Miyares 1998).

The nearly 34,000 Hmong in Wisconsin mostly reside in eight metropolitan areas that form a ring throughout the state (U.S. Bureau of the Census Summary File 2). This "Hmong zone" extending from Minneapolis eastward to Lake Michigan (Pfaff 1995, 67) has been prevalent since the early 1990s. The dispersion of Wisconsin's Hmong population is related directly to the activities of the Volags in these cities.

Sheboygan's Hmong Population

As in the U.S. and Wisconsin generally, Sheboygan relied upon Volags to bring Hmong to the city. The most notable were Lutheran Immigration and Refugee Services, Catholic Immigration and Refugee Services, and the Grace Episcopal Church (Yang 2005). On April 24, 1976, through the active sponsorship of Sheboygan pastor Dan Leonard, the first Hmong immigrants, a family of seven, arrived in Sheboygan as part of a larger resettlement.

At nearly 3000 in number (U.S. Bureau of the Census Summary File 3, 2000), the Hmong residents of Sheboygan constitute approximately 5 percent of the city's population. Data gathered from the phone directory revealed that the majority of Hmong population are relatively dispersed throughout the city. The greatest amount of clustering of the sampled Hmong population is along the 14th Street corridor (a heavily used north-south route that passes through the city's west side) and several blocks away from this route in either direction (Figure 9.1). This clustering appears most intense on both the east and west sides of this corridor north of the Sheboygan River. The mapped data also reveal that few Hmong reside near Lake Michigan on the city's north side, and few live west of Interstate 43 on the far west side.

Overall, the location of many of the mapped Hmong residents correlates with the sections of the city with lower property values and more numerous rental units. In contrast, the neighborhoods where the Hmong are absent are those where the property values are the highest in the city. Furthermore, the region hosts several Hmong-owned and operated businesses and churches that cater to the Hmong population. In all, it has seven Hmong-owned and operated businesses all within a mile of each other. While several are businesses oriented to the general population (i.e., a Thai restaurant, a dentist's office, a clothing store, and a therapeutic massage business), three are Hmong markets that deal in specialty items catering to Hmong culture. Access to these markets could certainly serve as a strong pull factor for settling in this neighborhood, especially given that the businesses are located near lower-rent housing.

Although the majority of Sheboygan's Hmong population is clustered in the city proper, they could hardly be viewed as residing in an ethnic enclave. For example, as compared to Hmong living in cities such as Minneapolis-St. Paul (where the majority of its Hmong population is clustered in one or two neighborhoods), Sheboygan's Hmong are well-dispersed in the city proper. The reasons for Sheboygan's Hmong residential dispersion are not clear, but are most likely dictated by simple factors such as affordable and available housing, access to public transportation, and to a lesser degree, access to retail establishments and cultural amenities that cater to Hmong cultural preferences.

The Hmong pattern in Sheboygan tends to fit the Zelinsky/Lee model of heterolocalism (1998). Rather than clustering in discernable ethnic neighborhoods like their immigrant counterparts of the 19th and early 20th centuries, Sheboygan's Hmong display dispersed residential patterns while maintaining ties with the overall ethnic community via technology such as telephones, televisions, the Internet, and automobiles, as well as organizations such as business associations, cultural centers, and ethnic churches.

Hmong Culture in Sheboygan

The dispersed residential pattern just discussed, coupled with the ephemeral nature of some of their cultural celebrations (as will be discussed), have led to a less overt Hmong presence within the city than might be expected for a group with such a distinctive culture.

The Hmong's rich culture has long been reflected in their ornate clothing: For hundreds of years, they have used intricate colorful patterns called *paj ntaub* or "flower cloth" on fabric (see below). The sewing of *paj ntaub*—as well as other forms such as story cloths—could be considered the signature of the Hmong culture. Beyond ornamentation, these cloths identify the wearer with one of the five traditional groups of Hmong, based on color and pattern: Black, Striped, Red-Headed, White, and Green.

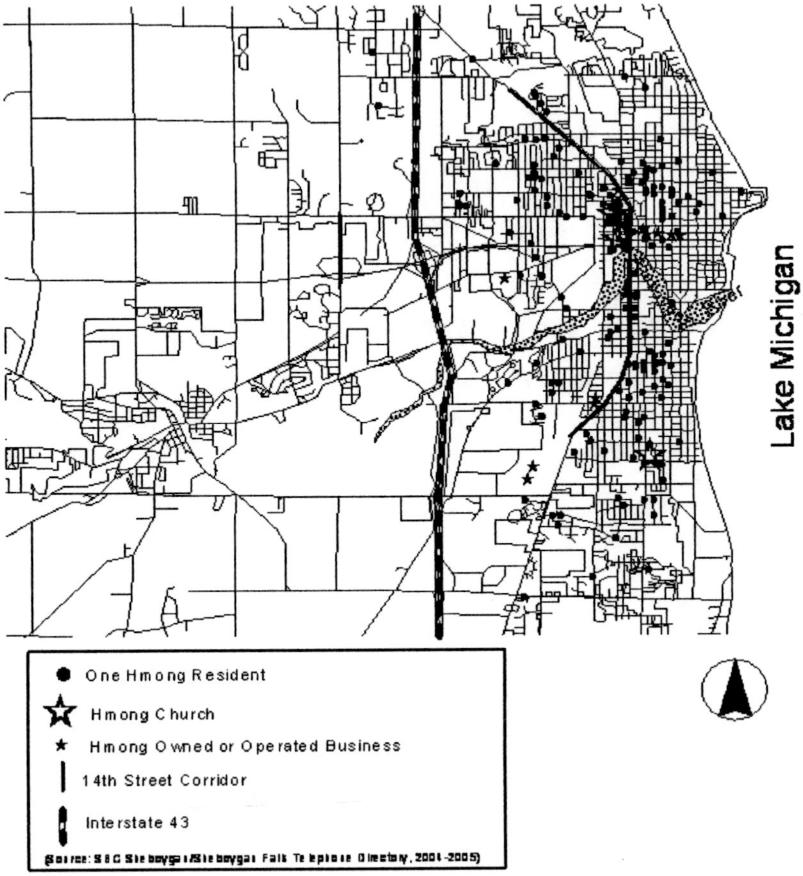

Figure 9.1 Hmong Residents, Businesses, and Churches in Sheboygan, Wisconsin, 2005

To best understand Hmong settlement patterns, one must consider that the Hmong retain these traditional groupings—and their secondary migration reflects this. According to Chasong Yang of the Hmong Mutual Assistance Association of Sheboygan (HMAAS), the majority of Hmong who migrated to Sheboygan are of the White and Green groups (2005, June 15).

The Hmong have also traditionally operated under a *xeng* or clan structure. In Laos, the Hmong organized socially and politically through a series of clans in which the leaders held the greatest authority. Morever, the clans operated as extended families to provide economic, social, and spiritual support. Clan ties have been strongly maintained in the United States, serving as a great impetus for secondary migration, especially as clan members raise money to help others migrate and provide the first few months rent as well as other necessities. The clans also provide an invaluable resource by helping new immigrants culturally adapt.

Traditionally, a person's clan name would be listed first and the given name second. However, many Hmong have chosen to follow U.S. custom and reverse that listing. For example, a Hmong man with the name Yang Song (Yang being his clan name) would change his name to Song Yang. However, not everyone chooses to reverse, causing confusion for some non-Hmong. There has also been an increasing tendency to give Hmong children Western names.[1]

Sheboygan's Hmong Belief Systems

Many of the Hmong have not only attempted to acculturate by changing their names, but also by altering their belief system. Traditionally, the Hmong were animists, believing that animate and inanimate objects (i.e., animals, trees, rocks, and streams) possess spiritual powers and can attract spirits (*dabs*), both benevolent and malevolent. For example, the spirit *Ndu Nyong* plays a Satan-like role that the Hmong try to counter through soul exchange: in medical treatments and funeral services, an animal is sacrificed for appeasement, so *Ndu Nyong* takes that soul instead.

Many Hmong in the United States have become "non-practicing," that is they selectively appropriate specific elements of their traditional faith while ignoring others. This selectivity may also be unintentional. In her study of the Hmong in Seattle, Donnelly observed that because many possess little knowledge of their Hmong rituals and cosmology, they've become what she termed "inadvertently secular" (1994).

Christianity has greatly influenced Hmong culture, with some 50 percent of the U.S. Hmong practicing a Christian faith (Duffy et al. 2004, 14). This stems in part from the fact that Hmong Christians comprised a disproportionate number of the U.S. refugee population (Donnelly 1994, 50). Sheboygan presents no exception to these findings, in that many were already converts before migrating. Others, upon arrival, have increasingly gravitated toward Christianity. Both of these trends are related to the impact of the Christian Volags. Refugees espousing Christianity were not only more likely to be brought to the United States to begin with, but once here, they were acculturated under the Christian umbrella, by the Volags. Initially in Sheboygan, those Hmong who wished to attend Christian services did so at already established churches. Some, such as Grace Episcopal Church, which served as a prominent Volag, provided separate services in the Hmong language. As the area's Hmong Christian population increased, they established three churches: the Hmong Community Alliance

Church, Hmong Christian Reformed Church, and Ebenezer Lutheran Church. Their congregations, ranging from 180 to 320 parishioners, hold both English and Hmong services.

When asked if they had observed their members engaging in traditional Hmong belief practices, the pastors of two Hmong churches here in Sheboygan both emphatically stated that they had not, as all the members had shed their animist beliefs. The third pastor, Kao Vang of the Hmong Christian Reformed Church, reported that while there are individuals in Sheboygan who still practice animism, none are members of his congregation (2005, March 24).

It nonetheless appears that many are selectively appropriating aspects of their former belief systems in an attempt to merge them with Christianity. Vang distinguished between those who practice animism (a practice whose renouncement is required by Christian churches), and those, like many in his congregation, who still engage in certain Hmong customs that do not qualify as animism, such as rituals related to traditional medicine and funeral ceremonies. Nevertheless, this distinction is a fine one; reviewing these customs shows that many are based on the animistic beliefs such as soul loss, transmigration of the soul, and others, that are seemingly incompatible with Christianity. The traditional Hmong belief landscape presents the potential for conflict with host culture norms.

Sheboygan's Hmong Business and Employment Landscape

Many non-Hmong in Sheboygan stereotype the Hmong as welfare dependent. Economic data reveal quite the contrary. In fact, 95 percent of Sheboygan's Hmong adults are employed, according to Cher Pao Vang, business and career counselor for the HMAAS (2005, March 21).[2] This is equivalent to the 95 percent overall employment rate in Wisconsin. Given the Hmong's relatively recent arrival to the United States, the population's lower levels of education attainment for first arrivals, their cultural isolation , and their low exposure to modern technology, Sheboygan's Hmong could be considered to be extremely successful at finding jobs.

Like other ethnic groups in urban areas, Sheboygan's Hmong population has successfully established businesses that effectively cater to many of its needs. Likewise, several have generated entrepreneurial success through certain advantages that native residents may not possess, supporting Kaplan's observations of Indochinese immigrants in Minneapolis-St. Paul who took advantage of a captive market and geographic proximity to co-ethnics, to become economically successful (1997). Kaplan's observations are similar to those of Evans (1989). As noted previously, however, Sheboygan's Hmong are loosely woven together spatially, so that market capture is less assured than in these other cases, and so Hmong entrepreneurs have had to diversify their offerings by providing a fuller range of goods to appeal to both Hmong and non-Hmong customers.

According to Kaplan (1997) and Portes and Manning (1986), through time businesses in ethnic enclaves tend to increasingly diversify in functions of the mainstream economy so as to offer a greater range of economic opportunities and achieve institutional completeness for the ethnic community. In short, a particular ethnic group who for varied reasons may initially gravitate toward one business venture, such as food stores and restaurants, will ultimately expand outward into other sectors of the economy (i.e., services such as insurance and real estate) to more adequately cater to the needs of members of their ethnic community.

An examination of the Hmong-owned businesses in Sheboygan shows that most have achieved this phenomenon internally rather than by "splintering off" into separate specialized economic activities. Specifically, they are providing a greater range of goods and services at each business location, rather than having separate businesses provide discrete activities.

For example, the four Hmong grocery stores in Sheboygan not only sell groceries, but also carry many other items, such as videos in the Hmong language, Hmong books, magazines, and other forms of literature, as well as many traditional Hmong clothing items. Even outside of the realm of grocery businesses, there is diversification. For example, the one Hmong-owned and operated video rental business in the city not only offers videos in Hmong, Thai, and English, but also sells traditional Hmong clothing, as well as bolts of fabric. By providing specialty items (i.e., traditional food and clothing) not attainable at non-Hmong retailers, these Hmong-owned stores are vital enclaves of Hmong cultural preservation.

For many years, grocery stores were the only form of entrepreneurship undertaken by Sheboygan's Hmong. According to Blia Vang, an agent for State Farm Insurance in Sheboygan, the past trend was that if a Hmong entrepreneur started a business and it was successful, others followed suit and started the same type, as there was timidity in exploring unfamiliar ventures (2005, April 5). Although store ownership changed hands among Hmong owners, the type of business tended to remain the same. In many instances, the entire business would be sold—equipment, inventory and all—to another Hmong resident. By not having to completely restock and equip the store, the new owner would almost instantly be able to restart the business. There were a few instances in which the actual type of business would change (i.e., from a Hmong grocery store to a Hmong restaurant), but nonetheless it would remain in the same building, giving a certain level of stability to these nodes within the Hmong cultural landscape. The changeover pattern is pretty typical and is primarily explained by the fact that in many instances the sale of businesses in the Hmong community is through word of mouth. As such, it is rare in Sheboygan for a Hmong-owned business to be reoccupied by someone who is not Hmong. In other words, despite the lack of propinquity found in ethnic enclaves elsewhere, there is considerable ethnic cohesiveness in the evolution of Hmong businesses in Sheboygan.

Blia Vang reported that there have been recent significant changes in the Hmong business landscape given that "a decade ago one only saw grocery stores as the primary type of Hmong-owned business and really nothing else" (2005, April 5). The Hmong in the city are increasingly breaking free of their sectoral concentration (defined by Kaplan as the concentration of ethnic economies within a few economic sectors [1997]), experimenting with and expanding into entrepreneurial activities, from Hmong clothing stores to a dentist office.

Even given the increase in the number and types of Hmong-owned businesses in Sheboygan, the overall employment pattern tends to be opposite of that observed within other ethnic economies, in which the majority of an ethnic group tended to be employed directly by members of the same ethnic community (Portes et al. 1989, Stepick 1989). In contrast, the majority of Sheboygan's Hmong population is employed by non–Hmong-owned businesses, most in lower occupational categories. Such an employment pattern may more rapidly acculturate the Hmong population (given that the majority of Hmong work with non-Hmong), while at the same time diminish their ability to preserve elements of their culture.

Hmong Adjustment Problems in Sheboygan

Coming from the isolated Laotian highlands, many of the Hmong were ill-prepared for being mainstreamed into U.S. culture. With the exception of the weaponry they were trained to use in the Secret War, most had never been exposed to Western technology or Western culture. The concepts of electricity and indoor plumbing were completely alien, let alone driving automobiles, paying rent, and filing tax forms. Thus the U.S. State Department implemented an Overseas Training Program for those in the second wave of migration. It offered such cultural training as how to answer a telephone, buy groceries, and interview for a job (Pfaff 1995). Even with this program, however, the Hmong's adaptation and assimilation have been difficult. Complicating the picture is that nearly all of these individuals were swidden agriculturalists, possessing few marketable skills that would translate well into employment in the United States. Thus their economic transition has been complex. The seismic difference in customs between the Hmong and their hosts has also played a role in this. For the Hmong, cultural preservation protects their identity and sense of community, but simultaneously it can generate cultural conflict and tension with majority community institutions such as health care, education, and work.

Hmong Health Care and Culture Conflict

A significant arena of cultural conflict in Sheboygan has been health care. According to Fungchatou Lo, the Hmong in Laos had four general tactics for health care: spirit appeasement with such practices as sacrificing animals and burning incense; herbal remedies; chants to ward off bad spirits; and the use of a *txiv neeb*—loosely translated as a shaman (2001). Chasong Yang of the HMAAS, as reported by *The Sheboygan Press*, defined a shaman as "a spiritual healer who finds out what is spiritually wrong with a person, much like a psychotherapist—not a magic healer as they are often portrayed" (2005, June 15).

A traditional view among the Hmong is that illness is caused by "soul loss." Specifically, one becomes sick when—for varied reasons such as sadness, fright, or theft by a *dab* or spirit—one's soul leaves their body. The Hmong patient then seeks out a *txiv neeb* to engage in a "soul calling" ceremony to beckon that soul back into the body. In general, Hmong traditional medicine uses a holistic approach aimed at treating the soul and body simultaneously because it is believed that treating just the body and not the soul is useless (Fadiman 1997).

Many scholars of Hmong culture have discussed soul loss and traditional Hmong medicine (Dao 1993; Duffy 2004; Lo 2001; Quincy 1988), but probably the most poignant account is Anne Fadiman's *The Spirit Catches You and You Fall Down* (1997). It not only shows how tenaciously an ethnic group can cling to its beliefs and selectively reject the beliefs of a host culture, but also reveals the close-mindedness of certain Western health care practitioners and some professionals' lack of understanding of and empathy for the Hmong culture.

Early accounts of the Hmong health care landscape in Sheboygan did not differ greatly from that of Fadiman, as local physicians at first had a difficult time meeting the health care needs of the newly arrived Hmong. One of these accounts was provided by Rolf Simonson, M.D. (2005), who has been working with Hmong patients since they began arriving in Sheboygan nearly 30 years ago. A pediatrician for the Aurora Sheboygan Clinic, Simonson related how the health care landscape has changed during this period. At first, the new Hmong residents tended to mistrust Western medicine. Moreover, doctors saw frequent evidence of folk remedies. Simonson shared that many Hmong patients would wear healing bracelets and amulets, and it was common to see minor burns from coining (a healing ritual in which heated coins are placed on bare skin). Furthermore, there were instances in which Hmong patients used folk cures from Laos that contained mercury compounds that actually made patients sicker (especially children).

The use of such folk cures are part of the Hmong's culture that was preserved because of a lack of understanding of Western medicine, which in turn made it more difficult for Simonson and colleagues to treat the Hmong. Other health problems arose because of a general lack of understanding of Western culture. Simonson related how Hmong patients were coming in with respiratory problems because they had used barbeque grills indoors. On a less serious note was a Hmong patient who covered every one of his many chicken pox marks with Band-Aids.

Since these initial misunderstandings, the health care landscape of Sheboygan's Hmong has changed greatly. Although Sheboygan's Hmong have not completely shed their traditional healing practices, many appear to be less leery and more accepting of certain Western medical tests and procedures and of medical advice in general. This acculturation was apparently assisted by the doctors striving to be empathetic towards Hmong culture.

Kristine Wake, M.D., started practicing in 2000 as a pediatrician at the Aurora Sheboygan Clinic. She reports that her Hmong patients and their families do not appear to deliberately distrust Western medicine (2005, March 9). However, she has found that the Hmong tend to be more selective in what they deem to be a medical problem. Specifically, her Hmong patients and families tend to take more seriously conditions with more tangible symptoms (i.e., skin rashes and coughs), while tending to ignore chronic illnesses with less tangible symptoms (i.e., anemia and diabetes). Wake relates that if an illness cannot be readily seen, patients tend to exhibit disbelief and are less likely to follow medical advice.

Myshoua Vang, the health educator for the HMAAS, also finds the above to be the case (2005, March 8). She added that many Hmong patients stop taking their prescribed medicine after they begin to feel better. Of course, non-Hmong patients often do the same, but anecdotal evidence shows stronger tendencies among Hmong patients. Vang relates that trying to explain the importance of taking, and finishing, medications, especially for chronic conditions, is one of the more difficult challenges of administering health care to the Hmong.

Vang further relates that while the Sheboygan Hmong now seem to be better accepting of common treatments, such as taking medication, some are still leery of invasive procedures, such as having their gall bladder removed, and they shy away from blood draws and spinal taps. She reports that this reluctance stems from the beliefs that all organs are vital to the body's functioning and the body has a limited amount of certain fluids that do not replenish.

In their experience, Wake and Simonson noticed that such reluctance has been decreasing among their Hmong patients. They report a great change in attitudes such that now few of their patients object to blood draws and spinal taps.

Other cultural differences still exist. Wake and Simonson report that Hmong patients tend to require more time to make medical decisions than their non-Hmong counterparts. They believe that delayed medical decisions relate to a desire to consult with a fellow clan member for advice. Their observations of some patients' dependence on clan leaders parallel those related by Fadiman (1997). Although these consultations may seem benign, Simonson related that they delay health care, which can be detrimental when the diagnosis requires immediate care.

One of the greatest difficulties in health care provision for the Hmong is the language barrier. This is a common observation among Sheboyganites since their German ancestors learned English much more quickly than the Hmong. However, the switch did not occur as readily as they portray. They depended on accommodation by the state, whose 1848 constitution was published in German and Norwegian as well as English. Parochial schools taught children in German. Many fought against a law requiring that all Wisconsin's children be educated in English; according to Wisconsin's Legislative Reference Bureau, they secured its repeal in 1891.

Many citizens fail to acknowledge that German and English belong to the same language sub-family (Germanic), whereas Hmong is a different language family altogether (Austro-Asiatic). It is a spoken language that is monosyllabic and tonal: as in Chinese, words can have completely different meanings depending on the tone. Shifting from a tonal language to a non-tonal language is much more difficult than shifting from German to English. Furthermore, until recently, the Hmong had no formal writing system. Combined with the illiteracy of many Hmong owing to denial of easy access to education, these factors severely limit communication.

Owing to the language difficulty, it is not surprising that in the Sheboygan County Hmong Healthcare Assessment Survey, 56 percent of the respondents reported they required the services of an interpreter for health care (Hmong Healthcare Needs Assessment Project 2001, 11). However, the past unavailability of interpreters in Sheboygan has caused some problems for both physicians and patients. According to Simonson, this scenario has been common: physicians provide medical advice, and not wishing to lose face, Hmong patients say that they understand the advice and agree to follow it. However, later doctors often found patients had little idea of what was being advised.

Translation needs generate great difficulty for Sheboygan's Hmong population given that the city's two hospitals and one clinic do not employ full-time Hmong interpreters, but rather hire them on an ad hoc basis, or rely on Hmong employees to volunteer. Thus, many Hmong use family members as cultural brokers. According to Myshoua Vang, children as young as seven translate for their parents given that youths are often the ones in a family who possess the greatest knowledge of the English language. Simonson relates that problems can arise given most children's limited vocabularies and general difficulties in translating complex terminology. Furthermore, using youths as a liaison causes other problems as it reverses the authority structure of the Hmong culture. Fadiman discusses this point: "[F]ailing to work within the traditional Hmong hierarchy, in which males ranked higher than females and old people higher than young ones, insult[s] the entire family but also yield[s] confused results, since the crucial questions ha[ve] not been directed toward those [with] the power to make the decisions" (1997, 65).

In recent years in Sheboygan, there has been a decrease in the trend to use children as translators. While Wake reports Hmong families who have been here the longest generally rely most on their children, she (and Simonson) related that, ironically, recent U.S. arrivals tend to come to the clinic with more competent cultural brokers. Usually these are sponsors (both Hmong and non-Hmong) who aided in their migration and who in almost all instances have been Sheboygan residents for a significant period of time and possess excellent English skills and a multitude of experiences in American culture, including medical treatments.

Given that many Hmong still require the services of a translator, it is fair to question why a full-time translator is not provided for Hmong patients at any of the city's health care facilities, especially when such is provided for the Hispanic population. According to Wake, one reason may be a general perception among local health care administrators that the Hmong are leery of answering what they would consider to be very private questions in front of a medical translator. Because of this, Wake related, it is rare that a Hmong patient comes in without an English-speaking family or clan member to do the translating for them.

Myshoua Vang related that this situation breeds a vicious cycle, with the patients turning to ad-hoc cultural brokers because there is no full-time translator, and the administrators thinking that is their preference, so they do not make further efforts to secure translators. Vang states that this problem is exacerbated by most Hmong patients being too meek to request translation services, even though law affords them that right.

According to Vang, this situation is problematic because most of the informal translators are inadequate, with at best a nominal understanding of medical terminology. Communication is further complicated because the Hmong language does not have equivalents to many medical terms. Moreover, the terms that do have equivalents can be extremely complex (i.e., the Hmong translation for "hormone" is 24 words long) (Fadiman 1997, 69).

The overall situation is improving, nonetheless. According to Simonson, the newly arrived Hmong population's communication with those who have seen the benefits of Western medicine has generated a greater, more immediate confidence in physicians and Western treatments. Therefore, recently arrived Hmong are less fearful of invasive procedures and much better about taking their medications than previous Hmong immigrants. Overall, according to Simonson, communication is better and the Hmong (especially the new immigrants) seem to be much more accepting and appreciative of Western medical services. The Sheboygan County Hmong Healthcare Assessment Survey conducted in 2000–2001 supports his observations: the majority of Hmong who responded sought a Western healthcare provider, not a *txiv neeb*, when illness occurred. The survey nonetheless reflected how traditional health care practices are still the sole treatment of choice for a minority of area Hmong. Others use both traditional and Western medicine. According to Myshoua Vang, there are at least seven *txiv neeb* in the Sheboygan area conducting healing ceremonies just about every weekend.

If the pattern of acceptance of Western medicine among Sheboygan's Hmong continues, one can assume that as the period of Hmong residence increases, the use of traditional Hmong medicine will decrease. However, given the continued prevalence of Hmong traditional medicine still practiced on the Sheboygan landscape, it is unlikely that these practices will disappear completely. Eventually, remnants will likely be performed for ritualistic reasons, to preserve selective cultural attributes rather than out of a belief in their healing powers.

Hmong Educational Attainment

Data from the 2000 U.S. Census reveals relatively little difference overall in post-secondary educational attainment between Sheboygan's two largest minority populations, Hmong and Hispanics, with Hmong males slightly ahead and females somewhat behind, their Hispanic counterparts (Table 9.2). Hmong women tending to marry much younger, may account for the latter disparity. On the other hand, Hmong males' greater attainment may be related to family pressures on male Hmong to go to college. These pressures will likely have an uplifting effect on Hmong male and eventually female occupational mobility.

Table 9.2 Hmong and Hispanic Educational Attainment in Sheboygan, 2000

Ethnicity/Gender	Undergraduate	Graduate/Professional
Hmong Males	3.8%	0%
Hmong Females	3.0%	0%
Hispanic Males	3.0%	0%
HispanicFemales	6.2%	1.8%
Sheboygan Males	3.4%	4.1%
Sheboygan Females	4.1%	0.6%

Source: U.S. Bureau of the Census, 2000 Summary File 4

Enrollment in graduate and professional programs (not shown) for Hmong as well as Hispanic males lags far behind that of Sheboygan's non-minority males; in fact, neither of each are enrolled in such programs. These differences in graduate/professional educational enrollment may reflect difficulties in local access, especially given the Hmong's tendency to want to keep close to their extended families. There are only two institutions near Sheboygan that offer graduate or professional degrees. The closest of these, the University of Wisconsin-Sheboygan, offers only one graduate program. The other is approximately twenty-five minutes (by automobile) outside of the city and requires private transportation to access. It also charges nearly $17,000 for tuition, a figure many first-generation college students might find intimidating

Having said this, the case of Hispanic females is somewhat different with nearly two percent of their population so enrolled. But this higher percentage, as compared to the enrollment of Sheboygan's non-minority females, is most likely reflective of a small total Hispanic population in Sheboygan, and not greater access to higher educational opportunities.

Hmong Occupational Mobility

Sheboygan's Hmong have yet to achieve a mass sectoral transformation into higher occupational categories. Compared to the city's population overall, the

Hmong are far from being proportionally represented in the professional and technical categories (Table 9.3).

Lower levels of occupational attainment within the Hmong population is reflected by their higher percentages in manufacturing and accommodation/food services, and lower percentages in education, health and social services, and other professions, compared to the total population.

Table 9.3 Hmong and Hispanic Employment in Select Occupational Sectors in Sheboygan, 2000

Occupational Category	Manufacturing	Accommodation and Food Services	Retail	Education, Health, and Social Services	Professionals
Hmong	63.8%	15.6%	2.8%	8.3%	1.6%
Total Population	39.9%	6.0%	10.4%	17.3%	2.4%

Source: Sex by Industry for the Employed Civilian Population 16 Years and Over, U.S. Bureau of the Census, 2000 Summary File 4.

There has been, however, an observable upward occupational trend among the Hmong since 2000. Several support themselves through informal but increasingly lucrative forms of employment. For example, about 25 Hmong sell produce at the Sheboygan farmers' market, and there are also several, mostly women, who sell traditional needle work, or *pandau.* Most of them do this on a part-time basis, but at least one woman does it full time. Sewing an average of 80 story cloths and other embroidery projects a year, Sheboygan resident Xao Lee managed to earn enough to help send two of her children to medical school. Her needle work, as illustrated by the *paj ntaub,* or story cloth, shown in Figure 9.2, is well-known throughout the region; in 2003 she won the Best Artist award for the John Michael Kohler Art Center's annual festival, which features artists from throughout the Midwest.

Many of Sheboygan's adult Hmong have moved up the occupational ladder by embarking on careers generally different from those worked in the past two decades. For example, although limited in numbers, Hmong professionals in Sheboygan now range from a police officer to a dentist, and also include a variety of jobs in finance, insurance, and real estate. According to Blia Vang, the State Farm agent, the trend appears to be that if a Hmong individual is college-educated, he or she generally tends to work as a professional; those without college degrees generally work in such sectors as manufacturing. Their pursuits bring Hmong professionals into a new relationship with the city's non-Hmong, reflecting a greater degree of cross-cultural contact and cultural adaptation on the part of the Hmong overall. The belief among the Hmong is that as residence time increases, more and more of their numbers will follow these examples.

Figure 9.2 Sheboygan Hmong Artist, Xao Lee with Her Story Cloth

Aids in Social and Cultural Adaptation

In realization of the difficulties of the average Hmong refugee in adjusting to a totally different culture and society, a non-profit organization the HMAAS (Hmong Mutual Assistance Association of Sheboygan) was created in 1980 to assist their cultural adaptation. The HMAAS helps Hmong migrants find housing and jobs, start their own businesses, learn English, and master basic living skills. Some other HMAAS programs include senior outreach and a program that provides cultural and linguistic services.

Overall, HMAAS has been an indispensable cultural broker for Sheboygan's Hmong population, as it also strongly encourages and sponsors events that help maintain their heritage. For example, with the annual New Year's celebration held every November at the Sheboygan Armory, about 3,000 to 4,000 Hmong gather for three days to celebrate their culture. Many dress in traditional garb, listen to Hmong music played on such instruments as the *qeej* (a wind instrument that somewhat resembles and sounds like a bagless bag pipe), play games such as *pov pob* (a courtship ritual with ball tossing), and enjoy Hmong cooking.

The annual Hmong Summer Festival, which attracts several thousand Hmong, provides an informal social gathering. Visitors can purchase traditional Hmong healing herbs, spices, and prepared and unprepared food items, as well as videos and compact disks in the Hmong and Thai languages, as well as other contemporary items. There are also sport competitions, such as *tuj lub* (a Hmong game that resembles Bocce ball but uses large tops).

Both of these annual events allow the Hmong to practice and therefore preserve selected aspects of their culture. Although they attract thousands of Hmong from the broader region, they do not leave a large cultural imprint on Sheboygan. There appear to be two reasons why. First, these are ephemeral manifestations, occuring annually for only about three days each. Second, the participants as well as the observers are primarily Hmong. In other words, Hmong culture has not yet made the crossover to attract admiration, or even general awareness, from the mainstream culture. In fact, to the average non-Hmong Sheboyganite, these events are landscapes to be avoided.

The Hmong have maintained cultural cohesion in other ways, especially through technology. To better communicate with and serve the cultural needs of Sheboygan's Hmong population, Vue Yang launched a radio program in 1982. Originally aired on a private station, the show had a five-minute time slot from 7:55 to 8:00 on Sunday mornings—a miniscule time slot considering Sheboygan's Hmong numbered 800 persons at that time. According to Yang, the owner of Union Oriental Market and an engineer with the local company Pentair, the time limitation was "funny and ridiculous" because most people were either at church or still in bed (2004). "Just think about what we could say with 5 minutes!" he observed.

In September 1983, Yang launched "*Suab Hmoob* Sheboygan" (literally translated as the "Hmong Voice of Sheboygan") on Sheboygan's radio station WSHS. Since then the program has run every Friday evening from 4:30 pm to 10:00 pm. It serves as a cultural touchstone for Sheboygan's Hmong community as its stated mission is to focus "mainly on developing and promoting the best of Hmong oral traditions and culture" (Yang). Since 2000, "*Suab Hmoob* Sheboygan" has been able to connect with an even larger Hmong population by broadcasting via the Internet. Yang reports, it "now reaches out to many Hmong living inside and outside the United States of America."

Until recently, television also directly served the Sheboygan Hmong population. In 2002 a Hmong program about healthcare issues began airing on a local access channel. "Families Eat and Live Well" (generally referred to as the "healthy family" show) aired weekly for about two years. Presented entirely in Hmong, it centered on a trained Hmong health care professional (Myshoua Vang, Health Care Educator for the HMAAS) bringing modern medical information directly into Hmong homes. Delivery through the media in their language, rather than interpersonally from a Western health care professional, proved far less stressful and thus aided their integration into the social norms of the community. Unfortunately, this program is no longer offered, because funding for it expired in 2004.

Sheboygan's Hmong have also benefited from a grant obtained in 1987 through the Library Services and Construction Act. This Act created a substantial collection of Hmong-language books, videos, and cassette tapes.

These programs, events, and media have provided the Hmong in Sheboygan with a means to preserve their traditional culture, but for the most part this culture has not projected itself into the larger cultural landscape of the community, and has not necessarily helped integrate the Hmong into the health-care educational, and occupational landscapes of the city (with the possible exception of the traditional crafts industry). Therefore, two distinct futures suggest themselves. One is that as the city's Hmong population continues to grow through high natural increase and low net out-migration, its culture will become more prevalent and more accepted. However, there is another possibility, that acculturation will outpace cultural preservation, thus reducing rather than increasing the Hmong imprint on Sheboygan's cultural landscape.

Discussion and Conclusions

Sheboygan's adaptation to the influx of Hmong over the last thirty years is still not finished or tension-free, in part because migration still continues. The overwhelming majority arrive from locations elsewhere in the United States, but some arrive from overseas, for example in 2005 when seventy-one families (about 350 persons) arrived in the city as part of a larger resettlement program. In all, some 15,000 Hmong had been granted asylum at a Buddhist temple for about ten years, but then the Thai government forced them out, with many immigrating to the United States (Chasong Yang 2005, June 15).

Unlike their counterparts who comprised the first wave of migrants to Sheboygan nearly thirty years ago, these new immigrants benefited greatly by being exposed to Western culture during their long stay at the Buddhist temple (with some even having access to e-mail). They also received very active sponsorship from Hmong families in Sheboygan. As such, acculturation difficulties appear to be minimal, certainly much less than in that first wave (Chasong Yang 2005, June 15). Furthermore, the only public demonstration against the resettlement consisted of a few letters of complaint to the local newspaper. The lack of an organized protest suggests the host culture is evolving in its acceptance of the Hmong migrants.

This increasing acceptance is further exhibited in the 2005 election of Myshoua Vang as the first Hmong member of the Sheboygan Area School District. Her victory reflects not only acceptance but also recognition of the board's need for proportional representation in terms of ethnicity. As of June 2005, 17 percent of the students enrolled in the Sheboygan Area School District were Asian (*Sheboygan Press* 2005, June 12). Myshoua's position is a first step, but still important. Only about 1 percent of the city's schoolteachers are Asian (the district reported in June 2005 that it was actively recruiting more), whereas just over 7 percent of the city's population is Asian.

Despite gains made by the Hmong in Sheboygan, negative attitudes still exist. Common rumors include the following: Hmong do not have to pay taxes; the government provides them all with vans; they are welfare freeloaders. Occasionally mean-spirited letters to the editor argue that "these people don't deserve anything" (*Sheboygan Press* 2005, January 6).

These negative attitudes are all the more tragic considering the United States' breaking its promises to the Hmong after their valiant efforts to assist the United States at the end of the Secret War; and also considering the Hmong's tragic history as a people without a homeland for hundreds of years.

In Sheboygan, the Hmong are finally receiving some of the formal recognition they deserve, through the creation of a forty-foot granite memorial honoring Lao, Hmong, and American Veterans of the Secret War. Initially, many Sheboygan citizens protested its creation. Some objected out of ignorance (i.e., many believed that the Hmong here were actually our enemies in the Secret War). Others were simply opposed to the memorial's being sited in a historic downtown park. However, over time, support grew for the memorial, especially after a new committee (of which this writer is a member) actively pursued a less controversial site. The site was donated by the city of Sheboygan, and is located in a lakefront park. It is a beautiful setting that many local residents visit daily and that is the locus for major festivals. It is also next to the city's well-used marina.

One hopes that this monument will garner some of the attention, respect, and appreciation for the Hmong community that heretofore has not existed in Sheboygan. The memorial's concept welcomes the visitor with festive exterior walls and ceramic mosaics designed by area children. The interior, however, is meant to be a somber and meditative space that educates the public about the lives sacrificed and the loyalty and valor shown by Hmong men who gave so much. It also honors the women and families who supported them and shows how the Hmong, Laotians and Americans all worked together in the cause of freedom. It is an important step towards participatory accommodation that can serve an ultimately positive example for future streams of immigrants to the American heartland.

Notes

1. A review of Sheboygan's Grant Elementary School yearbook shows that 47 percent of the 68 Hmong students (encompassing 17 percent of the student body) have American names, ranging from Alexander and Amy to Tommy and Yolanda. Also, several high school guidance counselors reported students whose first name is the surname of the doctor who delivered them; there are a number named "Marsho" after one particular physician.

2. Two to three percent are seniors and two to three percent are on disability.

References

Dao, Yang. 1993. *Hmong at the Turning Point*. Minneapolis: World Bridge Associates, Ltd.

D.C. Everest Area Schools. 2001. *The Hmong and Their Stories: The Secret Wars, Escape to Laos, the Legends*. Wausau: D.C. Everest Schools Publications.

Donnelly, Nancy D. 1994. *Changing Lives of Refugee Hmong Women*. Seattle: University of Washington Press.

Duffy, John, Roger Harmon, Donald A. Ranard, Bo Thao, and Kou Yang. 2004. *The Hmong: An Introduction to Their History and Culture*. Washington: Center for Applied Linguistics.

Evans, M.D.R. 1989. "Immigrant Entrepreneurship: Effects of Market Size on an Isolated Labor Pool." *Sociological Review* 54: 950-62.

Fadiman, Anne. 1997. *The Spirit Catches You and You Fall Down: A Hmong Child, Her American Doctors, and the Collision of Two Cultures*. New York: Farrar, Straus and Giroux.

Foo, Lora Jo. 2002. "Hmong Women in the US: Changing a Patriarchal Culture." In *Asian American Women: Issues, Concerns, and Responsive Human and Civil Rights Advocacy*. Ford Foundation.

Hmong Healthcare Needs Assessment Project. 2001. Sheboygan County, WI.: Promoting Access to Health Project Mini-Grant. Funded by the Office of Minority Health, through the Association of Asian Pacific Community Health Organizations. May 15.

Kaplan, David H. 1997. "The Creation of an Ethnic Economy: Indochinese Business Expansion in Saint Paul." *Economic Geography* 73:214-233.

Lai, Eric, and Dennis Arguelles. 2003. *The New Face of Asian Pacific America: Numbers, Diversity and Change in the 21st Century*. Berkeley: AsianWeek.

Lo, Fungchatou T. 2001. *The Promised Land: Socioeconomic Reality of the Hmong People in Urban America, 1976-2000*. Lima: Wyndham Hall Press.

Miyares, Ines M. 1997. "Changing Perceptions of Space and Place as Measures of Hmong Acculturation." *Professional Geographer* 49:214-224.

———. 1998. *The Hmong Refugee Experience in the United States: Crossing the River*. New York: Garland Publishing.

Pfaff, Tim. 1995. *Hmong in America: Journey From a Secret War*. Eau Claire, WI: Chippewa Valley Museum Press.

Pfeifer, Mark E. 2001. *Trends in Hmong Population Distribution across the Regions of the United States*. Minneapolis: Hmong Resources Center.

Portes, Alejandro., and R. Manning. 1986. *The Immigrant Enclave: Theory and Empircal Examples. In Competitive Ethnic Relations*, ed. S. Olzak and J. Nagel, 47-68. Orlando: Academic Press.

Portes, Alejandro, M. Castells, and L. Jensen. 1989. *The Informal Economy: Studies in Advanced and Less Developed Countries*. Baltimore: Johns Hopkins University Press.

Quincy, Keith. 1988. *Hmong: History of a People*. Cheney: Eastern Washington University Press.

SBC Sheboygan/Sheboygan Falls Telephone Directory, 2004-2005.

Schofield, Steve. 2005. Email, January 11.
Sheboygan Press. 2005. "Is There a Double Standard for Hmong?" Letter to editor from David Mohar, Sheboygan. Thursday, January 6.
———. 2005. "Handicapped Woman Assaulted." Thursday, June 16.
———. 2005. "Schools, Students Coming to Terms with Diversity." Sunday June 12.
Simonson, Rolf, M.D. 2005. Aurora Sheboygan Clinic. Telephone interview, March 23.
Stepick, A. 1989. "Miami's Two Informal Sectors." In *The Informal Economy: Studies in Advanced and Less Developed Countries*, edited by A. Portes, M. Castells, and L. Benton. Baltimore: Johns Hopkins University Press.
U.S. Bureau of the Census. 2000. Summary File 1, 100-Percent Data, QT-P7.
———. 2000. Summary File 2, 100-Percent Data, PCT1.
———. 2000 Summary File 4 Sample Data, PCT61.
Vang, Blia, Agent, State Farm Insurance. 2005. Interview, April 5.
Vang, Cher Pao, Business and Career Counselor for the Hmong Mutual Assistance Association of Sheboygan. 2005. Interview, March 21.
Vang, Kao. 2005. Pastor, Hmong Christian Reformed Church. Telephone interview, March 25.
Vang, Ker. "The Night My Family and I Left Laos Secretly." 2001. Paper written for Geography 102: Roots and Diversity, May 8.
Vang, Myshoua, R.N. 2005. Health Care Educator for the Hmong Mutual Assistance Association of Sheboygan. Telephone interview, March 8.
Wake, Kristine, M.D. 2005. Aurora Sheboygan Clinic. Telephone interview, March 9.
Yang, Chasong. 2005. Executive Director of the Hmong Mutual Assistance Association of Sheboygan. Telephone interview, June 15.
Yang, Vue. 2004. History of Hmong Sheboygan Radio. http://www.hmongunionmarket.com/05142004/LivxwmxovtoojcuaSuabHmoobSheboygan.htm.
Zelinsky, Wilbur, and Barrett A. Lee. 1998. "Heterolocalism: An Alternative Model of the Sociospatial Behaviour of Immigrant Ethnic Communities." *International Journal of Population Geography* 4:281-298.

Chapter 10

Getting Settled in the Heartland: Community Formation among First- and Second-Generation Iranians in Iowa City, Iowa

Mohammad Chaichian

The 1979 Iranian revolution and establishment of the Islamic Republic led to a massive out-migration and creation of an Iranian Diaspora at the global level. Those who chose the United States as their final destination either settled in major urban centers and metropolitan areas in large numbers, or formed small ethnic communities in many states including Iowa. Although Iowa has never been a major destination for Iranian immigrants, a small contingent of about 700 Iranians has found Iowa to be their home. In an earlier study (Chaichian 1997), I focused on the problematic of cultural adjustment and segmented assimilation of the first generation Iranian immigrant community in Iowa City, a university town located in eastern Iowa. But the article in particular focused on the extent of this ethnic community's integration into the host society's culture on the one hand, and maintenance of Iranian cultural and ethnic identity on the other.[1] Related to the former issue, more than half of respondents, both male and female, identified "adjustment to American society" and "social isolation and loneliness" as the two most pressing issues of concern for Iranians in the U.S. and Iowa.[2] Based on the findings I concluded,

> Thus, in spite of their educational, professional and economic successes, [first generation] Iranian immigrants' increasing isolation, psychological depression, and loneliness may signal a more serious problem of the existence of a subtle

> but pervasive form of prejudice and discrimination against them in rural areas on the one hand, and their failure to blend into the greater society on the other. (Chaichian 1997, 624-25)

As a follow-up to my earlier study of this ethnic immigrant community, in this chapter I will chronicle Iranian immigrants' gradual adjustment to their new home and various dimensions of "settling in." In particular, I will examine the processes of community formation for residents of Iranian ancestry by looking at settlement patterns; nature and types of their participation within their ethnic enclave and their immediate urban environment; the role of Iowa's only Iranian cultural association in community building; and the second generation's role in short- and long-term community sustenance. Regarding the last factor, I will examine the interface between the second generation's desire for professional achievement and personal fulfillment with the extent of their personal commitment to parents (first generation) and the Iranian community.

Settlement Patterns of Iranians in the United States

In his study of settlement patterns of Iranian immigrants who arrived in the United States from 1975 to 1993 Modarres (1998, 38) finds that more than one-third have chosen the greater Los Angeles area as their place of residence. Other Iranian immigrants have been attracted to San Francisco, New York, and the Washington, D.C.-Baltimore conurbations, although their numbers have been less significant.[3] In addition, Modarres documents that Iranian immigrants identified 7,194 ZIP codes, or one out of every four, as their place of residence.[4] However, his further analysis indicates that only 264 ZIP codes had 100 or more Iranian immigrants, comprising a little more than half the immigrant population. More specifically, 17 percent of all Iranian immigrants resided in 15 ZIP codes, each with 1,000 or more residents.

Spatial patterns of settlements for Iranian immigrants in the United States have four distinct tendencies. First, during the 1980-1990 period Iranians seem to have had a clear preference for the western states, mainly California, followed by states in the northeastern and southern regions. However, during the 1990-2000 period Iranian immigrants both came in fewer numbers and showed a regional preference for southern states, the latter reason most likely being due to market demands and job opportunities. In contrast, during both decades fewer Iranian immigrants were attracted and absorbed by Midwestern states (see Table 10.1). Second, the majority of Iranian immigrants have settled in two main geographic areas, the greater Los Angeles-San Francisco urban area (in California) and the Boston-Washington conurbation (a continuous stretch of metropolitan areas on the East Coast that includes Baltimore, Philadelphia, and New York). Third, Iranian immigrants have also chosen residence in selective urban centers outside these major conurbations. For example, cities with more than 1,000 Iranians include Seattle and Portland in the north-east region; Atlanta, Dallas, Houston, San Antonio, New Orleans and Miami in the south; and Minneapolis-St. Paul, Omaha, Kansas City, Chicago, Detroit and Cleveland in the Midwest. Fourth, although fewer in numbers and scattered spatially, Iranian immigrants have also chosen other less-populated and less urbanized states as their place of residence but have nonetheless resided in or near urban population centers. This is clearly the case for Iranians in Iowa. Based on the 1993 census data only 5 percent of 787 Iranians (44 individuals) resided in rural areas (Chaichian 1997, 615).

Table 10.1 Regional Preferences of Persons of "Iranian" Ancestry in the United States, 1980-2000

	1980	1990	% Change 1980 to 1990	2000	% Change 1990 to 2000
U.S.:	122,890	235,521	+91.6%	338,266	+43.6
Regions:					
West	52,116	123,496	+136.9%	182,938	+48.1%
Northeast	20,935	34,693	+65.7%	44,838	+29.2%
South	31,635	50,109	+58.3%	82,004	+63.6%
Midwest*	18,204	22,283	+22.4%	28,486	+27.8%
Iowa:	607	787	+29.6%	698	-11.3%

*For regional data the 1980 census uses "North-Central" instead of "Midwest."

Sources: For 1980, US Census Bureau, Ancestry of the Population by State: 1980 (Supplementary Report PC80-S1-10), April 1983. For 1990, U.S. Census Bureau, 1990 Census of Population: Detailed Ancestry Groups for States (1990 CP-S-1-2). For 2000, U.S. Census Bureau. 1990 Census and Census 2000 Special Tabulations.

In search of reasons for Iranian immigrants' decision to reside in rural states Modarres (1998, 48) concludes that in most cases these states have made a concerted effort to enroll Iranian students in their colleges and universities, some of whom have found employment after graduation and have decided to stay. This has often been followed by reunification with their immediate families. This also partially explains the case for Iranians in Iowa, as I will discuss in the following section.

Settlement Patterns of Iranian Immigrants in Iowa

As stated earlier, most states in the Midwest have not been major destinations for Iranian immigrants due to both personal preferences and unavailability of desirable employment opportunities. Among Midwestern states, Iowa attracted its fair share of Iranians but could not retain them due to the previously-mentioned factors, particularly during the 1990s (see Table 10.1). A review of census data for 1990 and 2000 reveals that not only Iranians in Iowa constitute a tiny portion of all Iranians in the United States; their numbers are also in decline (Table 10.2). For example, in 1990 there were 787 Iranians residing in Iowa, a meager 0.35 percent of all Iranians in the United States (Chaichian 1997, 615).

Table 10.2 Population Changes for Residents of Iranian Ancestry in Iowa Counties with a Major City or Metropolitan Area (1990-2000)

County	Residents of Iranian Ancestry				Major City/ Metropolitan Areas	Major Educational Institutions
	1990	2000	Change #	Change %		
BlackHawk	80	19	-61	-76.3	Waterloo-Cedar Falls	U. of N. Iowa
Des Moines	52	16	-36	-69.2	Burlington	
Dubuque	23	00	-23	-100.0	Dubuque	Clarke & Loras Col., U. of Dubuque
Johnson	167	296	+131	**+78.4**	Iowa City-Coralville	U. of Iowa
Lee	17	00	-17	-100.0	Fort Madison	
Linn	76	20	-56	-73.6	Cedar Rapids	Coe & Mount Mercy Col., Kirkwood Comm. Col.
Polk	92	116	+24	**+26.0**	Des Moines	Drake U.
Pottawatt-amie	04	05	+01	**+25.0**	Council Bluffs	
Story	182	40	-142	-78.0	Ames	Iowa State U.
Webster	21	05	-16	-76.2	Fort Dodge	
Total for Iowa	787	698	-89	-11.3		

Sources: U.S. Bureau of the Census 1990 (1993a:183), and U.S. Bureau of the Census 2000, Summary File 3, Matrices PCT15 & PCT18.
*Data in bold represent positive changes for metropolitan counties

By 2000 only 698 Iranians (0.2 percent of Iranian immigrants) were still in residence, an 11.3 percent decline (U.S. Bureau of the Census 2000).[5] Iowa counties which have a sizeable Iranian population are those with either a major metropolitan area such as Polk (city of Des Moines and West Des Moines), or the ones with college towns and medical facilities such as Story, Johnson, and Blackhawk Counties (the home of Iowa State University, University of Iowa and affiliated hospitals and clinics, and University of Northern Iowa, respectively).

A comparison of 1990 and 2000 census data for Iowa counties with Iranian residents in Table 10.2 indicates the development of two spatial patterns of population movement. The first is a net out-of-state migration of eighty-nine Iranian residents or 11.3 percent of all Iranians in Iowa during the last decade of the twentieth century. The second *emerging* pattern is movement of the remaining Iranians *between* Iowa counties that has resulted in convergence of Iranian residents in and around three vibrant metropolitan areas—Iowa City (Johnson County), Cedar Rapids (Linn County), and Des Moines (Polk County). The first two form a fast-growing "urban corridor" in eastern Iowa, with an economy based on education and health care. Des Moines, the seat of state government, is a major hub for insurance industry in the region, and in addition, is a thirty-mile drive from Ames, the home to Iowa State University.[6]

Table 10.3 Occupational/Professional Status of Iranian Immigrants in Southeastern Iowa and Iowa City

Occupation/	S.E. Iowa 2004[a]		Iowa City 1994[b]	
Profession:	#	%	#	%
Academic	1	2.0	1	4.1
Medical Field (physicians, dentists, surgeons, etc.)	25	51.0	6	25.0
Computer Science & Engineering	10	20.4	6	25.0
Managerial	1	2.0	1	4.1
Self-employed	2	4.0	4	16.6
Salaried employees/wage earners	8	16.3	5	20.8
Farmers	2	4.0	1	4.1
Total	49	99.7	24	99.7

Sources:
a. Based on a survey of membership list obtained from the Iranian Cultural Association of Iowa (ICAI), November 2004 (N= 65).
b. Based on a 1994 survey of Iowa City-Coralville Iranians (Chaichian 1997, N= 40).

The change of residence from rural counties to major metropolitan areas and urban corridors denotes a move toward further permanency for that portion of Iranian immigrants who have chosen to stay in Iowa. It is also an indication of this immigrant population's high level of education and skills, and their interest in certain occupations that could only be offered in major urban centers. This is supported by two sets of data collected for southeastern Iowa and Iowa City-Coralville area (see Table 10.3).[7]

On the other hand, Iranian immigrants who have left Iowa are a part of the greater statewide out-migration of educated and skilled workers. According to a U.S. Census report, during the 1995-2000 period "Iowa lost 11,691 more single, college-educated residents ages 25 to 39 than it gained," and in a state-wide opinion poll in 2000 more than 50 percent of college students indicated that they plan to leave Iowa after graduation. This puts Iowa above only North Dakota regarding the rate of out-migration (Jordan 2003). Thus related to the issue of community formation the remaining Iranian immigrants in Iowa are facing unique challenges in order to sustain the vitality of their tiny ethnic communities. What follows is a closer look at one such community in Iowa and its prospects for a long-term sustenance and survival.

Iranians in Iowa City: Settling In

Methodology

This study outlines the evolution of this immigrant population over the last two decades, and is based on my personal observations as a participant-observer and member of this ethnic immigrant community; careful examination and analysis of pertinent census data files for the past three decades at national, regional and state levels; findings of two surveys of small samples of first and second generation Iranians in Iowa City in 1994 and 1999; and a follow-up survey and interviews with second generation Iranians in 2005.[8] I have defined *second generation Iranians* as "U.S.-born children with Iranian-born parents," or "Iranian children born abroad who came to the United States before the age of twelve." With the help of the Persian Student Organization (PSO), a student-run group at the University of Iowa, I sent a letter to all second generation members via e-mail, directing them to a web page where they could fill out the questionnaire and submit it electronically. This technique was used to ensure confidentiality and facilitate data collection.[9]

Aside from demographic and biographical questions, two dimensions of the second generation's commitment to the Iranian community were identified, namely, their *degree of attachment to the Iranian community* and *level of commitment to parents*. The first was measured within the context of second generation's *participation in ethnic-specific events*, the *ethnic origins of their close friends*, and their *intention to stay in the Iowa City Hub after graduation*. As for the second dimension, subjects were asked questions about the *importance of staying close to one's parents* and their generation's *level of commitment to look after their aging and retired parents*.

Formation of an Ethnic Community[10]

With a population of 62,220 in 2000, Iowa City is the sixth largest city in the state and is home to the University of Iowa with a student population of 29,000. With close to 24,000 employees on its payroll, the University of Iowa is the largest employer in the Iowa City-Coralville hub which is also one of the fastest growing "urbanized areas" in Iowa. [11] By the year 2000 the hub had a population of 83,697, of which 296 were individuals of Iranian ancestry. Yet while the Iowa City-Coralville hub's population had a 13 percent growth during the 1990-2000 period, that of the Iranian population was 78.4 percent, an enormous growth in a state with declining native and Iranian immigrant populations.[12]

Iranians in Iowa City are highly educated, making this immigrant community quite distinct compared to larger urban concentrations of Iranians such as the one in Los Angeles, California (see Bozorgmehr and Sabagh 1987). For example, 85 percent of first generation Iranians in the Iowa City hub have a four-year college degree, 62 percent have masters or equivalent degrees, and 33 percent hold doctorate or other professional degrees. These percentages are more than four times those for the U.S. population overall.[13]

Like many other Iranian immigrant communities, it appears that the Iowa City community has grown out of the turbulent years of political and ideological clashes between various student and activist groups that polarized Iranians during the early years after the Iranian Revolution. For instance, while many Iranians in the early 1980s socialized along clearly drawn political boundaries (such as the left, the Monarchists and Islamic groups both opposing and supporting the Islamic Republic), the Iranian communities in the 1990s became more tolerant of and accommodating to political, ideological and religious diversity. The relative consolidation of various subgroups within the Iranian immigrant population of the United States is by no means an indication of the emergence of a cohesive and unified political block, but it can be considered as the first building block towards their integration into the host society culture.

In assessing the extent of adjustment and assimilation to the host culture it is crucial to study the process of *community formation* and its role in the sustenance of an ethnic immigrant population. One such study was conducted by Gilanshah (1990) in the Twin Cities area in Minnesota during the 1983-1989 period. Her findings indicated that a two-tiered Iranian community was established— an "Iranian-American community" comprised of those who immigrated prior to the hostage crisis and who have adopted parts of the host society's culture; and a younger "Iranian student colony" whose members have resisted integration into the American society and who were ambivalent about socializing with the "older" Iranian-Americans.

In a similar fashion I have also identified three distinct groups among Iranians in Iowa City.[14] The first group is comprised of *first generation middle age and older immigrants* and their *second* generation *offspring* form the core of Iranian community. They comprise of all Iranians thirty-five years and older and their families who know each other either through professional associations such as the physicians and college and university faculty/employees, or through family ties and friendship networks. Out of this group a few came to the United States in the 1960s and early 1970s, and are considered the "elders" of the community. The rest have come to the United States in the aftermath of the 1979 Islamic revolution in Iran, the majority of them were students at American universities at the time who decided to stay in the United States on a permanent basis. Socialization among this group has mostly been based on social interests of both adults and children, and one can find several sub-groups with different needs and social interests.

The second group is comprised of *first generation younger immigrants and the second generation implants* who are mostly in their twenties and thirties. Among this group, some have come to the United States for higher education and professional training purposes, either from Iran or other countries where their immigrant parents reside; and others have moved to Iowa from other states. Like the "older" enclave this group is comprised of several subgroups of individuals and families of similar social tastes and professional interest. While those belonging to the first group are mostly settled and with established careers and professional ties within the community, members of the second group are mostly university and college students or recent graduates who will most likely follow the job market and move out of the community. What is more, after the 1979 Iranian revolution fewer Iranian students were allowed to come to the United States, further contributing to shrinkage of the second group in the Iowa City hub.[15]

The *isolationists* form the third group of Iranian immigrants. This last group is comprised of those who are married to Americans and have culturally drifted away from Iranian community;[16] professionals who call themselves the "new implants" who have recently moved to Iowa City and its vicinity and have little or no contact with other Iranians; and some long-time residents who do not want to be associated with their Iranian compatriots for personal reasons.

Although the majority of Iranians in Iowa City are Muslims either by faith or by birth, most of them prefer to socialize with others on a secular and non-religious basis. Yet during the late 1980s and early 1990s there also existed a small *Muslim enclave* of Iranian families and individuals who observed all religious rituals and events within the Muslim faith, socialized with other devout Iranian and non-Iranian Muslims, attended religious ceremonies at the makeshift Islamic Center in town or the main mosque in nearby Cedar Rapids community, and taught their children the Holy Quran and appropriate codes of Islamic conduct. With the maturation of Iowa City Iranian community those families who have stayed have been dissolved into the Iranian niche and can no longer be identified separately on religious grounds.[17]

Socialization among members of the Iowa City Iranian enclave has also undergone two distinct phases of transformation that I call *convergence* and *divergence*.[18] During the first phase that lasted up until the late 1990s, social gatherings were large-scale, included more families, and were more inclusive in terms of one's social status and economic class. However, as the first generation got older, became more established, and got more entrenched in the local economy this once seemingly cohesive community began to experience polarization along the lines of social class and personal interests. Thus in the past five years the second phase has been marked with a decline in number of private parties ("Dowrehs") in which a large and often incongruous group were invited, and an increase in small gatherings of few like-minded families who usually have similar social class backgrounds and interests.

Settlement Patterns in Iowa City

With further institutionalization and routinization of the Islamic government in Iran, many non-resident status Iranians decided to stay in the United States on a permanent basis and focused their attention on career and professional advancement. A distinct feature of the Iranian community in Iowa City is the prevalence of home owners over renters. For instance, with the exception of those who for the reason of their job requirements have a temporary residence in the Iowa City hub and are renters, almost all other Iranian families and individuals in the area are home owners.

As a measure of this ethnic community's socio-economic status and the degree of its integration into the city I will examine two indicators: 1) average value of homes owned by Iranian households, and 2) the extent of residential dispersion. Regarding the first indicator, a survey of twenty one homes owned by residents of Iranian ancestry in the Iowa City/Coralville MSA indicates that their assessed values in 2004 ranged from $119,410 to $990,380. The median value of these homes in 2004 was $194,670, compared with $144, 458 for other residents identified as "white, not of Hispanic origin" and $133,147 for African American residents, placing Iranian residents in a much higher income bracket.[19]

Measuring the second indicator (degree of residential dispersion) for Iowa City Iranians, a survey of residential patterns for Iranian households indicates the *heterolocal* nature of residential units or absence of any preference for certain residential neighborhoods (formation of ethnic ghettoes) that have been the characteristic of certain other immigrant populations (see Conzen 1979). Research indicates that lower class urban residents have a higher dependency on services provided in their immediate communities (Foley 1950) and also are more attached to their residential neighborhoods (Fried 1963). This can have particularly negative effects on an immigrant population's extent and pace of integration into the urban host community. For instance, in his study of ethnic residential patterns Lieberson (1963) found that residentially segregated ethnic groups were:

> More sharply differentiated in their occupational composition, more deviant in patterns of occupational mobility, less likely to become American citizens, less likely to speak English and more likely to be endogamous (Yancey et al. 1976, 398).

Clearly, this is not the case for Iranians in the Iowa City-Coralville hub. In the absence of an ethnic immigrant "critical mass," there are no local businesses owned by Iranians that normally cater to specific needs of the Iranian community, in contrast to larger cities like Chicago, Washington, D.C., or Los Angeles. Likewise, those who can be identified as "working class" Iranians in Iowa City are not typical workers, as most hold a bachelor's or higher level educational degree.

The concept of *heterolocalism* was first used by Zelinsky and Lee (1998, 285) who questioned the validity of "assimilationist" and "pluralist" assumptions, and instead offered an alternative model for an immigrant population's settlement patterns.[20] In their assessment, heterolocalism is a late twentieth century phenomenon with at least three distinct attributes: an immediate dispersion of immigrants within the host society; separation of place of work and residence; and presence of strong community ties among immigrant population, partially due to new electronic means of communication.

As is illustrated in Figure 10.4, only two homes owned by residents of Iranian ancestry (designated by black circles) are located in census tracts that have areas of "concentrated poverty".[21] But it has to be noted that these tracts include the downtown area and older housing stock that have special appeal in a university town. Thus in most cases the higher median value of homes owned by Iranians is also translated into their preferences for urban tracts that cater to above average and high income bracket residents. In light of the small size of Iowa City's Iranian community it is not possible to calculate indices of dissimilarity or exposure.[22] However, Iowa City does not seem to be a segregated city even for newer immigrant populations with larger numerical representation.[23]

The heterolocal residential pattern for Iranian residents can also be explained by two important social factors. First, my research findings, based on two samples of first- and second generation Iranians in this community, indicate that despite their real and perceived ethnic and cultural differences with a host society of predominantly "white" European background, both groups report having a positive experience of living in Iowa with few or rare incidences of prejudice and overt discrimination either at school or in seeking employment. For instance, in a survey of a small sample of second generation Iowa City Iranians in January 2005 (N=15), almost all subjects responded that they have "never or rarely" been discriminated against while seeking employment or promotion, as well as by their employers and co-workers.[24] Second, in a 1994 survey of first generation Iowa City Iranians, 86 percent responded that they have "never or rarely" been discriminated against in housing because of their national or ethnic origin.[25] In presenting their heterolocal model, Zelinsky and Lee (1998, 285-286) correctly attribute this to the "affluence of many of these foreign-born newcomers," the "enactment of fair housing legislation," and "significant shifts in public attitudes and perceptions" that in turn have reduced spatial barriers between new and old residents.

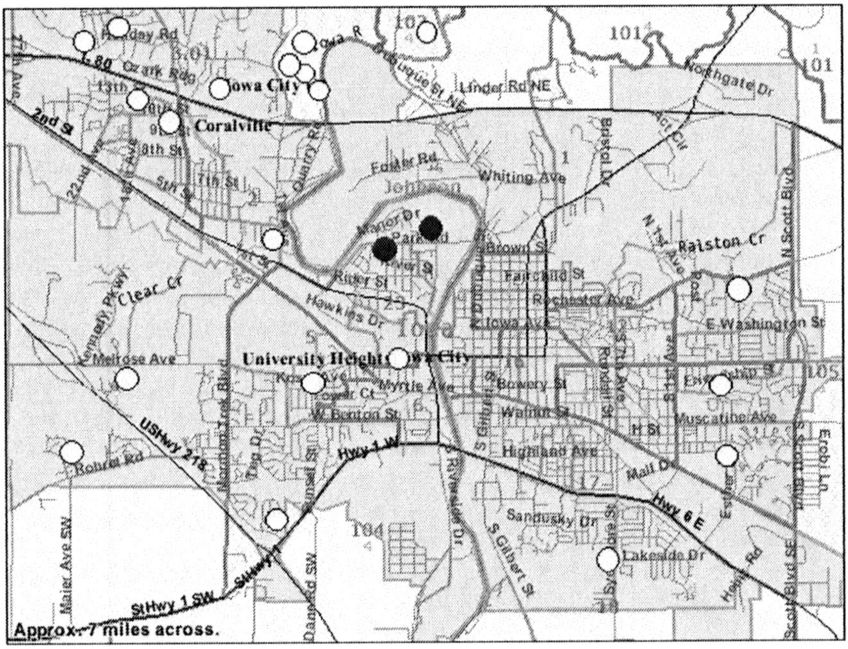

Figure 10.4 Location of 22 Residences Owned by Iranians within the Census Tract Boundaries for Iowa City-Coralville-North Liberty Metro Areas (2005). Black dots indicate areas of concentrated poverty.

The Role of the Iranian Cultural Association of Iowa in Community Formation and Maintenance

With the decline of political factionalism and ideological conflict characteristic of pre- and post-Revolution period (between 1978 and the mid-1980s) and relative stability in the Islamic republic in Iran, the political and ideological differences lost their practical social appeal for many Iranians outside Iran, particularly in the United States. In major American cities such as Los Angeles, Washington, DC, and Chicago a declining political activism was replaced by ad hoc Iranian cultural associations which were formed to bring Iranians closer together by promoting social and cultural causes.

Earlier observations by Gilanshah (1990) on the Iranian immigrant community of about 3,000 in the Twin Cities area indicate a clear tendency for the maintenance of Iranian culture and ethnic identity through the organizing of various social and cultural activities instead of forming groups based on political factionalism. In yet another study of Iranians in Los Angeles, Moslehi (1984) provides evidence for the importance of a growing organizational consciousness among Iranians, that may indicate both a need for and a desire to create a sense of cultural connectedness by maintaining an "Iranian" community.[26] This is also the case in Iowa City, as one no longer can identify "political enclaves" but divisions along family and social interests as well as professional affinities.

Among the larger Iranian communities in Iowa, the one in Iowa City has been most active in sustaining its ethnic and cultural identity. After several failed attempts (mainly by long time Iranian residents) the Iranian Cultural Association of Iowa (ICAI) was formed in Iowa City in the fall of 1993. A core group of about twenty-five individuals selected a president, vice president, and a secretary and approved the association's by-laws. Since then, ICAI has held poetry reading nights, established a Sunday Farsi school for children, and organized festivities marking major secular Iranian holidays such as NowRuz (the Iranian New Year and rite of Spring) and Mehregan (harvest fest).[27] The NowRuz celebration in March 2005 attracted about 160 residents of Iranian ancestry and their guests from Iowa City and other cities within hundred mile radius in eastern and central Iowa.[28] Outside community boundaries, the association has spearheaded at least two fundraising campaigns to help victims of natural disasters such as the 2003 Bam earthquake in Iran.

Some ICAI members in Iowa City have also made inroads into Iowa's political landscape through informal lobbying and fundraising efforts in support of state politicians. Of note is the proclamation of March 21st by Iowa's governor as *"Persian Heritage Day"* in 2001 and again in 2003; and a fund-raising event to support the re-election of current Iowa Governor Tom Wilsack. The Iranian community in Iowa City has therefore assumed a de facto leadership in bringing Iranian immigrants in the region closer together, as well as taking the first steps towards the immigrant group's secondary assimilation into host society. Furthermore, in spite of the heterolocal nature of residences and the increasing polarization of families along the lines of social class and personal interests, the Iowa City Iranian community has maintained its ethnic integrity in great part due to the role played by the ICAI. In rejecting the earlier models of ethnic community that considered "ethnic concentration" in urban "ghettoes" a necessary means of survival, Conzen (1979, 613) argues that:

> Under twentieth century conditions, even a structured ethnic community can maintain close patterns of interaction without residential concentration, and ethnicity defined by either cultural inheritance or interest is likewise independent of residence.

This is certainly the case for the heterolocal Iranian immigrant community that is brought together by an overarching cultural association. In this context, one cannot discount the increasing role played by electronic communication such as the internet and electronic mail (e-mail) for information dissemination; networking; fund-raising; and other organizational objectives, as well as increasing popularity of ethnic-oriented satellite programming that is connecting members of ethnic communities in ways that were unimaginable even ten years ago (see also Zelinsky and Lee 1998, 288-289). This new "virtual ethnic community" supersedes old forms of social interaction within and between ethnic communities, a tool that is comfortably used by the ICAI in the Iowa City hub.[29]

Despite strong initial support given by a considerable number of Iranian families and individuals to establish the Cultural Association in the early 1990s, ICAI has increasingly become a one-person endeavor, at least in the past few years. Although members have kept the association financially afloat through membership fees and generous donations, when it comes to organizational planning and sponsoring cultural events most members take a back seat and rely on the ICAI's president. Thus the ICAI faces an uncertain and unstable future due to a combination of factors such as a lack of cooperative effort, reluctance of community members to carry the torch, and a fast-aging first generation immigrant population.[30]

It is important to note that secular voluntary associations that are geared toward philanthropic objectives and helping mostly newer group members with limited resources did not have strong roots in Iranian culture, and hence have not played a significant role in adjustment of Iranian immigrants in the United States (see also Bozorgmehr 1998, 24). Similarly, at the local level the Iowa City Iranian community's unique socioeconomic characteristics such as high levels of education, skills, and income have not been conducive to formation of such voluntary associations. However, small informal self-help groups have emerged among more affluent Iowa City Iranians who in most cases have collaborated on economic projects and investment opportunities, particularly in real estate and related activities.

The Role of Second Generation Iranians in Community Sustenance and Continuity in Iowa City

A recent census report released in 2004 indicates that sixty-eight out of ninety-nine Iowa counties lost population between 2000 and 2003 (Morrison 2004). Of those with a net population gain, Johnson and Linn counties (with county seats Iowa City and Cedar Rapids, respectively) were among the top five.[31] According to one report the Iowa City-Cedar Rapids corridor is the "brightest spot" of urban growth in eastern Iowa that is "bucking the trend by luring young people for education and keeping them with jobs." The report also indicates that young people have ranked this urban corridor as Iowa's "coolest" urban area, offering its residents a myriad of cultural events and "about a thousand coffee shops and bars" (Jordan 2003).

The preceding exaggerated account of this urban community's "cool" qualities is obviously based partly on a desire to market the area to newcomers and partly on the younger population's experience in the community. Yet small communities can attract those who seek employment only if there are available and relatively secure long-term jobs. Within this context, the Iowa City Iranian community's considerable numerical increase in the last decade is mostly due to educational and training opportunities offered by the University of Iowa and its affiliated teaching hospital and clinics. However, it does not appear that there are long-term employment options for this population cohort. This is supported by findings of my survey of forty-two second-generation Iranians related to their employment choices and options in 2004. While almost all (95.2 percent) of second generation individuals pursued their post-secondary education in the Iowa City hub, of those working only two (14.4 percent) were employed locally and the rest (twelve individuals) were hired elsewhere.

At the same time, first generation Iranians have had considerable stability and job security which in turn has kept most of them in Iowa. For instance, among those Iranians who have left the Iowa City community (and Iowa) during the last ten years (1995-2005), there were only two first-generation families who followed their children after they graduated and secured employment elsewhere. Based on the preceding observation it appears that the long-term sustenance and viability of ethnic Iranian communities in small towns will in large part depend on the extent and nature of intergenerational interdependence, with the second generation playing a crucial role.

The Second Generation: Asset or Liability for Long-Term Community Sustenance?

In an interesting discussion on the question of "Iranian identity" and the way Iranians have wrestled with it after the Arab invasion and the Sassanids' defeat in the seventh century, Meskoob (1992, 44) convincingly argues that Iranians "discovered" their distinctive identity vis-a-vis an invading Arab army and its imperialist culture. This consciousness of one's cultural or national identity, argues Meskoob, is a reaction to another set of cultural values which appear to be an overpowering entity at the time:

> In essence, identity is a reactive matter. Attention to self becomes meaningful in relation to others and from being with them. Being oneself means not being another. It means having differences from another, and preserving separateness and distance while enjoying links or even intermingling. This perception is proper to human beings as social animals. Since it accrues meaning through

> and from others, they are naturally stimulated to greater attention to their own identity.

Meskoob's argument appears to be valid for contemporary Iranian immigrants and exiles as well. But an interesting dimension of the first generation's understanding of their ethnic identity is their realization that to maintain "ethnic purity" in a multi-ethnic society is impractical, if not impossible, particularly as it pertains to raising their offspring. To be more clear, first generation parents come to realize that in relative terms members of the second generation are better equipped to interact with the host culture and in turn better received by others, hence rendering "reactivity" almost obsolete, pertaining to one's ethnic identity. Related to Iowa City first generation Iranians, in an earlier study I reported that 77 percent of my sample stated "they are 'fully committed' to instilling a sense of ethnic pride and identity in their children." Yet 30 percent also expressed their approval of exogamous unions for their children, and 37 percent indicated that they will respect their children's decision (now or in the future) to marry outside the Iranian ethnic population (Chaichian 1997, 623). Thus, using the preceding example we may conclude that despite their rigidity and a relatively conservative approach to the question of cultural identity, first generation Iranians take a more liberal position when it comes to their children's independent judgment and their future plans. This, coupled with parents' higher-than-average socio-economic status makes this Iranian community a special case that probably will not be representative of other communities with a larger and more heterogeneous concentration of residents of Iranian ancestry.

In order to examine the extent of second generation's commitment to their parents and their cultural attachment to this small urban multi-ethnic Iranian enclave, in January 2005 I administered a survey to members of Persian Student Organization (PSO), a student-run group at the University of Iowa with the majority of its members being second generation Iranians. The respondents' pool consisted of seven second generation females and eight males, with eight respondents indicating their interest in being interviewed in person.[32]

Respondents' age ranged between eighteen and thirty-two, with a mean age of twenty-four. In terms of educational level, all but except one were enrolled at, or graduated from, a local college or the University of Iowa. Twenty-seven percent (four individuals) held Master's degree or higher, with another 33 percent (five individuals) holding bachelor's degrees.[33] The survey's findings relative to the second generation's commitment to the Iranian community are discussed below. It is important to note that the small sample size will not warrant any definite conclusions.

The Second Generation's Degree of Attachment to the Iranian Community

One indicator of the second generation's attachment to its ethnic enclave is the extent of their participation in events organized by the Iranian community. Three types of activities were identified for this survey. First, the annual event in celebration of the Iranian New Year (NowRuz) usually takes place on or before March 21st in Iowa City, bringing most Iranian families and individuals together. This ancient secular "rites of spring" event is celebrated in two different nights, one organized by the first generation and the other by the second generation. Second, several traditional events of lesser importance are also observed by Iranians, mostly the first generation, such as Mehregan (fall harvest fest), and Yalda (observance of the year's longest night). Finally, there are private parties organized by families who mostly invite a select group of friends and relatives, and other parties organized by second generation individuals that cater to the younger generation. Second generation Iranians seem to be more attracted to all three types of events organized by their peers, but also desire to maintain their close ties with parents and other older members of the community by at least attending the annual new year's party. As one eighteen-year-old female respondent put it, "up until ninth grade I was encouraged and sometimes pressured by my parents to attend, but now I go on my own since all my friends are going too" (see Table 10.4).

Table 10.4 Second Generation's Level of Participation in Various Events organized by the Iranian Community (N=15)

Type of Event:	Never (#)	Rarely (#)	Sometimes (#)	Often (#)
Attend NowRuz parties organized by 1st generation	3	1	2	9
Attend NowRuz parties organized by 2nd generation	3		3	9
Attend Seezdah Behdar	1	1	3	4
Attend Mehregan	7	3	3	2
Attend Yalda night	6	2	3	4
Attend 1st generation parties	2	3	8	2
Attend 2nd generation parties	3	2	4	4
Attend PSO parties	2	1	3	9

Overall, second generation Iranians demonstrate a positive attitude toward their "Iranian" side and also have a positive perception of their Iranian identity. For instance, respondents were asked to rate changes in self-perception and others' perception of their "Iranian" ethnic identity, particularly in the aftermath of September 11 events. While nine respondents (out of fifteen) rated changes in their self-perception as "highly positive" or "positive," an equal number also indicated that changes in others' perception has been "highly negative" or "negative." In an earlier study of Iranian American communities Ansari (1992, 132) also observed the negative correlation between Iranians' self perception and others' perception of their ethnicity and its role in strengthening Iranian ethnic identity:

> The dialectically interrelated anti-western action in Iran and anti-Iranian reaction in America not only transferred the already available marginal identity to a much larger group, but also reinforced the development of a new community.

This remarkable boost in the second generation's self-perception despite an increased negative attitude toward their ethnicity is partly a reflection of their higher-than-average social class and hence their higher level of self-confidence. In a study of ethnic and racial identities of second generation black immigrants in New York City, Waters (1994, 803-804) identifies four factors that help the second generation develop a positive perception of their ethnic identity: a middle or upper class upbringing; attending better schools; parents' involvement in ethnic voluntary organizations; and a more stable family structure. As discussed earlier, all four factors apply to second generation Iranians.

Another indicator of second generation's attachment to their ethnic community is their level of socialization both within and outside the ethnic enclave. Survey findings indicate that close friendship relations are established with both Iranians and others alike. For instance, nine individuals (out of fifteen) reported having three or more Iranian "close friends," and equal numbers also indicated having close friendship ties with Americans of European origin.[34] Also of note, is considerably high number of close friends from among traditionally identified ethnic/racial minorities, such as African Americans, Asians, and Hispanics.[35] Although there are no indications of overt prejudice and discrimination on the part of European Americans against second generation Iranians, some respondents find themselves being closer to ethnic minorities on both cultural and political grounds. For example, a teenage male college student responded to have three or more close friends from among black and Asian Americans and yet none among Americans of European origin. When asked about the reasons during our interview, he was quick to mention that he has "a lot more in common" with the former and "differences in political views" with the latter.[36]

Despite respondents' clear interest in, and attachment to tradition and events organized by the Iranian community, their ethnically diverse network of close friends speaks of their undifferentiated attitude in socialization that is not bound by their parents and tradition.[37] This desire and ability to expand their social network is also manifested in their future plans and intentions once they are graduated. For instance, ten individuals in the sample indicated that they will "definitely not" stay in Iowa City after graduation, and only two individuals (both females) responded that they will remain in the area only if "they find a desirable job." Furthermore, when asked for reasons from those who intend to leave Iowa, the majority indicated they desire to move to larger cities in order to have access to more cultural events. Half the respondents also wanted to move to larger cities that have higher concentration of Iranians. Finally, related to job opportunities, only two individuals believed that there is a shortage of available jobs in Iowa, and yet eight responded they will go where the job opportunities take them.[38] This desire to "move on" is best expressed in a farewell letter written by a second generation Iranian and long-time Iowa City resident to all "dear friends" before leaving Iowa City for Chicago in early 2005:

> I just got a job offer in Chicago, although I enjoyed living in Iowa City, but I felt like it is time to move on! Maybe Helen Keller was right when she said "life is either a daring adventure or nothing." . . . I moved to Iowa City almost 20 years ago and have worked for the University of Iowa Hospitals and Clinics for over 15 years, but what I did not expect was meeting so many kind, sweet, warm and passionate people (and I had no family members in this country therefore you were my family) (Rasteh, 2005).

Extent of the Second Generation's Commitment to Tend to Their Aging Parent's Needs

The second generation's interest in sustaining the Iranian community in the Iowa City hub was examined by measuring their desire to remain close with their parents, as well as their commitment to take care of them once their parents have retired. Only eleven respondents in the sample had their parents in the area, and none of them indicated that staying close to parents is a "very important" concern. Furthermore, while three individuals felt it is "important" to be with their parents, four respondents considered the issue as "not important." Yet all eleven individuals responded that they are "fully committed" or "committed" to look after their aging parents despite their desire to move elsewhere. During my interviews with several respondents it became clear that all are very close to their parents and quite passionate about their well-being, and a female respondent expressed her disdain even about the thought of "leaving her aging parents behind in a nursing home" in the future.

The contradictory nature of the two sets of responses above can be partially explained by another finding during the interviews, as five individuals (out of eleven whose parents were residing in Iowa City) predicted their parents will also leave Iowa City either immediately after their children have left or right after their retirement. Another partial explanation is parents' overall economic security and higher-than-average socio-economic status that may have influenced the second generation's opinion on this issue.[39] All things considered, it is clear that second generation Iranians are both capable and willing to leave their parents and the Iowa City community behind in search of better jobs or a more enriching urban and social environments. More than a decade ago in his study of the formation of Iranian communities in the United States Ansari (1992, 133) predicted that a "rapidly Americanizing" second generation ". . . will probably only last for one generation." Although the very small sample size prevents us from making any definite conclusions, looking at the second generation's overall levels of community attachment and commitment to parents, it can be argued that this small Iranian-American community has a limited chance, if any, of a long-term and sustained inter-generational survival.

Conclusion

A quarter century has passed since the 1979 Iranian revolution, and the Iranian immigrants who chose the United States for their final destination have formed ethnic communities of variable size in most states including Iowa. Notwithstanding the remarkable achievements and indications that Iranian immigrants are fast approaching the stage of permanency in the United States, there are signs that limited availability of economic and career opportunities in small urban communities such as Iowa city has not been conducive to the sustenance of a multi-generational Iranian community, as evidenced by out-migration of the second generation members in their pursuit of career and socio-cultural objectives. In addition, with the majority of first generation Iranians reaching retirement age, and given the strong cultural and emotional ties between first generation immigrant parents and their offspring, the long-term viability of this immigrant community is seriously questioned. As I indicated earlier, in my first study of first generation Iowa City Iranians 52 percent of men and 47 percent of women identified "social isolation and loneliness" as the second most pressing social problem facing Iranians in the United States, making out-migration of second generation individuals even more problematic (see Chaichian 1997, 625).[40] Although limited in scope, survey findings and interviews with second generation members indicate that their eventual departure will most likely be followed by out-migration of at least part of first generation Iranian families who will follow their offspring to new destinations. Thus the Iowa City Iranian community's uncertain future is not because of first generation's lack of commitment and resolve. Rather, it is the second generation's understandable desire to pursue its long-term objectives beyond the confines of this small metropolitan enclave that will eventually undermine the long-term stability of this Iranian American community in small town America. The reader is cautioned, however, that due to the study's small sample size and higher-than-average levels of income and education for first and second generation Iowa City Iranians, the findings in this case study may not be applicable to other Iranian American communities.

Notes

1. Iowa City is a moderate-sized university town that is home to the largest concentration of this ethnic group in the state of Iowa.

2. Male/female responses to these issues were 68 percent and 60 percent for the former, and 52 percent and 47 percent for the latter, respectively (Chaichian, 1997, 624).

3. A total of 224,456 Iranians immigrated to the United States during the 1975-1993 period (Modarres 1998).

4. Based on INS data for the 1983-1993 period. The respondent pool included both newly arrived Iranians as well as those who adjusted their non-immigrant status to immigrant.

5. This includes both Iran-born immigrants as well as those who were born to (one or both) Iranian parents in the United States.

6. Census data show Johnson County where the University of Iowa is located, and Story County with Iowa State University in Ames as its main center of urban population, were among top five counties for net population gain overall. Other counties were Dallas, Jasper, and Linn (Jordan, 2003).

7. I am grateful to Ali Rezai, an active board member of the Iranian Cultural Association of Iowa (ICAI) for providing me with valuable information about ICAI membership (see Table 3).

8. Readers are cautioned about my peculiar relationship with many members of this ethnic immigrant community which is based on close interaction, friendship, and socialization, definitely affecting my "objectivity" in conducting research. However, some social scientists also recognize the benefits gained by the researcher's immersion in the social environments they are studying, or what is referred to as "insider understanding" (see for example, Lofland and Lofland 1995:61).

9. I am indebted to Sahar Kashef, PSO's President, without whose support this project would not have been possible. I would also like to express my gratitude to Marilyn Murphy, Director of Library Services at Mount Mercy College who designed and administered the questionnaire for electronic dispatch and data collection.

10. It is important to note that although I use the term "Iranian" in its generic form, it does not imply that any community of "Iranian" ancestry is a homogeneous one. Iran is a diverse, multi-ethnic society with at least eight major ethnic groups that have a long history of interaction not devoid of socio-economic and political conflicts. Thus even a tiny "Iranian" ethnic community such as the one in Iowa City is ethnically heterogeneous by nature.

11. See "About Iowa City" (http://www.icgov.org/aboutic.htm#madeof, accessed 20 March 2005).

12. See "2000 Community Profile for Iowa City: http://www.icgov.org/documents/demoinfo.pdf. (Accessed 20 March 2005).

13. According to a recent study conducted by the Iranian Studies Group (ISG) at MIT in Cambridge, MA, 26 percent of Iranian Americans have Master's degrees or higher. This compares with 61.6 percent for Iranian Americans residing in Iowa City (See "Iranian-Americans Among the Most Educated in the U.S.," http://www.payvand.com/news/03/oct/1169html . (Accessed 20 March 2005).

14. The following categories are based on my observation of intra-group relations among Iranians in Iowa City during the 1993-2005 period.

15. For instance, the number of "non-immigrant" Iranian students (holding F-1, J-1 and tourist visas) admitted to the University of Iowa declined from 33 in 1988 to 10 in

1994 (Data supplied to the Institute of International Education, "The Open Doors Survey: 1988-94," Office of International Education, the University of Iowa, Iowa City, Iowa).

16. In a pioneering study of the process of dual marginality among first generation Iranian professional immigrants, Ansari (1975) calls this group "settlers" or "Persian Yankees," who were receptive of the host society's cultural values and had made up their minds to stay.

17. It has to be noted that some members of this small subgroup received scholarships from the Iranian Government and allegedly refrained from socializing with other secular Iranians on the assumption that secularists do not sympathize with the Iranian Government and Islamic movement in Iran. Thus partly on religious and partly on ideological grounds, this small group of Iranians dissociated itself from the larger immigrant community in town.

18. As a member of the Iowa City Iranian community I have had the privilege of an insider's view, that is based on both personal observation and evolving with other members of this immigrant community in the past thirteen years.

19. The median home value for whites and African Americans is calculated based on 2000 values ($144,458 and $133,147, respectively), assuming an average 3 percent rate of inflation/year.

20. Their model is based on a critique of both "assimilationist" and "pluralist" models, the former assuming a two-stage housing pattern of clustering-dispersion for immigrants depending on their level of assimilation, and the latter conceptualizing the formation of a "spatial mosaic" of ethnic enclaves in metropolitan areas (see Zelinsky and Lee 1998, 282-285).

21. In 2004 census tracts 11, 16 and 21 were all areas of concentrated poverty, where "greater than or equal to 40 percent of the population lived at poverty level." See Scattered Site Housing Taskforce (2004).

22. The Dissimilarity Index (D), measures whether one particular group is distributed across census tracts in the same way as another group; and the Exposure Index (P) refers to the racial/ethnic composition of the tract where the average number of a given group lives.

23. For instance, in the year 2000 residents of Mexican ancestry comprised 1.42 percent of city's population (1,581 individuals) yet they resided in census tracts whose Mexican ancestry population was on average two percent of the total. The dissimilarity index for Mexican ancestry versus the non-Hispanic white population was 28, a fairly low index (Hispanic Population and Residential Segregation: Iowa City, Census 2000).

24. In the 2005 survey of second generation Iranians I did not ask about housing discrimination.

25. However, 47 percent of respondents reported being discriminated against "all the time" or "sometimes" in seeking employment (N=40).

26. On this issue see also Ansari (1992, 136).

27. Despite its successful start and enthusiastic support by both parents and children, the Sunday Farsi school was discontinued after two years, mostly due to a growing resistance by students (second generation).

28. An interesting emerging pattern is increasing participation of non-Iranians in these festivities. For example, of the 160 participants in the 2005 Noruz party 48 guests were non-Iranians, mostly friends and/or relatives of American spouses, including 40 native Iowans of "European origin," 7 Afghanis, and one Iraqi immigrant.

29. Most communication among ICAI members is done via e-mail, and the association maintains a website that is kept up-to-date by one of the ICAI board members (see http://iowairan.com).

30. Personal interview with Abbas Rezayazdi, ICAI's president, 23 March, 2005, Iowa City, Iowa.

31. Johnson County is home to the University of Iowa and its affiliated teaching hospital and clinics. Two private colleges, Mount Mercy and Coe, and Kirkwood Community College, are located in Linn County.

32. I am greatly indebted to the following members of the Iranian-American community for their willingness to be interviewed and sharing their insights on this issue with me: Yashaar Chaichian, Mariam Hafezi, Ali Jabbari, Sarvenaz Jabbari, Diana Mina, Rose Rezai, and Idean Vasef.

33. This corresponds with the national average for Iranian Americans. See the ISG report: http://www.payvand.com/ news/03/oct/1169htm.

34. This is in sharp contrast with first generation Iranians' socialization outside the ethnic enclave. In an earlier study of first generation Iranians in Iowa City (Chaichian 1997, 622), I reported that about half the respondents reported to have "close American friends." But during personal interviews it became clear that most of their close "American" friends were those of non-European origin.

35. Out of a total of fifteen, ten respondents reported having one or more African American, six having Hispanic, and twelve having Asian American "close friends."

36. Based on the 2000 census data, the three ethnic/racial minorities comprise five, seven, and four percent of Iowa City-Coralville hub's population, respectively. See *The 2000 Community Profile for Iowa City,* http://www.icgov.org/documents/demoinfo.pdf. (accessed 20 March 2005).

37. It is important to note that most, but not all parents of second generation Iranians reside in the Iowa City area.

38. Also of note is the second generation Iranians' positive experience in Iowa city, as none of those who intend to leave indicated that they are leaving Iowa in order to escape from prejudice and discrimination aimed at Iranians.

39. Of the eleven respondents whose parents are in Iowa City area, four identified their parents' social class as "upper class" and the rest considered them as "middle class." For the Iowa City first generation Iranians' socio-economic status also see Chaichian (1997, 615-16).

40. The first pressing issue was "adjustment to American society."

References

Anasari, Ma'boud. 1975. "A Community in Process: The First Generation of the Iranian professional Middle Class Immigrants in the United States." *Internatonal Review of Modern Sociology* 7:85-101.

———. 1992. *The Making of the Iranian Community in America.* New York: Pardis Press.

Bozorgmehr, Mehdi. 1998. "From Iranian Studies to Studies of Iranians in the United State. *Iranian Studies* 31(1):5-30.

Bozorgmehr, Mehdi, and George Sabagh. 1987. "Are the Characteristics of Exiles Different from Immigrants? The Case of Iranians in Los Angeles." *Sociology and Social Research* 71:77-84.

Chaichian, Mohammad. 1997. "First Generation Iranian Immigrants and the Question of Cultural Identity: The Case of Iowa." *International Migration Review* 31(3):612-627.
Conzen, Kathleen N. 1979. "Immigrants, Immigrant Neighborhoods, and Ethnic Identity: Historical Issues." *The Journal of American History* 66(3):603-615.
Foley, Donald L. 1950. "The Use of Local Facilities in a Metropolis." *American Journal of Sociology* 56:238-46.
Fried, Marc. 1963. "Grieving for a Lost Home," Pp. 151-71 in *The Urban Condition*, edited by Leonard Duhl. New York: Basic Books.
Gilanshah, Farah. 1990. "The Formation of Iranian Community in the Twin Cities from 1983-1989." *Wisconsin Sociologist* 27(4):11-17.
Jordan, Erin. 2003. "Iowa is Next to Last in Keeping College-Educated Young People." *Des Moines Register*, November 20.
Lieberson, Stanley. 1963. *Ethnic Patterns in American Cities*. New York: Basic Books.
Lofland, John, and Lyn H. Lofland. 1995. *Analyzing Social Settings: A guide to Qualitative Observation and Analysis*. Belmont, CA: Wadsworth.
Meskoob, Shahrokh. 1992. *Iranian Nationality and the Persian Language*. Washington, D.C.: Mage Publishers.
Modarres, Ali. 1998. "Settlement Patterns of Iranians in the United States." *Iranian Studies*, 31(1):31-49.
Morrison, Jeff. 2004. "Refusing to Join the Exodus from Iowa." *Iowa State Daily*, April 22.
Moslehi, Shideh. 1984. *Iranian-e-Burun Marzi v Nemoune-ye Angelesian* (Iranians Abroad: the Case of Los Angeles). Los Angeles: Ketab Corporation (in Persian).
Rasteh, Mehdi. 2005. *A Farewell Letter*. http:// iowairan.com/ page1/ default.htm, retrieved February 6, 2005.
Scattered Site Housing Taskforce. 2004. Taskforce Minutes, City of Iowa City, November 8, retrieved March 21, 2005.
U.S. Bureau of the Census. 1993a. *1990 Census of Population: Social and Economic Characteristics, Iowa*, CP-2-17, Table 137, P. 183. Washington, D.C.: U.S. Government Printing Office.
———. 2000. *Census of Population and Housing, 2000:* Hispanic Population and Residential Segregation: Iowa City MSA. http://mumford1.dyndns.org/cen2000/HispanicSeg/HspSegData/3500 msa.htm, retrieved March 22, 2005.
———. 2000. *Census of Population and Housing, 2000:* Summary File 3, Tables PCT 15 & 18. Washington, D.C.: U.S. Dept. of Commerce..
Waters, Mary. 1994. "Ethnic and Racial Identities of Second Generation Black Immigrants in New York City." *International Migration Review* 28(4):795-819.
Yancey, William, Ericksen, Eugene; and Richard Juliani. 1976. "Emergent Ethnicity: A Review and Reformulation." *American Sociological Review* 41(3):391-402.
Zelinsky, Wilbur, and Lee, Barrett. 1998. "Heterolocalism: An Alternative Model of the Sociospatial Behaviour of Immigrant Ethnic Communities." *International Journal of Population Geography* 4:281-298.

Chapter 11

The Untraditional Geography of Hispanic Settlement in a New South City: Charlotte, North Carolina

Heather A. Smith

There is a growing awareness among geographers that traditional patterns of Hispanic migration and settlement in the United States are changing. Over the 1990-2000 decade, Hispanics/Latinos emerged as the largest and fastest growing minority group in the country, increasing from 22.4 million to 35.3 million persons.[1] An unexpected feature of this growth has been a growing Hispanic presence in areas of the country previously bypassed by non-Anglo immigrant streams. While states with already long established Hispanic populations continued to experience growth over the decade, a number of states in the traditionally bi-racial South experienced sudden and substantial influxes of Hispanic residents. North Carolina, for example, experienced a 386 percent jump in its Latino population between 1990 and 2000.

While the story of Hispanic settlement in North Carolina is in no small part a function of opportunities in the state's rural based economies where migrant labor as early as the late 1970s and 1980s could find frequent, lucrative and sometimes permanent work in agricultural fields and food processing plants, by the early 1990s a growing proportion of the state's Hispanics were clearly gravitating to urban centers (Cravey 1997; Johnson et al. 1999; Johnson-Webb and Johnson 1996; Fink 2003; Johnson-Webb 2003). Between 1980 and 2000 the metropolitan areas of Raleigh, Greensboro and Charlotte each experienced rates of Hispanic population growth of about 1,000 percent, leading them to be classified as three of the top five Hispanic "hypergrowth" cities in the nation

(Suro and Singer 2002). Such remarkable growth is linked not only to the evolution of finance, business services and high tech economies in these cities but also to the range of industrial and agricultural opportunities available in their broader urban regions. These are cities in which Hispanic migrants, both native and foreign born, can tap into opportunity structures across the occupational spectrum and in which healthy economic growth minimizes the risks of failure and possibly mitigates conflict with already established groups. Still, the rapid insertion of Hispanic populations into once non-Latino cities raises challenging issues for historically bi-racial and nativist communities who must deal with the new economic, social, cultural and spatial realities Hispanic immigrants initiate as they establish themselves in their new urban environments. There is also, of course, the experience of immigrants themselves. The migration and settlement experiences of immigrants to cities in North Carolina is likely to differ from that experienced in cities with social, institutional, cultural and economic infrastructures already developed by waves of previous immigrant groups.

This chapter charts the untraditional and evolving geography of Hispanic in-migration and settlement in Charlotte, North Carolina, a city in which the officially charted Hispanic population has grown by more than 614 percent over the course of the 1990s. Augmenting statistical data drawn primarily from the U.S. censuses and field observation detailing the city's changing Hispanic and broader cultural landscapes with a series of interviews conducted with both Latino and non-Latino community leaders and service providers, the chapter also assesses the complex issue of adjustment for both the receiving and arriving populations.[2]

The chapter will begin with a brief review of literature detailing traditional Hispanic immigrant settlement patterns in the United States focusing on how and why those patterns have altered in recent years. Paying particular attention to the experience of the Southeastern United States, the chapter will explore the temporal and spatial dynamics that have made this region an unexpected magnet for recent Latino settlement outside traditional settlement destinations. North Carolina's story of Hispanic growth will provide an important contextual bed for the case study analysis of Charlotte to follow which highlights not only the dynamics and dimensions of Latino settlement in the city but also the adjustment and integration challenges, cultural landscape transitions and service provision implications that have accompanied the unexpected and large scale arrival of Latinos in this very "new southern" city.

From Traditional to Non-Traditional Locations

Scholars increasingly frame the settlement patterns of immigrants in terms of traditional and non-traditional locations (Frey 2002; Frey 2003; Suro and Singer 2003; Singer 2004; Gozdziak and Martin 2005). Traditional settlement locations for Hispanics have concentrated in the urban and rural communities of the American Southwest, primarily in New Mexico, California, Arizona, and Texas.[3] Florida, New York and New Jersey have also served historically as states with large Latino populations. The 2000 Census, however, confirmed that throughout the 1990s the settlement patterns of Hispanics clearly broadened into non-traditional locations in the Midwestern and Southeastern United States (Brewer and Suthan 2001; Arreola 2004; Kandel and Cromartie 2004). While traditional settlement locations continued to experience the highest absolute growth in their Hispanic populations, their rates of proportional growth were outpaced by increases in states such as Georgia, Tennessee, North Carolina, South Carolina, Alabama and Mississippi, all of which experienced more than 200 percent increases in their Hispanic populations between 1990 and 2000. Given that Nevada was the only state outside of the southeastern region to experience Latino growth at a similar level, there can be no doubt that the American South has emerged as a non-traditional and growing location for Latino settlement (Brewer and Suthan 2001; Singer 2004; Smith and Furuseth 2006).

In their work exploring the changing geography of Mexican immigration to the US, Durand et al. (2000) emphasize that any analysis seeking to explain why migrants are shifting away from traditional and gateway locations must factor in political and economic changes that have occurred on both the sending and receiving side of the border. In the Mexican context, they cite the recessionary crisis of 1994 as encouraging the working age population to seek economic opportunities and a better life in America. Within the US, particular attention is paid to the implementation and effect of the 1986 US Immigration Reform and Control Act (IRCA) which is viewed as a critical institutional context encouraging newly documented Latinos to look beyond California and Texas and identify alternative locations in which to settle (Durand et al. 2000; Massey et al. 2002). In part an attempt to regulate and monitor the flow of undocumented immigrants into the country, the IRCA granted legal immigrant status to undocumented migrants able to prove continued residency in the US prior to 1982 and provided an official mechanism for the agricultural industry to hire temporary workers to address labor shortages. The granting of amnesty to more than 2.3 million Mexicans between 1987 and 1990 initiated a dramatic shift in the geography of settlement among Mexicans resident in the US at the time. As Durand et al. (2000) explain,

> (W)hereas illegal migrants generally seek to find and hold a steady job, avoiding mobility to minimize the risk of detection; newly legalized immigrants suddenly had full U.S. labor rights and lost their fear of arrest. Not only did they have the freedom to move, other changes provided them with strong incentives to do so, for the legalization occurred against a backdrop of new employer sanctions (for the hire of illegal workers), deteriorating economic conditions (especially in the cities of the southwest), and growing hostility

toward immigrants in California (and other traditional gateway states) (Durand et al. 2000, 9).

During the late 1980s many Mexican migrants left California and Texas and relocated to other states within the southwestern region such as New Mexico, Arizona and Colorado that had already established but smaller Latino communities. Many also gravitated to a broadening array of non-traditional Hispanic locations—Idaho, Utah, Oregon in the west, Kansas and Indiana in the Midwest and Georgia, North Carolina and the other states of the southeast (Murphy et al. 2001; Driever 2004; Millard and Chapa 2004; Gozdziak and Martin 2005; Smith and Furuseth 2006). Durand et al. (2000) show that "by the mid-1990s, nearly one-third of all Mexicans were settling somewhere other than gateway states" (11).

Kandel and Parrado (2004) show that in the southeast a significant component of Hispanic settlement has occurred in non-metropolitan areas and is linked to employment opportunities in industrial sectors such as poultry production, meat processing, carpet manufacturing and forestry where work conditions are less than desirable and pay is especially low. In the absence of sustainable levels of local labor, employers recruit specifically for Latino workers despite the risks involved in running afoul of immigration law should recruits be undocumented (Johnson-Webb 2003). In these non-metropolitan communities Hispanic migrants are able to escape the kind of labor market competition they encountered in traditional settlement locations and, as Kandel and Parrado (2004) point out, also avoid the pitfalls of city living (higher cost of living and lower quality of life). If migrants are undocumented, smaller or non-metropolitan communities in need of laborers may be ideal places in which to find a steady job and raise a family without raising suspicion. Indeed, much of the research exploring non-metropolitan Hispanic settlement in the southeast has noted the relative ease with which Latinos settle and are welcomed into the fabric of the community. As a general rule, the type of native versus foreign born discrimination and conflict characteristic of traditional gateways is not yet a *defining* feature of settlement and adjustment in these areas (Engstrom 2001; Studstill and Nieto-Studstill 2001; Fink 2003; Johnson-Webb 2003; Torres et al 2003; Kandel and Parrado 2004). As Hernández-León and Zúñiga (2001) demonstrate in their case study of Carpet City, Georgia, there is a stage-based process of arrival, settlement and permanent community formation in these new destinations that often begins with "trailblazing" young men. By way of traditional gateway locations, these young men arrive alone or with other young males to scout out the potential of a new destination. Over time these young men decide that non-traditional, southeastern rural places are sufficiently receptive and opportunity laden and relocate their partners and/or family from Mexico (or other Latin American originations) thus initiating the creation of a permanent newcomer community.

North Carolina

As has been the case in other southeastern states, considerable attention in North Carolina has focused on the settlement of large numbers of foreign born Latinos into communities that have no previous experience with culturally distinct and/or non-English speaking groups (Cravey 1997; Dale et al. 2001; Hernández-León and Zúñiga 2001; Fink 2003; Johnson-Webb 2003; Torres et al. 2003). For most of the twentieth century, North Carolina experienced little domestic or international in-migration. Indeed between the turn of the last century and the 1970s the state experienced net-migration losses with more people leaving than arriving. In this context, the racial balance within the state remained fairly stable, and social and economic relations were constructed around the long-standing black/white binary (Orr and Stuart 1999). By the 1980s, however, the state's migration patterns were adjusting with migration into the state exceeding natural increase as the largest component of population growth—especially on the part of African Americans coming from the de-industrializing northern and central states (Johnson-Webb and Johnson 1996). A smaller but no less significant component of migration into North Carolina was the arrival of Hispanics looking for work in rural based agricultural, food processing and textile industries. Both foreign and American born, documented and not, young male Hispanics began arriving in growing numbers. In their study of Hispanic newcomers in the state, Johnson et al. (1999) found that between 1985 and 1990 most Latino migrants came to North Carolina by way of the traditional settlement states of California, Texas, Florida and New York. These states contributed to North Carolina's population between 2,600 to 15,000 Hispanic persons each. A smaller number of Hispanic migrants to North Carolina (8,873) arrived directly from a foreign country. These migration streams contributed to an overall increase in the state's Latino population from 56,667 in 1980 to 76,726 in 1990.

The greatest numeric and proportional increases in North Carolina's Hispanic population, however, have occurred since 1990 and have been centered not only on those rural communities that acted as the state's first internal gateways but also on the state's largest cities.[4] By 2000 the number of Hispanics in North Carolina had increased substantially to reach a total of 372,964 persons. As described above, the IRCA played an important role in accelerating the pace of Latino settlement in the state over the late 1980s and early 1990s. For North Carolina where demand for temporary workers to plant seedlings and harvest crops was (and continues to be) high, the IRCA facilitated the hiring of a steady stream of Hispanic temporary laborers (through the H2A program) who quickly realized that when the agricultural season was over, work could be found in any number of poultry, seafood, hog and textile plants across the state. And, if Latinos were so inclined, even broader opportunities could be found in the state's cities.

Throughout the 1980s and 1990s North Carolina's major urban areas—Raleigh, Durham, Greensboro and Charlotte—all experienced significant growth in their Hispanic populations. Linked together by what is referred to as the I-85 corridor these cities not only house the state's largest urban populations but also its most significant concentrations of job growth and economic development (Johnson-Webb and Johnson 1996; Orr and Stuart 1999; Bailey 2005). It is not surprising, then, that the state's most recent waves of Latino growth and community development have been centered in its major cities.

Of 18 metropolitan areas across the nation designated by the Brookings Institution as Hispanic hypergrowth, Raleigh, Greensboro and Charlotte all emerged as ranked within the top five (Suro and Singer 2002).[5] While Raleigh experienced 1,180 percent growth in its Hispanic population between 1980 and 2000, Greensboro experienced a 995 percent increase and Charlotte a 932 percent increase. In the Charlotte case, the vast majority of that growth occurred over the 1990s—614 percent to be precise. The balance of this chapter focuses on the character, causes and geography of Latino settlement in the City of Charlotte and pays particular attention to the challenges and opportunities of adjustment on the part of both new and more established residents as the cultural landscapes around them transition and re-define what it means to be Charlottean.

The Emergence of a Hispanic Hypergrowth City

Between 1990 and 2000, the City of Charlotte's Hispanic population rose from 5,571 to 39,800, representing a growth in population representation of 1.4 percent to 7.4. While these figures rank far below absolute and proportional thresholds for gateway cities, in this traditionally black/white city the arrival of a rapidly growing Hispanic population has been accompanied by a significant diversification of the city's population, a transformation of its economic, cultural, social and political landscapes and a process of adjustment on the part of both the Latino community and the predominantly bi-racial community in which it is embedded. Quite clearly, "Charlotte (today) is no longer the Black and White city it used to be" (Martin 2002).

It is important at this juncture to stress that while the statistics used in this chapter's analysis are drawn largely from the U.S. Census Bureau, leaders and Latino representatives in the City of Charlotte consistently emphasize that these numbers fall considerably short of actual population counts. Citing the number of undocumented immigrants resident in the city, the reluctance of many persons, even if documented, to answer the personal questions of census takers, and the hidden and/or transient nature of many sub-communities within the Latino population, many interviewees in this research argued that more realistic counts would likely double the official numbers. Many among Charlotte's Latino leadership cite a more realistic figure of 70,000 to 80,000 persons (Ortega 2004; Hernandez-Paris 2004; Villamarin 2004).

Two theories commonly explain the reason immigrants are drawn to particular locations—social networks (often accompanied by the presence of ethnic enclaves) and economic opportunity. We have already seen in this chapter that in North Carolina's rural context economic opportunity is prioritized, with social networks developing once a decision is made on the part of multiple individuals to settle in a place more permanently and begin the process of family and community building. Using Charlotte as our example a similar pattern seems to hold in the state's cities as well.

Prior to the significant upswing in Hispanic population growth in the early 1990s, Charlotte's Latino population was relatively small (3,091 persons in 1980 and only 5,571 in 1990) and skewed towards established and middle- to upper-class residents of Euro-Latin descent, either American born or hailing from South American countries of birth (Hernández-Paris 2004; Ortega 2004). Networks existed but they were loose and largely revolved around business interests rather than co-ethnic ties (Cooper 2004; Hernández-Paris 2004).

Figure 11.1 shows that in 1990 there were no clear concentrations of Latino settlement. The small Hispanic population resident in the city at that time was fairly evenly scattered with only one tract in the city showing a proportional concentration of Hispanics above 10 percent (tract 4) and only two others showing rates between 5 and 9.9 percent. While the city's average proportion of Hispanic concentration across all census tracts was 1.3 percent, in tracts 7 and 17.00 Latinos represented 6.8 and 5.2 percent of the population respectively. While it is true that these tracts are not contiguous, the map obscures the fact that they are loosely bound together by a series of tracts with levels of Hispanic proportional representation of at least twice the city-wide average (above 2.6 percent). Still, given the very small number and proportions of Hispanics in these tracts, the presence of an already established residential enclave cannot be claimed (a fact supported by the interviewees). It appears, then, that at least in the early 1990s neither a preexisting enclave nor an established social network between already settled Latinos acted as primary reasons drawing Hispanic newcomers.

A stronger draw came in the form of Charlotte's exploding and bifurcated economy which was reflected in a building boom both in the city's downtown core and throughout its suburbs and regional commuting sheds. Although anecdotal, the story told about the role played by the construction of a single office tower by at least three interviewees for this research is reminiscent of the point made by Durand et al. (2000) that we cannot understand migratory adjustments without understanding the dynamics of place in both receiving and sending locations. In Charlotte, its fortune as a city on the rise with a growing population, economy and reputation was paired in the early 1990s with growing controversy about immigrant rights, racial tensions and declining quality of life in the nation's traditional gateway cities and states.

The building of the Bank of America Headquarters between 1992 and 1993 is believed to have acted as a catalyst drawing to the city a sudden and large number of pioneering Hispanic young men. Crews on that project were contracted from Texas and were largely comprised of laborers of Mexican descent (Hernandez-Paris 2004). When the crews arrived in Charlotte, they discovered a city undergoing a commercial and residential building boom, a

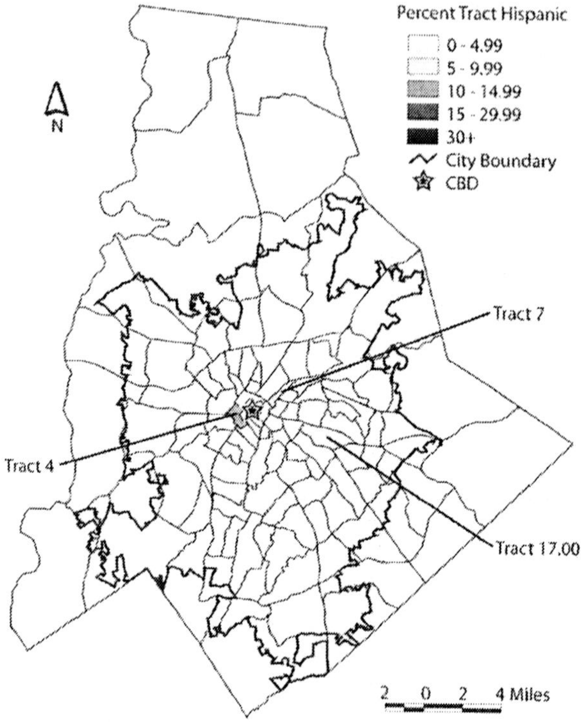

Figure 11.1 Percent of Tract Hispanic, 1990

climate that supported year round landscaping and construction work and a population unaccustomed to absorbing large, culturally different or ethnically distinct groups into their midst. Employers, interviewees noted, did not necessarily ask for immigrant documentation, rewarded those eager to work and did not seem to mind if laborers had nonexistent or limited English language skills. Beyond this, pay rates on construction jobs here were higher than in other states. Over the course of their work on the Bank of America project, many laborers established contacts with local construction companies and decided to stay (Cooper 2004). It was also noted that Charlotte's pro-business climate was particularly keen to welcome newcomers with entrepreneurial initiative. Charlotte, at least at first glance, had a comparatively welcoming and open milieu into which Hispanics could settle themselves with relative ease.

Following the longstanding tradition of immigrant trail-blazing, many young men whose first embarkation point in the United States had been the American southwest, relocated to Charlotte to "test the water"—establish whether it was a place where steady work could be found, determine the balance of remuneration and cost of living and assess whether it was a city from which to move on or to where families could be raised and communities formed. In many cases the young men decided to stay and very quickly, interviewees emphasized, a form of transnational commuting developed especially among those without official U.S. resident or immigrant status (Ortega 2005; Villamarin 2004; Cooper 2004). When asked to describe the experience of Hispanics in Charlotte in the mid 1990s, interviewees spoke about a cycle in which young men would live and work in Charlotte for several months (often sharing accommodation and living costs with one another), and then travel home to Mexico for an extended period each year. This return to home most commonly took place in the months immediately surrounding Christmas when both construction and landscaping work experienced a lull or hiatus and an extended trip didn't jeopardize future job placement (Ortega 2004).

While the Bank of America story marks a rising tide in the pace and the scale of Latino settlement in Charlotte in the early 1990s, it is important to take a brief step back and recall that migrants already resident in other locations within the state were also looking to Charlotte as a place in which a better life could be built. The increasing number of Latinos drawn to North Carolina's rural communities throughout the 1980s by agricultural opportunities in the tree, tobacco and fruit industries, and job availability on hog farms and poultry processing plants also began to see broader and perhaps more lucrative opportunity in the burgeoning construction and landscaping trades centered in Charlotte and the state's other expanding cities.

In Charlotte, the small stream of internal rural to urban migrants were augmented by Latinos who by the early 1990s had re-evaluated earlier settlement decisions and relocated to Charlotte after having spent time in other U.S. cities. By the turn of the century, this group was joined by a growing number of Latinos arriving directly from Latin America as social networks and word of mouth quickly spread that Charlotte was an attractive place to live across a range of criteria. The 2000 Census shows that while 3.3 percent of Charlotte's Hispanic population over the age of five years resided in a North Carolina county other than Mecklenburg in 1995, 24.6 percent lived in another state and 37.7 percent lived outside the United States entirely. Thirty-four percent of the city's Hispanics over five years were resident in the same Charlotte based county (Mecklenburg) in 1995.

Figure 11.2 shows the residential distribution of the City of Charlotte's Hispanic population across census tracts as of 2000. Immediately apparent when comparing this map to 1990 (see Figure 11.1), is the phenomenal growth of this population over the decade and its suburban presence radiating out from those tracts with higher than average Latino representation in 1990.

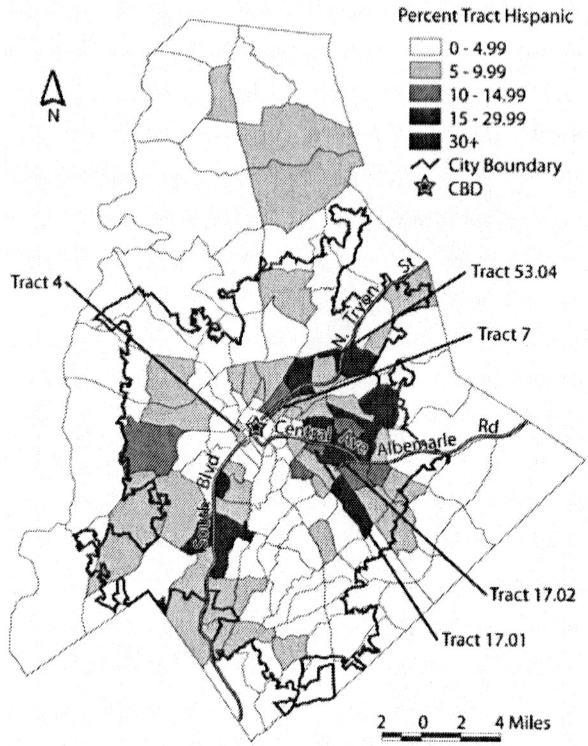

Figure 11.2 Percent of Tract Hispanic, 2000

The Cultural and Economic Landscape of Charlotte's Hispanics

Throughout the 1990s, Charlotte's Latinos clustered in three broad suburban districts—one in Northeast Charlotte centered on North Tryon Street, a second in East Charlotte focused around Central Avenue and a third in Southwest Charlotte following South Blvd. While in different parts of the city, these districts share similar development stories and common land use dynamics. At the center of all three are small collections of tightly bound census tracts where Hispanics represent more than 15 percent of the tract population. Phelan and Schneider (1996) establish the 15 percent threshold as defining a community with significant minority group representation. In their work looking at race, ethnicity and class in American suburbs, a Hispanic/multi-ethnic suburb is a community with more than 15 percent Hispanic residents. Only one census tract (number 53.04 lying in the northeast area) with a Latino population of 44.7 percent, comes close to meeting the higher benchmark set by Lobo, Flores, and Salvo (2002), wherein a census tract must have at least 50 percent Hispanic residents to be classified as a Hispanic neighborhood. Interviews with community leaders confirm the expectation though that while officially no majority Hispanic tract has emerged in Charlotte, the reality is that a number of Latino majority tracts do exist and are found in the core areas of each of the three clusters. Together the boundaries of the three broad areas encapsulate the residential location of more than 75 percent of the city's total Hispanic population.

Historically, these areas were targets of residential suburbanization as early as the 1960s. Following a distinctive sectoral model along major thoroughfares, neighborhoods in these areas were built to satisfy the middle class, White, single detached, single family housing market (Hanchett 1998). Small-scale businesses serving nearby residents occupied strip commercial centers and particularly along Central Avenue and South Blvd. amenity oriented multi-family apartment complexes were spread out along the arterial roadways. North Tyron Street was more heavily commercial.

Over the 1970s and 1980s as continuing suburbanization pulled new growth to peripheral green field sites, these areas attracted a growing number of middle income African Americans and the businesses, retailers and service facilities that met their needs and preferences. As the districts continued to age and face competition from newer development in the outer suburbs, by the 1990s middle class whites and blacks had both begun to move away from these areas towards the expanding and more affluent periphery. Into the growing number of vacant apartments, for-lease offices, and depreciating properties, stepped an increasing number of Hispanic households and business enterprises.

When interviewees were asked why these suburban areas were attractive to Latinos coming to the city in the early 1990s, they cited in priority order the abundance of available, affordable and flexible housing, proximity to public transit, and centrality to the job opportunities across the urban region (Smith and Furuseth 2004). While none of the clusters is the site of, or immediately adjacent to, the city's major employment hubs or rapidly growing edge cities, all three are well served by public transit and in the case of the southwest and east clusters are characterized as walkable based upon pedestrian accessibility to retailing and services (City of Charlotte 2002).[6] These particular attributes are especially important to a population that has limited funds for private transportation. The clusters are also positioned around three of the city's major roadways (Central Avenue, Tryon Street and South Blvd.) which cross-cut the city and link the center to its outlying urban/rural fringe—particularly important given the fluid work arrangements of many Latinos who, say, might one month work in the poultry processing plants on the city's outskirts and then the following month on a construction site in the downtown core. The three districts are also the sites of significant concentrations of aging multi-family rental housing. That landlords compete for tenants in a market that has frequent turnover and vacancies contributes to an environment that respondents describe as flexible and anonymous—attractive features for a young, pioneering and increasingly undocumented immigrant population.

Interviewees also spoke about the importance of a visible landscape of opportunity and community in attracting Latinos to these areas for settlement. While we have already established that identifiable Latino neighborhoods and tightly bound co-ethnic social networks did not exist in the city in 1990, both were very quickly established once increasing numbers of Latinos began arriving in the city around 1993-1994. Within each of the districts, Spanish language billboards quickly sprouted up along major roadways to advertise Latino products and services and, in some cases, jobs. Latino stores and businesses clustered into the previously vacant units in the strip malls and office buildings. Parking lots became sites for weekend markets and weekday pick up points for workers shuttling to and from construction or landscaping job sites. Spanish language signage advertising a month or two of free rent became, and remains, commonplace. Whereas Latino restaurants and grocery stores were rare a decade ago, there has been an explosion of such establishments since the mid 1990s. Indeed, recognizing growing competition from independent retailers catering to Hispanic clientele, a local Walmart built and stocked a dedicated wing with merchandise from Mexico, Central and South America (Hernandez 2004). The city's first Spanish language cinema opened in 2004 in the mall off Central Avenue and the local telephone book now has its own Spanish language yellow page section with a clear spatial skew towards businesses and services located in one of the three main settlement areas. Not surprisingly given the trajectory of the areas immediately prior to the Latino's arrival, interviews with city planners and community leaders, particularly those who have been in Charlotte for ten or more years, reveal a common belief that the arrival and clustered settlement of Hispanics along South Blvd. and Central Ave in particular has revitalized two areas of the city that might otherwise have fallen into decay and abandonment.

In addition to changes that have occurred within the suburban settlement clusters, the speed and impact of Charlotte's new Latino presence is also evidenced in the growing attention focused on Hispanics as a consumer group. Consider that in a span of less than ten years, Charlotte has become home to competing Spanish language radio stations and newspapers (Figure 11.3). *La Noticia*, the city's leading Spanish-language newspaper with a weekly readership of 91,000, has recently been joined by *Que Pasa*'s expansion into Charlotte from the Raleigh/Durham/Greensboro area. Arguing "that the Charlotte metro (area) is an underserved market in terms of quality Hispanic news, sports, entertainment, and information reporting" the President of the Hispanic Group which owns *Que Pasa* is also looking to buy a local radio station (Hispanic Business 2004). Furthermore, at least two residential sub-divisions have recently been developed with the Latino population specifically in mind. In addition to building near the Southwestern Hispanic cluster (so possible buyers would notice the development as they drove by), construction has involved a "tweaking" of design to meet the needs of first time home buying Latino families who often pool resources, live together with their extended family and thus require more living space. For the first time in their development history, Liberty Homes has offered a package that allows buyers to convert garage space into living space—most commonly an added bedroom and bath (Norwood 2004).

Demographic and Socio-Economic Integration of Charlotte's Hispanics

We turn now to a detailed profile of Latino Charlottean's demographic and socio-economic characteristics as reflected in the 2000 U.S. Census and local statistics provided by service agencies and government departments. As a generalization Charlotte's Hispanic population in 2000 was predominantly male and young, of Mexican descent and foreign born, poor with limited education and English language ability and occupationally concentrated in construction, production (assembly, textiles, furnishings) and general service trades in the food, cleaning and landscaping industries. Table 11.1 offers a statistical profile of this characterization and highlights how it compares with the City of Charlotte as a whole.

Reflective of the pioneering stage of settlement that still existed in the city as of 2000, 62.5 percent of Charlotte's Hispanics were male. That this figure was only 52.6 percent in 1990 and much closer to the rate for the city as whole at that time captures the trailblazing spirit of young Hispanic men arriving in the city from both domestic and foreign originations. However, anecdotal evidence drawn from interviews and informal discussions with community representatives stresses that the overwhelmingly male character of Charlotte's Latino population post 2000 has changed dramatically—particularly in the wake of 9-11 when community service providers and leaders began to see an increasing number of undocumented women and children among their community and client constituencies.

While a significant tightening of the U.S.-Mexican border and new enforcement practices targeting Latino males followed the passing of the 1990 Immigration Act, the 1996 Illegal Immigration Reform and Immigrant Responsibility Act and Operations "Blockade," "Gatekeeper," and "Hold the Line" in Texas and California (Massey et al. 2002), the safety and feasibility of transnational commuting is thought to have become even more challenging after the terrorist attacks of 9-11. Latino service providers in Charlotte noted that a growing number of their clients were sharing stories of paying increased fees to ensure safe passage and/or of having to travel to ever more obscure places in which to cross undetected. In this context, many Latinos began to reevaluate the wisdom of transnational commuting and prolonged absences from loved ones.

Anecdotal evidence of the growing number of women and children now present in the city is supported by locally derived data from the Charlotte Mecklenburg School Board which show a doubling of school enrollment for Hispanic students between 2000 and 2004. Whereas Hispanic children comprised only 4.5 percent of student enrollment in 2000, four years later that proportion had

Figure 11.3 Advertisement for Spanish Language Broadcasting along South Blvd. Charlotte, NC. Photo by Author.

jumped to 9.4 percent. Medicaid data drawn from the Mecklenburg County Department of Social Services also speak to this trend of family reunification and development among the city's Hispanic community, post-2000. Between 2000 and 2004, Medicaid assistance to Hispanic children grew by over 115 percent, from 4,078 to 8,788 cases.

It is important to note that these data are both a function of family formation and development among the city's more established Latino community as well as recent trends family reunification. Indeed, that the bulk of Charlotte's growing Hispanic community are within their prime child-bearing years harbingers even greater rates of increased population growth in the immediate future. As Table 11.1 details, in 2000, 54 percent of the city's Latino population was between fifteen and thirty-four years old, compared to only 37 percent for the city at large.

In addition to their youthfulness and the implications that this is having for already strained service infrastructures,[7] a growing concern of community leaders and service providers is that the Hispanic community in Charlotte is also increasingly poor. In 1990, 9.7 percent of the city's resident Hispanics fell below the poverty line. By 2000, that proportion had more than doubled, rising to 23.9 percent. Given that the citywide incidence of poverty in 2000 was 10.6, and that poverty rates for the city's black and white populations have been falling over the decade, there is clear cause for concern. That the majority of Charlotte's Hispanics are recent immigrants certainly plays a role in their poverty—the classic immigrant narrative is one of upward social mobility from a point of comparative deprivation—but there is also the fact that as of 2000, the city's Hispanic population showed high levels of very limited educational

Table 11.1 Statistical Profile of the City of Charlotte's Hispanic Population, 2000

	Number	Percent	City Comparison
Hispanic population male	24,712	62.0	48.9
Hispanic population between 15 and 35 years of age	21,560	54.2	37.0
Hispanic population of Mexican ancestry	22,168	55.7	NA
Hispanic population foreign born	28,037	70.0	11.0
Hispanic population below poverty level	9,483	24.0	10.6
Hispanic population 25 yrs + with less than 9th grade education	6,548	31.2	5.0
Hispanic population 5 yrs+ speak English less than very well	22,371	61.5	7.8
Hispanic population 15 years and over never married	13,449	42.7	32.7
Hispanic males above 16 years in construction, extraction, maintenance occupations	7,253	47.4	14.6
Hispanic males above 16 years in production, transportation and material moving occupations	3,020	19.7	15.7
Hispanic females above 16 years in service occupations (i.e. cooks, food preparation, building and grounds cleaning)	1,503	27.7	14.9
Hispanic females above 16 years in production occupations (i.e. textiles, furnishings, assembly)	1,048	19.3	5.0

Source: US Census Bureau, Census 2000, Summary Files 1 and 3.

attainment, minimal English language proficiency, and occupational concentration in low remuneration sectors and average household incomes that fell short of city wide averages. While only five percent of the citywide population over twenty-five years of age have failed to attain more than a ninth grade education, the figure for the city's Hispanics is 31 percent. In terms of language ability, 67.7 percent of Latinos report speaking English less than "very well." Officially, 47.7 percent of the city's Hispanic males are employed in construction, extraction and maintenance occupations. Unofficially, respondents suggest that the figure is as high as 80 percent. Although to a lesser degree, Hispanic women are also concentrated in occupations characterized by low pay. The census shows that 27.7 percent of the city's Hispanic females are employed in service occupations such as cooking, food preparation, building and grounds cleaning. That Charlotte's Latinos are comparatively poorer than the city population at large is reflected in the fact that their median household income for 2000 at $38,298 was only 81 percent of the city wide mean.

As has already been emphasized, the statistics reported here are those derived largely from the U.S. Census and as such only capture the component of the Latino population that was invited, able and willing to answer census takers' questions. Interviews with community leaders stress that the growing poverty among this group is particularly apparent among the most recent arrivals many of who are undocumented, young, of indigenous descent, and directly from rural backgrounds in their native countries. It is this group that they see as the most threatened by poverty and the most challenged in terms of adjustment and integration. Although not frequently repeated, interviews did reveal concern that this group experiences particular hardship adjusting to life in an American urban area—their rural Latin American backgrounds simply do not equip them to know how to immediately handle the vagaries, high density and complexity of city life. And, in some cases linguistic isolation—even in Spanish language contexts—contributed to the growing poverty levels among Latinos in the city. Among the newest arrivals the use of a native language other than Spanish or English and basic illiteracy are believed to be increasingly common.

Acculturation amid Cultural Diversity

One of the most overlooked features of Charlotte's Hispanic population is its ethnic diversity. While it is true that a considerable majority of the city's Hispanics are of Mexican descent (55.7 percent), this fact has tended to overshadow the experience and contribution of those Hispanics from other national backgrounds.

Table 11.2 details the city's Hispanic population by type. Collectively, Central Americans are the next largest Hispanic group in the city representing 12.6 percent of the Latino population. Following them are Caribbean groups representing 10 percent, and South Americans representing 6.9 percent. When these categories are broken down more specifically, the numeric dominance of Mexicans becomes even more apparent. Behind Mexicans, Puerto Ricans and Salvadorans are the most populous groups capturing only 6.1 and 4.8 percent of the Latino population. Following them are Hondurans, Cubans and Columbians representing 4, 2.8 and 2 percent respectively. Although in no way as numerically or proportionally dominant as the Mexicans, these other Hispanic groups have each experienced immigrant, settlement and/or adjustment processes differently and are leaving their own distinctive mark on the transition of Charlotte from a quintessentially bi-racial city to a more multi-cultural one. A case in point, although not a positive one, is the growing presence of youth gangs in the city. While portrayed in the media as generically Latino, these gangs are strongly associated with persons of Central American heritage (Couch 2004). Police representatives explain that gangs take root in Charlotte via two pathways. Either they are dispersed here from larger (read gateway) cities in the US or are established here on the part of the new arrivals coming from countries (i.e., El Salvador) where gang membership and its associated power are characteristics of everyday life. Either way, their presence is new for this city and illustrative of one of the ways in which Latinos are establishing themselves and securing some measure of personal/collective control over new lives in a new location.

While interviews did not reveal tensions between different Hispanics based on place of birth, they did reveal tensions based on time of arrival in the city and ancestry, particularly between Latinos of European descent (who represent the pre-established Hispanic power structure in the city) and those of indigenous descent. As one anonymous interviewee noted (Anonymous interviewee 2004a), "the established Latinos look down on new immigrants," concerned that they will erode the good standing they have worked to achieve in the city. Indeed, there seems to be unease that many of the city's most recent arrivals are among the indigenous and under-classes of their home countries. Notes another anonymous interviewee, "within the Latino community, levels of prejudice vary depending on where one is from" (Anonymous interviewee 2004b) and this can have powerful affects for the accessing of job openings, housing opportunities and involvement in community building initiatives. "It is not uncommon," it was emphasized, "for members of the established Latino community to advocate for the limiting of opportunity to new immigrants." There is an attitude of "now that I have made it, close the doors for those who follow'' (Anonymous Interviewee, 2004a).

As Driever's (2004) research in Kansas City illustrates, this kind of disunity between established and newly arrived Latinos is not unique to Charlotte. However, Driever focuses less on tensions based on ancestry and race and more on immigrant generation. It may well be that in the south, where racial constructs are a powerful historically entrenched avenue through which belonging and place-based citizenship are conferred, tensions between Latinos are taking on a distinctively regional flavor.

In the same way that the dominance of Mexicans has obscured the internal diversity of Latinos in the city, it has also drawn attention away from the fact that Charlotte is experiencing rising rates of in-migration from other international groups as well. Of Charlotte's 59,849 immigrants in 2000, 50.3 percent were from Latin America, 26.5 from Asia, 12.5 percent from Europe and 8 percent from Africa. These immigrants accounted for 11 percent of the city's total population and were overwhelmingly recent arrivals. Sixty-four percent arrived in the U.S. between 1990 and 2000, 45 percent after 1995. Profiling only the Hispanic population we see that they are predominantly (70 percent) foreign born with 56 percent arriving in the country between 1990 and 2000. Of the Hispanic foreign born, 27.9 percent were born in Mexico while 11.6 percent were born in the other countries of Central America. It should be noted that the increasing number and recency of arrival of the city's diverse immigrant population has led to Charlotte's metropolitan area being categorized as a pre-emerging immigrant gateway (Singer 2004).

Table 11.2 City of Charlotte's Hispanic Population by Type, 2000

	Number	Percent
Hispanic or Latino of any race by type	39,800	100.1
Mexican	22,168	55.7
Other Central American	5,001	12.6
Puerto Rican, Dominican and Cuban	3,985	10.0
South American	2,732	6.9
All other Hispanic and Latino	5,914	14.9
Mexican	22,168	55.7
Puerto Rican	2415	6.1
Salvadoran	1891	4.8
Honduran	1577	4.0
Cuban	1098	2.8
Colombian	835	2.1
Ecuadorian	800	2.0
Spanish	653	1.6
Dominican	472	1.2
Nicaraguan	459	1.2
Guatemalan	449	1.1
Peruvian	417	1.0
All Others	6566	16.5

Source: US Census Bureau, Census 2000, Summary File 1

In addition to the intra and inter group dynamics that frame their adjustment and acculturation experiences, Charlotte's Latinos must also navigate relationships that arise from their residential geography. Not emphasized in the discussion above, but apparent on the map in Figure 11.2, is the fact that the population in the *Latino settlement clusters* is still overwhelmingly black and (non-Hispanic) white. While interviewees also did not reveal tensions between newly arrived Hispanic and white residents in the clusters, they did allude to growing tensions between black and Hispanic residents. When asked to describe this relationship, one interviewee said there was a "nervousness" between the two communities that stemmed from cultural misperception and insensitivity (Villamarin 2004). While there was animosity on the part of some blacks about perceived Latino encroachment into their neighborhoods and employment niches, and some fear on the part of Hispanics about victimization at the hands of blacks, outright tension was rare. Indeed, a representative of the Charlotte-Mecklenburg police department emphasized that given the rapid arrival and settlement pattern of Latinos, he was surprised that problems between groups were so minimal. In fact, he said, there is "very little infighting between the groups and tensions are in no way explosive" (Couch 2004). He offered that one possible explanation for the relatively minor social friction between blacks and Hispanics is the luxury of expansive space. In Charlotte, conflict over space and neighborhood territory may be mitigated by the fact that in this rapidly growing city with large swaths of green field development, there is always somewhere else for people to go. Simply put, if people don't like changes underway in their neighborhood, they move. Given new construction of housing units across the socio-economic scale, this mobility seems an option for all but the poorest citizens.

Still, the adjustment experience of Latinos in the city is undoubtedly affected by the relationships they establish with their residential neighbors and while relations between blacks and Hispanics in the city appear at the time of writing to be relatively calm, there is concern that this may change with downward adjustments in the economy (translating into growing job competition) and/or the envy that might come of improved socio-economic status among Latinos as they become more integrated into mainstream opportunity structures.

Adjustment for Latinos is also about the transitions and challenges they face within their own households. Interviews revealed concern about two recent issues arising from the growing trend towards family reunification and the increased presence of women among the city's Hispanic population. As one interviewee explained, when women arrive in Charlotte and begin the process of incorporating themselves and their children into everyday American life, shifts occur in the traditional dynamics families often observed while at home in Latin America. Once in Charlotte many women enter the labor market and begin to bring money into the family as wage earners and feel increasingly empowered and independent in the process. This "power shift" is not always embraced by husbands or partners, and Latino service and advocacy agencies have begun to see significant increases in domestic violence. Representatives of the medical community confirm this within their professional context and add that these domestic adjustments are also translating into increased mental stress (depression) on the part of Hispanic men who may perceive their wives and partners working as a failure on their part to provide for their families and a personal inability to make a success out of life in America.

Depression is also on the rise among Hispanic women. But in this case mental stress is often an adjustment outcome for newly arrived, undocumented and non-English speaking women who have come directly to Charlotte from rural (remote) places in Mexico and Central America. Once they arrive in the loud, busy, car-dependent and sprawling city, they can become quickly overwhelmed and isolated if they choose to cope by staying in their homes and limiting contact with outsiders.

Policy Aspects of Adjustment in Charlotte

Another element that frames the adjustment and acculturation experience of Charlotte's Latinos is the efforts made by the public sector, represented by local government agencies and service providers, who have quickly (and in some cases not so quickly) restructured their programs and service delivery procedures to meet the language and cultural needs of newly arriving Latinos. The Charlotte-Mecklenburg Police Department, for example, has established an International Relations Unit a primary focus of which is meeting the needs of the city's rapidly growing and frequently victimized Latino community. To assist with cultural integration, the city government has developed a series of Spanish language brochures that outline procedures for trash collection and utility payment as well as access to public transit and libraries. Charlotte Mecklenburg Schools (which have seen more than a 550 percent increase in their Latino student population since 1994) have hired a permanent translator to assist Spanish speaking parents enroll their children in school (Martin 2002).

Underneath the surface of ease with which Latinos to Charlotte seem to have settled in and been welcomed into the city thus far, lies a much more nuanced and complex adjustment experience on the part of both the receiving society and the Hispanics themselves. While it is true that some service agencies have been quick to respond to the Latino presence by providing bilingual and culturally sensitive outreach, they are doing so in the context of having to also provide services to their traditional constituencies. In an era of social service cutbacks and limited funding, providers increasingly struggle with the balance of where funds should be allocated. This can be a delicate and emotionally charged decision given the continued and very pressing needs of large components of the city's impoverished African American community.

Compounding this dilemma is a spatial mismatch between the location of established services meeting the needs of the city's poorest residents and the residential location of the city's fastest growing poverty population. Given the legacies of segregation, and that poverty in Charlotte has historically been concentrated among African Americans, many of the city's public and non-profit sector service agencies for the poor are located in the city's western and predominantly black neighborhoods. As Figure 11.2 illustrates, these areas are not the ones in which Hispanics are settling, yet as the statistics noted above show, as poverty rates for blacks in the city are falling, those for Hispanics are growing rapidly. Do providers leave facilities where they are and try to entice Latinos who need their services to travel across the city? While it is true that those areas with the most well integrated public transit correspond with the settlement clusters of Hispanics, service becomes less frequent and well integrated in the city's west suburbs. Alternatively, should the city close the facilities and relocate them to one of the three cluster areas of Latino settlement?

Adhering to its mandate to meet the needs of indigent and under-served populations, CMC relocated one of its family practice clinics into the eastern cluster of Hispanic settlement. Despite their location on Central Avenue and in the heart of a contiguous set of census tracts with comparatively high levels of Latino settlement, the clinic's patient base in no way reflected the Hispanic constituency it sought to serve even two to three years after the move (Dulin 2004). Through a process of research and dialogue with local Latino leaders, the clinic has come to recognize that location alone will not bring Hispanics through their doors. Without insurance many undocumented Latinos were previously utilizing hospital emergency rooms for care, or availing themselves of the services of lay healers familiar with approaches used in Mexico or Central America. At the most basic level, the clinic did not initially have a Spanish-speaking translator or staff person. Nor were there bilingual materials to assist patients with directions for care. And, given that the clinic did not have a pre-existing Hispanic patient base and did not advertise its presence in Spanish, word of mouth did not draw patients in. The clinic is now partnering with a neighborhood Latino service agency to conduct focus groups with Latino residents to determine how the clinic can adjust their practice and procedures to better and more sensitively meet the needs of the community it wishes to serve.

The pace of growth and the youth of Charlotte's new Latino population is a particular challenge for the school system. As noted above, the number of Latino students entering the Charlotte-Mecklenburg School System in the last several years has been staggering. These increases in a largely poor, linguistically challenged and not always stable population have come on the heels of the system's legally mandated cessation of racially based busing. There is also the issue in North Carolina that undocumented students cannot access in-state tuition breaks for post secondary education. Educators and community leaders are increasingly concerned about the disincentive for learning this situation places in front of young Latino students (Ortega 2004).

Conclusion

At first glance then, Latino migration and settlement in Charlotte has followed an uncommon path with migrants bypassing traditional gateways and coming to this New South city in increasing numbers. And, once here they have settled in loosely bounded clusters in the city's aging inner suburban ring. But the adjustment experience as relayed by the interviewees also reminds us that even in non-traditional locations, the age-old challenges of relationship building, access to and competition for services, cultural misunderstandings, and tensions between old and new populations still rear their heads. Whether the nuances of the adjustment process differ significantly in the context of a southern, pre-emerging immigrant gateway is the subject of future study, but at this juncture it seems fair to say that at least to some degree the experience of migration has some universal and timeless elements.

By charting the untraditional and evolving geography of Hispanic in-migration and settlement in Charlotte and touching upon the complexities of adjustment for both new and established communities, this chapter has hopefully shed light onto what might be a distinctive geography of Latino immigrant settlement in this city in particular and the transitioning south more broadly, and contributed to an evolving understanding of how and why traditional theories of immigrant settlement and process drawn from established gateway cities require continued reconsideration.

Notes

1. While the U.S. Census of Population and other government sources use Hispanic as the identifier for persons of Latin American ancestry, the term Latino is the preferred descriptor among members of this community. In this chapter the terms are used interchangeably and refer to persons of both male and female gender.

2. Interview participants were identified through a two stage snowball sampling process in which a small subset of key informants known to the researchers were invited for initial interview and then asked to identify others in both the Latino and non-Latino communities who could speak to issues of Hispanic settlement processes and outcomes in the Charlotte urban area. In total the project encompassed over forty interviews with representatives of city or county service agencies whose positions involved direct outreach to the Hispanic population (teachers, police officers, health care providers, social service workers, etc.) and leaders of non-profit and/or advocacy agencies also focused on meeting Latino needs. The initial set of interviews took place in late 2004, and are those cited specifically in this chapter. The second set of interviews took place in 2005, were conducted anonymously, and are used in this chapter primarily for the purpose of informing the analyses. All interviews were semi-structured with a small set of common questions focusing on the changing character of the city's Latino population and the challenges and opportunities that were presented by their recent large-scale arrival in the city.

3. In 2000, the U.S. Census Bureau showed New Mexico as having 42.1 percent its population of Hispanic ethnicity, California at 32.4 percent, Texas at 32 percent, Arizona at 25.3 percent, Nevada at 19.7 percent and Colorado at 17.8 percent. In Florida, Hispanics comprised 16.8 percent of the population while in New York and New Jersey, Hispanics represented 15.1 and 13.3 percent of the total state populations respectively.

4. High increases in Hispanic population growth have also been noted within North Carolina counties military bases such as Fort Bragg and Pope Air Force Base in Cumberland County and Camp Lejeune in Onslow County.

5. It is not insignificant in the context of this chapter that Atlanta, GA and Orlando, FL were the other two of the nation's top five "Hypergrowth" Latino Destinations. Suro and Singer (2002) show rates of increase in these cities over the 1980 to 2002 period of 995 and 859 percent respectively. Of the eighteen cities listed with rates of Latino population growth over 300 percent across the twenty years (the definition of a Hispanic hypergrowth metro), eleven, including Washington DC, are found in the Southeastern United States.

6. See Greene (1995) and Frey (2001) for analyses of suburbanization trends among immigrants and diverse ethno-racial groups.

7. Particular points of strain are the school and health care systems. Given that Latinos to Charlotte are settling in three broad suburban areas of concentration, Hispanic children stream into only a handful of neighborhood-based schools. That the school board confirmed its first majority Latino elementary school in 2003 is a sign of the staggering pace of transition faced. The health care system also cites strain (Dulin 2005) with significant challenges surrounding healthcare provision for children and expectant mothers as well overwhelming use of emergency rooms on the part of non-English speaking, uninsured patients seeking routine assistance (flu, colds, etc.).

References

Anonymous Interviewee. 2004a. Latina community worker. Interview with author, summer 2004.

Anonymous Interviewee. 2004b. Latina community worker/activist. Interview with author, summer 2004.

Arreola, Daniel D. 2004. "Hispanic American Legacy, Latino American Diaspora." Pp. 13-35 in *Hispanic Spaces, Latino Places: Community and Cultural Diversity in Contemporary America,* edited by Daniel D. Areola. Austin: University of Texas Press.

Bailey, Raleigh. 2005. "New Immigrant Communities in the North Carolina Piedmont Triad: Integration Issues and Challenges" in *Beyond the Gateway: Immigrants in a Changing America,* edited by Elzbieta M Gozdziak and Susan F. Martin. Lanham, MD: Lexington Books.

Brewer, Cynthia A. and Trudy A. Suthan. 2001. *Mapping Census 2000: The Geography of U.S. Diversity*, U.S. Census Bureau, Census Special Reports, Series CENSR/01-1. Washington, DC: U.S. Government Printing Office.

City of Charlotte. 2002. *Charlotte Neighborhood Quality of Life Study 2002.* Charlotte: City of Charlotte Neighborhood Development and Charlotte-Mecklenburg Planning Commission.

Cooper, Wayne. 2004. Honorary Consul of Mexico. Interview with author, August 4, 2004.

Couch, Chris. 2004. Head, International Relations Unit, Charlotte-Mecklenburg Police Department. Interview with author, July 30, 2004.

Cravey, Altha J. 1997. "The Changing South: Latino Labor and Poultry Production in Rural North Carolina." *Southeastern Geographer* 37(2):295-300.

Dale, Jack G, Susan Andreatta, and Elizabeth Freeman. 2001. "Language and the Migrant Worker Experience in Rural North Carolina Communities." Pp. 93-104 in *Latino Workers in the Contemporary South,* edited by Arthur D. Murphy, Colleen Blanchard and Jennifer A. Hill. Athens: The University of Georgia Press.

Driever, Steven L. 2004. "Latinos in Polynucleated Kansas City." Pp. 207-223 in *Hispanic Spaces, Latino Places: Community and Cultural Diversity in Contemporary America,* edited by Daniel D. Areola. Austin: University of Texas Press.

Dulin, Michael F. 2005. Family Physician, Eastland Family Practice, Carolinas Medical Center Department of Family Medicine. Interview with author, October 2004.

Durand, Jorge, Douglas S. Massey, and Fernando Charvet. 2000. "The Changing Geography of Mexican Immigration to the United States: 1910-1996." *Social Science Quarterly* 81(1):1-15.

Engstrom, James D. 2001. "Industry and Immigration in Dalton, Georgia." Pp. 44-56 in *Latino Workers in the Contemporary South,* edited by Arthur D. Murphy, Colleen Blanchard, and Jennifer A. Hill. Athens, GA: The University of Georgia Press.

Fink, Leon. 2003. *The Maya of Morganton: Work and Community in the Nuevo New South.* Chapel Hill: The University of North Carolina Press.

Frey, William H. 2001. *Melting Pot Suburbs: A Census 2000 Study of Suburban Diversity.* Washington, DC: The Brookings Institution, Center on Urban and Metropolitan Policy.

———. 2002. "U.S. Census Shows Different Paths for Domestic and Foreign-Born Migrants." *Population Today*, August/September:1-5.

———. 2003. *Metropolitan Magnets for International and Domestic Migrants.* Washington, DC: The Brookings Institution, Center on Urban and Metropolitan Policy.

Gozdziak, Elzbieta M., and Susan F. Martin. 2005. *Beyond the Gateway: Immigrants in a Changing America.* Lanham, MD: Lexington Books.

Greene, Richard. 1995. "Chicago's New Immigrants, Indigenous Poor, and Edge Cities." *The Annals of the American Academy of Political and Social Science* 55:178-190.

Hanchett, Thomas W. 1998. *Sorting Out the New South City: Race, Class and Urban Development in Charlotte, 1875-1975.* Chapel Hill: The University of North Carolina Press.

Hernández, L. 2004. "New Wal-Mart will cater to Hispanics." *News 14 Carolina Online*, www.news14charlotte.com.

Hernández-León, Rubén, and Victor Zúñiga. 2000. "'Making Carpet by the Mile': The Emergence of a Mexican Immigrant Community in an Industrial region of the U.S. Historic South." *Social Science Quarterly* 81(1):49-66.

Hernández-Paris, José. 2004. Executive Director, International House, Charlotte, NC. Interview with author, August 2004.

Hispanic Business. 2004. "*Que Pasa* Expands into Charlotte Metro." *Hispanic Business Online*, www.hispanicbusiness.com/news.

Johnson, James H., Karen Johnson-Webb, and Walter C. Farrell, Jr. 1999. "A Profile of Hispanic Newcomers in North Carolina." *Popular Government* 65(1):225-235.

Johnson-Webb, Karen. 2003. *Recruiting Hispanic Labor: Immigrant in Non-Traditional Areas.* New York: LBF Scholarly Publishing.

Johnson-Webb, Karen, and James H. Johnson. 1996. "North Carolina Communities in Transition: An Overview of Hispanic In-Migration." *The North Carolina Geographer* 5:21-39.

Kandel, William, and John Cromartie. 2004. *New Patterns of Hispanic Settlement in Rural America.* Washington DC: United States Department of Agriculture, Rural Development Research Report, Number 99.

Kandel, William, and Emilio A. Parrado. 2004. "Hispanics in the American South and the Transformation of the Poultry Industry." Pp. 255-76 in *Hispanic Spaces, Latino*

Places: Community and Cultural Diversity in Contemporary America, edited by Daniel D. Areola. Austin: University of Texas Press.

Lobo, Arun Peter, Ronald J.O. Flores, and Joseph J. Salvo. 2002. "The Impact of Hispanic Growth on the Racial/Ethnic Composition of New York City Neighborhoods." *Urban Affairs Review* 37(5):703-727.

Massey, Douglas S., Jorge Durand, and Nolan J. Malone. 2002. *Beyond Smoke and Mirrors: Mexican Immigration in an Era of Economic Integration*. New York: Russell Sage Foundation.

Martin, K. 2002. "A City Transformed: A Latin Flavor in Charlotte, NC." *Planning* 68(7):14-19.

Millard, Ann V., and Jorge Chapa. 2004. *Apple Pie and Enchiladas: Latino Newcomers in the Rural Midwest*. Austin: University of Texas Press.

Murphy, Arthur, Colleen Blanchard and Jennifer Hill, editors. 2001. *Latino Workers in the Contemporary South*. Athens: University of Georgia Press.

Newbold, Bruce K., and John Spindler. 2001. "Immigrant Settlement Patterns in Metropolitan Chicago." *Urban Studies* 38(11):1903-1919.

Norwood, A. 2004. "'*Primera casa*' Has Latinos Excited." *The Charlotte Observer*, July 17, 2004: 1A and 15A.

Orr, Douglas M., and Alfred W. Stuart. 1999. *North Carolina Atlas: Portrait for a New Century*. Chapel Hill: University of North Carolina Press.

Ortega, Angeles. 2004. Executive Director, Latin American Coalition, July 27, 2004. Interview with author.

Phelan, Thomas J., and Mark Schneider. 1996. "Race, Ethnicity, and Class in American Suburbs." *Urban Affairs Review* 31(5):659-680.

Singer, Audrey. 2004. *The Rise of New Immigrant Gateways*. Washington, DC: Center on Urban and Metropolitan Policy, The Brookings Institution.

Smith, Heather, and Owen Furuseth. 2004. "Housing, Hispanics and Transitioning Geographies in Charlotte, NC." *Southeastern Geographer* 44(2):76-95.

Smith, Heather, and Owen Furuseth, editors. 2006. *Latinos in the New South: Transformations of Place*. London: Ashgate Publishing.

Studstill, John D., and Laura Nieto-Studstill. 2001. "Latin Immigrants in Southern Georgia." Pp. 68-81 in *Latino Workers in the Contemporary South*, edited by Arthur D. Murphy, Colleen Blanchard and Jennifer A. Hill. Athens: The University of Georgia Press.

Suro, Roberto, and Audrey Singer. 2002. *Latino Growth in Metropolitan America:Changing Patterns, New Locations*. Washington, DC: Center on Urban and Metropolitan Policy, The Brookings Institution.

Torres, Rebecca, Jeff Popke, Holly Hapke, Matilde Elise Saurez, Heidi Serrano, Brian Chambers, and Paola Andrea Castaño. 2003. "Transnational Communities in Eastern North Carolina: Results from a Survey of Latino Families in Greene County." *The North Carolina Geographer* 11:88-107.

Villamarin, Theresa. 2004. Program Supervisor, Catholic Social Services, Diocese of Charlotte, NC. Interview with author, August 3, 2004.

Chapter 12

"An Anchor of Hope": Refugees in Utica, New York

Ellen Percy Kraly

In *Managing Displacement*, Jennifer Hyndman reflects on her experiences working in refugee camps in Kenya in provoking her to reconsider the conceptualization of "mobility of 'people out of place'—those uprooted from their homes because of fighting, famine, and fear . . ." (2000b, xvi). She argues for a more accountable theory of humanitarianism, which she defines as the "site at which the projects of development and relief are being contested and recast in light of a new geopolitical landscapes and neoliberal economies that transgress the boundaries of states" (xv). A good distance from east Africa, Utica, New York, exists within the international landscape of humanitarian aid for refugees and refugee resettlement. Since 1979, the Mohawk Resource Center for Refugees has worked with federal authorities and international agencies to receive and resettle over 11,000 refugees in the city of Utica. As humanitarian programs structure the space of displaced persons in regions of origin, refugee migration has made a significant imprint on the social, economic and political landscape of this city of resettlement. In the face of net population loss spanning three decades, the foreign born population of Utica nearly doubled its size between 1990 and 2000, increasing its proportion of the city's population from 5 to 12 percent (U.S. Bureau of the Census). These demographic metrics reflect the confluence of global, national and local geographies of refugee migration and resettlement.

In this chapter, I first examine how processes of refugee resettlement have changed the urban landscape and institutional capacities within the Utica community, and second, how initial processes of adjustment and acculturation are understood and interpreted as sources of community change and urban development. In focusing on the meanings of refugee migration and settlement, my research complements that of Gouveia, Carranza and Cogua (2005) who seek to understand the institutional climate for the incorporation of Mexican and Latino labor migrants within rural communities in Nebraska. Grey and Woodrick's (2005) study of Mexican immigration to Marshalltown, Iowa also considers the ways in which immigration is understood as a source of economic and cultural revitalization for the rural community. In Utica, the largest group of international migrants originate from Europe, specifically, Bosnia. My findings underscore the critical importance of community context and modes of incorporation and institutional mechanisms for understanding social geographic outcomes for both migrant households as well as the larger community.

There is a growing research literature on new "gateway" cities for immigrant settlement in the United States to which the present volume makes a contribution (see for example, Gozdziak and Martin, 2005; Singer, 2004; Zúñiga and Herandez-León 2005; Durand, Massey and Capoferro 2005; see also Capps, et al. 2003). While several studies have considered the implications of recent and rapid immigration to small cites and rural communities in the United States (see for example, Griffith 2005; Donato, Stainbank and Bankston 2005; Dunn, Aragones and Shivers 2005), the role of immigration, and refugee resettlement, specifically in revitalizing declining urban geographies, has received somewhat let attention in the academic literature.

Social Adjustment among Settled International Migrants

The conceptualization of processes of immigrant adjustment and incorporation continues to command extensive scholarly discussion and debate across the social sciences (Hirschman, Kasinitz and DeWind 1999; Rumbaut and Portes 2001; Estaville et al. 2003; Berry and Henderson 2003; Foner, Rumbaut and Gold 2000; Silvey and Lawson 1999). Research on the second generation has challenged existing paradigms on segmented assimilation theory (Kasinitz, Mollenkopf, and Waters 2004; Alba and Nee 2003). City-based research on immigration settlement, such that included in this volume, underscores the significance of context and place-based characteristics in mediated processes of social adjustment and incorporation (see Waldinger 1996, 2001; Waldinger and Lichter 2003; Foner 2000, 2001). Geographers have given sharp focus to this analytic discourse by framing migration research within critical social theory. Underscoring the connections between theory and method, geographers have used ethnography and other qualitative approaches to reveal transnational and gendered dimensions of contemporary international migration that are less than observable through quantitative models and reliance on census and survey data (see for example, Hardwick 2003; Bailey 2001; Lawson 2000; McHugh 2000; Hyndman 2000a).

This research is guided by these developments in migration and migrant scholarship. Portes and Rumbaut (2001) underscore the interaction between characteristics of immigrants and immigrant streams and the conditions of reception and initial settlement in influencing the settlement experience and patterns of change among first generation immigrants to a community. Immigrant characteristics include not only social capital but also circumstances of migration. Thus, refugees seeking permanent resettlement in the United States arrive with a distinctive relationship to both their homeland and their new community of resettlement, and with meager resources as well. Different groups of refugees, moreover, may vary significantly in terms of personal resources and background characteristics concerning household structure, education, occupation, and religiosity. Conditions of reception then filter the transfer of the characteristics and resources of immigrants and immigrant households into the new community. Portes and Rumbaut (1996, 2001) specify the salience of modes of incorporation—government programs, local social and economic structures, community receptivity toward immigrants and ethnic groups, the characteristics and resources of earlier immigrants (co-ethnic groups)—for segmented paths of assimilation among immigrants (see also Hardwick 2003; Newbold and Foulkes 2004).

Drawing on "new institutionalism," Alba and Nee (2003) underscore the salience of institutional mechanisms in structuring patterns and processes of immigrant assimilation. Hardwick (2002) distinguishes between initial adaptation and acculturation and subsequent patterns of integration and assimilation and identifies the important of language, residence and religion in influencing the experience of resettlement of refugee groups in the United States. Early stages of settlement involve processes of "adaptation to the pressures of daily life" (2002, 260), and acculturating to life in a new society. Given the conditions of refugee migration and resettlement, processes of adjustment and acculturation are often dramatic and abrupt. Institutional modes of incorporation, such as community groups sponsoring refugees, can be expected to play a critical role in the initial stages and experiences of resettlement. A former refugee in Utica has described social adjustment as "starting with spoons."

This study of refugee resettlement in Utica draws on these conceptual relationships by considering the interaction between the characteristics of refugees and families and the context of reception for refugees in the city. I underscore and empirically explore the significance of community and institutional context for the ways in which processes of social adjustment unfold among resettled refugees. To this are added the ways in which the social geography of adjustment and acculturation are observed, understood and interpreted by key members of the Utica community, including members of the refugee community. For a city facing challenges in the present and for the future, there may be a role for a particular path of refugee resettlement and acculturation in policies seeking to promote sustainable urban development.

Approach

The analysis is embedded within the context of interacting social, demographic and economic trends in Utica and its region. Social demographic and qualitative research methods are combined to follow an extended case methodology (Burawoy 1998) in order to interconnect macrostructures with local processes and individual experience. The extended case method is particularly relevant for drawing general theoretical relevance from unanticipated social situations. A growing and prominent immigrant population within a city experiencing significant population loss would seem to fit this analytic circumstance.

Perspectives on the social adjustment of resettled refugees are drawn from a series of interviews with key informants in Utica. Because the participants in the study occupy positions as formal or informal community leaders, or occupy an expert vantage point on the macro-level processes of urban change in Utica, the analysis yields data in which knowledge, perception and position intersect for a specific and privileged group of community actors. My approach represents a "repositioning of the academic gaze" to consider the "institutions, organizations, and bodies that govern human relations, rather than to study the governed themselves" (Hyndman 2000b, xvii). Respondents were identified through several routes. Key sectors of the community were selected for study: political offices and public administration, prominent community groups (churches, civic, cultural and ethnic interest groups, etc.), educational programs, urban research groups, business and commercial interests, foundations, and social service groups. A "snowball" approach was also used to identify possible respondents based on suggestions made by previous respondents.

To promote candor in the conversations, the interviews were anonymous; quotes are attributed to the respondent only by community role or sector. With the assistance of two undergraduate research assistants, Lorraine Coulter and Theresa Murray, sixteen largely open ended interviews lasting between forty-fi ve minutes and two hours were conducted. Respondents were asked to reflect upon the effects of refugee resettlement on the city of Utica as well as the potential advantages or problems posed by continued refugee migration and settlement in the city. Respondents were encouraged to offer both general perspectives as well as views specific to his or her area of expertise and role in the Utica community. The interviews were tape recorded and later transcribed.

This chapter begins by establishing the institutional context of international migration by describing the process of refugee resettlement in Utica, and specifically the programs of the Mohawk Valley Resource Center for Refugees. An overview of the social demographic effects of international and refugee migration on Utica's population is presented, followed by a description of the urban landscape and economy. Within these contexts and drawing from the results of the interviews, I present perspectives on the social adjustment of refugees organized around three themes: human capital and household characteristics, residence, and social capital and community building. Similarly, perspectives on the impacts of refugee resettlement on the city—both present and anticipated—are organized around four dimensions of urban change: economic development, housing and neighborhoods, capacity building, and multiculturalism. The paper concludes by considering social adjustment and integration of international migrants as a potential asset for positive community development in Utica.

Refugee Resettlement: Agents and Agency

The influx of international migration to Utica during the 1990s overwhelmingly reflects the resettlement of refugees through U.S. refugee law, policy and programs.[1] The Mohawk Valley Resource Center for Refugees (hereafter the Refugee Resource Center or MVRCR) was organized in 1979 and incorporated as a non-profit organization in 1981. Its sponsor is Lutheran Immigration and Refugee Service, thus exemplifying the public-private association which has characterized the administration of the resettlement process in the United States since the end of the Second World War. Since its founding in 1979, MVRCR has been the sponsor (officially, the Executive Director of the Refugee Resource Center is the named sponsor) of resettled refugees. The Center is located in downtown Utica in what was previously a parochial school.

Utica's major refugee groups reflect different histories embedded in major political events around the globe since the mid-1970s. The city's emergence as a multi-ethnic destination stems from the U.S.'s involvement in those events as well as Utica's reputation as a sponsor of refugees.

Persons fleeing the fall of Saigon were first paroled into the United States in 1975; in fact the first refugee to Utica in this era was a Vietnamese man sponsored by a group of clergy in that same year. The Indochinese Refugee Adjustment Act provided the means by which persons admitted as parolees could adjust to permanent resident status. The Amerasian Homecoming Act of 1987 authorized the admission to the United States of children fathered by U.S. military personnel during the war in Vietnam. Persons arriving under this act are technically immigrants but receive refugee benefits. Political turmoil and ultimately transformation in the Soviet Union in the late 1980s increased the number of persons seeking refugee resettlement. Persons from the Soviet Union, largely Pentecostal Christians, began to be resettled in Utica in 1988.

By far the largest group of refugees resettled in Utica are the Bosnians. The Bosnian refugee program was initiated by Congress in 1993 in response to the violence caused by the breakup of the Yugoslav federation. Utica received 104 refugees from Bosnia-Herzegovina in that first year. Bosnians resettled in Utica were predominately Muslim, largely secular. Many of this resettled population originated from northwestern Bosnia in the vicinity of the city of Kladusa, a region experiencing severe violence in seeking independence from the Sarajevo government. With the defeat of the civil rebellion in 1995 many of these Bosnians fled to UN camps in Croatia. Other Utica Bosnians originally found asylum in Germany, Austria, Sweden, and even Pakistan (see Coughlan and

Owens-Manley 2002). Nearly 2000 Bosnians arrived in Utica in 1996-1997. Arrival continued in large numbers in the latter years of the 1990s, reflecting in part requests by applicants to settle in what they had heard was a welcoming place for refugees from Bosnia. While the Bosnian program ended in 2001, immediate relatives of resettled refugees continue to migrate to Utica through granted affidavits of relationship. These family members receive some federal assistance through the programs of the Refugee Resource Center.

In the summer of 2003 the Refugee Resource Center began receiving a number of Somali Bantu refugees. Refugees from western Africa (Liberia) are also being resettled in Utica as well as a small number of Sudanese men. Refugees from the former Soviet Union also continue to arrive. At the end of 2005, the largest refugee stream was from Myanmar.

Figure 12.1 presents data on the national origins of refugees resettled in Utica by the Refugee Resource Center since 1979. Bosnians comprise nearly two- fifths of total arrivals. Approximately one fifth are persons from Vietnam (including Amerasian-Vietnamese), and another fifth are from areas of the former Soviet Union. The diversity of the total refugee population, however, is striking, with several hundred persons (between one and four percent of the total) resettled from Cambodia, Myanmar (Burma), Laos, Sudan and Somalia, for example. This cultural diversity has obvious implications for the programs of the Center which currently maintains thirteen different language translation programs. The Refugee Resource Center receives funding for its programs from the federal government largely on the basis of the number of refugees resettled by the Refugee Resource Center. The programs of the Refugee Resource Center focus on fostering the employability of its "clients." This goal is implemented through stability in housing, health assessment, English language training, cultural orientation and employment counseling. Several of its employees are former clients of the Refugee Resource Center, that is, persons who came to Utica as refugees. English language instruction is supported in large part with resources from the Utica City Public Schools.

In addition to employment counseling and training, the Refugee Resource Center has promoted the cause of its clients to businesses in the Utica labor market by alerting employers to the benefits of employing clients of the Center. The Center underscores the work ethic and prior professional and occupational experience of refugees, the support for cultural orientation and job placement available through the programs and administration of the Center, and even the cultural effects of refugee workers. This approach is illustrated in a statement in one of its publications: "Increase the diversity of your staff by adding workers from around the world" (Mohawk Valley Resource Center for Refugees, 2003).

The agency has received attention for both the extent and organization of its operations and its rather unexpected location in upstate New York. Within the city and the metropolitan region, there is recognition of the Refugee Resource Center as a multicultural institution. Its programs, initiatives, and clients are covered regularly in the regional newspaper, the *Observer-Dispatch*, which also includes a weekly page devoted to the Bosnian community, written in Bosnian.

Both the scale of the refugee resettlement and the programs of the MVRCR have drawn national attention (see for example, Zielbauer 1999). In 2005, the magazine, *Refugees*, published by the United Nations High Commissioner for Refugees (UNHCR) devoted an entire issue to refugee resettlement in Utica, "The Town that Loves Refugees" (UNCHR 2005).

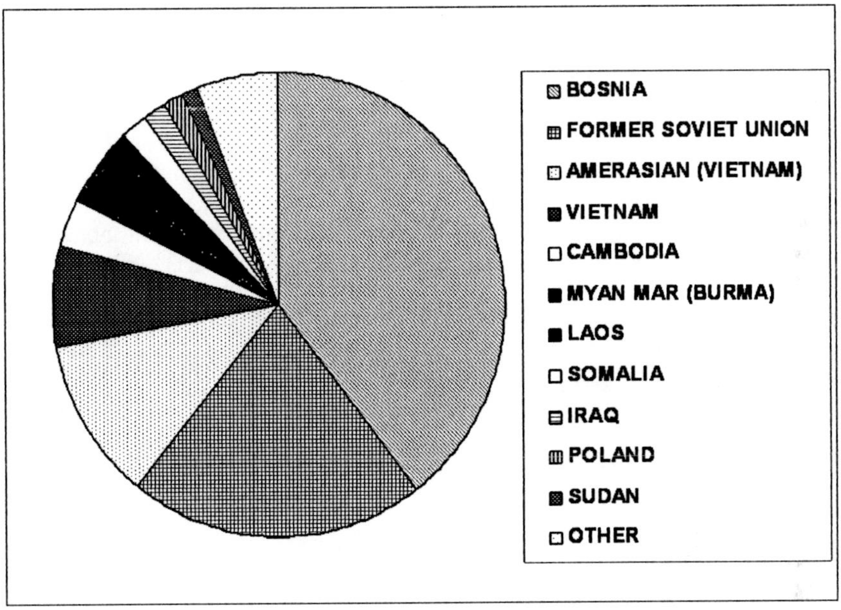

Figure 12.1 Refugees Resettled in Utica, by country of Birth, 1979-2005 (total = 11,213)

In the aftermath of September 11, 2001, U.S. resettlement of refugees has been curtailed, causing some refugee programs to contract services and lay off employees and other smaller centers to close their doors entirely. While the Utica Refugee Resource Center currently remains in full operation, changes in both staffing and programming have occurred. The mission of the Center has been expanded to serve both refugees as well as other international migrants in the city and region. The message sent is one of assistance to immigrants and refugees as well as connections to the larger community:

> We promote the well-being of culturally diverse individuals and families within our community by welcoming our new neighbors, refugees and immigrants and by providing individual and community-centered activities designed to create opportunity and facilitate understanding (Mohawk Valley Resource Center for Refugees 2006).

As is evident from perspectives shared below, the Center is increasingly central in both promoting multiculturalism in the urban community and fostering cultural capacity throughout public and private sectors by promoting interagency collaboration and exchange regarding efforts to support refugees and immigrants. Finally, social, demographic and economic trends in the local and regional community continue to frame the policy and administrative context of refugee resettlement in Utica.

International Migration, Refugee Resettlement and Population Change

Several recent studies have documented the role of international migration in the dynamics of demographic change in selected U.S. metropolitan areas. Salvo and Lobo (1996) have revealed the importance of immigration in metropolitan and intra-metropolitan population trends in New York City, perhaps the most "traditional" of immigrant gateways (see also Lobo, Salvo and Flores 2002; Kraly and Miyares 2001). Singer (2004) identifies the emergence of new location for U.S. immigrants during the 1990s, anticipates future magnets for immigrant settlement in both suburban areas and small metropolitan areas (see also, Camarota and Keeley 2001), and heralds increasing diversity in the immigrant settlement patterns (see also Bump, Lowell and Pettersen 2005; Durand, Massey, and Capoferro 2005; Alba and Nee 2003, 248-260).

The Utica-Rome MSA (metropolitan statistical area) is located on the Mohawk River near the geographic center of New York State. Between 1970 and 2000, the population of the metropolitan area declined from 340,670 to 299,896, a loss of about 40,000 persons or 12 percent. Based on the results of the 2000 census, the Utica-Rome ranked third out of 280 MSAs in the United States in *both* absolute and relative population decline since 1990 (U.S. Bureau of the Census). Relative population change has been even more dramatic for the City of Utica. Decennial census data show the city's population declining from 91,611 in 1970 to 60,670 in 2000, a relative loss of 34 percent. Between 1970-1980 and 1980-1990 the foreign born population declined by about one third and one fourth, respectively, reflecting in part the older age structure of the resident foreign born population.[2]

The most recent intercensal period has witnessed a reversal in the trajectory of growth of the foreign born population in Utica. Between 1990 and 2000, the foreign born population increased from 3,718 to 7,231, a near doubling. Kraly and VanValkenburg (2003) estimate that in the absence of international migration during the decade, population loss in the city would have been on the order of 20 percent in comparison to the 12 percent decline actually registered.

Table 12.1 presents 2000 census data on nativity and country and region of birth of the foreign born population of Utica.

Table 12.1 Nativity and Country of Birth of Foreign Born, Utica City, 2000

Nativity and Country of birth	Number	Percent
Total Population	**60,679**	**100.0**
Foreign born Population	**7,231**	**11.9**
Country of Birth of Foreign Born		
Total	**7,231**	**100.0**
Europe:	**5,340**	**73.8**
Germany	193	2.7
Italy	440	6.1
Poland	253	3.5
Belarus	602	8.3
Russia	244	3.4
Ukraine	461	6.4
Bosnia/Herzegovina	2,596	35.9
Asia	**1,335**	**18.5**
Vietnam	819	11.3
Africa	**43**	**0.6**
Oceania	**0**	**0.0**
Latin America	**434**	**6.0**
Caribbean	301	4.2
Central America	25	0.3
South America	108	1.5
Northern America	**79**	**1.1**

Source: U.S. Bureau of the Census, 2000 Census of Population, Summary file 3.

Of the foreign born population nearly three quarters were of European birth. Over one third of Utica's immigrant population in 2000 was born in Bosnia-Herzegovina (a proportion quite similar to that of the Italians in Utica in 1920). Nearly a fifth of the foreign born population was born in regions in the former Soviet Union, and also a significant proportion in Vietnam.

The Urban Landscape

Figure 12.2 illustrates the residential concentration of the largest group of refugees resettled during the period, Bosnians, in eastern neighborhoods of the city. When asked, Bosnians often say that they live in "East Utica," shown in the figure. These neighborhoods were initially attractive to arriving Bosnian households because the availability of two-family houses, cheap housing and proximity to shopping and other services. Successive arrivals from Bosnia have also been drawn to the area because of the presence of a growing Bosnian community. To date, it is estimated that Bosnians have made over 400 home purchases in the city of Utica.

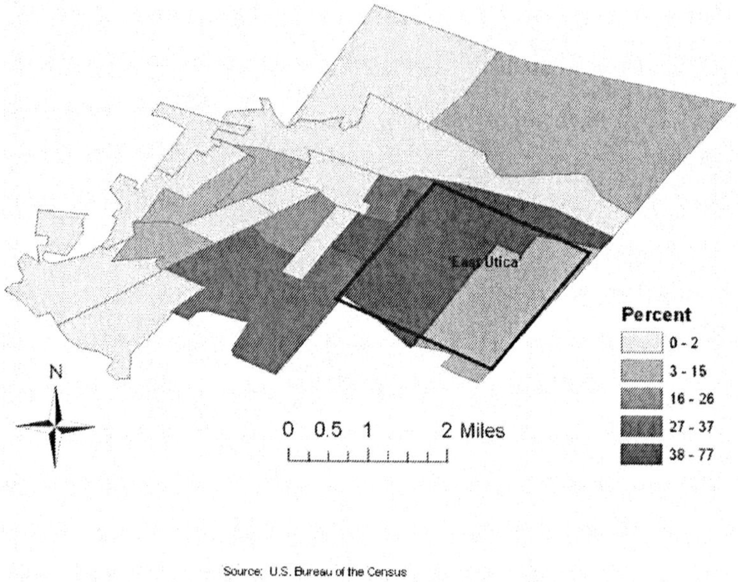

Figure 12.2 Percent of Total Population Born in Bosnia-Herzegovina: Utica City, by Census Tract: 1990-2000

Utica is characterized by old housing stock: 54 percent of the housing units in the city were built before 1939 (U.S. Bureau of the Census). While some areas in the city are characterized by closely built structures, many houses are situated on relatively large lots along tree-lined streets (Figure 12.3). Recalling the loss of population in Utica in recent decades, it is not surprising that the proportion of housing units which are vacant increased from 5 percent in 1970 to 14 percent in 2000 (U.S. Bureau of the Census). Spatial analysis reveals that neighborhoods with large percentage increases in the foreign born population, including high proportions of recent immigrants, have significantly lower levels of housing vacancy (U.S. Bureau of the Census).

In lockstep with population loss, the Utica-Rome metropolitan area has experienced economic decline in the past three decades. Between 1977 and 2002, the number of manufacturing establishments declined from 411 firms to 339, and the number of wholesale trade companies declined from 419 to 257. Not surprisingly, and corresponding to both economic and demographic change in the labor market, the number of retail trade establishments declined sharply,

Figure 12.3 Illustration of Housing in Eastern Areas of Utica

from 3,044 to 1,136 during this twenty-five year period (Slater and Hall 1994; U.S. Bureau of the Census).

The Economy

Clients of the Refugee Resource Center generally begin work in the Utica labor market within about four months of arrival in the city. According to tracking done by the Center during the 1995-2000 period, clients have been hired by some 236 employers in the Utica-Rome metropolitan area. The vast majority of these employers, nearly two hundred, employed fewer than ten refugees; thirteen establishments employed over fifty refugees. These firms were largely manufacturing and assembly plants but also included several textile mills (a legacy of Utica's past as a mill town), meat processors, and greenhouses (Hagstrom 2000).

Figure 12.4 Business Establishments in Utica: from left to right, the Ruznic Grocery Store, on Albany St.; the Café Caruso and Nyguyen Phat Oriental Store, on Bleeker St.

In addition to labor force participation, home ownership, and patterns of consumption, we may also consider economic enterprise among refugees as a potential source of urban economic development. Types of entrepreneurial activities include restaurants, book keeping and tax services, convenience stores, beauty shops and barbershops, boutiques, car repair and mechanics, car sales, real estate, construction, dance bands, and at least one Bosnian nightclub. These establishments cater largely to co-ethnics, hence serving as evidence of an ethnic enclave, as well as other refugee groups. The grocery store shown in Figure 12.4 offers fresh baked goods and imported foods from throughout Europe to appeal to Bosnians and Russians. The owner of the store, a Bosnian, intends to open another market, and has recently opened a restaurant adjoining the grocery. He remarks, "If they (Bosnians and Russians) stop buying, I'd have to change to something else. This business really is for some groups of people" (Kline 2006).

Acculturation and Integration of Refugees

Perspectives on the process of social adjustment among refugees are embedded within this context of resettlement programs as well as the urban geography of Utica. The views of informants that follow in this section are organized around three dimensions of adjustment/acculturation and integration: (1) human capital and family characteristics; (2) the geography of resettlement; and (3) social capital and cultural preservation.

Human Capital and Family

Several interviewees comment on the human resources and family values that refugees, particularly Bosnians, bring to the community. For example, two respondents comment on the strong work ethic of refugees:

> I think part of what has helped is the refugees themselves have shown themselves to be very strong workers, and reliable workers . . . That's the key requirement is show up and be there every time. (economist)

> And, so the Bosnian community in particular has been extremely well received by our local employers . . . In the early development of that community . . .someone . . . would be injured or sick or unable to show up at work on a given day, and they would send either a brother or a cousin to literally take their place. They would be concerned about losing their job, and would send a family member to take their place for the day, . . . So, they've been extremely well received into the broader economic base and economic model in terms of employers, with their skill set, their willingness to work, their work ethic, all those sorts of things. (economic development official)

Bosnians are considered to bring good character, a commitment to learning for themselves and their children, and strong family values:

> . . . they have to begin again and have roots. And they want their kids to prosper. And, I can see that in N . . . , how precious his kids are to him and what he wants for them. For them to have good schooling, and education, and a future. (ESL instructor)

The growth in refugee children enrolled in the public school system has resulted in more families committed to educational achievement in the community:

> The refugees have been tremendous for the school system because in many ways, they come with a different outlook about public education, and their willingness to seize every opportunity. (city educational administrator)

A former refugee reflects on the role of language (cf. Hardwick 2003) in the occupational mobility of his family and that of his co-ethnics:

> Both of us, my wife and me, [were] faculty in our country, bachelor degrees, but we know we have to work very hard to make future for our children much better. Little by little we start to learn the language. Refugee Center help us in the beginning, five first months, then my wife, she went to BOCES here, then school. We tried to make improvement in our employment, every time, better and better position, depend on language skill. (former refugee-researcher)

This same individual also reflects on the strains deriving from household economic strategies, illustrating aspects of dissonant acculturation described by Portes and Rumbaut (2001, 308).

> Now kids come first, they are not supervised very well because both parents work, and they have a lot of freedom, and they have cars at 16 instead of 18 . . . And there are all kinds of people, and things that you can do here that parents don't know too much about. There's some trouble.

The Geography of Resettlement

Informants were cognizant about the geography of refugee resettlement, especially Bosnians, in the city, speculating on the value of home ownership within the refugee community. Themes of of heterolocalism (Zelinsky and Lee 1998) also emerge:

> Bosnians . . . come here with what appears to be a real definite goal of owning a home in the community. And not necessarily creating a Bosnian neighborhood, if you will . . . but that the Bosnians are looking to buy homes wherever they can buy them in the community. And outside the community, apparently,

> in neighboring communities. . . . I'm also keenly aware that although in the Bosnian community they may be scattered about—they may not all necessarily [be] living in a four-block area . . . you're going to find Bosnians living from Clinton to wherever in Utica, but they're staying together as their own community, with that sense of community, that shared experience that they brought here, through the newspaper. (foundation representative)

Social Capital and Cultural Preservation

The formation of ethnic community groups represents a particular mode of incorporation (Portes and Rumbaut, 2001) and is understood as an ongoing and multidimensional process, intrinsic to processes of adjustment:

> We have different groups trying to create their own community within the larger community. Those who are electing to stay are assimilating into the community, in one way or another, but definitely in different ways. (foundation leader)

There is an appreciation of social capital in processes of social adjustment among refugee groups. The formation of formal as well as informal supports for community development is viewed as a critical dimension of the process of adjustment and cultural preservation, again playing out over time:

> . . . more and more people going in their own business so we have a few restaurants, a few café-bars, mechanics, groceries . . . So now people more interact at that level. You know, through trying . . . events, some celebrations . . .There is now one radio station, that I just learned, another one . . ., you know, they're going developing slowly, but it's going always progressing up. There are two [Bosnian newspapers]. . . . You have everything that you need really and that takes time in your ethnicity. (former refugee-research)

This individual also commented on the safety and security of Bosnian neighborhoods: "So our neighbors feel safe, old people who [experienced] those changes now feel confident that nobody will leave the area."

Human and social capital is also understood in the process of economic integration in the urban community. Note this statement linking both forms of resources:

> These are individuals who carry with them a skills set, an experience set; they're contractors, they're engineers, they're chefs, they're business owners, they're shop owners, they're retailers, they're restaurateurs that have, have come over as a large group, as a displaced group, into the US, and into Utica in particular. And so we readily see them assimilate to the community, in terms of now serving their own community . . . someone who was a restaurateur in their homeland, now the community as such has taken on a vibrancy within the city proper . . . it's really a community unto itself, in terms of now generating addi-

> tional economic activity, catering to that community. (economic development official)

Impacts of Refugees on the Urban Community

The community effects of refugee resettlement and immigrant households constitute important issues for both community leaders and refugee informants who have made Utica their home. In this section, observations are presented concerning the consequences of resettlement, acculturation and integration of refugees and migrants for a community characterized by decline in many urban sectors, organized around four specific themes: (1) economic development, employment and production, (2) housing and neighborhoods, (3) institutional capacity building, and (4) multiculturalism.

Before exploring these specific themes, however, it is important to summarize the overarching message of respondents. Resettlement and the social adjustment of migrants and their families were placed by those interviewed within the context of the social and population geography of Utica. While different dimensions of urban change were addressed, there was a consistent recognition of the special opportunity for urban development afforded by refugee settlement largely because of the cultural traits and "cultural capital" possessed and expressed by refugee populations.

> The most important potential is that this is the rebirth of the city. We were going, as a community, downhill, fast, in terms of job growth, population growth. We're an aging community. And the refugees have provided many challenges, but also a shot in the arm for this community. . . . We've gotten the opportunity, an influx of new people that are coming to a region that was really going downhill, in terms of enrollment. . . . And this gives us an opportunity to grow, and to do new things, potentially. (city education administrator)

> So . . . we have a lot of abandoned houses, and we have a lot of absentee landlords, which is very bad. Now, all of a sudden, we have this influx of the refugees—of many denominations there—we have the Russians, we have the Bosnians, who are the newest group, and we had the Vietnamese, and they've bought these homes and revitalized them, which has given us new strength and new growth in the city. (ESL instructor)

> The refugee resettlement has been a notable anchor of hope in changing that direction, whether it's east Utica or here in Corn Hill, or wherever. The Bosnian community, because of its size, is just an example of just a wonderful rebirth of the old neighborhoods. Now, with some side businesses starting up, and corner businesses and things, restaurants—that is a total reversal of the trend in the last thirty years, forty years in this area. So that's a great sign of hope. (religious leader)

These general perspectives on context were also evidenced by the fact that many respondents began their reflections by remarking on the palpable impact of refugee arrivals and settlers on demographic change in the city and its neighborhoods:

> I mean, those are people who want to be there, who're happy to be there, who haven't left, who may put down roots, and so provided a much-needed people-boost when the city really needed it. (community development scholar).

> I will say that the one [effect] that may not be significant, but it's obvious, is that the contribution that immigration is making to reversing the trends of downward populations in the county. (arts leader)

Correspondingly the issue of retention of refugees in Utica was also a recurring theme:

> I worry that, that, just like a lot of the young people in Utica are now leaving, this next generation of refugees coming through is going to pick up and move as well. How do we make this a community that, despite the fact that it's frigid in the winter, and the fact that it's got a lower-income potential, how do you entice people to come, but then encourage people to stay once they have come? (social program director)

In her remarks at a naturalization ceremony[3] in Utica, Deana Smiljic, Councilwoman-at-large on the Utica City Counsel and a former refugee from Bosnia, encouraged the new U.S. citizens to remain in the Mohawk Valley and to participate in community-building. These sentiments illustrate the general appreciation of interconnections among international migration, population growth, economic trends and community development.

Economic Development, Employment, and Production

Turning to the issue of economic development, respondents comment on both the emergence of refugee owned and operated businesses as well as the importance of refugee workers for large and small employers in the region:

> The other is the economic impact, both of federal money coming in, but also of bright, ambitious, hard-working people that are willing to work jobs that otherwise are not great jobs. So, you know, that has become important for a number of smaller businesses and I think larger businesses that have enjoyed the good labor quality. (community development scholar)

The positive and less positive dimensions of retaining the business enterprises that employ refugees are also noted:

> Basically, keeping refugees here means keeping people here, you know, and keeping many jobs open here. Most, in the beginning, refugees, they would take the lowest paying jobs, work in the factories, and I think without the refugees, probably many of these companies would, you know, not have enough employees. (former refugee)

> The difficulty is that once refugees have gone into small manufacturing type jobs that are less and less popular in this area, so it really puts the burden on local business and political figures to promote to small manufacturing firms in other places that this is a perfect place to come. In other words, there isn't a natural tendency right now for those types of businesses to just spring up in this area. If you were thinking of doing that you'd probably move to Tennessee or Kentucky or someplace and start that type of business where taxes are so much lower, energy is so much lower. (economist)

Several respondents described the multiplier effects of the process of settlement, adjustment, and integration in the form of upward economic mobility. For example:

> The refugee population really brought able-bodied people, young enough to take any job, . . .now it is noticeable that people are taking a lot more complicated duties and jobs. At the same time we have a college population, finishing college and taking jobs, on their part, by their education, taking better jobs. I think from that side we can make positive things for Utica—more growth, more money, and a higher standard in the city. The kind of important thing I think is if their standard grows—more money so they can start to purchase other things. (former refugee-research)

> The Bosnian community in particular is noted for their efforts at, I'll use the term "homesteading." And what they're doing is buying up residential property in the core urban area that perhaps you might otherwise recognize as being distressed, shall we say. Buying it up and paying cash, or taking out a nominal mortgage, typically self-funded, and regentrifying neighborhoods, buying them up and fixing up properties, and more families coming in and buying the property next to them, and then they just proliferate. . . . They're a terrific boon to our tax base in terms of stabilizing the core urban fabric, residential urban fabric, and fixing up these properties. (economic development official)

Housing and Neighborhoods

Respondents emphasize the ways in which refugee families have changed Utica's neighborhoods. As evidenced above, the topic of housing maintenance and renovation is prominent:

> Bosnians have come in and purchased some of these homes, and fixed them up—painted them, replaced—and they have done fantastic, and on very little. They have very good work skills, they are very good carpenters, they can make

> almost anything and fix anything. So this is what we've needed. And you can go up and down the streets now and see the improvement in the area, and you know that they are Bosnian people that are there. (ESL instructor)

> Before the ink is signed on the paper, they're out painting the house, and getting the lawns cleaned up, and there's a win-win-win for everybody. The owners of the homes who've had a hard time selling them, they give them to us as a tax write-off. We find a family who fixes the houses up, and the neighborhood's better off, and everybody's happy. So those are just little examples of the Vietnamese community, and how they've been such a blessing, certainly to our church, but in the bigger picture, to the greater community. (religious leader)

Neighborhood and street life also benefits from Bosnian culture:

> What the Bosnians brought to the neighborhoods, that they tended to do things in a way that you might have done, let's say in the 1950s: they tended to sit on their porches, and . . . just tended to be out in the neighborhood. Tended to be very friendly, you know, calling out to you when you came in, and in a way you . . . just that they brought this feeling of neighborhood that, uh . . . the Americans thought had been missing for them, for a while. (social researcher)

Institutional Capacity Building

Refugee resettlement and support for the adjustment of refugees in the community has amplified the institutional capacity of Utica. The establishment of the Refugee Resource Center represent a mode of incorporation specific to refugee resettlement; one respondent said it simply: "The first and foremost is that Utica is lucky that it has one more really strong, really stable non-profit organization" (community development scholar). Another respondent noted how the Center had evolved as a result of the process of refugee resettlement:

> Well what really changed that was the coming of the Bosnians, because they came in such large numbers that two things happened. I do think the Bosnians coming in such, such large numbers then sort of inundated the school district and the Department of Social Service and maybe other community services like that, that made it impossible to ignore. And, then I think the Board [of the refugee center] made changes. . . . the Refugee Center had a role to play in making sure the people got integrated into the community and became a part of the community, and not just that they got here. So I think those things combined to start making it more visible. (social researcher)

Public education programs have also been provoked to change as a result of dramatic and rapid refugee settlement. Additional students have brought revenue but also changes in resource allocation, curriculum, and instruction:

> Anytime a district is growing, it presents problems, but certainly some challenges and some opportunities. As your enrollment increases, there's an additional funding that comes with enrollment. There's additional growth and space that you need, but . . . it's a challenge in some ways, but it's also a sign of prosperity, that's you're growing. . . . It's forced us to change the way we deliver instruction into every classroom, because every single teacher is forced to deal with students that English wasn't their native language . . . And I see that as an advantage, because I think as teachers look at kids individually and how they learn, it not only helps kids that are refugees, but it helps [those] that may not learn the same way as everybody else. (city educational administrator)

Refugee settlement has stimulated changes in social administration and programs, particularly by encouraging, perhaps demanding, linkages among agencies and organizations:

> Now, I think the community response has been good in that I think the community has really endeavored to, for instance in the Department of Social Services, to have very strong links with the Refugee Center, and then to hire people that are bilingual. So I think we're getting there, but we're like this community in transition. (social researcher)

> The positive impact of youngsters going to school put pressures on the school system both ways. That really caused us to make a major partnership, as a college, with the school district, almost as a social responsibility. (higher educational leader)

There is also the recognition that enhanced social infrastructure benefits both migrants and migrant households as well the larger community:

> But it's building a community's capacity to, to provide their services and engage cultural development at a relevant level. So, we take the agencies that do counseling for domestic violence, or alcohol abuse, or, any kind of those areas, you take traditional American-geared services and try to have them work effectively and efficiently with, say, the Sudanese population. . . . the resettlement process is enhanced if there is a community connection. And it's enhanced both for the refugees that come in, but it's also enhanced for the local community, as it welcomes and engages with the refugees. (social program director)

> Programs like ESL, English as a Second Language, and academic intervention services, are very important to these young people, learning, growing, and becoming the work force of the future for us. (political leader)

> Many other services, service-oriented businesses in the community are hiring individuals from that particular community who have some multi-lingual skills; banks, by way of example, being the most, perhaps one of the more obvious. To . . . really have a bank teller stand there and be able to speak Croatian, and to give . . . and, and word spreads that this is a Bosnian-friendly organization, and it brings in business. (economic development official)

Multiculturalism

Persons interviewed also value the effects of refugee migration stemming from the settlement of many different ethnic and racial groups in creating opportunities for learning about and experiencing diversity and multiculturalism:

> In terms of culturally and the diversity, what the kids from different countries bring to the school is really immeasurable. We . . . if you go into any of our schools, elementary, middle, or high school, and you look at the faces of the kids, you can tell they reflect, you know, the United Nations. They really reflect all different countries all over. And I think that's great for them, and for kids that were born here. They, they learn different cultures, they learn from different kids. So that's a real plus, I think for the kids that go to school here. (city education administrator)

> The fact that we have such a wonderfully diverse population here, a very, very good thing for this community, and for the young people in this community to be in school with people from all over the world. . . . That's amazing. . . . And so you're sitting next to someone from somewhere else in the world; what a great geography lesson. What a great sociology lesson; what a great history lesson. So, so I think that our children are having the opportunity to be more accepting, to have a bigger world view. I see this as extremely positive for our community, on every level that I can possibly think of. (foundation leader)

Within this discussion there is also the recognition of emergent tensions over scarce resources: ". . . in the community development field, you know, one of the old truisms is that the smaller the pie, the more people fight over the pieces. And that's what you see in a lot of the urban areas" (community development scholar).

Summary and Conclusions

Perspectives offered by Utica community leaders and key informants on the effects of refugee resettlement connect well with scholarship on processes of immigrant adjustment and acculturation in North American cities. Our respondents identify the importance of the characteristics of individual refugees and their families, including their occupation and skills, work ethic and commitment to education, and family values. Respondents also recognize the importance of social capital in the form of community-building among refugees. Community organizations, churches, newspapers, and economic enterprises are described as mechanisms by which refugee families are incorporated into the urban society and economy. Political leaders also encourage civic participation. These interpretive domains of community leaders resonate with the framework of segmented assimilation developed by Portes and Rumbaut (2001) and Portes and Zhou (1993). Moreover, the diversity effects of refugee resettlement are considered a stimulus for the development of the cultural capacity of urban institutions, for example, schools and businesses, as well as integration among public and private groups to provide services to a growing multicultural community. While Alba and Nee (2003) conceptualized institutional mechanisms for immigrant assimilation largely on the national scale concerning civil rights and changing public discourse regarding equal opportunity and opportunity structures, I would argue that changes in public and private institutions at the local scale, as recognized by community actors, constitute a complementary expression of institutional arrangements fostering acculturation and integration among refugees, immigrants and potentially other minorities in Utica.

These specific findings point to three general sets of conclusions and questions for Utica. Similar to the perspectives of Grey and Woodrick (2005) on the relationship between activism and community research, my hope is that the results of this research will contribute not only to scholarship on international migration to smaller cities in North America, but also to productive exchange among policy actors and community interest groups, including refugees, concerning the potential for refugee settlement to contribute to positive change (see also Hyndman 2000a, 2000b).

First, the perspectives on refugee resettlement, adjustment, and integration expressed by the informants in this study are consistently embedded in the context of demographic and economic change, in this case, decline. Community leaders and key informants offered largely positive perspectives on the implications of refugee integration for Utica. The many challenges faced by the city for sustainable economic and community development are the starting point, however, for this assessment. Economic growth, or even stasis, can not be assumed for Utica; the converse—urban decline both in economy and population – is the prominent expectation. Processes of social adjustment of refugees are understood within this context.

Grey and Woodrick's (2005) study of Marshalltown, Iowa, provides a useful comparison to Utica. While not directly comparable to Utica in terms of the causes and trajectory of demographic and economic change, Marshalltown (like Utica) came to recognize the positive impacts of immigration, specifically in terms of (Latino) businesses emerging in response to the influx of Mexicans and Latinos for work in the food processing plant. However, in Marshalltown (as in Utica), there was an important moral component to the acceptance of immigrants—i.e,, a decision to help them not just because they could revitalize the community, but on deeper humanitarian grounds. One respondent in this study suggested that

> I think you have to accept this as a humanitarian effort that can have real positive effects on the community; not as an endeavor to repopulate and redevelop your community. I think once you divorce it from the humanitarian, aspect of it, you're sure to run into some problems because there's no guarantee who the next wave of refugees is going to be.

Second, and related, the cultural traits of refugee groups are also placed in relief to the needs of the urban community for revitalization. Thus cultural traits such as work ethic and entrepreneurship, investment in housing, commitment to family and neighborhood, efforts at community building, are considered direct benefits, a form of social and cultural capital afforded by refugee settlement, benefiting the city and providing an "anchor of hope" for the future of the city. Indirect effects which may, or may not, unfold for the future, include the possibilities for retaining employers and businesses, improving physical infrastructure in the city, notably housing stock, and stimulating positive change in civic organizations and institutional relationships. Research focusing specifically on the Bosnian community in Utica has revealed that factors such as a strong refugee resettlement infrastructure, job opportunities, and affordable housing are also reasons for the choice of Utica among successive stream of Bosnian migrants (Coughlan and Owens-Manley 2005).

Third, the connection between urban context and appreciation of the possible benefits of cultural diversity deriving from refugee migration and settlement is a provocative result of this research with implications for models and strategies for urban development (see Kraly, Coulter, Weinberg, and Murray 2005; see also Gouveia, Carranza, and Cogua 2005):

> I think the refugees, for some people in the area, have reminded people from time to time that Utica actually exists. At a time when we were desperate for something bright, the refugees were one of the bright spots. I think that gives people hope for Utica, and just keeps Utica on people's minds. But also, it's a city that's historically been known as having really interesting people and communities. (community development scholar)

> We're this community in transition . . . a much more diverse community, a community that is more visible and multi-cultural, instead of this little place tucked away where you wouldn't know it unless you know how to find it. . . . To really support . . . not these people losing their ethnic identities, but really celebrating them in a much more visible way that we can all be enriched by. It seems to me that downtown Utica would like that, and it would be a wonderful contribution to the community. (social researcher)

Thus, in addition to building cultural capacity or a multicultural infrastructure for social services and support throughout the community, there are voices for building the "multicultural capital" of Utica—to promote the cultural as well as human resources of the city:

> So what are we going to do with what we have? And what we have is an extremely multi-cultural community. And so, that's a richness that to me sets us aside from someone else. I think that the future of Utica is having a unique opportunity to have a more worldly understanding, than most communities of our size. (foundation leader).

Such perspectives have implications for processes of social adjustment and integration among refugees and other international migrants. Councilwoman Deana Smiljic not only encouraged the congregation at the citizenship ceremony to stay in Utica and build a strong and prosperous community, she also appealed to the new U.S. citizens to retain and express their culture: "No one wants you to forget."

Notes

1. The 1980 Refugee Act consists of amendments to the Immigration and Nationality Act. The 1980 act "[p]rovided the first permanent and systematic procedure for the admission and effective resettlement of refugees of special humanitarian concern to the United States" (U.S. Department of Justice 1997, A.1-18). The law defined refugee in accordance with the 1967 United Nations Protocol on Refugees, thus theoretically eliminating flight from Communism as the criterion for refugee status. The law also authorized the adjustment to permanent resident status of all persons admitted as refugees after one year's residence in the United States and established a federally funded domestic program of refugee resettlement (U.S. Department of Justice 1997, A.1-18).

2. In order to develop comparability in geographic units over time, I have collapsed census tracts identified in decennial census operations prior to 2000. Data maps were prepared by Meg Reed, undergraduate student in geography, Colgate University.

3. This ceremony was held on February 28, 2003, at the Legislative Chambers of Oneida County.

References

Alba, Richard, and Victor Nee. 2003. *Remaking the American Mainstream*. New York: Russell Sage.

Bailey, Adrian. 2001. "Turning transnational: notes on the theorization of international migration." *International Journal of Population Geography* 7:413-428.

Berry, Kate A., and Martha L. Henderson. 2002. *Geographical Identities if Ethnic America: Race, Space, and Place*. Reno: University of Nevada Press.

Bump, Micah, Lindsay Lowell, and Silje Pettersen. 2005. "The Growth and Population Characteristics of Immigrants and Minorities in America's New Settlement States." Pp. 19-53 in *Beyond the Gateway,* edited by Elzbieta M Gozdziak and Susan F. Martin. Lanham, MD: Lexington Books.

Burawoy, Michael. 1998. "The extended case method." *Sociological Theory* 16:4-33.

Camarota, Steven A., and John Keeley. 2001. "The New Ellis Islands: Examining Non-traditional Areas of Immigrant Settlement in the 1990s." Center for Immigration Studies *Backgrounder*. September.

Capps, Randolph, et al. *The New Neighbors: A User's Guide to Data on Immigrants in U.S. Communities.* Washington, DC: The Urban Institute.

Coughlan, Reed, and Judith Owens-Manley. 2002. "The New Face of Immigration: Bosnian Refugees in Transition." In *Ethnic Utica*, edited by J. Pula. Utica, NY: Oneida County Historical Society.

———. 2005. Surviving War, Starting Over: Bosnians Resettle in Upstate New York. In *Refugees' Resettlement in the West: Economic, Social and Cultural Aspects,* edited by V. Colic-Peisker and P. Waxman. New York: Nova Science Publishers, Inc.

Donato, Katharine M., Melissa Stainback, and Carl L. Bankston III. 2005. "The Economic Incorporation of Mexican Immigrants in Southern Louisiana: A Tale of Two Cities." Pp. 76-100 in *New Destinations: Mexican Immigration in the United States,* edited by Victor Zúñiga and Rubén Hernández-León. New York: Russell Sage Foundation.

Dunn, Timothy, Ana Maria Aragones, and George Shivers. 2005. "Recent Mexican Migration in the Rural Delmarva Peninsula: Human Rights versus Citizenship Rights in a Local Context." Pp. 155-183 in *New Destinations: Mexican Immigration in the United States,* edited by Victor Zúñiga and Rubén Hernández-León. New York: Russell Sage Foundation.

Durand, Jorge, Doulgas Massey, and Chiara Capoferro. 2005. "The New Geography of Mexican Immigration." Pp. 1-22 in *New Destinations: Mexican Immigration in the United States,* edited by Victor Zúñiga and Rubén Hernández-León. New York: Russell Sage Foundation.

Estaville, Lawrence, Susan Harwick, James Allen, and Ines Miyares. 2003. "American Ethnic Geography: Development Contributions, and Challenges." In *Geography in America at the Dawn of the 21st Century,* edited by Gary Gaile and Cort Willmott. Oxford: Oxford University.

Foner, Nancy. 2000. *From Ellis Island to JFK: New York's Two Great Waves of Immigration.* New Haven, CT: Yale University; New York: Russell Sage Foundation.

———, ed. 2001. *New Immigrants in New York.* New York: Columbia University.

Foner, Nancy, Ruben Rumbaut, and Stephen J. Gold, eds. 2000. *Immigration Research for a New Century.* New York: Russell Sage Foundation.

Gouveia, Lourdes, Miquel A. Carranza, and Jesney Cogua. 2005. "The Great Plains Migration: Mexicanos and Latinos in Nebraska." Pp. 23-49 in *New Destinations: Mexican Immigration in the United States*, edited by Victor Zúñiga and Rubén Hernández-León. New York: Russell Sage Foundation.

Gozdziak, Elzbieta, and Susan F. Martin, Editors. 2005. *Beyond the Gateway.* Lanham, MD: Lexington Books.

Grey, Mark A., and Anne C. Woodrick. 2005. "'Latinos Have Revitalized Our Community': Mexican Migration and Anglo Responses in Marshalltown, Iowa." Pp. 133-154 in *New Destinations: Mexican Immigration in the United States,* edited by Victor Zúñiga and Rubén Hernández-León. New York: Russell Sage Foundation

Griffith, David. 2005. "Rural Industry and Mexican Immigration and Settlement in North Carolina." Pp. 50-75 in *New Destinations: Mexican Immigration in the United States*, edited by Victor Zúñiga and Rubén Hernández-León. New York: Russell Sage Foundation.

Hagstrom, Paul. 2000. Materials prepared for presentation at Colgate University.

Hardwick, Susan W. 2002. "Russian Acculturation in Sacramento." Pp. 255-278 in *Geographical Identities of Ethnic America: Race, Space, and Place,* edited by Kate A. Berry and Martha L. Henderson. Reno: University of Nevada Press.

———. 2003. "Migration, embedded networks and social capital: towards theorizing North American ethnic geography." *International Journal of Population Geography* 9:163-179.

Hirschman, Charles, Philip Kasinitz, and Josh DeWind, eds. 1999. *The Handbook of International Migration: The American Experience*. New York: Russell Sage Foundation.

Hyndman, Jennifer. 2000a. "Interrogating borders: a transnational approach to refugee research in Vancouver." *The Canadian Geographer* 44:244-258.

———. 2000b. *Managing Displacement: Refugees and the Politics of Humanitarianism*. Minneapolis: University of Minnesota Press.

Kasinitz, Philip, John Mollenkopf, and Mary C. Waters, eds. 2004. *Becoming New Yorkers: Ethnographies of the New Second Generation*. New York: Russell Sage Foundation.

Kline, Allissa. 2006. "Immigrants Eased Region's Population Drop." *Observer-Dispatch*. March 16, 2B.

Kraly, Ellen Percy, Lorraine Coulter, Theresa Murray, and Adam Weinberg. 2005. "Refugee Resettlement and City Revitalization: Prospects for Change in Utica, New York." Mansucript in preparation.

Kraly, Ellen Percy, and Ines Miyares. 2001. "Immigration to New York: Policy, Population, and Patterns." Pp. 33-79 in *New Immigrants in New York*, edited by Nancy Foner. New York: Columbia University Press.

Kraly, Ellen Percy, and Kristin VanValkenburg. 2003. "Refugee Resettlement in Utica, New York: Opportunities and Issues for Community Development." Pp. 125-148 in *Multicultural Geographies: The Changing Racial/Ethnic Patterns of the United States*, edited by John Frazier and Florence Margai. Binghamton, NY: Binghamton University Press.

Lawson, Victoria. 2000. "Arguments within the Geographyof Movement: the Theoretical Potential of Migrants' Stories." *Progress in Human Geography* 24:173-89.

Lobo, Peter, Joseph Salvo, and Ronald Flores. 2002. "The Streets and Byways in All of New York: Stories, Statistics and Styles in a High Immigration Era." Joint Statistical Association Meetings, American Statistical Association, Section on Government Statistics, Social Statistics Section. New York, August 10-15.

McHugh, Kevin. 2000. "Inside, Outside, Upside Down, Backward, Forward, Round and Round: a Case for Ethnographic Studies in Migration." *Progress in Human Geography* 23:71-89.

Mohawk Valley Resource Center for Refugees. 2003. *Mohawk Valley Resource Center for Refugees*.

———. 2006. *Mohawk Valley Resource Center for Refugees*.

Newbold, Bruce, and Matthew Foulkes. 2004. "Geography and Segmented Assimilation: Examples from the New York Chinese." *Population, Space and Place* 10:3-18.

Noble, Allen George. 1999. *An Ethnic Geography of Early Utica, New York: Time Space, and Community*. Lewiston, NY: E. Mellen Press.

Portes, Alejandro, and Ruben Rumbaut. 1996. *Immigrant America: A Portrait*. Berkeley: University of California Press.

———. 2001. "Conclusion—The Forging of a New America: Lessons for Theory and Policy." Pp. 301-317 in *Ethnicities: Children of Immigrants in America*, edited by Ruben Rumbaut and Alejandro Portes. Berkeley: University of California Press, and New York: Russell Sage Foundation.

Portes, Alejandro, and Min Zhou. 1993. "The New Second Generation: Segmented Assimilation and Its Variants." *Annals of the American Academy of Political and Social Sciences* 530:74-96.

Rumbaut, Ruben and Alejandro Portes, eds. 2001. *Ethnicities: Children of Immigrants in America.* Berkeley: University of California Press; New York: Russell Sage Foundation.

Salvo, Joseph, and Peter Lobo. 1996. *The Newest New Yorkers, 1990-1994.* New York: Department of City Planning.

Silvey, Rachel, and Victoria Lawson. 1999. "Placing the Migrant." *Annals of the Association of American Geographers* 89:121-132.

Singer, Audrey. 2004. "The Rise of New Immigrant Gateways." The Living Census Series. Washington DC: The Brookings Institution.

Slater, C., and G. Hall. 1994. *1994 County and City Extra.* Lanham, Md.: Berham Press.

United Nations High Commissioner for Refugees. 2005. "The Town that Loves Refugees." *Refugees* 1:138+.

U.S. Bureau of the Census. 2000. Selected data from Census 2000.

Waldinger, Roger. 1996. *Still the Promised City: African-Americans and New Immigrants in PostIndustrial New York.* Cambridge, MA: Harvard University.

———, ed. 2001. *Strangers at the Gate: New Immigrants in Urban America.* Berkeley: University of California Press.

Waldinger, Roger, and Michael Lichter. 2003. *How the Other Half Works: Immigration and the Social Organization of Labor.* Berkeley: University of California.

Zelinsky, Wilbur, and Barrett A. Lee. 1998. "Heterolocalism: an Alternative Model of the Sociospatial Behavior of Immigrant Ethnic Communities." *International Journal of Population Geography* 4:281-298.

Zielbauer, Paul. 1999. "Utica Welcomes Refugees as the Hope for a Prosperous Future." *New York Times.* May 7, A21.

Zúñiga, Victor, and Rubén Hernández-León, eds. 2005. *New Destinations: Mexican Immigration in the United States.* New York: Russell Sage Foundation.

PART FOUR

EPILOGUE

Chapter 13

The Contributions of Immigrants: From Megalopolis to Mainstream

Richard C. Jones

The four corners where Bushwick Avenue meets Flushing could be a movie set for quintessential New York blight. The 360-degree view offers the sweat-beige brick of a public housing project, the charred black of a burned-out liquor store, and the smoky gray of a 24-hour discount gas station, its attendants attending behind thick yellow-toned plexiglass. . . . Homeboys in hooded sweatshirts pass in and out of a nearby restaurant to make quick calls from a public phone by the entrance. Lookouts, no doubt, for the local drug lord. This is a neighborhood that the police have dubbed "The Well." Brooklyn, New York in the 1990s.

Down the block at 913 Flushing, a line of customers snakes into the gutter, silent figures waiting for their daily fix. Crack cocaine? Heroin?

No, señor. Tortillas.

They line up like this every Saturday at Tortilleria Piaxtla, Inc., and on Sunday, too. Brooklyn's first tortilla factory is one of five manufacturers of the Mexican staple to open in the city since 1986. As the long line attests, business is booming for owner and founder Fernando Sanchez, [who] processes roughly two hundred tons of corn flour into saucer-sized pancakes every month. Sanchez [had] eked his way through a series of factory, then restaurant jobs, rising from dishwasher, to cook, to chef's assistant at a Midtown French restaurant. In 1986, he called in some of the favors he had earned through a decade of money-lending to friends and relatives [to found the tortilleria]. From just two co-workers when he started, Sanchez now employs fifty, "Puros Poblanos," like Sanchez, from the Mexican state of Puebla. Tortilleria Piaxtla is named for his hometown.

Economists, viewing the output of Tortilleria Piaxtla and the other new tortilla vendors, would see something different. Call it the Tortilla Index. If the index were converted to cover neighborhoods, it would show an expansion spreading out from New York's poorest quarters—East Harlem, Bushwick, and

> the South Bronx of the Savage Skulls—to less desperate but still poor districts, like Kensington, Corona, Sunset Park, and the Lower East Side. Every hundred tortillas would be a family, representing rent being paid, baby clothes being bought, movies being seen, and wages being earned. . . . Ten thousand households spending their incomes on the margins of the working class. [At first], teenagers from the nearby projects preyed on the Mexicans who came to Tortilleria Piaxtla to work or shop. But as the block filled with new families, robbing got harder to do. Mexicans filled The Well. By filling the old garment lofts, they filled their pockets, which filled the apartment houses and filled Fernando Sanchez's dream to open his store. "Now the whole block is Mexican people, Sanchez said. "Everyone working, no one on welfare. That's why no more they rob my people." (Millman 1997, 19-24).

This story is one of many in a richly ethnographic book by Joel Millman entitled *The Other Americans: How Immigrants Renew our Country, our Economy, and our Values.* It takes place far from the Heartland. In fact, it is situated in the very heart of Megalopolis. Yet this story reflects several deep communalities with other immigrant success stories all across the United States, over the past several decades. Thus, it emphasizes the points that I wish to make in this final chapter.

Immigrants bring with them a strong work ethic, a fierce independence, a strong desire to succeed, and family networks that enable them to do so despite poverty and community hostility. Their ambition and drive are traits that are quintessentially American. Instead of eroding national identity and values, immigrants reinforce them in a rather spectacular manner. Their attitudes are matched by their accomplishments. They obtain advanced degrees, found businesses, create new jobs, and revitalize neighborhoods. Their social costs to local areas are temporary, and in whatever time frame, are exceeded by their economic benefits to these same areas. Whether they "assimilate" culturally to the traditional mainstream is not the right question. Do their cultures benefit U.S. society? The answer to this question appears to be a resounding "yes." Apart from their adoption of the U.S. work ethic, their family-oriented, communal, and principled approach to life provides a great many benefits and lessons for a society that has become, in many ways, individualistic, self-centered, and hedonistic. It is not just the "model minorities" who contribute to U.S. society in these ways. Lower-status immigrant groups have these same values and even with the supreme challenges they face, they succeed—although it may require a generation to do so. And if second and third generation Latinos and Asians in traditional gateway cities have adjusted and prospered—and mastered English and married outside their ethnic group—is there any reason to believe that this won't occur for new gateway cities and towns in the Heartland?

Immigrants and American Values

Nativists worry that core Anglo-Saxon and European values are being pushed aside by new national groups with strong outside loyalties and customs. Arthur

Schlesinger, Jr. (2005), warns against jettisoning European ideas and traditions for new African, Asian, Middle Eastern, or Latin American traditions, simply as anti-hegemonic backlash. He takes aim at Afrocentric curriculum in universities (dating his argument), but his reaction to "ethnic revolt" clearly resonates with recent arguments by immigration restrictionists against ethnic politics. He identifies an "American Creed" (a concept originally Myrdal's) springing from European cultural roots and whose branches are individual liberty, human rights, the rule of law, and cultural freedom. These stand in contrast to the "collectivist cultures" (comprising 70 percent of the world's population) in which the good of the group overrides personal goals and rights—obviously not a good thing in his estimation. The most widely-quoted proponent of these ideas currently is Samuel Huntington (2002), who sees the history of the world as a perpetual conflict along national, ideological and (now) cultural fault lines. Unfortunately, according to Huntington, this fault line now splits apart America from within—a "deconstruction" that began in the 1960s as the civil rights movement (a good thing) was carried too far, resulting in balkanization along ethnic, linguistic, and political lines. The vanguard of this deconstruction is new immigrants who challenge our core (WASP) values. To him, America was, and clearly should be, a *nation state* with a common political, ethnic, racial, and cultural identity. For 165 years (1775-1940) the country fit all these criteria—but afterwards rapid cultural fragmentation pruned away everything except our common political identity. He denies that we are a "nation of *immigrants*," arguing instead that it was the early English *settlers* (the "charter group") who formed our lasting institutions. Immigrants have simply built upon that base. Finally, he attempts to link work ethic, religiosity, pride in nationality, and American greatness in a unique and inseparable whole that if adulterated will lead to our peril as a nation. He cites the breakup of the USSR, and the devolution of the U.K., as warnings to the United States of what can happen when ethnic and cultural sub-identities are carried too far. In fact, Huntington believes that the southwestern U.S. may soon reunite with Mexico, led into battle by Mexican and Mexican American political leaders whose statements he cites as evidence of their irredentist motives (see also Yeh Ling Ling 2004). Schlesinger's and Huntington's views are magnified in the arguments of Patrick Buchanan (2002) and Roy Beck (1996). Buchanan depicts a "war against the past" in which an intimidated majority refuses to reassert itself against a "foreign enemy" (immigrants) who threaten the future of western civilization. Beck envisions an "irreparable change" in U.S. lifestyle (racial strife, overpopulation, and environmental degradation) as a logical outcome of "too many" immigrants.

I have tried to understand these arguments. They are not without interesting historical insights. Our roots are indeed deep; it is true that these roots are becoming intertwined with new, faster-growing rootstocks; and indeed, once-great political states like the United States have withered and disintegrated. But I reject the nativist arguments. There are two major dimensions to my rebuttal: (1) the uniqueness and resiliency of the American political experiment; and (2) the selectivity and values of immigrants themselves.

To begin with, the "American Creed" is unique and rather more durable than assumed by nativists. The political birth of the United States was as much a reaction to European institutions as an embracing of them. The founders were not concerned with ethnic or cultural origins of newcomers (blacks and Indians being important exceptions)—as great as they were then perceived to be—but with class-based political ideas they might have brought with them from Europe (in particular, from monarchic Europe of the late eighteenth century). The Founders' ideas that all men are created equal and should be treated equally, that inherited status is unimportant, and that government should prevent the majority from tyrannizing the minority, were offered as an alternative political creed to Europe's class society. As Tamar Jacoby has written, "the framework that the founders established was close to a perfect scaffolding for what would become a nation of immigrants" (Jacoby 2004b). Thus, the ethnic, class, and religious divisions of Europe would be removed once an immigrant reached America. Only political allegiance was required. This view contrasts markedly with Huntington's notion of a "nation state" with its requirement for cultural unity. Jacoby's interpretation of U.S. values resonates with that of the early-twentieth century philosopher Horace Kallen as well as many recent writers. It is starkly different in many ways from that of Huntington, Buchanan, and Beck. The "American Creed" includes not only freedom and respect for immigrant and minority rights, but also freedom for the reassertion of majority rights. For example, in recent years minority successes in the form of bilingual programs, race-sensitive political redistricting, minority college admission quotas, black and Asian study programs in universities, and H1B visa expansions (to admit skilled immigrants) have all been eroded by subsequent legislation or judicial decisions. These decisions may have been flawed. But they do not support the nativist claim of an intimidated, estranged majority.

Contrary to the assumptions of nativists, immigrants do not replicate the demographics or values of their home countries. They may be poorer and less educated than the average for their countries (as in the case of Mexicans or Haitians) or they may be better off (as in the case of Asian Indians or Chinese). They do tend to be younger, more ambitious, and less likely to commit crimes than those who stay behind. Notably, they tend to be more politically liberal than people in their home countries, and in fact are frequently opposed to the policies of their home governments. These latter traits suggest that immigrants are to an important degree pre-adapted to life in the United States. It can be argued that they believe in the ideals of the Founding Fathers—opportunity, freedom, and individual rights—more fervently than the average American does. Consider these statements, by educated immigrant entrepreneurs to the United States:

> I came to the United States frightened and scared. But I found if you do well and if you have a dream you will find people in America willing to help and give you an opportunity (Nancy Chang, Taiwanese-born Co-Founder of Tanox, a medical research company in Houston; quoted in Anderson and Platzer 2004).

> It's a filter system: First, ambitious people come. Second, an environment for growth exists that encourages and accelerates ambition, which doesn't exist in other parts of the world (Ronnie Vasishta, English-born of Indian ancestry, CEO of eASIC, a producer of computer chips, in Santa Clara, California; quoted in Anderson and Platzer 2004).

These quintessential U.S. values are not restricted to higher-status immigrants. In *Villages*, Richard Critchfield describes the magnetic pull that the United States has for Mexican villagers from Puebla:

> One thing that we have going for us is the curious love affair most villagers have with America; they can even be a bit possessive about it. America is becoming everybody's second country. America as a symbol, an idea, of the good life, of oomph and vitality and freedom and fun (quoted in Millman 1997, 13-14).

A related and final point about values is the alleged positive relationship between national Christian religiosity, pride in nationality, and American greatness (a relationship lauded by Huntington and also Buchanan). But this is an ambivalent correlation at best. Huntington (2002) concludes his book with a graph showing a strong positive relationship between religiosity and pride in country, stating that "in a world in which religion shapes the allegiances, the alliances, and the antagonisms of people on every continent, it should not be surprising if Americans again turn to religion to find their national identity and their national purpose." Let us hope not. Inspection of the graph places the U.S., with high values on both religiosity and nationalism, in the company of Northern Ireland, South Africa, Nigeria, Turkey, and Brazil. For all their progress in recent years, these countries are lacking in various degrees the very democratic ideals and personal freedoms that Huntington champions. Moreover, considerable research has positively linked high religiosity to intolerance. When the American majority seeks renewal of purpose and security in religion and patriotism, this has the negative effect of eroding the very freedoms (of minorities and "others," including immigrants) that are at the core of the "American Creed."

The Economic Impact of Immigrants

There has been a substantial literature on this topic, but little agreement. Some studies stress the costs to American society while others emphasize the benefits. Few indeed are the studies that attempt to arrive at net benefits in a particular category (say, social services received vs. taxes paid, or "American" jobs lost to immigrants vs. jobs created by immigrants). Even fewer are those that attempt an accounting of overall net benefits across all categories.

Concern for the economic costs of immigration centers around two issues: (1) *social service* costs for the provision of health care, education, and welfare to immigrants and their children, and (2) *labor market* costs in the form of displacement and wage depression in jobs held by natives. Regarding social service costs, George Borjas (2004) concludes that less-skilled immigrants, particularly Mexicans, are taking much longer to assimilate economically than earlier immigrant waves (see also Smith 2001; Ortiz 1996; Pastor 1999; Jones, Chapter 7, this volume), thus placing a greater social service burden on American society. In 2000, Mexico accounted for over one-fourth of the foreign-born in the U.S., and an estimated two-thirds of lower-status foreign-born. One outcome of Mexicans' lack of advancement is the social service burden it may create. Although poor, undocumented migrants often avoid seeking medical help and welfare or the services of the police or a lawyer, when their situations deteriorate they may be forced to seek emergency aid for illness, accident, childbirth, shelter, food, abuse, criminal victimization, etc. These emergency services are expensive and their costs must be principally borne by local jurisdictions. Beyond this, the longer-term issue of educating children whose first language is not English has placed a financial burden on local school districts. The social overhead costs of immigration may be especially high for cities and towns outside of Megalopolis that have recently faced unprecedented growth in immigration (Kochhar et al. 2005; Foust et al. 2002)—including Garden City (Beck 1996, 203-207) which is the focus of Chapter 6 in this volume.

Regarding labor market costs, consider the arguments of Roy Beck (1996). Beck feels that immigrants have advanced economically "on the backs of black Americans" (pp. 156-202). He cites Booker T. Washington's impassioned speech to northern industrialists in 1895, in which he recounted the story of a trans-Atlantic sailing ship whose crew was dying of thirst. The captain sighted another vessel and signaled his plight, but the ship merely signaled back "Cast down your bucket where you are." This made no sense until the captain realized that his ship was in the 200-mile-wide mouth of the Amazon River, where the water was fresh and life-giving! Washington drew on this story to decry his audience's importing of immigrants to fill their factory jobs, when they were surrounded by "vast pools" of loyal black workers in dire need of work, given the failure of Reconstruction. "Cast down your bucket where you are," implored the great educator and black leader. "Cast it down among the eight millions of Negroes whose habits you know. . . ." Washington was, unfortunately, unsuccessful in his crusade. Beck sees a direct analogy to the post-1965 situation in the United States when again immigration has been promoted to fill jobs that Americans supposedly won't take or can't fill. Relevant to this analogy and to the theme of this book is Beck's discussion of post-1980 immigration to the "poultry crescent" in the Southeastern U.S. In this non-megalopolitan region, employment has boomed but wages have dropped, as Mexican and Central American workers have systematically replaced the traditionally black labor force. Beck believes that poverty and joblessness among the "failed black third" are to a large degree the result of immigration into this region. His interviews with employers appear to support a decline of black as well as Euro-American employment not only in the poultry industry but in seafood processing, forestry, and meatpacking, and a concomitant increase in Latino employment in these sectors. These interviews and those of others reveal preferences for, and stereotyping of, Latinos as the preferred workers owing to their exemplary diligence and lack of complaining on the job (Beck 1996, 176-78; Johnson-Webb 2003, 79-84; Griffith 2005; Gouveia et al. 2005).

The argument for economic displacement of natives by immigrants extends beyond extractive industries of the Southeast. In large cities, it is argued, blacks and poor whites are bypassed when it comes to job offerings by businesses such as janitorial services in Los Angeles, restaurants in Washington, D.C., and construction firms in New York City (Beck 1996, 180-83). There is some statistical evidence for this trend: in Los Angeles, between 1970 and 1990, black male janitors decreased in number by one-third, while male Mexican immigrant janitors increased sixteen-fold, and by 1990 unemployment among the former group was over three times that of the latter (Rosenfeld and Tienda 1999). In "high immigration areas" (traditional gateway metros like those above), net out-migration has been recorded for poor black and white residents, purportedly compelled by competition with low-status immigrants (Frey 1999; Frey and Liaw 1999; Frey 2002). Economic displacement, it is contended, also occurs for foreign students and professionals in the sciences, business, and academia. Immigrants entering the country as graduate students or on H1B work visas are preferred (it is argued) over eager domestic applicants who are equally qualified (Beck 1996, 136-155).

There is no doubt that these types of social service burdens and worker dislocations have occurred. The question that must be addressed is whether these burdened or displaced groups as a whole (not just particular subgroups of them), and society as a whole, are ultimately better off with immigration than without it—that is, whether immigration creates jobs and economic savings in other aspects of the labor and product markets that benefit them in the long run. Immigration lends itself to maritime analogies—cast-down buckets, rising tides, seas of immigrants, etc. To continue this thought current, we may ask whether this "tide" of immigrants has swamped the boats of entitled minorities and domestic workers, who are (presumably) anchored to the seafloor? Or we may ask whether it has raised all the boats in the harbor, including poorer workers who are not anchored to the seafloor or who are able to cut loose from their anchors?

Regarding the cost of social services, contrary to popular belief immigrants do pay, indirectly if not directly, for these services. At the federal level, an estimated three-fourths of undocumented immigrants submit earnings statements and pay wage deductions, even though their employers may be aware that they are illegal (but do not want to admit it). Since undocumenteds use fictitious social security numbers, their social security payments pile up in a special "earning suspense file" to the tune of $6-7 billion per year—money that helps bail out this beleaguered fund in the service of American retirees (Porter 2005), including a large proportion of minorities. Social Security is the largest wage deduction of undocumented migrant workers. However, these workers are not entitled to federal benefits. Therefore, at the federal level their presence is a net income earner for the government. At the state level, undocumented migration is also a net income earner. A study by the Texas State Comptroller (Strayhorn 2006) concludes that undocumented migrants to the state contribute almost 40 percent more in revenue (in the form of taxes, federal program funding, and fees) than they consume in state funds for education, health, criminal justice, and other programs. Local jurisdictions may find themselves paying the costs of these programs. But the logical solution is not to get rid of the migrants; it is to transfer funds from the federal and state levels to the local level to pay for the services that they use.

Speaking broadly, and including all immigrants, Julian Simon's comprehensive study of the economic consequences of immigration concludes that immigrants contribute far more to public coffers in deductions, transfers, taxes, and fees, than they withdraw in social services (Simon 1999, Chapter 5). His accounting does not even include other considerations that would push the net benefit calculations higher, namely: (1) Working-age immigrants' education has already been paid for by their countries of origin, which constitutes a savings to the United States (Lynch 2001); (2) First generation Latino immigrants and their children tend to be mentally and physically healthier than their U.S.-born counterparts, and thus less of a health burden (Hancock 2005); and (3) Social support for immigrant families should be viewed as an investment in economic growth and future prosperity, not as an expense (Massey 2004), for without it the country incurs a high opportunity cost that must be paid many-fold by subsequent generations.

Regarding labor-market impacts of immigrants, research has clearly established that displacement of domestic workers in some sectors is more than compensated by the creation of jobs in other sectors. In our boat analogy, some (anchored) boats will be submerged by immigrants while many more (unanchored) boats will be buoyed by the immigrant tide to higher levels of economic attainment. For example, Rosenfeld and Tienda (1999) found for selected U.S. cities that although immigrants displaced black and white janitors, maids, and apparel workers, domestic workers retained or improved their positions in higher-paying jobs in high-tech manufacturing and in skilled service occupations—where English-speaking ability and education are important. In other cases immigration appears to be the driving force behind job creation for domestic minorities. For example, Mexican American teachers are hired to teach in districts with a high influx of Mexican immigrant children. For another example, immigrant entrepreneurs create businesses with employment and income multipliers that work to the benefit of U.S. born minorities in the communities where immigrants settle (see below). Rosenfeld and Tienda (1999) conclude that "It may be that an influx of low-skilled immigrants can help push some native groups up the occupational hierarchy" (p. 97). This statement receives support in another study outside of megalopolis over the 1990s (Kochhar et al. 2005). The authors discover that in 36 rapid-growth counties of the "New South" (accounting for over half of Hispanic growth in the six-state region of NC, AR, GA, TN, SC, and AL), Hispanic and non-Hispanic employment went up together. That is, those counties that had the highest growth of Hispanics also had the highest growth in non-Hispanics, and this was true for blacks as well as whites. This trend held for both rural counties where extractive and manufacturing jobs were created and filled by Hispanics at the same time that new service jobs were filled by others, and for booming metropolitan or adjacent counties where construction jobs were filled by immigrant Hispanics, while white-collar jobs in transportation, education, health, finance, etc., were filled by non-Hispanics. The authors conclude: "There is little evidence that the gains for Latinos were accompanied by losses for non-Latinos. . . . Economic growth in the New South appears to have delivered significant new job opportunities for most workers during the 1990s" (p. 27). The conclusions of Kochhar et al. are supported by those of Heather Smith (Chapter 11 of this volume), who notes that Charlotte's rapid growth has created new job opportunities for black as well as Hispanic workers. Other research supports the conclusions of these studies, both within and outside megalopolis (Bean et al. 1999; Portes and Zhou 1999; Simon 1999, 175-96; Murphy et al. 2001). Chris Airriess' contribution to this volume (Chapter 8) suggests that Vietnamese re-territorialization of black areas in Versailles (New Orleans) was not contested; this process led to the eventual founding of almost 100 Vietnamese businesses that supported both co-ethnic demand and a larger extra-community demand. In Chapter 5 of this volume, Nancy Hiemstra illustrates the clear economic benefits of Mexican migrants in Leadville, Colorado. They fill seasonal jobs in the nearby ski industry that given its exponential growth, is hard-pressed to find enough workers in construction, maintenance, and resort services. It is evident that the Mexicans' hard work and incredible sacrifices benefit immeasurably both the ski towns and the families who visit them.

Additionally, there are labor market benefits from immigrant entrepreneurship and scientific expertise, as well as non-labor market benefits from the improvement in urban land values and the cost of living. Regarding entreneurship, Joel Kotkin tells the story of Charlie Woo, a Hong Kong immigrant who in the early 1970s established "Toytown" in a formerly derelict industrial area just east of downtown Los Angeles (Kotkin 2000, 2004). This wholesale district today handles 60 percent of U.S./Mexican toy imports from Asian suppliers. Its location here generates 4000 jobs for inner-city residents. Toytown also has *multiplier effects* in the hundreds of small toy-making, design, and distribution firms that have agglomerated at the site. Kotkin proceeds to give other examples of immigrant businesses, including those in non-megalopolitan metro areas where suburban ("midopolitan") ethnic enclaves have become focal points for investment and employment. One example is the south side of St. Louis where the Bevo Branch of Southern Commercial Bank doubled its deposits in two years from the activities of an eclectic mix of Bosnians, Somalis, Vietnamese, and Mexicans who moved there. Another is the Harwin corridor outside Loop 610 in Houston, where 800 shops have created an "Asian frontier sprawl" of Chinese, Korean, and Indian furniture, luggage, car parts, electronics, and related businesses. Indeed, it was largely immigrant investments that resurrected Houston from its 1980s oil bust. In Tucson, Arizona, Chinese entrepreneurs have been very instrumental in the city's economic evolution (Weng 2001).

In regard to scientific expertise, in contrast to the fears of Beck (1997) that immigrants are crowding domestic college students and PhDs out of university seats and scientific positions, Anderson and Platzer (2004) describe a situation in which immigrants (most of whom entered the U.S. as students) are taking scientific/research positions and starting new firms in the United States that hire thousands of domestic college graduates. These firms compete in the lucrative global market for microcomputers, internet search engines, medicines, medical equipment, and software publishing (see also Farrell 2002). In fact, fully one-fourth of all U.S. venture-capital backed public companies established since 1990 have been founded by immigrants (including Intel, Sun Microsystems, Solectron, eBay, Yahoo!, Google, and many small medical and software firms). These firms hire a quarter million workers in the U.S. and bring in substantial investment capital from abroad. Anderson and Platzer contend that the recent U.S. cutback in H1B visas is not creating more jobs for U.S. citizens. Instead, it is resulting in the flight of high-tech entrepreneurs—and the jobs they have generated—to Europe, Canada, and Australia. It is also resulting in the out-sourcing of work to teams of researchers and technicians living in foreign countries such as India or the Philippines.

Less easily-measured but equally important are the effects of immigration on urban revitalization and the cost of living. One type of revitalization is that which brings life to a dying area. This is exemplified by the story that opened this chapter, of Fernando Sanchez whose Mexican countrymen brought life to the decaying Bushwick area of Brooklyn. Millman (1997) also recounts the story of Brownsville, another Brooklyn district that was the focal point, in July of 1977, for riots and looting—based on pent-up racial tensions that surged forth during an infamous power blackout. This incident precipitated the closing of businesses, the out-migration of middle-class blacks, and the subsequent isolation of a residual black underclass in the inner-city, in a downward spiral of unemployment and crime. But black West Indian immigrants looked past the racial hatred and run-down buildings and homes, and saw opportunity here. As Millman states it, "After Blackout Night, West Indians were just about the only Brooklynites, white or black, moving in" (p. 83). Not harboring the racial baggage of American blacks, these new residents found a niche in health care (hospitals, nursing homes, and home health care), where their English speaking ability was an asset in understanding the needs of their largely white patients. This niche led to the formation of renewed black neighborhoods clustered around the central Brooklyn hospitals, and became the nucleus of economic renewal in all of Brooklyn. Over the 1980s, the borough gained population for the first time in three decades. Millman concludes:

> Far from displacing American-born blacks, these [West Indian immigrants] restore life in the black community, rejuvenating all the institutions—black-run stores, black-run schools, black churches, black sports teams, black block asso-

> ciations—that withered during the years of the great exodus. . . . The benefits of black gentrification may not devolve equally to all blacks, but without immigrant enterprise, few might benefit at all (Millman 1997, 95).

This type of revitalization, with immigrants bringing life to dying areas, has occurred all across inner-city areas in megalopolis—Chinese, Taiwanese, Koreans, and Vietnamese in Los Angeles' Toytown (Kotkin 2000 2004); African Muslims and Uzbek/Tajik Jews in New York's Lefrak City, in Queens (Onishi 1996); and Haitians in Miami's Del Ray Beach (Millman 1997, 285-312).

Another type of revitalization is that which transforms small-town economic stagnation to economic growth. It is well-illustrated by economic restructuring of the meatpacking industry in conjunction with Mexican immigration to downward-transitional towns of the U.S. Midwest—a trend well described in Donald Stull and Michael Broadway's work (chapter 6 in this volume). Over the 1980s and 1990s, a plethora of new Hispanic workers, homes, businesses, and school programs revitalized the Garden City economy and transformed the urban landscape. This process has been repeated in Nebraska (Gouveia et al. 2005) and in Iowa. Marshalltown, Iowa, in addition to its meat packing plant, like Garden City is now a city with Latino tiendas, restaurants, and auto repair shops in addition to new teachers and offerings in the schools (where 70 percent of the elementary students are Hispanic). Many residents agree that Mexican immigration has revitalized their city. Marshalltown has accommodated its new residents better than most, with the help of its "sister city" ties with Villachuato, Michoacán (the hometown of most of its immigrants), which now include regular visits to the Mexican town by Marshalltown's civic leaders (Grey and Woodrick 2005; Baker and Hotek 2003).

Finally, in diverse urban settings immigration has lowered the cost of living for immigrants and residents alike. In large cities such as New York, enclave retail and service offerings make it possible for immigrants to make ends meet on bare survival incomes. The lower prices within these enclaves have the corollary effect of lowering prices outside the enclave. Millman (1997, Chapter 1) relates how immigrants to inner city New York brought back "the ten-cent phone call, the $1.50 round-trip bus fare, and the $2.95 all-you-can-eat buffet." How did this happen? The ten-cent call was a special line connecting New York to the Dominican Republic (the home of the largest Latino immigrant group to the city), but was a come-on for international and inter-metropolitan "local" service that undercut MCI by between 15 and 60 percent. Just like back home, immigrant customers walked up to storefront parlors, paid cash, entered a booth, and the call was dialed for them—a benefit for those without telephone credit cards or with bad experiences using public phones. Ultimately, these parlors became broadly popular in the inner-city. The $1.50 metropolitan bus fare resulted from the need for cheaper transportation to the subway stops for those traveling into Manhattan. A "guerilla army of minivans" driven by black West Indians filled this need, offering fast service for 40 percent less than the city buses along these same routes. The city had no choice but to lower its rates.

Millman calls it "Perestroika on wheels" (p. 26). The $2.95 lunch special was in Indian restaurants in Manhattan's "Bengali Alley." This special, at a time when New Yorkers couldn't buy a cheese sandwich for that price, was one factor in the competitive reduction in the prices of restaurant meals throughout Lower Manhattan, following the "distorted laws of supply and demand" that result from critical population mass and dire necessity (Millman 1997, 26-27).

Lowered prices also occur in smaller places with large immigrant presence. In San Antonio, a large foreign-born Mexican population of some 100,000—possibly half of which is a "shadow population" of undocumented migrants—labor in a variety of jobs that lower the cost of living for everyone in the city. The price of a home, the cost of home remodeling, the fee for landscaping a yard, the salary of a maid, the price of a restaurant meal—are all low in San Antonio because of an immigrant labor force in the city. The same types of benefits are beginning to accrue in towns of the South and Midwest, where immigrants came to work in factories or extractive industries, but have branched out into retail and service activities benefiting the general population. In small-town Iowa, Latino entrepreneurs started out providing service to Latino customers. Later, they expanded their Anglo customer bases "to the consternation of many established Anglo [businessmen]"—but presumably to the delight of the rest of the population (Grey and Woodrick 2005, 138-39).

The Cultural Impact of Immigrants

Some writers foresee major cultural problems stemming from immigration. Unlike past immigrant waves, it is argued, the new immigrants are failing to *acculturate* (adopt American culture as their own). This is believed to have two negative repercussions: it undermines America's national identity and global influence; and it inhibits the *integration* of these groups, in an economic and social sense. However, other writers dispute these points and in fact they cite numerous examples of precisely the opposite. Furthermore, they note that immigrant culture has many positive benefits today just as it did in the past. Immigrants bring new foods, music, art, customs, attitudes about leisure, etc. They rejuvenate an aging population. Their moral ideals complement and strengthen mainstream American ideals. Immigrants help reposition the family at the center of national life.

Regarding the alleged problems of low acculturation, Samuel Huntington (2004) worries that within the U.S. (as globally) we have a "clash of civilizations" in which immigrant cultures lack an appreciation of our Anglo-European roots and Christian values. He laments the emergence of "social polarization, cultural conflict, a decline in trust and community, and the erosion of traditional concepts of national identity" (p. 180). He fears that the United States is grappling with centrifugal forces similar to those faced by the USSR or Yugoslavia prior to 1990. These forces will in his estimation split the country apart (see also

Brimelow 1995). But Huntington worries even more that immigrant cultures are tending to preempt American culture. He is anxious that a "cosmopolitan alternative" in which the world reshapes America rather than the reverse (p. 363), is occurring. He prefers a "national alternative" that basically rejects the notion of a new American mainstream shaped by many cultures (Alba and Nee 2003; Jacoby 2004b). He believes that "America cannot become the world and still be America" (p. 365). Patrick Buchanan (2002) expresses these anxieties more strongly, as suggested by the title of his book (*The Death of the West*). He laments high minority birthrates, revisionist history, the de-Christianization of public life, and the swelling of the armies of affirmative action—in all of which immigration is suspected to play an overwhelming role. To these authors, "multiculturalism" is synonymous with national decline—a loss of national self-confidence, power, and influence in the world.

Many of these same authors believe that lack of acculturation impedes the *integration* of immigrant groups into U.S. society. The lack of integration of lower-status groups in the United States is not at issue here; various studies have shown that the first-generation integration is poor for groups such as Mexicans (Smith 2001; Foust et al. 2002; Ortiz 1996; Pastor 1999; Jones 2007, Chapter 7 of this volume), Dominicans (Pessar and Graham 2001), sub-Saharan Africans (Stoller 2001); and Hmong (Faruque 2002). What is at issue is whether the lack of cultural assimilation is the basis for poor integration into U.S. society. There is evidence that in the case of language, poor English ability indeed creates economic and social adjustment problems, because it limits the immigrant's choice of jobs and friends (e.g., Lopez 1996; Alba and Nee 2003, 223).

However, the concerns of restrictionist writers about integration extend considerably beyond language skills. Robert Samuelson, a columnist with *Newsweek* magazine, writes "...the huge and largely uncontrolled inflow of unskilled Latino workers into the United States is increasingly sabotaging the assimilation process" (Samuelson 2005). Interviews with Steven Camarota, Lawrence Katz, and George Borjas lead him to the "dispiriting" conclusion that poor school performance and low earnings are due (perhaps) to poor schools and to factors identifiable with Latino "culture" that remain unspecified. Samuelson finishes with the question for his readers, "Will immigration continue to foster national pride and strength or will it cause more and more weakness and anger?" Analogously, Roy Beck focuses on the upsurge of immigration of Southeast Asians to the upper Midwest and West Coast. Beck argues (citing Gerald Scully) that "increasing the number of languages and cultures in a country actually harm(s) economic progress." Despite the compassion he believes was shown these immigrants by residents of towns like Wausau, Wisconsin, and Worthington, Minnesota, the immigrants for their part have brought only poverty, welfare dependency, and crime (Beck 1997, 216-18). He deplores "the stark lines of social, economic, and cultural differences between the native-born in these cities and the large—and largely poor—new Southeast Asian population" (p. 50). These authors claim, then, that immigrant culture is incompatible with U.S. culture, and deleterious to immigrants' economic integration in U.S. society.

These arguments do not stand up well against recent research. First, other than the case of English language acquisition, maintenance of ties with the ethnic community does not appear to damage either the country or the immigrants in their personal efforts to integrate. For example, many Asian groups possess what Kibria refers to as ethnic identity capital (2002, 97)—advantages that their ethnicity has for extracting benefits in U.S. society and for benefiting U.S. society in the process. Korean, Chinese, and Japanese immigrants, who are familiar with the language and customs of their countries, may be valued employees of rapidly globalizing U.S. firms that have operations in those countries. Cubans, such as those in Phoenix and Miami noted by Emily Skop in Chapter 3 of this volume, are another group with ethnic identity capital, which along with legal status greatly aids their acculturation and integration into U.S. society. Reiterating a previous argument, the attraction of foreign scientists and entrepreneurs to the United States depends not just on economic opportunities here, but on how tolerant and appreciative we are of their culture. For example, Arab women in the U.S. may wear head scarves, but this right has been denied in France and the United Kingdom (see also Naím 2005). Portes and Rumbaut (1996) cite numerous examples (e.g., Cubans, Vietnamese) in which groups benefit from *selective acculturation*, wherein they maintain ties with their ethnic community while adopting English and integrating in a social and economic sense (pp. 242-253), even though in other ways they are quite traditional. In Chapter 4 of this volume, Pawan Dhingra gives us an excellent illustration of selective acculturation among second-generation Asian Indians in Dallas, who are Americanized and successful professionally, but who have simultaneously strengthened ties with their temple and established an Indian networking association to preserve their cultural heritage. Susan Hardwick provides another example of this in Chapter 2, in the "community of choice" within which Russians and Ukranians in Portland wherein accept some aspects of U.S. culture (identification with communities of color) while retaining their traditional culture in other aspects (religious and familial).

It might be argued that the case of high-status immigrants such as Asian Indians or Chinese is quite different from that of low-status groups such as Mexicans or Hmong, who have not integrated well. However, even for these latter groups maintenance of ethnic community ties does not appear to impede social and economic integration. It is quite likely that lack of acculturation is the result rather than the cause of poor integration for both high and low-status groups (see Alba and Nee 2003, 261). The immigrant arrives with high hopes for freedom and economic opportunity; however, these may not materialize (despite his hard work) because of discrimination, gatekeepers, and the highly competitive nature of U.S. society. The immigrant is thus compelled to seek the psychological and cultural (in addition to economic) resources of the ethnic enclave and the family, in order to survive. In the case of Mexicans in San Antonio (Chapter 7 of this volume) I refer to this as *cultural retrenchment*. Similarly, it can be argued that the poor acculturation of Southeast Asians in Wisconsin and Minnesota (Beck 1997, above) is not the cause of their low incomes, but an effect of their poverty coupled with their less than cordial treatment by residents. On the other hand, the Hmong in Sheboygan as described by Karl Byrand (Chapter 9 in this volume) appear to be integrating and acculturating better owing to their more favorable reception as refugees who served the U.S. in the Indochinese War rather than as "immigrants" to be lumped with other low-status groups.

Evidence that Mexican Americans in the Southwest are serious about rejoining Mexico—the *reconquista* (Huntington 2004; Buchanan 2002, 123-146; Ling 2004)—is tenuous in the extreme. Such claims are based on the statements of Mexican leaders speaking allegorically about the "Mexican nation" extending into the U.S., or of occasional pronouncements of Mexican Americans whose views on "liberation of the Southwest" represent a miniscule and mis-quoted proportion of the Mexican-American community. Mexican Americans are well acculturated and identify themselves as Americans first, Mexicans a distant second (if at all) (Jacoby 2004a). Their struggles to become "American" and the historical animosity between Mexico and the U.S., have distanced them significantly from their mother country (Jones, Chapter 7, this volume)—a situation quite different, for example, from that of Asian, African, and Latin American immigrants to Western Europe, who maintain their original national identities across many generations.

Are new immigrants failing to acculturate? This argument is unconvincing. Within the first generation, evidence is mixed. In terms of language, Mexicans along with Dominicans and Salvadorans show little improvement in English-speaking dominance with years since entry, while Koreans, Chinese, and Vietnamese show significant improvement (Alba and Nee 2003, 223). The second generation, however, is a different story. For Latinos in 1990, English dominance rose from around 5 percent for the first generation to nearly 40 percent for the second generation (Alba and Nee 2003); in 2000 almost 50 percent of second generation Latinos were English-dominant (Jacoby 2004a, 24). Regarding intermarriage, the 2000 figures are astonishing. Among the second generation a half of Asians and a third of Latinos marry outside of their ethnic group (Jacoby 2004a, 25). On other cultural measures, however, selective acculturation appears to be the norm, with various groups, both low and high-status, seeking refuge within their ethnic communities as regards food, music, and friends, while at the same time speaking English and following American customs regarding time, work habits, media preferences, and material possessions. Intermarriage statistics, at least those regarding Latinos and Asians, suggest that in several generations immigrants will have blended ethnically into what can only be called a new mainstream.

Unfortunately, the aforementioned arguments, pro and con, tend to obscure the positive contributions that new immigrants are making to this new cultural mainstream. Their contributions are most evident in megalopolis. However, the positive imprint of immigrants outside megalopolis is becoming increasingly evident. Ellen Kraly, in Chapter 12 of this volume, provides resounding evidence for this in Utica, New York, where Bosnians and other groups have brought a rebirth of downtown neighborhoods and businesses, taken gritty manufacturing jobs, stimulated multicultural programs in the schools, and "provided a geography lesson" for residents on world cultures. These new residents have given an "anchor of hope" to a declining city. In many other cities across the country, these influences are increasingly salient in the form of ethnic businesses, festivals, and media that have brought bona fide rejuvenation to some places and a multicultural flavor to others. Immigrant dining experiences are becoming more diversified and mainstream. In San Antonio, a bi-cultural city only 1.7 percent of whose population is Asian, there are now Indian, Korean, Thai, Turkish, Vietnamese, and Mongolian restaurants, complementing the many Chinese and Japanese ones. In ethnically homogenous states like West Virginia, Maine, and Vermont, none of whose Hispanic population reaches 1 percent of the total, Mexican restaurants are becoming popular. In non-megalopolitan cities from Utica to Yuba City and Atlanta to Sedona, cultural fairs and festivals celebrate these cities' new cultural diversity. Karl Byrand (Chapter 9) mentions the Hmong Summer Festival celebrated in Sheboygan and Mohammad Chaichian (Chapter 10) notes the Iranian New Year festival held in Iowa City. Houston and Atlanta have their celebrations of Diwali, the Indian festival of lights. Milwaukee wants tourists to know about its Arab World Festival, and Kansas City advertises its Taiwanese Festival. Salt Lake City is proud of its Pan Asian Festival and Macon, Georgia, of its Pan African Festival. If immigration has caused a cultural crisis and loss of identity in these cities, it is evident that their Chambers of Commerce don't think so.

In addition to cultural revitalization, there is labor force rejuvenation. Immigrants, who accounted for 11 percent of the U.S. population in 2000, were responsible for a third of total population growth in the United States over the 1990s, and one-half of the new entrants into the U.S. labor force (Martin and Midgley 2006). One reason for this is their age profile: almost four-fifths (79 percent) of the foreign-born were between the ages of eighteen and sixty-four in 2000, compared to just over three-fifths (61.7 percent) for the U.S. population as a whole (Schmidley 2001, 27) [The comparable figures for under eighteen were 10 percent and 26 percent, respectively—which will be a surprise to those who assume a large foreign-born child population]. The infusion of young, working-age persons was just as prevalent among Asians as among Latin Americans, suggesting that across the spectrum of socioeconomic status and job categories there was young blood to fill the demands of agriculture, manufacturing, science, and the professions. To realize the importance of this, one might reflect on the deep problems of labor force aging in the other global economic powers—Western Europe, Japan, and more recently, China. China's total fertility rate is now 20 percent below that of the U.S. (1.6 vs. 2.0). A young U.S. labor force not only boosts productivity. It supports a rapidly aging dependent population.

Finally, there is ample evidence that immigration reinforces U.S. values and restores the family to the center of U. S. life. As noted in the first section, because immigrants are selected in their villages and cities of origin on such traits as ambition, perseverance, intelligence, independence, and resourcefulness, they bring these character traits to the United States. But they also come with other cultural capital. Among East Asians, Confucianism instills the importance of education, discipline, and respect for authority as well as family honor; these values create a social environment that is strongly conducive to educational achievement among children of the second generation (Zhou and Kim 2006)—an environment that may be critical in countering the temptations and negative influences of U.S. culture, and avoiding dissonant acculturation (Portes and Rumbaut 1996, 242-247). Among Muslims, there is a strong sense of community and support of the less fortunate that springs from the teachings of Islam. These traits help explain the professional success of Muslims in the United States. We have seen an example of this in Mohammad Chaichian's case study of Iranians in Iowa City (Chapter 10, this volume). Blacks from the English and Dutch Caribbean enter the United States with superior educational preparation and professional aspirations, and indeed from their ranks, in New York City alone, have emerged such leaders as Ralph Bunche, Roy Innis, Stokely Carmichael, Louis Farrakhan, and Colin Powell (Millmann 1997, 77).

The immigrant family is the central and nurturing unit in all of these success stories. Its authority structure, its role as cultural reservoir and as creator and monitor of expectations, constitute an alternative model to the looser-structured, more individual-focused U.S. family. The immigrant family is also an economic unit, in which everyone cooperates for the economic success of the group. This includes children. In an incisive article, Marjorie Orellana (2001) highlights the work that immigrant children do to support their families, households, and schools, in her study of Mexican and Central American families in the Pico-Union area of Los Angeles. Rather than considering children as "emotionally priceless but economically useless"—the view that appears to predominate nowadays in "progressive," upwardly-mobile WASP families—the families in her study saw children as "economically useful," as "actors and agents" in the functioning of the family as an economic unit. Around the house, these children (in particular, the girls) washed dishes, vacuumed the house, answered the door and made guests feel at home, unpacked groceries, did laundry and folded clothes, answered the telephone, cleaned up after the baby, helped siblings with homework. Farther afield, they took siblings to school and the library, ran errands, ordered food in restaurants, and (most importantly) served as translators between English and Spanish for mother and father. Finally, children participated in the waged labor market, selling food and other merchandise alongside adult vendors, caring for children, mowing lawns, cleaning tables in the family restaurant, sweeping the floor of the family beauty salon. Of course, these behaviors are nothing unusual to families in their countries of origin. In the United States, however, they are novel. They may provide measurable economic benefits to society. Just as importantly, they are likely to make for more responsible, resourceful, cooperative, and tolerant adults. These are not qualities usually inbred in a society where children are given many opportunities but few responsibilities, where winning and success are often more important than getting along.

If immigrant families can help teach us this, even as we instill competitiveness and productivity in them, we will all be better off.

Conclusion

U.S. assimilation today has been described as a salad bowl or fruit salad. Arguably, a better term is "alloy" (Hamill 2004), because immigrants' music, food, pastimes, and language have been so thoroughly enjoined to the country's soul that it is impossible to identify the seams. However, the alloy metaphor is different from that of the melting pot. An alloy is not a dumbed-down, average amalgam of ingredients in which the negative qualities of some groups are smoothed out by the positive qualities of others. Immigration is not a zero-sum game. An alloy is functionally better than its individual components. In smelting, different metals are mixed with steel—chromium, manganese, molybdenum, nickel, tungsten—and a new product results. These other metals make the native steel *better* —less corrosive, harder, more malleable or ductile. The process must nevertheless be controlled, for under unfavorable conditions (in the case of immigration, if the context of reception is unfavorable) the alloying metal may become defined as an impurity. But assuming the right temperature and mixtures, the alloy is worth far more than its components separately. Immigration doesn't just divide the pie into small pieces, it grows the pie. It does not inundate the boats in the harbor, it raises them. It is a positive sum game.

It is true that immigrants are coming in larger and larger numbers and that they are ethnically and culturally very different from the traditional "mainstream." However, American attitudes have changed, becoming more tolerant than in those earlier times. Definitions of race, ethnicity, and cultural appropriateness have been transformed. Intermarriage is more common. In the second and third generations, pronounced acculturation occurs. Thus, the mainstream is redefined and reconstituted, as the proportion of Latinos and Asians in the population increases. The more tolerant attitudes towards immigrants are in part a function of the fact that over time, the respondents to these questions are more and more likely to be immigrants or children of immigrants.

In larger cities, especially those that are experiencing dynamic economic growth, *uncontested accommodation* of immigrants (the sharing or relinquishment of residential and commercial spaces without interaction or conflict) appears to be the norm (Bach et al. 1993). We saw this phenomenon in Chapter 8, in the case of Vietnamese in New Orleans, whose residential insertion into the Versailles community was part of an evolutionary, non-conflictual succession process. We also witnessed it in Chapter 11, in the case of Mexicans in Charlotte, where rapid economic growth and suburbanization benefit immigrants and native minorities alike, resulting in surprisingly few conflicts. In smaller towns and cities, with less dynamic economies and more homogenous populations, the situation is different. Immigrants stand out more noticeably on the cultural and social landscape in these places, and, at least initially, *reactive accommodation* (a polarization of newcomers and residents as the result of perceived wrongs and discrimination) is the norm. We have seen this well-illustrated in Chapter 5, for the case of Mexicans in Leadville, Colorado, where cultural and language misunderstandings have created a tense situation between the two groups. However, as accumulating evidence from both new and non-traditional gateway cities shows, these communities do change to acclimatize to this influx, and many achieve *participatory accommodation* (in which groups interact in various ways). Garden City, Kansas, the focus of Chapter 6, has made progress towards this type of accommodation. Immigrants and established Hispanic residents cooperate in school activities and soccer, patronize each others' businesses, and jointly support Hispanic political candidates, although interaction between Anglos and immigrants is more limited. One of the best examples of participatory accommodation of immigrants, however, is Utica, New York, the subject of Chapter 12. Not only have immigrants there been accepted; they have become a new spiritual center and economic rallying point for the city. They have revitalized the manufacturing labor force, upgraded neighborhoods with a myriad of home improvements, invested in businesses that give a European and Asian flavor to downtown Utica, and encouraged their children to excel in the schools, thus stimulating educational achievement in the whole community.

The original purpose of this book was to investigate the dynamic interaction between these two processes—the creation of new cultural landscapes and the negotiation of social adjustment—in cities outside of megalopolis. My personal belief was that these processes were often at odds with one another—the maintenance and championing of cultural uniqueness often hindered social adjustment. Now I am not so sure. No one can ignore the burdens of discrimination and maladjustment faced quietly by immigrants, and particularly by lower-status immigrants. But as a whole immigrants are holding up remarkably well. They work very hard, but they are healthier, more family-oriented, more motivated, less likely to get into trouble than the average American. In this process, adherence to their own culture appears to foster their adjustment better than immersion in U.S. culture, that is, segmented assimilation appears to be the norm among new immigrant populations today. Their culture is not only a refuge for them, but a reservoir of values and practices that make U.S. society better in the long run.

The voluble fear by restrictionists that these new immigrants will not assimilate is misplaced. Assimilation is not necessary for economic integration, which is arguably the ultimate goal of immigrants and of U.S. society on behalf of immigrants. However, their insidious fear that immigrants *will* assimilate, submerging the old stock European population, is just as misplaced. The values that founded this country are as strong among immigrants as the general population; they come here to see these values in practice and apply them to their own lives. Immigrants may bring new languages, foods, music, and customs, but it is unlikely that these will alter the values of individual freedom, equality, and protection of minority rights, which they hold as strongly as anyone. The immigrant second-generation is out-marrying at a surprising rate, and adopting English, but this ethnic blending of the population will not alter basic values either. Instead, it will result in a more tolerant, enriched culture who become "American" every bit as rapidly as their immigrant European predecessors.

References

Alba, Richard, and Victor Nee. 2003. *Remaking the American Mainstream*. Cambridge, MD: Harvard University Press.

Anderson, Stuart, and Michaela Platzer. 2004. *American Made: the Impact of Immigrant Entrepreneurs and Professionals on U.S. Competitiveness*. Washington, DC: National Venture Capital Association.

Bach, Robert, Rodolfo de la Garza, Karen Ito, Louise Lamphere, and Niara Sudarkasa. 1993. *Changing Relations: Newcomers and Established Residents in U.S. Communities*. New York: The Ford Foundation.

Baker, Phyllis, and Douglas Hotek. 2003. "Perhaps a Blessing: Skills and Contributions of Recent Mexican Immigrants in the Rural Midwest," *Hispanic Journal of Behavioral Sciences* 25(4):448-68.

Bean, Frank, Jennifer Van Hook, and Mark Fossett. 1999. "Immigration, Spatial and Economic changed, and African American Employment." Pp. 31-63 in *Immigration and Opportunity: Race, Ethnicity, and Employment in the United States*, edited by Frank D. Bean and Stephanie Bell-Rose. New York: Russell Sage Foundation.

Beck, Roy. 1996. *The Case Against Immigration: the Moral, Economic, Social, and Environmental Reasons for Reducing Immigration Back to Traditional Levels*. New York: W.W. Norton.

Borjas, George. 2004. "Economic Assimilation: Trouble Ahead." Pp. 199-210 in *Reinventing the Melting Pot: The New Immigrants and What it Means to be American, edited by Tamar Jacoby*. New York: Basic Books.

Brimelow, Peter. 1995. *Alien Nation: Common Sense about America's Immigration Disaster*. New York: Random House.

Buchanan, Patrick. 2002. *The Death of the West: How Dying Populations and Immigrant Invasions Imperil our Country and Civilization*. New York: St. Martin's Press.

Farrell, Christopher. 2002. "Anti-Immigration Fervor is Un-American," *Business Week*, April 26.

Faruque, Cathleen Jo. 2002. *Migration of Hmong to the Midwestern United States*. Lanham, MD: University Press of America.

Foust, Dean, Brian Grow, and Aixa Pascual. 2002. "The Changing Heartland: An Influx of Newcomers both Buoys and Burdens Small-Town America," *Business Week*, September 9.

Frey, William. 1999. "New Black Migration Patterns in the United States: Are They Affected by Recent Immigration?" Pp. 311-44 in *Immigration and Opportunity: Race, Ethnicity, and Employment in the United States*, edited by Frank D. Bean and Stephanie Bell-Rose. New York: Russell Sage Foundation.

———. 2002. "U.S. Census Shows Different Paths for Domestic and Foreign-Born Migrants." *Population Today* September/October.

Frey, William, and Kao-Lee Liaw. 1999. "Internal Migration of Foreign-Born Latinos and Asians: Are they Assimilating Geographically?" Pp. 212-30 in *Migration and Restructuring in the United States: a Geographic Perspective*, edited by Kavita Pandit and Suzanne Davies Withers. Lanham, MD: Rowman and Littlefield.

Grey, Mark, and Anne Woodrick. 2005. "Latinos have Revitalized our Community: Mexican Migration and Anglo Responses in Marshalltown, Iowa." Pp. 133-54 in *New Destinations: Mexican Immigration in the United States*, edited by Victor Zúñiga and Rubén Hernández León. New York: Russell Sage Foundation.

Griffith, David. 2005. "Rural Industry and Mexican Immigration and Settlement in North Carolina," Pp. 50-75 in *New Destinations: Mexican Immigration in the United States*, edited by Victor Zúñiga and Rubén Hernández León. New York: Russell Sage Foundation.

Gouveia, Lourdes, Miguel Carranza, and Jasney Cogua. 2005. "The Great Plains Migration: Mexicanos and Latinos in Nebraska." Pp. 23-49 in *New Destinations: Mexican Immigration in the United States*, edited by Victor Zúñiga and Rubén Hernández León. New York: Russell Sage Foundation.

Hamill, Pete. 2004. "The Alloy of New York." Pp. 167-79 in *Reinventing the Melting Pot: the New Immigrants and What it Means to be American*, edited by Tamar Jacoby. New York: Basic Books.

Hancock, Tina. 2005. "Cultural Competence in the Assessment of Poor Mexican Families in the Rural Southeastern United States," *Child Welfare* 84(5):689-711.

Huntington, Samuel. 2002. *Who are We? the Challenges to America's National Identity*. New York: Simon and Schuster.

———. 2004. "The Hispanic Challenge." *Foreign Policy*, March/April:1-17.

Jacoby, Tamar, 2004a. "The New Immigrants: a Progress Report." Pp. 17-45 in *Reinventing the Melting Pot: the New Immigrants and What it Means to be American*, edited by Tamar Jacoby. New York: Basic Books.

———. 2004b. "What it Means to Be American in the 21st Century." Pp. 293-314 in *Reinventing the Melting Pot: the New Immigrants and What it Means to be American*, edited by Tamar Jacoby. New York: Basic Books.

Johnson-Webb, Karen. 2003. *Recruiting Hispanic Labor: Immigrants in Non-Traditional Areas*. New York: LFB Scholarly Publishing LLC.

Kibria, Nazli. 2002. *Becoming Asian American: Second Generation Chinese and Korean American Identities*. Baltimore: The Johns Hopkins Press.

Kochhar, Rakesh, Roberto Suro, and Sonya Tafoya. 2005. *The New Latino South: The Context and Consequences of Rapid Population Growth*. Washington, DC: Pew Hispanic Center, July 26.

Kotkin, Joel. 2000. "Movers and Shakers," *Reason* 32(7), December.

———. 2004. "Toward a Post-Ethnic Economy." Pp. 183-98 in *Reinventing the Melting Pot: The New Immigrants and What it Means to be American*, edited by Tamar Jacoby. New York: Basic Books.

Ling, Yeh Ling. 2004. "Mexican Immigration and its Potential Impact on the Political future of the United States," *Journal of Social, Political, and Economic Studies* 29(4):409-431.

Lopez, David E. 1996. "Language: Diversity and Assimilation." Pp. 139-63 in *Ethnic Los Angeles*, edited by Roger Waldinger and Mehdi Bozorgmehr. New York: Russell Sage Foundation.

Lynch, Michael. 2001. "Migration Math," *Reason* 33(7), December.

Martin, Philip, and Elizabeth Midgley. 2006. *Immigration: Shaping and Reshaping America*. [Population Bulletin 61(4)]. Washington, DC: Population Reference Bureau. December.

Massey, Douglas. 2004. "The American Side of the Bargain." Pp. 111-21 in *Reinventing the Melting Pot: The New Immigrants and What it Means to be American*, edited by Tamar Jacoby. New York: Basic Books.

Millman, Joel. 1997. *The Other Americans: How Immigrants Renew our Country, our Economy, and Our Values*. New York: Viking Press.

Murphy, Arthur, Colleen Blanchard, and Jennifer Hill, eds. 2001. *Latino Workers in the Contemporary South*. Athens: University of Georgia Press.

Naím, Moisés. 2005. "Arabs in Foreign Lands," *Foreign Policy* 148, May/June, pp. 96-97.

Onishi, Norimitsu. 1996. "Stabilizing Lefrak City: Jewish and Muslim Immigrants Help Revive Troubled Complex," *New York Times*, June 6.

Orellana, Marjorie F. 2001. "The Work Kids Do: Mexican and Central American Immigrant Children's Contributions to Households and Schools in California," *Harvard Educational Review* 71(3):366-89.

Ortiz, Vilma. 1996. "The Mexican-Origin Population: Permanent Working Class or Emerging Middle Class?" Pp. 247-77 in *Ethnic Los Angeles*, edited by Roger Waldinger and Mehdi Bozorgmehr. New York: Russell Sage Foundation.

Pastor, Manuel, Jr. 1999. "Economics and Ethnicity: Poverty, Race, and Immigration in Los Angeles County." Pp. 102-38 in *Asian and Latino Immigrants in a Restructuring Economy: the Metamorphosis of Southern California*, edited by Marta López-Garza and David R. Díaz. Stanford, CA: Stanford University Press.

Pessar, Patricia, and Pamela Graham. 2001. "Dominicans: Transnational Identities and Local Politics." Pp. 251-73 in *New Immigrants in New York*, edited by Nancy Foner. New York: Columbia University Press.

Porter, Eduardo. 2005. "Illegal Immigrants are Bolstering Social Security with Billions," *The New York Times*, April 5.

Portes, Alejandro, and Ruben Rumbaut. 1996. *Immigrant America: a Portrait*. Berkeley: University of California Press.

Portes, Alejandro, and Min Zhou. 1999. "Entrepreneurship and Economic Progress in the 1990s: a Comparative Analysis of Immigrants and African Americans." Pp. 143-71 in *Immigration and Opportunity: Race, Ethnicity, and Employment in the United States*, edited by Frank D. Bean and Stephanie Bell-Rose. New York: Russell Sage Foundation.

Rosenfeld, Mark, and Marta Tienda. 1999. "Mexican Immigration, Occupational Niches, and Labor-Market Competition: Evidence from Los Angeles, Chicago, and Atlanta, 1970 to 1990." Pp. 64-105 in *Immigration and Opportunity: Race, Ethnicity, and Employment in the United States*, edited by Frank D. Bean and Stephanie Bell-Rose. New York: Russell Sage Foundation.

Samuelson, Robert J. 2005. "The Hard Truth of Immigration," *Newsweek*, June 13.

Schlesinger, Arthur M., Jr. 2005. "E Pluribus Unum?" Pp. 4-13 in *Taking Sides: Clashing Views on Race and Ethnicity*, edited by Raymond D'Angelo and Herbert Douglas. Dubuque, IA: McGraw-Hill/Dushkin.

Schmidley, Dianne. 2001. *Profile of the Foreign-born Population in the U.S.: 2000*. Current Population Reports, U.S. Bureau of the Census. Special Study P23-206. Washington, DC: U.S. Government Printing Office, December.

Simon, Julian. 1999. *The Economic Consequences of Immigration*. Ann Arbor: The University of Michigan Press.

Smith, Robert C. 2001. "Mexicans: Social, Educational, Economic, and Political Problems and Prospects in New York." Pp. 275-300 in *New Immigrants in New York*, edited by Nancy Foner. New York: Columbia University Press.

Stoller, Paul. 2001. "West Africans: Trading Places in New York." Pp. 229-49 in *New Immigrants in New York*, edited by Nancy Foner. New York: Columbia University Press.

Strayhorn, Carole Keeton. 2006. *Undocumented Immigrants in Texas: a Financial Analysis of the Impact to the State Budget and Economy.* Austin: Texas Comptroller of Public Accounts, Publication #96-1224, December.

Weng, Wensheng. 2001. "Chinese Americans in the Tucson Community," *Chinese Studies in History* 34:82-96.

Zhou, Min, and Susan Kim. 2006. "Community Forces, Social Capital, and Educational Achievement: the Case of Supplementary Education in the Chinese and Korean Immigration Communities." *Harvard Educational Review* 76(1):1-29.

Index

About the Contributors

Christopher Airriess (Ph.D. in Geography, University of Kentucky) is professor of geography, Department of Geography, Ball State University, Muncie, Indiana. His research interests include cultural and ethnic landscapes, focusing on the adjustment experiences of Southeast Asians in the United States, development, Southeast and East Asia, and ports and maritime transport.

Michael Broadway (Ph.D. in Geography, University of Illinois Urbana-Champaign) is professor and head of Northern Michigan University's geography department. His research expertise focuses on the meatpacking industry's community impacts in small towns on the Great Plains and Prairies, as well as demographic and economic change in the region.

Karl Byrand (Ph.D. in Geography, University of Maryland) is associate professor of geography, Department of Geography and Geology, University of Wisconsin-Sheboygan. His research is concerned with changing cultural landscapes, particularly those of Southeast Asian refugees in the United States, racial change, and perception of the physical environment.

Mohammad Chaichian (Ph.D. in Sociology, Michigan State University) is professor of sociology and chair, Department of Sociology, Mount Mercy College, Cedar Rapids, Iowa. His research expertise includes immigration issues particularly pertaining to first- and second-generation Iranian immigrants; political economy of urbanization in Iran, Egypt, and China; and race relations in the United States.

Pawan Dhingra (Ph.D. in Sociology, Cornell University) is associate professor of sociology, Department of Sociology, Oberlin College, Oberlin, Ohio. His research interests include ethnic and racial identity formation and performance among second generation Asian Americans, ethnic entrepreneurship of Indian American motel owners, and immigrant adaptation within the Midwest and South.

Susan Hardwick (Ph.D. in Geography, University of California at Davis) is professor of geography, Department of Geography, University of Oregon. Her research interests include refugee settlement in the Pacific Northwest, the role of religion among Russians in California, urban ethnic landscapes, refugee hetero-localism and social networks, cultural landscapes in California and Texas, and international geographic education.

Nancy Hiemstra (M.A. in Geography, University of Oregon) is a Ph.D. student in geography at Syracuse University. Her research interests include Latino immigration to the U.S. West, changing patterns of migration worldwide, national immigration policies, and human smuggling from S.America to the U.S.

Richard C. Jones (Ph.D. in Geography, Ohio State University) is professor of geography, the University of Texas at San Antonio. His research interests include patterns and adjustment of Mexican immigrants in the United States, the impact of remittances on Mexican origins, immigrant experiences in San Antonio, migration from the EU periphery, and economic development in peripheral regions. This edited volume is his third book on immigration.

Ellen Percy Kraly (Ph.D. in Sociology, Fordham University) is William R. Kenan Jr. Professor, Department of Geography, Colgate University. Her research expertise involves international migration and population dynamics, refugee resettlement, immigration reform and its impacts on immigrant integration, and demographic data and human rights.

Emily Skop (Ph.D. in Geography, Arizona State University) is assistant professor of geography in the Department of Geography and Environmental Studies, The University of Colorado at Colorado Springs. Her research centers upon Latino and Asian immigrant experiences, residential segregation, and social inequality in the contexts of U.S. and Latin American cities.

Heather A. Smith (Ph.D. in Geography, University of British Columbia) is associate professor of geography, Department of Geography and Earth Sciences, the University of North Carolina at Charlotte. Her published research investigates immigration and poverty in Canadian cities, immigrant residential patterns, and the reconstruction and "Latinization" of New South cities.

Donald Stull (Ph.D. in Anthropology, University of Colorado at Boulder) is professor of anthropology, University of Kansas. For the past two decades his research has focused on the meat and poultry industry and its impact on workers and host communities in the midwestern and southern United States. Tobacco farmers in his native Kentucky are his current research interest.